Transatlantic Fascism

⇥ Transatlantic Fascism ⇤

Ideology, Violence, and the Sacred in

Argentina and Italy, 1919–1945

FEDERICO FINCHELSTEIN

Duke University Press

Durham and London 2010

© 2010 Duke University Press
All rights reserved
Printed in the United States of America
on acid-free paper ∞
Designed by Katy Clove
Typeset in Dante by Keystone Typesetting, Inc.

Library of Congress Cataloging-in-Publication Data
Finchelstein, Federico
Transatlantic fascism : ideology, violence, and the sacred in
Argentina and Italy, 1919–1945 / Federico Finchelstein.
p. cm.
Includes bibliographical references and index.
ISBN 978-0-8223-4594-7 (cloth : alk. paper)
ISBN 978-0-8223-4612-8 (pbk. : alk. paper)
1. Fascism—Argentina—History—20th century.
2. Fascism—Italy—History—20th century.
3. Fascism and the Catholic Church—Argentina—History—20th century.
4. Fascism and the Catholic Church—Italy—History—20th century. I. Title.
F2848.F566 2010
320.53′30982—dc22   2009037181

Para Lauri y Gabriela

Contents

Acknowledgments

I want to thank Dominick LaCapra for his support and encouragement. Dominick was the ideal advisor when this book began its journey as a doctoral dissertation. It was he who suggested, in 2001, that Argentina should remain a central part of my research on fascism. I would also like to thank the other members of my doctoral committee: Vicki Caron, Tulio Halperín Donghi, Mary Roldán, and Michael Steinberg. Each of them added significant meaning to my work, and each, in his or her own way, influenced my historical thinking.

I wish to say *muchísimas gracias* to Sandy McGee Deutsch, the foremost expert on the Argentine (and Latin American) Right, for her encouragement and advice over the years.

My gratitude to Enzo Traverso is, as always, significant. I enjoy and learn from our dialogical transatlantic friendship.

I would like to thank Ben Brower and Ray Craib for their critical insights and friendship. My colleagues Chris Bilodeau, Chris Cantwell, and Will Harris read and corrected countless versions of my work, suggesting ideas and endowing me with their friendship.

The list of colleagues who discussed my research in Ithaca is extensive. From Cornell, I want to thank Ed Baptist, Holly Case, and Derek Chang. In addition, I thank Oren Falk, María Cristina Garcia, Karen Graubart, Mary Gayne, Franz D. Hofer, Isabel Hull, Alison Kallet, Taran Kang, Steve Kaplan, Emma Kuby, Tracie Matysik, Yael Nadav-Manes, John M. Najemy, Ryan Plumley, Camille Robcis, Richard Schaefer, Peter Staudenmaier, Barry Strauss, Eric Tagliacozzo, and Adelheid Voskuhl. Also at Cornell, I thank

Acknowledgments

Barb Donnell, Maggie Edwards, and Katie Kristof from the History Department; and Mary Ahl, Linda Allen, and Lisa Patti from the A. D. White House. At the Cornell Center for the Humanities, I spent a fruitful and enlightening year. I thank my fellow Mellon colleagues and the director, Brett de Barry, for providing an environment where critical thinking reigned. The same applies to the Summer School of Criticism and Theory directed by Dominick LaCapra; from the school, I wish to thank Michael Warner, in particular.

My thanks, more generally, to the members of the European History Colloquium, the Latin American seminar, and the Mellon seminars at the Cornell Center for the Humanities. In Ithaca, I would also like also to thank Jonathan Ablard, Mabel Berezin, Bruno Bosteels, Tim Campbell, Medina Lasanski, and Suzanne Stewart Steinberg. Not least, I would like to thank my friends and teammates of La Maquina *futbol* team, the team of the Cornell History Department. The brave community of scholars who participated in the team helped mitigate the rigid Ithaca winters. The basement of McGraw was also another place for academic exchanges over coffee; Gimme Coffee, right by Cascadilla Creek, was the closest Ithaca version of an Argentine café. I wrote and read many things over my personal customized version of *cortado*. Matoula and Greg Halkiopoulos provided their friendship and advice in "gorgeous" Ithaca.

My short stay at Brown University provided a unique context to work on this book while thinking about the day-to-day concerns of teaching the history of fascism. From Providence, I thank Omer Bartov, Deborah Cohen, James Green, Maude Mandel, and, once again, my mentor and *amigo, a lo Argentino*, Michael Steinberg. At Brown, I would also like to thank the chair of the History Department, James L. McClain. My thanks also to Julissa Bautista, Mary Beth Bryson, Cherrie Guerzon, and Karen Mota.

Around the world my thanks go to many people in many countries. In Israel, to Haim Avni, David Bankier, Manuela Consoni, Amos Goldberg, Raanan Rein, Leo Senkman, and Alberto Spectorovsky. In Italy, to Fulvio Cammarano, Maddalena Carli, Marcello Flores, Emilio Gentile, Massimo Mastrogregori, Michele Nani, Roberta Pergher, Paolo Pombeni, and Loris Zanatta, and my colleagues at the editorial board of *Ricerche di Storia Politica*. Loris Zanatta's generosity (in terms of suggestions, advice, and last but not least help and advice with the documentary materials of the Italian Foreign Ministry Archive) is boundless. In Brazil, I thank João Fábio Bertonha, Luiz Fernando Dias Duarte, and Maria Luiza Tucci Carneiro; in Germany,

Acknowledgments

Tim Muller; and in France, Sonia Combe, Geneviève Dreyfus-Armand (director of the Bibliothèque de documentation internationale contemporaine [BDIC]), Bruno Groppo, Philippe Minard, Fabiola Rodríguez López, and Enzo Traverso, as well as the members and participants at the seminar of the BDIC (Département d'études ibériques et ibero-américain de Paris 10, Laboratoire du LASP [CNRS]), in Nanterre, France, where I presented my work during my stay in Paris. Enzo and Bruno kindly opened their homes to me in Paris. I thank, too, Roger Chartier, from whom I learned many historical lessons, in France, Argentina, and the United States.

In Argentina, *los amigos y colegas son incontables y esta vez por una cuestión de espacio quiero agradecer particularmente a* Ale Cattaruzza *y asimismo a* Lilia Ana Bertoni, José Emilio Burucua, Lila Caimari, Luciano De Privitello, Patricia Flier, Jorge Gelman, María Victoria Grillo, Alejandro Katz, Daniel Lvovich, Hector Pavón, Mariano Plotkin, María Ester Rapalo, Hilda Sábato, Leandro de Sagastizabal, Guillermo Saidon, César Tcach, Hugo Vezzetti, y Eduardo Zimmermann. Perla Wasserman deserves special mention. Once more, I would like to thank my *maestros argentinos*: Luis Alberto Romero and José Sazbón. *Mi gratitud va más alla de lo que pueden expresar estas palabras.*

I owe textual gratitude to many librarians. My special thanks go to David Bloch, Cornell's own Latin Americanist librarian. Thank you, David, for buying the Filippo collection for Cornell when I needed it most. I want to thank Carmen Lugones for allowing me to read her family's archive. In addition, I want to thank librarians at Brown, The New School library, the New York University library, the BDIC, and the Archivio Centrale dello Stato; the Argentine archivists and librarians at the Archivo General de la Nación Argentina, the Archivo del Ministerio de Relaciones Exteriores y Culto, the Archivo Fundación IWO, Archivo Cedinci, the Bibilioteca del Congreso Argentino, and other libraries. My thanks, too, to Abel Roth from the Instituto Ravignani. I have special thanks for Ritta Saccal from the Latin American rabbinic seminary in Buenos Aires and Gail Shirazi from the Library of Congress in Washington, D.C.

In New York City, I thank my "uptown" friends and colleagues. Nara Milanich, Pablo Piccato, and Caterina Pizzigoni read and discussed two chapters of the manuscript; their comments and suggestions were extremely helpful. I also thank Claudio Lomnitz and José Moya, whose readings and suggestions were essential; Paul Gootenberg and Pablo Piccato for inviting me to present one chapter at the New York City Latin American History Workshop; the participants of that seminar for their feedback; and Diego

Armus, Brenda Elsey, Jeffrey Mehlman, Anson Rabinbach, Sinclair Thomson, Barbara Weinstein, and Eric Zolov.

The New School has provided an ideal intellectual context to complete this book. The New School for Social Research was founded by a group of antifascist intellectuals who situated their work at the crossroads of European and American critical thinking, including historiography and critical theory. My own orientation is more insistently and comprehensively transnational, but I nonetheless identify with this intellectual endeavor and situate my own approach within this broad intellectual tradition. At The New School I would like to thank my colleagues in the History Department: Elaine Abelson, Robin Blackburn, Carol Breckenridge, Faisal Devji, Oz Frankel, Orit Halpern, Victoria Hattam, Julia Ott, David Plotke, Paul Ross, Ann Laura Stoler, Neguin Yavari, Eli Zaretsky, and Ari and Vera Zolberg. I have learned a great deal from them. Also at The New School, I thank Andrew Arato, Richard Bernstein, Nancy Fraser, Neil Gordon, Andreas Kalyvas, Jonathan Veitch, and Val Vinokur. My New School for Social Research colleague Carlos Forment took the time to read and discuss my work, which has benefited immensely from his comments and suggestions. My research assistants at the New School for Social Research, Diego Cagueñas and Monica Fagioli, provided great help with the materials. I thank Luis Herrán Ávila for his help in preparing the index.

Different fellowships and grants allowed me to conduct my research and write. They include the Sage Fellowship (Andrew W. Mellon Foundation), Cornell University, 2005–2006; Mario Einaudi Fellowship, Fondazione Einaudi, 2004–2005; Graduate School Travel Grant, Cornell University, 2004; Tinker Grant, Latin American Studies Program, Cornell University, 2004; School of Criticism and Theory, Tuition Fellowship, 2004; Bowmar Research Travel Grant, Cornell University, 2004; Mellon Graduate Fellowship, Cornell University, 2003–2004; Graduate School Travel Grant, Cornell University, 2003; Sage Fellowship (Andrew W. Mellon Foundation), Cornell University, 2001–2002.

Parts of chapter 1 were published as an article in *Constellations: An International Journal of Critical and Democratic Theory* 15.3 (2008). I would like to thank the editors of the journal, as well as Blackwell Publishing.

Mary Roldán insisted that Duke University Press, one of the most important publishers of Latin American Studies in the United States, would be the ideal venue for this work. Many thanks, Mary, for your trust and encouragement. Vicki Caron read the manuscript in its transitional stage and suggested important editorial innovations. Many thanks as well to Michael Steinberg and Dominick LaCapra for their editorial suggestions.

I would like to thank Valerie Millholland, my editor at Duke University Press, for her confidence in this project. This book would not be what it is without her understanding. I would also like to thank the two anonymous readers for the press. I believe that the book has benefited immensely from their comments, criticisms, and suggestions.

I thank the students of my courses on fascism and on history, memory, and trauma at Brown University. I would also like to thank the students of my doctoral and undergraduate seminars on the history and theory of fascism at The New School for Social Research and Eugene Lang College of The New School. I learned a great deal from our exchanges.

Finally I would like to thank my family. *Mis viejos*, Norma and Jaime, *y mis hermanos*, Diego and Inés, were there as they have always been.

This book is dedicated to *dos mujeres*: Laura, my wife and *compañera*, and Gabriela, our daughter.

Introduction

Pero, bajo la piedra pesada de los tiempos la flor va a darnos su escándalo.

—LEÓN GIECO

I met Perla Waserman in 1994 when we were both first-year undergraduate students at the University of Buenos Aires. Our differences in age—she was sixty-nine, I was nineteen—were pronounced; our life experiences were even more different. I was born in Argentina some months before the last military dictatorship; Perla was born in Poland, but she had escaped to Argentina some years before the Holocaust. But what began as a simple acquaintanceship among two students in one of Latin America's largest public universities gradually evolved into an enduring friendship, one that I would recall years later when I was working on this book.

As someone who had been persecuted by the dictatorship in Argentina from 1976 to 1983, Perla was for me a larger-than-life figure. She and I shared classrooms for more than five years. Perla had a long and sad past behind her. Her daughter, Susana Margarita Martínez Wasserman, had been "disappeared" by the dictatorship, and Perla herself had been a political prisoner between 1975 and 1977. Susana was twenty-eight years old at the time and never returned, but Perla was ultimately released and became a Mother of Plaza de Mayo. As a member of Madres, the human rights organization constituted by a group of mothers of the disappeared, Perla found historical and personal meaning. I discovered, in the course of our conversations that her daughter Susana had been a history student at our university (this may have been a reason for the military to perceive her as an internal enemy). And much later, after Perla's departure, I understood that she was at the university to continue the studies that her daughter was not allowed to complete.

During those years, my conversations with Perla were mostly focused on the meaning of history. If anything, the return to democracy in Argentina along with the series of legal absolutions and presidential amnesties accorded to the military perpetrators of violence during the governments of presidents Raúl Alfonsín (1983–1989) and Carlos Menem (1989–1999), seemed to make it all the more significant for Perla to give public voice to her experiences. At the same time, the "pizza and champagne" lifestyle, the culture of "winners and losers" that had become widespread throughout Argentine society in the 1990s among the elite and nonelite alike, and the neoliberal reforms that accompanied them, threatened to deprive Perla of the vocabulary she needed to convey her own brutal brush with history to those of us in the next generations who did not have any immediate, first-hand political and conceptual experience with the dictatorship.

Perla worked as a cook, studied history, and was critically engaged in politics. When we discussed my interest in the development of Argentine fascism and nationalism in the 1930s, she underscored the subterranean links between it and the military dictatorship of the 1970s in ways that had eluded me. Perla's lived experience of history enabled her to appreciate the political and moral implications of my study far more lucidly than I did. Her uncanny ability to extract meaning from the past in order to illuminate the present was a lesson that remains with me to this day.

Even at this moment, when I am writing these lines, I can recall the vivid image of Perla's generous smile. It was in 1999, during the presentation of my first book in Buenos Aires. I remember her smiling in the first row of seats. She had arrived at the event with other Mothers of Plaza de Mayo and some veteran antifascists that she had invited as well. Later, she told me that these veterans did not agree with my professional (for them "nonpolitical") approach to history, but she expressed her approval of my work and stressed the more significant dimensions of my project, exploring through the interpretative and disciplined scrutiny of sources, why, where, and how residues from the past become embedded in the present and shape our understanding of both.

Perla never finished her studies. She was just beginning to think about her senior thesis when she suddenly passed away on January 22, 2000. Unfortunately, history almost never provides redemption. But from Perla I learned that history implies extracting meaning, including political meaning, from both collective and individual experiences. History can be the interpretation of human change over time in a given society. But history, as I have intimated, is also a critical and restrained attempt at disclosing the sources of signification that made this past real, sometimes too real, to its contemporaries and to us, its interpreters.

It is within this particular historiographical framework, in this specific but meaningful sense, that my understanding of history is inscribed. I am interested in the politics of Latin American authoritarianism and, more specifically, the history of Argentine fascism. I am a historian of fascism and definitely not a fascist historian. In a different dimension, I am an Argentine historian dealing with Argentine history and a public intellectual interested in the long-term ramifications of this history.[1] Having these two different identities at the same time is central to self-reflectivity; that is to say, to my understanding of my work and of history at large. Whereas many historians often identify with their subjects, if I had to choose an identity at all it would be clearly that of the victims of the Argentine fascists, who were also known as *nacionalistas*.

As an Argentine, I believe that an understanding of fascism would help decipher the roots of Argentine political violence and its illiberal political culture in the last century. This century observed a radicalization of the split between a democratic-leaning civil society and an authoritarian political society, which, especially after 1930, rested heavily on its military control of the state. This disjuncture partly explains the political instability that has been the mark of Argentina's recent history. The unprecedented, even exceptional, state violence of the "dirty war" of the 1970s represents a historical turning point and defines Argentina's current collective memories.[2] But it would be difficult to understand this violence without taking into account the longstanding legacy of the Argentine idea of "Christianized fascism" and its open contestation of secular Argentina.[3]

And yet, as a nonfascist or even an antifascist, how can I understand fascism?

One, of course, does not need to be a fascist in order to understand fascism, but my point is that the act of emphasizing an antifascist reading of fascism, as many historians have done and continue to do, provides a very limited understanding of fascism; a reading that is often derogatory and always simplistic.[4] On the other hand, there are some historians—some quite established in the field—who tend to sympathize with fascism at large or with some fascist nacionalista intellectuals.[5] These negative or sympathetic readings of fascism are inscribed within a broader Argentine history of dichotomous representations: namely, the idea of two Argentinas, one being truly "national," the other a mere mimetic foreign commodity adopted by Argentines with false consciousnesses or worse.[6] These negative or positive readings of fascism are devoid of contextual distance, but paradoxically they were also shared by many contemporary sources. There is a telling anecdote in this regard. Some Argentine writers—Jorge Luis Borges, Adolfo Bioy Casares, Ezequiel Martínez Estrada, and Ulises Petit de Murat—met in a Chinese restaurant in downtown Buenos Aires to discuss fascism and antifascism in the early 1940s. When confronted with Martinez Estrada's ambiguous fascist leanings, Petit de Murat convincingly argued that for "us" the "matter is simple": "On one side there are the decent people and on the other side there are the sons of bitches [hijos de puta]."[7]

I hope that readers of my work will agree with this position; I do, on a personal and political level. However, I do not think that this vision allows a nuanced historical understanding of fascism or political history at large. The point for me is not to establish whether fascism was good or not. Personally, I believe that it was a political catastrophe. Rather, I want to understand its ideological workings in their context and beyond, that is to say, in terms of its connections with the Argentine past and the present. Argentine antifascists saw fascism as a group of "hijos de puta" who had no ideology but only simple aims: to defend the status quo, to gain power, and so on. Similarly, for Italian antifascists, fascism was essentially a historical aberration. In other words, it was a reaction against modernity, a parenthetical regression into barbarism, and more generally a moral disease, as Benedetto Croce famously stated.[8] For Croce and for many other antifascist historians, fascism was a bad joke: it had no culture, it was not a revolutionary phenomenon, and most important, it had no ideology.[9]

But fascism was not a joke for its victims. For them, fascism was a very serious matter. It tortured and killed people and destroyed political systems across the Atlantic and beyond. Fascism was a modern phenomenon, a political ideology that engaged democracy on its own terms in order to destroy it. The study of fascism provides a new meaning to standard ideas of modernity, modernization, and nation building.[10] For fascists, fascism represented the "civilizing process"; that is, they believed fascism represented the "West" and stood against barbarism. Fascism was indeed a historically situated ideology like liberalism or Marxism. If we are to understand fascism on its own terms, self-understanding is a central reference point that should be combined with antifascist voices from the past as well as with interpretations from the present. My work lets the sources speak for themselves, but only to the extent that these voices provide a window into the fascist structures of meaning and meaning making. In other words, fascist self-understanding implies a particular kind of experienced subjectivity. It lies at the boundary between the fascist inner self and the external word. It is, in sum, a "subject in motion," constantly putting forward an ideological formation located between "high theory" and practice.[11]

To be sure, I am very critical—even suspicious—of my fascist sources, but if we are to understand the workings of fascist ideology, it is essential to see in what way the fascists saw themselves and how they related this vision to the external world. I focus on fascist patterns of signification, rather than using the sources to illustrate a personal theory of fascism. My stress on fascist self-understanding on both sides of the Atlantic provides a new interpretation of "fascism in motion."[12] Fascism thus observed represents many things at the same time: a political religion, but also in the Argentine case the political arm of an established religion. It was a secular ideology, but also an ideology that presented itself as emanating from God. It was a historical movement with totalitarian views of Argentine and Latin American history. And finally it was a violent political culture that stressed torture, repression, political violence, and civil war.

In historical terms, fascism can be defined as an ideology, a movement, and a regime. Emilio Gentile, who is perhaps the most insightful Italian historian of fascism, presents fascism as a modern revolutionary phenomenon that was nationalist and revolutionary, antiliberal and anti-Marxist. Gentile also presents fascism as being typically organized in a militaristic party that had a totalitarian conception of state politics, an activist and antitheoretical ideology, and a focus on virility and antihedonistic mythical foundations. Gentile also argues that a defining feature of fascism was its character as a secular religion, which affirms the primacy of the nation understood as an organic and ethnically homogenous community. Moreover, this nation was to be hierarchically organized in a corporativist state[13] with a warmongering vocation, which searches for a politics of national expansion, potency, and conquest. Fascism, in short, was not merely a reactionary ideology; rather, it aimed at creating a new order and a new civilization.[14]

Gentile's approach to fascism is advantageous in its attentiveness to the fascist definition of fascism. Gentile chooses not to select one defining aspect (for example, radical nationalism, totalitarianism, statism, or national rebirth) but provides a fascist catalogue that should work as a starting point for any research on the subject. My work builds on Gentile's in this respect and hence addresses his conception of fascism. Argentine *nacionalismo* fits this definition. But beyond its conception, fascism in history becomes a much more complicated subject—one that has to be understood as a global ideology undergoing constant transformation. Beyond national contexts and restricted theories, fascism then becomes a traveling political universe, a radical nationalism affected and, to some extent, constituted by transnational patterns. In terms of the big picture, fascism exists as both its classic form, as represented by Mussolini's fascist ideology, and its varied reformulations on both sides of the Atlantic and beyond. As opposed to standard binary notions of fascism and religion, fascism in its Argentine version was actually conceived as an instrument of the sacred, namely, an instrument of God that Argentine fascists put forward with the aim of modernizing the nation. But before this actually happened in the Southern Cone, Italian fascism was created in Europe. In Italy, fascism was born a radical nationalism that could at the same time be an ideology "for export." It would be limited to understand Argentine fascism, or for that matter any fascism, without understanding the first fascism of all: Mussolini's fascism. This book, in short, unfolds a transnational itinerary.

Whereas comparative works generally study different national cases, the new trend of transnational and transatlantic studies tends to focus on cross-territorial exchanges. Transnational history has been highly resisted by many historians, particularly Latin Americanists in the United States and, less so, those in Latin America. One general criticism of transnational studies, particularly those focusing on the so-called national periods, is that they do not sufficiently stress the specific national contexts, and consequently do not exhaustively engage national archival reservoirs, that shaped these cross-territorial exchanges in the first place. A second criticism implies that transnational history is just another name for comparative history. Whereas the latter objection is easily rebutted by the fact that traditional comparative studies did not address exchange across political borders as transnational studies do, the former criticism is a more serious accusation that needs to be addressed.[15] This book, the first historical study of transatlantic fascism, might be read as an answer to this objection. My aim is to transcend the artificial boundaries between comparative and transnational histories by focusing on their varied strengths, connections, and commonalities. I will analyze two national ideologies and their transnational relations.

My previous book on Argentine fascism is, in part, inscribed in this historiographical trend.[16] Rather than reducing intellectual history to yet another branch of the "new cultural history," my aim here is to provoke a dialogue between intellectual history and social and cultural concerns as well as to link it with political history and the study of international relations.[17] All these perspectives are central to the comparative intellectual study of fascist ideology as an ideology whose artifacts are "frontier texts."[18] These texts cannot be clearly classified (or reduced) by disciplinary or sub-disciplinary borders and distinctions.

My work addresses the relation between structural and ever changing elements of fascist ideology. I stress both how fascists depicted themselves and how they understood themselves.[19] Ideas played a central role in fascism, particularly in the enactment of fascist ideology. Fascism was often seen—and indeed it presented itself to the world—as an aesthetic movement, but, more important, it always considered itself a political movement that had a distinctive political subjectivity situated between theory and practice. I focus on this generally ignored aspect of the historiography, specifically with respect to Argentine and Italian fascism.

I conceive my approach as a continuation, and sometimes a complement, to the perspectives that I have just synthesized. Comparative contextual research on fascism is not extensively undertaken in fascist history. Most historians still tend to disregard theory when analyzing fascism and focus on specific national cases, downplaying or ignoring the central cross-national aspect of fascism. This is particularly problematic when dealing with Latin America. Mainstream historians of fascism tend to argue that fascism was not a reality in Latin America. For them the reason is simple: fascism is a modern complex phenomenon, and Latin America (like Asian and African societies) was simply unlike Europe during the fascist era.[20]

There are deeper currents behind these stereotypical notions of Latin America as reproduced by Europeanists. Many of the stereotypes about fascism in Latin America were originally "created" by the "imperial eyes" of European and North American antifascist travelers.[21] These travelers saw Latin Americans as lacking agency and presented South American territories as passive topographies of fascism or, as one of them put it, "jungles of fascism."[22] According to this view, Latin Americans were easy targets— puppets, even—of the European fascist empires. They were, in other words, colonial subjects of fascist imperialism. But global circuits of knowledge production were not abstract; they were moving and changing realities that involved people, ideas, and identities.[23] The Latin American translation of European fascist imperialism was a process of appropriation and reinvention. Decentering Europe is a healthy exercise when one is confronted with traditional stereotypes about the "non-Western other" and the West.[24] But what is the West? Latin America and Spain, for example, were, for centuries and until very recently, part of an intertwined intellectual world of exchanges, of dialogical "gazes across the Atlantic."[25] And Latin American mores and intellectual traditions "have as much of a claim to Europe as does the United States."[26]

In sharp contrast to stereotypical images of "third world" societies presented in mainstream fascist historiography, a few interpreters have demonstrated the possibility of thinking about fascism outside Europe and specifically in Latin America.[27] But whereas Chilean, Brazilian, and Mexican fascisms were suppressed in the late 1930s, leaving an indistinct legacy, Argentine fascism thrived during the 1930s and 1940s, when the proportion of fascist sympathizers in the population was at its highest, and it continues to be a political and intellectual force.

Generally speaking, historians of Argentina find themselves in a position of "inferiority" with respect to their Argentine fascist sources. Argentine fascists knew more about European fascisms than their historians currently do. My work presents precisely this Argentine fascist "knowledge" about the universal experience of fascism. My aim is to provide readers with an understanding of fascist connections across the Atlantic; with the help of Argentine, North American, French, and Italian archival materials, I try thus to overcome the obstacles that have limited other historians' understanding of fascism.

My work demonstrates that Argentine fascism was different from European fascisms. But this is not my main point. My aim is a more ambitious one. I want to emphasize the global connections that were essential for fascist ideology to travel (or replicate itself, so to speak) from one side of the ocean to the other. As an ideology, fascism is transnational (and often transtextual), and not necessarily European or Italian, as some Italian fascists in the past, as well as several contemporary historians, claim. One of my primary aims is to denaturalize standard notions of what is Latin American and what is European. These categories are used by intellectuals working in the northern hemisphere either to demonstrate the derivative nature of Latin American thought and practice with respect to European sources or to affirm the rather dubious notion of an essentially detached form of Latin Americanness devoid of any external "European" connotations. Neither representation really works for my historical subject. My aim is to study how different fascist theories of fascism changed over time and how fascism, when set in motion, resists standard geohistoriographical categories.

Moreover, I show the similarities and differences between the fascist movements across the Atlantic and follow up by arguing that Argentine fascism was not an inferior version of fascism. Argentine fascism was in tune with both "European" and "Latin American" realities of a country like Argentina. With almost half its population of Italian origin and enjoying remarkably high standards of living,[28] Argentina in the first half of the twentieth century was often presented on both sides of the Atlantic as a natural receptacle for fascism. As we will see, Mussolini himself certainly thought in these terms, and he targeted Argentina as the most important country for fascist imperialism in Latin America.

There are some excellent academic studies on the Italian community's relationship with fascist Italy.[29] But surprisingly there are no books specifically on the relations between Argentine nacionalistas and Italian fascism. In addition, the spectacular Nazi emigration to Argentina after 1945 has created a historiographical imbalance. Many historians believe that Nazis were the predominant force vis-à-vis nacionalismo.[30] This is an image that needs to be corrected. As this work will show, the diffusion of fascist propaganda preceded the Nazi initiative—in this respect the longevity of the Italian fascist regime had a role to play—and in the nacionalista universe Italian fascism was perceived as having a greater influence than its Nazi ideological cousin. To be sure, as many Italians complained, the Nazis had more means and poured more money into the nacionalista universe, but in matters of belief this did not count. In short, from the historical point of view of the nacionalista sources, Italian fascism was always more important for the Argentines than German Nazism. This link did not, however mean that nacionalista ideology was derivative. Nacionalistas actually regarded Italian fascism in the same way that the Nazis—and indeed Hitler himself—did at the beginning of the Nazi movement. Until the Nazi seizure of power in 1933, they perceived Italian fascism as the original matrix of a worldwide extremist movement.[31] Argentina itself was a major player in international politics, a longstanding contender with the United States in the western hemisphere. And last but not least, Argentina was the last country to go to war against the Axis powers. Literally, Argentina entered the war just before the war was over.

The links between Argentina and Italy, Mussolini often said, were not the kind one found in standard diplomatic practices because they were "arterial links" of blood.[32] From the very beginning, Italian fascism proclaimed itself to be a global ideology, extending naturally into Argentina. Italian fascism had colonial notions of Latin America that were inscribed in the broader context of Mussolini's idea of fascist imperialist universality; for Mussolini, Argentina was not really a nation. This was a view that Argentine fascists did not accept. In fact, the Argentine nacionalistas never adopted the model that the Europeans put forward. Through a comparative exploration of fascist ideology across the Atlantic, I will show why and how the Italians nevertheless continued to sell fascism and how and why the Argentines refused to buy it.

My work addresses different layers of meaning that could also be described as national and transnational; that is, it opens a critical dialogue with at least seven interlocutors: (1) the history of fascism; (2) traditional Latin American historiographies on authoritarianism, nationalism, religion, and nation building that present Argentina as having a *Sonderweg* or special path of unchecked liberalism until 1945 and the emergence of Peronism; (3) the history of political violence; (4) the history of anti-Semitism; (5) the debates about the origins of Argentina's unique brand of political violence that lead to the "dirty war" and the "desaparecidos" of the 1970s; (6) European and Latin American understandings of processes of secularization and desecularization; and (7) traditional approaches to intellectual and cultural processes in Europe and Latin America. This book attempts to bring theoretically oriented intellectual history and political history together and to go beyond traditional discussions about the "nature" of fascism. By grounding my research in archival and other hitherto unresearched materials from Europe and the Americas, I present fascist ideology as a global phenomenon. By tying these materials into a general analysis, I show the multifaceted, nonrational, and incoherent nature of fascist ideology as the fascists understood it—though for them, fascism was a coherent political ideology. Moreover, this book will show why these dangerous ideas made sense to fascists. I do not expect, nor would I like, readers to make sense of fascist ideas, or the fascists' rationale for the way they understood their world; rather, I hope to help my readers understand fascist processes of meaning making, their global links, and the messianic political ramifications of these ideas in the present.

An intellectual and cultural history of fascism, and particularly its foreign policy, must include the history of fascist ideological propaganda.[33] This book tells the transatlantic dimension of this history. Chapter 1 deals with the different layers of fascist thinking with respect to Argentina and Latin America. It provides a historical and theoretical introduction to fascism and then deals with the Italian, and European, side of the fascists' transatlantic equation, namely, how fascism saw Latin America as a larger, and often poorer, version of Argentina. In the chapter, I analyze how this conflation affected fascist international relations and policy-making decisions for South America. In the following chapters I deal with how fascism was received in Argentina, particularly by the Argentine state and the mainstream press, as well as the Left, the Right, and the radical Right, which at times called itself Argentine fascism and more generally nacionalismo.[34] Chapter 2 deals with the more institutional side of the story by providing a new account of previously underresearched diplomatic materials. The chapter also analyzes the different layers of the Argentine reception of fascism and provides an introduction to the history of Argentine nationalism, from liberal democracy to the Uriburu dictatorship and beyond.

Chapter 3 addresses the actual politics of fascist propaganda in Argentina, as well as the nacionalista reformulation of the Italian fascist experience. In this chapter, I investigate how Mussolini's propaganda endeavors included the fascist rethinking of Argentine history, fascist transatlantic flights, and the extensive use of radio, cinema, cartoons, and bribes. But Argentines did not merely adopt this "fascism for export." Interpretative appropriation was central to this reception. I show how the nacionalistas developed an original appropriation of fascism, which they understood as a generic version of their own political movement. In other words, they saw European fascism as an example and not as a prefabricated model that simply needed to be assembled. The chapter also stresses the question of Argentine fascist self-understanding. I pay special attention to the different fascist efforts to create a political doctrine. Without the presence of a leader and a regime such as those of fascist Italy, Argentine fascists had a greater intellectual autonomy in conceiving an ideological canon and defining their political culture in doctrinal and "sacred" terms.

Chapters 4 and 5 are concerned with the Argentine fascist or nacionalista conception of fascism as the political expression of the will of God. In chapter 4 I trace the origins of the particular attachment the Argentine nacionalistas had with the Catholic Church as it was informed by ongoing political discussions in Argentina and the world. Chapter 5 also deals chronologically with the contradictions and debates that the fascists encountered in their "sacred" journey of doctrinal and programmatic searching, including the questions of Nazism and the Spanish Civil War, imperialism and anti-imperialism, and the nacionalista creation of "the enemy."

Fascism was a cross-regional civic religion in its most extreme form. In certain Catholic countries, fascism reoccupied places previously held by institutional religion, but it also let itself be invested by the "sacred." This intertwining of the secular with the sacred is central to an understanding of Argentine fascism and is thoroughly explored in this book. Avoiding an oversimplified notion of secularization, I stress the complex interaction between secularizing processes and religious tradition and practice. I focus on the quasi-religious dimensions of fascism that overlapped with the Catholic "sacred." This relation was not devoid of conflicts, but anti-Semitism, and with it anticommunism, provided both fascists and Catholics on the far right with a common intellectual battlefield on which to join forces, as well as a symbolic shared space for enacting fascist ideology. As a political religion Argentine fascism was embedded in Catholicism, as the fascists understood it. In this context they resorted to anti-Semitism as the best metaphor to represent the internal enemy. Finally, chapter 5 provides a transnational recapitulation of the topics raised in this book.

The epilogue deals with the strong political and ideological legacy of Argentine fascism and, more specifically, its central role in the birth of Peronism. Visions of political apocalypse were central to the many fascists who could reposition themselves as an early right wing of the Peronist movement. In addition, the epilogue briefly treats the political and conceptual legacy of Argentine fascism after Peronism, especially the nacionalista idea of the internal enemy, which represents the intellectual genealogy of the last military dictatorship (1976–1983).[35] The epilogue, like the book as a whole, highlights the essential differences between Argentine nacionalismo and Italian fascism. Paradoxically, in terms of Argentine fascist self-understanding these differences show the ideological possibility of fascism as a global ideology.

This historical process of global reformulation constitutes the kernel of my interpretation of fascism. In short, it shows how fascism was many things in different times and places and yet it remained a transnational political ideology with theoretical, national, and contextual variations.

1

Transnational Fascism

It was always a too little noted hallmark of fascist propaganda that it was not satisfied
with lying but deliberately proposed to transform its lies into reality.

—HANNAH ARENDT, 1945

On April 16, 1939, Mussolini and his son-in-law, Count Galeazzo Ciano,
met with Marshall Hermann Göring in Rome. The international context was fragile. England and France were extremely worried, and the smell
of war was in the air. The Nazis seemed unsatisfied with the section of
Czechoslovakia accorded to them as a gift in Munich in September of 1938.
Italy, with its invasion of Albania and its presence in the Balearic Islands, was
threatening the status quo in the Mediterranean. As was customary in Nazi-
fascist conclaves, great matters were discussed: master plans for world domination, invasion of countries, and disquisitions about spheres of influence.
As usual, Mussolini tried to stress the originality of fascism vis-à-vis Nazism.
He emphasized his own sense of political imperatives, and when referring to
the "political situation," he declared that he "considered a general war to be
unavoidable." Mussolini also exaggerated the Italian military capacity. He
knew his military assessments were incorrect, but when meeting with the
Nazis he could not display any uncertainty.[1]

At one point, the conversation reached an astonishing detachment from
reality, at times typical of fascist rhetoric. Göring dismissed American peace
negotiations and leadership, suggesting President Franklin D. Roosevelt suffered from a "mental disease." Mussolini, in turn, mocked Roosevelt for his

supposed ignorance of geopolitical matters. The Duce refused to show the Nazis any weakness in his knowledge or determination, and, as opposed to Roosevelt's "ignorance," he claimed to know everything about everything. He felt compelled to confirm to the Nazis what for many years anyone could read on walls throughout Italy, or in Italian papers: "Mussolini is always right."[2]

But neither leader believed that the Americas could be ignored. Göring remarked that the United States was central to world opinion, particularly in the western hemisphere. Hopefully, he said, Roosevelt would not be reelected and "things could become very different." As was true of the Mediterranean, the Nazis wanted Mussolini to believe that they recognized Latin America as an Italian sphere of influence. Göring told Mussolini that "by means of her good connections with South America, Italy could certainly successfully counteract American influence on that continent." Upon the mention of Latin America, Mussolini uncharacteristically betrayed a lacuna in his knowledge when he admitted "that, for some reason which he could not quite understand, Italy's relations with Argentina were not particularly good."[3]

Without noting that Göring was referring to South America in general, Mussolini had shifted the topic of conversation to just one of its countries. This book addresses a number of different questions symptomatically present in Mussolini's musings about Argentina. Why were relations between fascism and Argentina "not particularly good"? Why did Mussolini believe that relations with Argentina should be different? Why did he care about this transnational problem when the discussion turned to the New World order? What was the "reason" that he could "not quite understand"? What was his vision of Latin America and the special place he reserved in it for Argentina? What do all these questions tell us about the transnational nature of fascism? This chapter and the following ones provide historical and theoretical answers to these questions. As I hope to demonstrate, Mussolini's vision, and the connections between Italian and Argentine fascism, provide a window onto the transnational and imperialist dimensions of fascist thinking on a global scale. This is the story I am going to tell. But first I provide a brief historical assessment of Italian fascism, and how it changed over time. What was fascism in its "classic" form? This chapter provides a brief analysis of the rise of fascism in Italy and Europe, and gives the reader an equally brief historical engagement with fascist theory. Last but not least, I discuss Italy's connections with Argentina and Latin America, which predated Mussolini's global ambitions and his desire to propagandize Argentina. In short, in this chapter I introduce the reader to fascism as a historical and theoretical international reality. By emphasizing the ambivalent transnational and national dimensions of fascism, I provide a necessary correction to the theoretically static and nationally limited presentation of fascism that the book as a whole calls into question.

Fascist Histories

Fascism is a political ideology that encompassed totalitarianism, state terrorism, imperialism, racism, and, in the German case, the most radical genocide of the last century: the Holocaust. Fascism in its many forms did not hesitate to kill its own citizens as well as its colonial subjects in its search for ideological and political closure. Millions of civilians perished on a global scale during the apogee of fascist ideologies in Europe and beyond. Like liberalism and Marxism, fascism assumed many national variations and political interpretations.

The word "fascism" derives from the Italian word *fascio* and refers to a political group (such as the group lead by Giuseppe Garibaldi during the times of Italian unification). "Fascism" also refers visually and historically to a Roman imperial symbol of authority. Its birthplace as a modern political ideology was northern Italy, the year was 1919, and its founder was Benito Mussolini. Thus, "fascism" as a term and as a political movement was born in the Italian peninsula. Its ideological origins, however, predate its name. The fact that fascism was born as a concept before its birth as a movement is central to any understanding of fascism. The ideology of radical nationalism that made it possible was part of a larger intellectual reaction to the Enlightenment.[4] This tradition was both European and, in the Latin American case, "non-European" as well. To be sure, the original ideology behind fascism was born as a reaction to the progressive European revolutions of the long nineteenth century (from the French Revolution of 1789 to the American and Latin American revolutions of 1776 and the 1810s). The ideology of the anti-Enlightenment is the major root of the longstanding ideological tradition that created fascism. Its branches constituted a reaction against liberal politics. And yet fascism did not oppose the market economy and put forward a corporatist organization that aimed to be functional to capitalist accumulation. Equally important, fascism is a philosophy of political action that ascribes value to absolute violence in the political realm. This ascription was boosted by one radical outcome of the Enlightenment: Soviet communism. The rise of Bolshevism in 1917 encountered global opposition as well as emulation. By presenting itself as the opposite of communism, fascism took advantage of this widespread rejection and fear of social revolution and at the same time incorporated some of its dimensions.[5]

A new age of total war ultimately provided the context of fascism more than the Soviet experiment did.[6] In fact, it was with the First World War that the ideology of fascism emerged in the trenches. Adolf Hitler and Benito Mussolini openly stated that war constituted their most meaningful experience. After the war, these two former soldiers found violence and war to be political elements of the first order. When this ideology of violence fused with extreme right-wing nationalism and imperialism and non-Marxist leftist tendencies of revolutionary syndicalism, fascism as we know it today crystallized. This moment of crystallization was not exclusively Italian or European. In Argentina, former socialist intellectuals such as the poet Leopoldo Lugones soon understood the political implications of this fusion. Like Lugones, the Brazilian fascist Plinio Salgado saw fascism as the expression of a universal transnational ideology of the extreme Right. During the same period, young Hitler, a disenfranchised war hero, began to give political expression to his basic violent tendencies. And he did it from the new trenches of modern mass politics.[7] Hitler first adopted, and then shaped, the ideology of a small German party of the extreme Right, soon to be called the National Socialist Party. Hitler early on recognized his debt to the thought and practice of Mussolini, but both leaders also shared a belief that the world as they knew it was in crisis. Both adopted fierce anticommunist and antiliberal stances.[8] This antidemocratic modernism combined modern politics with technological innovation, aesthetic notions, and a discourse of war.

The modernity of fascism has preoccupied major thinkers over the course of the last century. Whereas Sigmund Freud saw fascism as the return of the repressed, namely, the mythical reformulation of death and violence as a source of political power, Max Horkheimer and Theodor Adorno in their *Dialectic of the Enlightenment* presented fascism as modernity's worst outcome.[9] Overall, although I agree with Horkheimer and Adorno's analysis, their thesis is nonetheless limited to European developments and the "continental" frame of reference. In order to grasp the global and transnational dimensions of fascism it is, however, necessary first to understand its history, beginning with its national articulation, and second to relate this manifestation of fascism to intellectual exchanges across the Atlantic Ocean and beyond.

Fascism as a political movement was created in Italy by Mussolini, in Piazza San Sepolcro, Milan, on March 23, 1919, in front of about fifty followers, and it reached power there in 1922, ten years before Nazism. Italian fascism was the first successful fascist model, and other kindred movements of the radical Right, including Nazism, regarded it as such throughout the interwar period. Besides fascism and Nazism there were other movements and ideologies of the fascist variety in Europe. The historian Robert Paxton presents five stages of fascist development in the region: (1) the creation of movements, (2) their taking root in the political system, (3) their seizure of power, (4) the exercise of power, and (5) the long "duration," during which the fascist regimes chose either radicalization or entropy.[10] To be sure, only some fascist movements completed these five stages, but fascist movements were a reality in most countries on the European continent. Their success or failure was related to national and international currents. The Nazi occupation of France or Norway, for example, literally placed native fascists in a position of power. Spain would not have seen the emergence of a fascist regime without the military assistance that Hitler and Mussolini provided. Conversely, the apparent sustainability of the British and Russian political systems, the entry of the United States into the war, and the ultimate failure of the Nazi invasion of these countries saved these countries from fascism.

Military historians are right to point out this external evidence, but in all these cases, fascism would not have existed without an ideological synthesis as important as socialism or liberalism. Fascism was the product of an ideological concoction that combined a deformed version of socialism and a deformed version of liberal nationalism. Once socialists such as Benito Mussolini replaced notions of class struggle with ideas of national struggle, the road to fascist imperialism and war was open; Mussolini's proletarian imperialism (he declared the fascist empire in 1936) was a result of exactly this fascist synthesis. Even in his socialist youth, when Mussolini opposed state-sanctioned imperialism, he nonetheless stressed the supposedly superior traits of Italian national spirituality. For Mussolini every language was the expression of the "need, the attitudes, and the spirituality of a given people." (He claimed that "not even" the Zulus as a linguistic group should be denied their national pride.) Thus, even before his famous renunciation of socialism, Mussolini believed in the possibilities of nationalist politics as a transnational theory and practice adapted to the spirituality of every country.[11] Mussolini's "internationalism" should be considered within the framework of his idea of specific nationalist needs. More than an institution or a state, "Italianness" for

Mussolini was an ethnic and linguistic identity, and it was this that he identified with; he had never identified with the politics of the Italian pre-fascist state, even in the socialist period of his life (when, according to his hagiographers, he had been a staunch patriot). He actually saw the liberal state as representing the established bourgeois order that he opposed. His opposition to the Italian colonial adventure in Libya in 1911–1912 propelled him to national attention within the Italian socialist movement, and, more important, the radicalism of his anti-imperialist position gave him national exposure—on the strength of that position, when he was just twenty-nine years old, he became editor of Italy's most important socialist paper, *Avanti*.

At the outbreak of the First World War, Mussolini briefly hesitated but finally joined the tiny prowar camp of the Socialist Party and thereby isolated himself from the mainstream party as well as from almost all his socialist acquaintances. He told a party gathering, "You persecute me because you love me." He was soon expelled from the party. By the end of 1914, he had founded a newspaper, *Il Popolo d'Italia*, which was subsidized by the French government in its effort to persuade Italy to enter the war on the Allied side. (The paper was also supported by Italian industrialists.) In 1915, Mussolini was thirty-two, already old in military terms, but he successfully lobbied to be sent to the front, where he rose to the rank of corporal. Mussolini killed some of his fellow soldiers when apparently mishandling a grenade thrower,[12] but then he was badly wounded, and when he returned to Milan, he presented himself as a war hero.

The self-proclaimed status of *Il Popolo d'Italia* as the organ of "producers" and "combatants" signaled the nationalistic sense of Mussolini's new understanding of politics. The slogan of the paper was a quote from Napoleon: "The revolution is an idea that has found bayonets." What kind of revolution did it refer to? This was of minimal importance to Mussolini. At the time, he considered it the revolution put forward by revolutionary syndicalism. But perhaps more important, he believed that bayonets, and violence, epitomized politics in general. He was ready to lead an ampler movement than socialism, and so, fascism was born.

The earliest fascists were a group of war veterans, former Milanese revolutionary syndicalists, socialists, republicans, futurists such as Filippo Tommaso Marinetti, anarchists, and even some liberals and Catholics. They represented a gray zone within the Italian political system. These groups did not necessarily share a strictly defined ideology, but they did hold the same messianic ideas about crisis, revolution, violence, war, and nation that Mus-

solini put forth. Like him, they replaced class struggle with nationalism and
spiritual imperialism. Their ideological displacement to a field of meaning
generally occupied by the traditional Right created a political hybrid. In
short, the outcome was an ideology that was radically rightist, even "reactionary," as Mussolini often said. At the same time, Mussolini used a language of revolution and change typical of the Left. Fascism was thus neither
right nor left but a combination of both.[13] This political turn to the Right,
the "overcoming of socialism," had other motives beyond the ideological
ones, including careerism and financial perspectives. If the new fascists had
advocated war during a time of international war, once the war was over
they advocated civil war in a time of peace. War, whether international or
civil, was a defining trait of fascism. The founding fathers of fascism advocated violence, expansionary nationalism, and a Spartan ideal of the Italian
people as an "armed nation." Yet in contrast to the traditional Right, they
proposed the confiscation of church property, antimonarchism, an imperialist foreign policy understood as one that would protect Italy from "the
hegemony of the current plutocratic powers" (i.e., England, France, and the
United States), the abolition of the Senate, the defense of libertarianism and
free speech, a progressive tax on capital and a fixed minimum wage, the vote
for women, expropriation of land and factories, the nationalization of the
war industry, and confiscation of war profits. In other words, the early
fascists proposed the radical eradication of the "social-bourgeois" order as
they understood it.

Turning the world upside down was the overall premise behind the
pseudocarnival program of the early fascist movement that Mussolini created. With the exception of violence, nationalism, imperialism, and a militarism of a new type radically opposed to traditional reactionary "military
dictatorships," the fascist regime never followed the other elements of the
"program." Soon, Mussolini began to downplay these other goals or strip
them of practical meaning. They were not "his" program. He had endorsed
the original program, but it had been mainly shaped by the futurist elements of fascism and not by Mussolini himself. For example, F. T. Marinetti,
the founder of the literary vanguard group of futurism, warned against
the danger posed by the presence of the pope in Italy and proposed "de-
Vaticanization" as a central aim for fascism.[14] But more important than
such futurist projects for the nation were the actions of the main group
within original fascism that actually made fascism possible: the war veterans. The veterans were instrumental in injecting political violence into

Italian life, and tellingly, in the first fascist ballot, Mussolini was identified as one of the veterans.[15] He was clearly more interested in channeling their seemingly uncontrolled violence than in forging a dogma for the incipient movement.[16]

During this earlier period, Mussolini carefully followed and ultimately betrayed Gabriele D'Annunzio's nationalist military adventure in Fiume and was able to assert his power over the messy fascist movement.[17] The need to assemble a massive constituency and to present himself as the only *duce* of the movement motivated Mussolini to appreciate that fascism if it wanted to reach power had to, first, stop being an antiparty; second, regulate its violence; and third, become a party with a central organization under Mussolini's command. This explains, in part, the absence of the most radical "social" topics of 1919 in the life of the fascist national party (Partito Nazionale Fascista), created from the fascist movement in 1921.[18]

Violence, radical "nonreactionary" militarism, and national expansion seemed to be the only elements that remained in the pragmatic versions of the party that unfolded in the 1920s. And these were precisely the elements that the earlier fascist Mussolini preferred to stress. In 1919, he had explained "the meaning" of fascism by appealing to its radical opposition to the traditional democratic politics of electoralism: "Our fight is a political fight but we also do not mean this word [politics] in its traditional sense."[19]

Violence, or more precisely the violent terrorist actions of the fascist squads against socialists and communists, placed the party in a national context. Mussolini described this violence in 1921 as "aristocratic, surgical, . . . and humane."[20] Although fascism was crushed in its first election, this violence, and the long-term social and political problems of the endemically dysfunctional Italian democracy, created a collective sensation of disorder, a political void that many members of the elite, including the Italian king, thought fascism could fill. Instead of crushing the fascists, who were threatening the Italian political order, the king decided to call Mussolini to Rome and asked him to be the next prime minister. Mussolini did not refuse this invitation. Thus, after the so-called March on Rome on October 28, 1922, fascism took over power on October 31. By the end of 1922, Mussolini had a state and a monopoly of violence to regulate the violence of the fascist squads. Now, Mussolini could finally impose "discipline" on fascism. The history of fascism from 1922 onward is the history of the Duce's successful attempt to bend the fascist movement to his will—first politically and then ideologically. A singular step in this direction was the fusion of

Italian nationalism and fascism. With the theoretical assistance of the Italian right-wing nationalists who were merged with fascism in 1923, Mussolini created the structure of his totalitarian state. Finally in 1925, after some unstable political moments (e.g., the fascist assassination of the socialist representative Giacomo Matteotti, one of the leaders of the antifascist opposition), fascism defined itself as a full-blown totalitarian dictatorship. After 1925, when democracy was finally destroyed from within, "true" fascism was born. Opposition was suppressed, and the fascist dictatorship affirmed its "totalitarian" will to dominate all aspects of Italian life. It also affirmed the need to have a unitary ideology of its own. The period between the signing of the concordat with the Vatican in 1929 and the imperialistic adventure in Ethiopia that finished with the declaration of the fascist empire in 1935–1936 signals the most successful era of fascism, that of its broadest consensus among Italians.[21] During this time, Mussolini's megalomania expanded and the cult of his personality grew to totalitarian proportions. Primo Levi, who was a young man at the time (and soon to become a Jewish victim of fascism and Nazism), would later document the idolatry surrounding Mussolini's persona.[22] Federico Fellini's recollections of childhood in this period, in his film *Amarcord*, stress the overpowering presence of Mussolini's body image in every aspect of life, including coins, pictures, and dreams. Another writer who was a child at the time, Italo Calvino, later wrote, "You could say that I spent the first twenty years of my life with Mussolini's face always in view, in the sense that his portrait hung in every classroom as well as in every public building or office I entered." The cult of Mussolini was internalized and occupied every aspect of life, including the games one played with children, creating a collective reflection of the face of the "thinking" dictator that was carried for generations of Italians. In Calvino's words:

The other salient feature of these first official images of the dictator was the pensive pose, the prominent forehead seeming to underline his capacity for thought. In one of the affectionate games that people used to play at the time with children of one or two years, the adult would say, "Do Mussolini's face," and the child would furrow his brow and stick out angry lips. In a word, Italians of my generation carried the portrait of Mussolini within themselves, even before they were of an age to recognize it on the walls, and this reveals that there was (also) something infantile in that image, that look of concentration which small children can have, and which does not actually mean that they are thinking intensely about anything.[23]

An incapacity to think defines fascist instrumental rationality, namely, the idea that subjects are objects and should be treated as such. This was the fate of the colonial enemies of fascist imperialism in Africa. Fascist imperialism, war, and racism were cemented in fascist notions of a global ideological civil war against antifascism.[24]

Mussolini conceived fascism as a universal movement of the extreme Right, and during the 1930s, fascism organized a "fascist international." Asvero Gravelli, a dynamic fascist ideologue, was, along with General Eugenio Coselschi, its most conspicuous representative.[25] In his inaugural speech in the first of the two global meetings of international fascism in 1935, Coselschi argued that the need for a "universal fascism" was apparent in the face of "a monstrous phenomenon, the alliance of capitalism and the anarchist and Bolshevik movements."[26] For Coselschi, acting out in the fascist meeting the subject position of ventriloquist of Mussolini and Italian fascism, the enemy represented a united front against fascism. Fascism, he thought, had to be universalized in order to fight this front. The idea that paranoia, that is, an ideologically biased perception that involves fears of persecution, should be taken as truth shaped fascist politics and created new realities. In short, the perceived enemy, presented as a persecutor, deserved to be persecuted. Coselschi's notion that aggressive warlike strategies and actions were acts of self-defense resembles Hitler's famous self-fulfilling prophecy in his very public Reichstag speech of January 30, 1939:

> One thing I should like to say on this day which may be memorable for others as well as for us Germans: In the course of my life I have very often been a prophet, and have usually been ridiculed for it. During the time of my struggle for power it was in the first instance the Jewish race which only received my prophecies with laughter when I said that I would one day take over the leadership of the State, and with it that of the whole nation, and that I would then among many other things settle the Jewish problem. Their laughter was uproarious, but I think that for some time now they have been laughing on the other side of their face. Today I will once more be a prophet: If the international Jewish financiers in and outside Europe should succeed in plunging the nations once more into a world war, then the result will not be the Bolshevization of the earth, and thus the victory of Jewry, but the annihilation of the Jewish race in Europe![27]

To be sure, Hitler was more certain and explicit than Coselschi, or Mussolini, about the Jewish nature of the enemy. But both fascist "thinkers" based their universal fascist wars on two related fictions. First, the enemy existed and could be easily defined as an alliance of capitalism and communism; second, the enemy was going to attack and fascism had to defend itself. For fascist ideology, totalitarian aggression became self-defense. All subsequent fascist wars in Europe can be seen through this lens, namely, the idea of a self-defensive war between total good and absolute evil. "Universal fascism" helped the Spanish fascists in the Spanish Civil War (1936–1939). Some 78,000 Italian fascists, 19,000 Nazis, and 10,000 Portuguese fascists fought against democracy in Spain.[28] In 1938, Mussolini, without any pressure from his German friends, decided to follow the Nazi pattern of anti-Semitism and established racial laws against the Jewish population of Italy. In 1940, Mussolini made the worst and contextually the most unpopular political decision of his life when he made Italy enter the Second World War on the Nazis' side. The failure of the Italian armies in Europe and Africa increasingly indebted the fascists to the Nazis. By 1942 Mussolini had lost most of his autonomy to Hitler. And yet Hitler regarded Mussolini as perhaps his only equal ideological partner. Thus, despite the overall lack of autonomy, Mussolini's had more "independence" than other fascist regimes in Nazi Europe.[29] By 1943, most Italians had lost their confidence in their Duce. Fascists increasingly voiced the previously unspeakable idea that Mussolini was wrong on the war and perhaps on other issues as well. Even some noted fascists believed that because of Mussolini's actions fascism and Italy were destined for total destruction. Old and ill (Mussolini suffered from somatic gastric pain), the dictator increasingly believed in the myth of his own infallibility. Millions of Italians should die if that was necessary, he claimed, to achieve his major ideological aims: securing imperial dominance in the Mediterranean and the Latin Atlantic and forging a new Italian race of violent, soldierly men.

Finally, in a secret session of the fascists' Grand Council on the night of July 24, 1943, Mussolini was ousted from power by a group of rebellious fascists that included Count Ciano, Mussolini's son-in-law, whom Mussolini later would make pay for this "treason" with his life. After he was deposed, Mussolini was put in prison, but not for long. A German commando liberated the Duce and sent him to Germany. With the help of the Nazis, Mussolini returned to Italy and established a republican fascist regime in the northern part of the country. The south was, however, soon occupied by the Allies, and civil war erupted in the Italian peninsula. The Fascist Social Republic (1943–1945) that Mussolini founded, the so-called Republic of Salò, was a Nazi puppet regime. But ironically, without the actual means of power, most of its fascists dedicated themselves to thinking about theoretical issues in addition to enacting radical violence against Jews and antifascists (along with their German masters). The republic was indeed radical through its brief life, as famously depicted by the film director Pier Paolo Pasolini. Pasolini's description of social fascism as a degraded reactionary ideology inspired by the Marquis de Sade is idiosyncratic; in reality, the fascism of 1943–1945 implied a return to the social radicalism, anticlericalism, and antimonarchism of 1919.[30]

Fascism as a movement and as a regime rose and fell promoting civil war. This was in the end the Italian legacy of Mussolini: a country divided, and a near apocalyptic fight that required radical violent means, including fascist collaboration in sending Italian Jews to Auschwitz.[31] But perhaps, more important, the legacy of fascism goes beyond Italy and Mussolini: fascism not only sent Italian Jews to Auschwitz after 1943; transnational fascism was the global ideology that made that crime possible.

To put it simply: without fascism, there would have been no Nazism as we know it. Nazism represented a radical outcome of transnational fascist ideology, an outcome so different from its ideological cousins that some historians argue that it was something else: a totally unique ideology.[32] Nazism and its outcome, the Holocaust, dwarf the gruesome Italian use of chemical weapons against African colonial subjects in the 1930s and the crimes of Spanish fascism, which involved the killing of 200,000 civilians and perceived political opponents[33]—it is only when contrasted with the Holocaust that the enormous crimes of other fascist formations seem to become lesser violations of normative humanity. Yet the comparison with the extremity of the Holocaust, the radical standard of political evil, should not excuse fascism at large. Fascism was an ideological network of national and, in some cases, transnational state terror. In the Nazi case, the fascist notion of the primacy of political imperatives and the reification of violence was literalized to the extreme. Nazism, in its radical spiral of integral terror against the Jews, left the fascist pack behind. It was in the Nazi empire in the east that the Nazis decided to literalize in the concentration camps the most circular notion of Nazi fascism, the notion of the abject; in Auschwitz, a closed and controlled laboratory of fascism, the Nazi idea of the abject enemy, the most detached and psychotic aspect of Hitler's ideology, became a reality.[34] The Nazis found and took advantage of a transnational European network of genocidal collaboration. Fascists and radical rightists from Romania to France and from Norway to the Ukraine and Croatia collaborated in the enterprise. Still, Nazism seems to represent, as far as the Holocaust is concerned, a radical departure from standard versions of fascism that fascist Italy epitomizes so well. Nazism is not an "ideal type" of fascism but its most radical possibility.[35]

Whereas the Nazi radical version of fascism stressed the perceived enemy as the defining aspect of its ideology, most fascisms ascribed to it a less fixed place. These key differences notwithstanding, fascism was a global phenomenon that included Nazism. There is no such thing as a fascist Platonic ideal type. Italian fascism was the first fascist movement in Europe and the original point of reference for other fascist movements. It was not, however, a Platonic form of fascism from which all other fascisms were derived. Understanding the Italian case is central to the general understanding of fascism, but fascism as a term and a reality refers to a transnational network of shared ideological subjectivities. Fascists in Europe and across the Atlantic were identified with the "idea." Above all, fascism was, and is, an idea about the world that occluded other readings of reality. Fascism confuses reality with truth. Hannah Arendt defines ideology as providing a circular vision of the world that occludes perception and empirical experience—fascism represented the ultimate ideological gaze in this Arendtian sense.[36] Fascist thinking represented an ideological lens to see and read the world. Paradoxically, fascism implied a denial of reality, an ideological detachment from it, that changed it and even created a new reality and a new definition of the possible in ideological politics. Fascism is, first and foremost, a political ideology. Its articulation through contextual political practices, aesthetics, and rituals across the Atlantic is the subject of the last section of this chapter and the chapters that follow, but before we examine those tendencies, we need to address fascist theory as Mussolini and most fascists understood it.

On Fascist Ideology

One theoretical problem that I want to address early on in contextual terms is what I mean by the ideology of fascism. Many times I have been asked: What is your theoretical definition of fascism? My answer to this question is that there are simple and complicated ways of dealing with definitions in history. The simple way is to finish a book (or a class) with a definition of the subject; the more complicated way, the way I would prefer, is that of starting with a general working definition of fascism and then complicating it. In other words, I want to deessentialize the topic.

Like liberalism and socialism, fascism never had a closed canonical apparatus. Its ideas changed over time, and only now, with the benefit of hindsight, is it possible to provide an analytical account of its major ideological patterns. Most fascists perceived fascism as a new political ideology in the making. It was radically opposed to traditional democratic politics, what they called Western "electoralism."[37] Benito Mussolini, the creator of fascism, argued that only decadent and old-fashioned ideologies had a closed body of knowledge. For Mussolini, ideas were useful when they had a practical value, that is to say, when they could confirm his own confused intuitions about social regeneration and the rebirth of nations, the leading role of elites, politics as an art, and more generally his noted antihumanitarianism. In short, for the creator of fascism ideas were useful when they provided legitimacy for short-term political goals.[38]

Mussolini was a strategist who believed that political needs should determine theoretical formations. Many historians have concluded that this belief made Mussolini a kind of antitheorist and that fascist theory was not important to the movement.[39] To be sure, Mussolini at some moments of his career had antitheoretical biases. But all the political needs that shaped Mussolini's strategic view of fascism were informed by a set of unarticulated thoughts and aims. These ideas about power, violence, the internal enemy, empire, and his own messianic expectation to be the virile leader of his people drove Mussolini's political practice over the years. These ideas were abstract enough to inform his political priorities, and concrete enough to be considered noncomplex elements for fascist politicians who often wanted to void conceptual complications. Antonio Gramsci, an astute Italian observer and theorist, preferred to stress the "concretism" of Mussolini as a defining characteristic of the fascist leader and, perhaps, of fascist ideology at large.[40] Mussolini's concretism was related to the idea of the primacy of politics over "rigid dogmatic formulas." With some wishful thinking, Mussolini himself argued that "theological" or "metaphysical" discussions were foreign to his movement. Fascism was not dogma but a "special mentality." In typical anti-intellectual terms, Mussolini usually merged his concretism, namely, the fascist preference for violent "immediate action," with a simplistic understanding of reality. Early on, Mussolini posed his "heretical" realism against the "prophecies" of liberalism, socialism, and communism. In other words, Mussolini defended the "reactionary," "aristocratic," and yet "anti-traditional" character of fascism by juxtaposing it to the "orgy of the revolution of words."[41] Fascism was essentially modern.[42] It saw itself as a child of the present and even as a "primitive" dimension of the future. Past causes, past theoretical formations, and even past experiences were not as important to Mussolini as present political "action." However, present strategies could for him only be manifest acts of a significant whole, a set of meaningful formations that constituted the basis from which political strategies emerged. The search for a symbiosis between this common ground from which fascist practices emanated and varied theoretical justifications for these strategies constituted the most dynamic element of fascist ideology and also presented its most obvious limits to full canonization. At the end of the day, the creation of a fascist canonical corpus was an endless task. It tried to combine varied short-term strategies with a longstanding basic preconception of the world. The fascist synthesis was based on this impossible transition from the politics of daily life to dogma. Fascist interpreters across the Atlantic had to articulate the often tense relation between fascist practice (strategy) and ideal (theory).

Fascist aesthetics played a central role in how fascism showed itself to the world, but fascism as a political ideology cannot be exclusively encompassed by aesthetics.[43] There was a deeper articulation between a more static fascist matrix and a constantly changing strategy. Ultimately, fascist practice was not related to day-to-day mundane politics, or aesthetics, but rather focused on a set of gendered rituals and spectacles that were aimed at objectifying fascist theory.[44] Fascist theory never became an articulated system of belief. It was always a changing set of tropes and ideas. Mussolini personally disliked systems of belief because he considered them to be necessarily dysfunctional. If economics or art were elements that the Duce deemed irrelevant to a person of his stature, he considered fascist ideology or fascist theory to be subordinated to practice and thereby capable of adaptation. But behind, or above, adaptation there was something more grandiose: the definition of fascism as an epochal turning point, a mental and practical "sacred" revolution. Indeed, despite his contempt for theory, Mussolini believed in the existence of high theory: the master narrative that represented immediate intuitions about the world—namely, a belief in the primacy of fascist basic meaning over the external world. Intentional, self-affirmative inner meaning was thereby the hard-core attribute of fascist ideology.

Inner fascist meaning represented the fascist matrix, its sacred founding dimension. This inner meaning expressed the supposed purity of the fascist ideal, the "fascist feeling" that kept the fascist universes of people and specific ideas tied together.[45] Tellingly, even as early as 1919, Mussolini had represented the different groups that formed fascism as sharing the same "unique soul." Fascism, he claimed, may have been "distinctive in form but it is fused and confused in substance."[46] To borrow a Saussurean metaphor, fascism is to be understood as a specific code, a language of political interpretation and action that had a changing set of signifiers attached to a less malleable signified. Mussolini called this signified the fascist *fondo commune* or "common denominator." It was the meaningful nucleus, the core contained within the less coherent changing dicta or set of fascist signifiers. The common denominator was a master cursor, a point of orientation. It was, in short, the fascist minimum, which contained the most basic premises of fascism, that which was relatively constant in fascist ideology as opposed to variable forms of fascist expression. The "fondo commune," the fascist primal notion of the world, was more important than its contextual practices or strategic presentations. The latter were the manifest contextual enactments, the strategic instantiations of a more stable "substance of fascism." As Mussolini put it in an uncanny moment of full disclosure: "Everyone of us has his own temperament, everyone has his own susceptibility, everyone has his own individual psychology, but there is a common denominator through which the whole is equalized."[47]

For the Duce, this equalized whole, the matrix of fascism, was the most basic level or core of fascist notions about politics and the world. It was a set of master tropes, distorted values and feelings about violence, war, nation, the sacred, and the abject. For some interpreters in the present it may be difficult to make sense of the sheer charge of irrationality and instinctual force that fascism embodied, what Antonio Gramsci had earlier presented as a fascist embrace of the "mysterious" coupled with a "psychology of war."[48] Although fascists in the past often understood this "psychology" in mystical, or even esoteric terms as imbued with unsignifiable, or unrepresentable, hidden meaning, its main components can perhaps be defined by historians in the present.

The fascist matrix was constituted by traditional binaries such as "us versus them" or "civilization versus barbarism," among others. But the fascist importation of this notion of the other as a totally abject being provided a central dimension to its ideology. Thus, fascism also presented central victimizing dimensions. That is to say, it had negative drives that represented what it stood against as opposed to what it stood for. My definition of fascism presents these dimensions as central to fascism across the Atlantic. More specifically, racism and anti-Semitism forged the links between Italy and Argentina, particularly but not exclusively during the early 1930s.[49] Against the enemy, fascism proposed its sacrifice for the sake of the national organism.

The notion of sacrificial violence not only concerned the abject (the enemy) but also the fascist self, as Mussolini often repeated. This also can be perceived in the powerful depiction by Jorge Luis Borges of the imaginary Nazi Otto zur Linde, or in the fascist leanings of the celebrated French theorist Georges Bataille.[50] Fascist racism and anti-Semitism are the consequences of this continuous search for the ideal enemy, who was increasingly dehumanized from 1919 onward. However, fascism comprised not only "anti" or negative dimensions. The more assertive elements of a definition of fascism would include a messianic "religious conception" that stressed the centrality of a dictatorial leader—embodied in the persona of Mussolini—who presented violence, war, and the accumulation of power as the categorical premises for a desired turning point in Italian and world history: the fascist empire. In fascist ideology, violence and aggression were considered the best expressions of power, as embodied in the Italian "race" and its "normal" masculinity.[51]

Fascism represents a particular understanding of the state and its monopoly of violence, namely, totalitarianism.[52] Whereas the Italian antifascists that coined the term "totalitarianism" in the 1920s meant it as a modern tyranny presenting fascism as a contemporary version of absolutism, Mussolini had a different take on totalitarianism. He appropriated the term, changing it from a negative political adjective to a self-assertive concept and reformulating it as a full identification of fascist ideological imperatives (violence, war, imperialism, and a particular notion of the abject) with regard to the state.

> The Fascist State is not a night watchman, solicitous only of the personal safety of the citizens; nor is it organized exclusively for the purpose of guaranteeing a certain degree of material prosperity and relatively peaceful conditions of life; a board of directors would do as much. . . . The State, as conceived and realized by Fascism, is a spiritual and ethical entity for securing the political, juridical, and economic organization of the nation, an organization which in its origin and growth is a manifestation of the spirit. The State guarantees the internal and external safety of

the country, but it also safeguards and transmits the spirit of the people, elaborated down the ages in its language, its customs, its faith. The State is not only the present, it is also the past and above all the future. Transcending the individual's brief spell of life, the State stands for the immanent conscience of the nation. The forms in which it finds expression change, but the need for it remains.[53]

The state that fascism presents as being above and beyond everything else is not every state but a fascist state personified in the leader and his ideological imperatives. It is the state that fascism had previously conquered and dominated. This state eliminates the distinction between the public and the private. Moreover, the fascist state swallows civil society and eventually destroys it.[54] As many antifascists noted at the time, fascism used democracy, and even democratic alliances, in order to destroy democracy.[55] The fascist revolution that the state impersonated was supposed to exterminate the bourgeois order once and for all. Fascism presented itself as the antithesis of gradualism, the "antiparty," the "anti-Europe" that would move Europe and the world to the future. Fascism is essentially revolutionary. Like Soviet Russia, it eliminated political discussion, pluralism, and diversity. Like "real socialism," it obscured the distinction between the state's legitimate use of power and the use of unlawful violence. In short, in totalitarianism, the state becomes a criminal and abhors enlightened normativity. However, if Stalin was totalitarian in practice, he never rejected the legacy of the Enlightenment from a theoretical point of view. This was, of course, the ethical failure of communist ideology.[56] The fact that Nazis could enjoy listening to Beethoven in the midst of Auschwitz stands in contrast to Lenin's incapacity to listen to the German composer in the midst of communist terror. Lenin believed that listening to Beethoven would make him softer while he was engaged in the gruesome repression of political opponents. For Lenin, Beethoven's music represented reason, the legacy of the Enlightenment. This is a symptom of Lenin's recognition of the fact that one could not listen to reason while acting against it.[57]

In contrast, for the Nazis, the German composer represented bare beauty and violence. One may recall, in this regard, Stanley Kubrick's depiction of Alex DeLarge, leader of postfascist urban squads in the film *A Clockwork Orange* (1971).[58] DeLarge shared his musical taste with Nazis such as Hitler, Goebbels, and Mengele.

Fascist totalitarianism, unlike Soviet Russia, did not spread fear, violence, and death with the sole objective of silencing real and imagined dissent. Violence, and the lawless use of violence, was one of its defining aspects, in both fascist practice and fascist theory.

Structural violence was a mark of fascism and found its best expression in the war ideal and the concentration camps. Violence, as Primo Levi cogently put it, became an end in itself.[59] Fascism brandished power and violence as ideological aims rather than means. In fascist ideology, violence is not only instrumental; it is mainly a form of intuition, of creation. It is not only a mobilizing myth but a negative sublime, namely, an object of political desire.[60] For Mussolini, violence is power without restraints. It is a nonrational state that provides the nation and the individual with the security of being protected from the menacing outer world. For Max Weber, Karl Marx, or even partly for Georges Sorel (who nonetheless exalted violence in regenerative and redemptive terms), violence has a primary role in politics but needs to be restrained after having usefully achieved an end. In the fascist ideal, violence loses its instrumentality and becomes a direct source of knowledge.[61] Violence is perceived as a sublime experience that renders politics an almost sacred field of action. Moreover, violence was for Mussolini an ethical force that helped fascism achieve a radical break from ordinary concerns.

Here, the notion of sacrifice is central. Over time Mussolini best expressed this idea in the famous fascist catchphrase "I don't care" (or "I don't give a damn") that was inscribed in the showrooms of the permanent fascist revolution in 1942. For Mussolini this action of not caring was related to the acceptance of death and "purifying blood" as redemptive forces.[62] Even as late as 1942, when considering the future of the Italian nation, he could not (or did not want to) conceal the fascist embrace of violence that the Nazi war of destruction promised him.[63] As they were for Hitler, the Spanish fascist Primo de Rivera, or the Argentine nacionalistas, violence and war were for Mussolini sources of political orientation and personal and collective redemption.[64] A feeling of present danger embedded in violence was part of the fascist way of life. As Mussolini declared: "Living dangerously should mean always being ready for everything—whatever the sacrifice, whatever the danger, whatever the action, when the defense of the fatherland and fascism are concerned."[65]

Violence was for fascism essentially expressed in the totalitarian fascist state and its "spiritual" and "ethical" imperialism. As Mussolini stated:

The Fascist State expresses the will to exercise power and to command. Here the Roman tradition is embodied in a conception of strength. Imperial power, as understood by the Fascist doctrine, is not only territorial, or military, or commercial; it is also spiritual and ethical. An imperial nation, that is to say a nation which directly or indirectly is a leader of others, can exist without the need to conquer a single square mile of territory.[66]

Imperialism is for fascism a state of becoming rather than a state of being. To be sure, fascism does not differ in this sense from other imperialist formations.[67] However, it differs in that it is presumably a "proletarian imperialism" when it is viewed as the ultimate expression of Mussolini's nationalist displacement of class struggles onto national struggle. Paradoxically, for Mussolini, fascist imperialism was the ultimate form of anticolonialism. Imperialism was the political antithesis of "decadence." In other words, an active new fascist form of imperialism eliminates the possibility of "becoming a colony."[68] Fascist imperialism presented itself as heir of roman imperial traditions. But the importance of Romanness notwithstanding, in contrast to the ancient Romans, fascism promoted the idea of a war without end.[69] In other words, Mussolini conceived of war as preemptive action to strengthen Italian leadership in the Latin world, indeed, as an imperialist move against "plutocratic empires": "a war of civilization and liberation. It is the war of the people. The Italian people feel it is its own war. It is the war of the poor, the disinherited, and the war of the proletarians."[70] When projected onto a global stage, fascist imperialism is the ultimate form of violence and power: "Fascism sees in the imperialistic spirit—i.e., in the tendency of nations to expand—a manifestation of their vitality. In the opposite tendency, which would limit their interests to the home country, it sees a symptom of decadence. Peoples who rise or rise again are imperialistic; renunciation is characteristic of dying peoples."[71]

For fascists, imperialism was at the center of the fascist matrix. It provided them with a sense of moving from theory to practice through war and violence. In brief, it represented a tangible expression of fascist action situated beyond ritual and theory. The different failed attempts to create a formal fascist international have to be understood within the larger framework of fascist spiritual imperialism. This book traces the specific ways through which these theories were put into practice across the Atlantic. Thus, this short foray into the fascist matrix as Mussolini and other fascists understood it becomes my starting point, the point that I will attempt to problematize and deessentialize.

So far, I have sketched the major ideological patterns of fascism, and these sketches may provide the reader with a comparative frame of reference for fascist theory before it crossed the ocean. As we will see, Mussolini's fascist matrix fits some major ideological patterns of Argentine nacionalismo perfectly but also differs in other respects. Complicating the fascist definition that I have briefly analyzed above, fascism was in constant ideological and practical movement. This book proposes one possible point of entry to the changing ideological world of fascism, a point that informs its global nature from the perspective of the transatlantic dimensions of the fascist idea and its voyages in Argentina and Latin America.

Fascism, Argentina, and Latin America

A full-fledged fascist regime never existed in Argentina or anywhere else in Latin America. Although state policies in Argentina were to a great extent shaped by internal considerations and ideological presuppositions, the level of conflation between personalized politics and the state never reached the totalitarian level that Italy witnessed.

The connections between Italy and Latin America began with the actual "discovery" of the region by an Italian: Christopher Columbus. Another Italian, Amerigo Vespucci, provided the continent its name. Italians were perhaps the most significant group in the tiny European minority of non-Iberian foreigners during colonial times. Argentina, of course, received massive Italian immigration at the end of the nineteenth century and the early twentieth century. There is a famous joke in Latin America that whereas Mexicans descended from the Aztecs and Peruvians descended from the Incas, Argentines descended from ships (punning on the word "descends" to denote ancestral origins but also the act of disembarking from ships). These ships, the joke assumes, were full of Italian migrants.[72] As a youth, Mussolini actually thought about migrating to South America for a while.[73] When fascism came to power in 1922, its actions and perceptions were informed by these longstanding links that regarded South America as an informal colony, with Argentina and the Pampas as its point of reference. Fascism claimed to follow an imperial tradition of spiritual and practical colonization that previous Italian administrations had embraced. These claims were rooted in the past but increasingly changed once they acquired a fascist frame of reference. They reached a point where ideology was fused with propaganda. Fascist external propaganda in Latin America was progressively shaped by the workings of Italian internal propaganda, where the thought and practice of the Duce were determining forces. The Duce's disregard for diplomatic norms and traditions in fact significantly diminished the power of the Italian diplomatic corps to shape foreign relations. Fascist strategy, as the Duce understood it, was the more important factor in fascist Italy's changing attitudes toward Latin America and the River Plate region. Like Mussolini, fascist propaganda strategists naively believed that Argentina would be a kind of showcase for other Spanish-speaking Latin American countries because it had a population of Italian heritage. In actuality, fewer than half of Argentina's inhabitants had Italian origins or were Italian citizens. But for many fascists this demographic or "racial" trend differentiated Argentina quantitatively and qualitatively from other Latin American countries. Behind this assumption there was a racist belief in the putative superior qualities of the Italian white race that Mussolini clearly embraced. This belief helps explain the bewilderment and frustration he expressed at the poor state of Italian–Argentine relations in his dialogue with Göring.

Fascism had an original geopolitical interest in Latin America that was later cultivated to suit the needs of its foreign policy. Thus, during the international crisis triggered by the imperialistic war in Ethiopia, Mussolini needed Latin America's help. The same consideration applied to the early stages of the Second World War. In addition, for fascism, Latin America was an exotic land. There were no differences between the exotic and traditionally gendered accounts of fascist travels in Latin America and those in Afghanistan, India, or Turkey, including the fascist interest in the "eternal feminine" nature of the Orient (from Buddhism to the *Kama Sutra* and Mount Everest).[74] Fascist orientalism was clearly imbued with imperial readings of these regions as sites of Western civilizational engagement. Even in the barbaric fascist conquest of Ethiopia, where Italy made extensive use of chemical weapons, the "civilizing" character of the conquest was compulsively repeated.[75]

But as opposed to the Asian or African realities, Latin America was paternalistically considered an area discovered by an "Italian" (Columbus) and thereby a vital space for fascist "Latin" reclamation. Some observers even resented "the poetry" and "sentimentality" of the countless exotic travel accounts and argued that regarding Latin America "the most essential aspect from an Italian perspective . . . is the current and future interference between Latin American advancing civilization and the needs of our colonial expansion."[76]

The importance of the region as a battleground for the fight against communism and against British and U.S. imperialism was a recurring theme during the fascist period.[77] The emphasis on the Latin aspects of Latin America sometimes led fascist observers to project Argentine trends onto Latin America in general.[78] The Italian fascists ordered Latin American regions hierarchically. Mexico and Central America were seen as lost to communism, "Indo-Americanism," or American imperialism. Conversely, South America seemed to be the region that attracted the most attention from fascism insofar as at least a large part of it was believed to be "white" and "Latin" and thereby more open to fascist persuasion. Fascists considered South America always one step behind to European intellectual trends, noting that it was "in this sense a mere and retarded reflex of Europe."[79]

Expressing widely shared thoughts, the Italian fascist Sandro Volta did not see South America as a homogeneous region but one racially divided in three major regions: "Brazilian America with 31 million inhabitants of the prevalent black race, Andean America with 27 million Indians, and white America (Argentina, Uruguay, and four states of southern Brazil . . . with 25 million inhabitants." It was clear for the fascists that "white America" was closer to Italian racial and imperial interests. The stereotype of the premier Latin American form of leadership, "South American *caudillismo*," was strongly enforced by, but definitely not equated with, fascist forms of leadership. Unlike the Duce, the Latin American caudillo was a result of the region's "infatuation" with democracy. Moreover, in the "tyrannical" character of Latin American politics, fascists saw another example of their recurrent ideological assertions about the crisis of liberal capitalism.[80] To be sure, they considered this crisis to be terminal. But nonetheless, countries like Argentina, Brazil, and to a lesser extent Uruguay were seen as different from the rest of Latin America. As Mussolini explained in 1928, relations with them were not only of a political and economic character but of a "moral one" as well. The countries that received massive Italian immigration could not be presented as lands of low civilization. The fascist press even vaunted that in Brazil, 7 percent of the population was Italian, and that even larger "is the percentage in Argentina, where in a population of ten million people 45 percent of the population has Italian origins. This documents the unbreakable force of a thousand-year-old race."[81]

Throughout this book, I will deal with what I call the thematic engagements of fascist thinking in Argentina. These included exoticizing renditions of the Argentine Pampas, historical revisions and fantasies, transatlantic flights, and finally the articulation of a major propaganda strategy. Especially from 1934 to 1943, fascist transatlantic propaganda included both public and covert operations, subsidies to the Argentine press and political movements, and most important, the exporting of fascist ideology regarding the myth of Mussolini and fascist imperialism.

There were of course variations over time regarding these processes of thematic propaganda. However, certain tropes remained unchanged during the entire period under study. These included the view of the Italian community in Argentina as an arena to work out fascist internal politics and even to carry out imperialist expansion, and, more generally, the negative vision of the Argentine nation as an irredeemable land of unchecked liberalism.

Fascist perceptions of Argentina were colored by the massive immigration of Italians into Argentina, the most significant group of immigrants in the country. Italian fascism had an ideological bias against this immigration and opposed it in principle. Typical of the earlier fascist years were denunciations of Argentina as a negative place for the Italian people and as a reservoir for antifascists. Mussolini himself closely followed the activities of antifascism in Argentina.[82]

This consideration implied, as did the question of Italian immigrants, a point of internal politics. Mussolini argued that emigration was a thing of the bourgeois Italian past.[83] The Duce often observed with respect to Italians living abroad, including those in Argentina, that Italy was the place where Italians belonged, and he urged them to return. Mussolini, who claimed to be personally interested in the question of emigration insofar as he had been an "emigrant" himself, recognized the "physiological" need for emigration. He clearly agreed with the poignant argument made by Italian nationalist and fascist Enrico Corradini in 1923, that "political parties should begin to recognize that not all of Italy is encompassed by the borders of Italy."[84] The same year Mussolini claimed that the fascist state should impose a paternalistic watch over Italian emigration for this was "a problem of life and death for the Italian race."[85] If it could not be avoided, Italian emigration, he argued, should be seen as an act of "expansion." Mussolini thought that Italians abroad should be representatives of fascism. This constituted a subversive understanding of the role of Italians abroad, since Argentina considered many of these Italians to be Argentine citizens or permanent residents.[86] During the period between 1922 and 1925, emigration from Italy, especially to the United States and Argentina, and the activities of Italian fascists and antifascists abroad were the central focuses of Mussolini's American and Latin American concerns.[87] These concerns point to a recurrent conflation in Italian fascism of external and internal politics, a conflation that permeated Mussolini's relationships with Argentina and Latin America as a whole.

As regards Argentina, this unbalanced combination never dissipated, and fascist propaganda was aimed at two imagined audiences: Argentine society and Italian immigrants. To be sure, these audiences were often the same imagined communities, but fascism never addressed this situation.[88] In its early years, fascism seemed to have been almost exclusively concerned with the "internal aspects" of Argentine reality. However, the reality check of day-to-day governance, and the recurrent complaints of Argentine diplomats, eventually moderated—or, to be more precise, reduced—Mussolini's need to control emigration and antifascism to sporadic official announcements or to mere internal communications to his ambassador in Buenos Aires.[89] Although Mussolini eventually moderated his stance on these issues, the fascist press never ceased to criticize the disadvantages of emigration.[90]

The negative, or at best ambiguous, presentation of Argentina continued throughout the period between 1922 and 1945, along with the fascist attempts to politicize the Italian communities abroad. In 1928, Mussolini enacted the Statute of the Fascists Abroad, which not only attempted to regulate the activities of the fascists living abroad but also forbade Italian immigrants from taking part in the domestic politics of foreign countries. More generally, as Mussolini's brother, Arnaldo Mussolini, explained, the statute signaled "the need to affirm to the world that the symbol of the lictor [the fascist symbol] is the new potency of Italy."[91] Ironically, from an Argentine perspective, the ban on immigrant involvement in Argentina's domestic politics was an intrusion insofar as it implied an open disagreement with the longstanding Argentine desire that immigrants participate in Argentine political life even before they acquired Argentine citizenship.[92] Italian fascists were in principle against an absolute notion of national territoriality such as the Argentine one, and they regarded that notion as especially problematic when it was applied to those they considered Italian citizens by blood.

Argentine multicultural tendencies that so deeply troubled the Argentine fascist nacionalistas were, for the Italian fascists, marks of Latin America's problematic liberalism. The risk of losing population, which Mussolini and his followers often understood in terms of losing military power, was matched by the distaste for the liberal state that, as we now know with hindsight, was increasingly losing ground in Argentina.[93] But Italian fascists did not see this trend. They actually blamed liberal Argentine culture for the successful assimilation of Italians. They often pointed out that Argentina's insistence on Argentinizing its citizens of Italian origin was the reason behind the migrants' explicit desire to integrate into Argentine society, and they continually blamed Argentina for the migrants' lack of interest in Italy and fascism. In short, for the fascists, the "Italians of Argentina" were not to be blamed for being eager to become Argentines because they were victims of a powerful "process of assimilation." The fascists presented Argentina as a cultural medium for the "dispersion" of Italians that "disappear in the 'mare magnum' of native citizens, reneging on their fatherland of origin."[94] In short, Argentina was a radical example of the American continent as a whole—a place where "hybridity" reigned and Italians were transformed into Argentines.[95]

This Latin American "hybridity" clearly challenged racial, imperialist, and transhistorical fascist notions of the world. In Latin America, and especially in Argentina, the fascists conflated their fears of racial miscegenation with an actual context of cultural mixing and assimilation. In 1926, Mussolini had already argued that fascism should adopt an explicit policy for the "defense of the race." In his 1927 "ascension" speech, Mussolini linked the "destiny of the nation" to demographic patterns. In other words, Mussolini called for a demographic battle that would provide full "potency" to Italy by encouraging Italians to reproduce themselves within the borders of fascist Italy.[96] This longtime fascist concern for demography became particularly acute when confronted with the drainage of people to the Americas. In an important article published in 1934, Mussolini used Argentina as an example of a decadent trend that also affected other "white" countries such as France, the United Kingdom, and Germany.[97] But in contrast to their view of other countries, Mussolini, and Italian fascists more generally, considered Argentina as made up of Italian "colonists." Thus the "lethal" demographic situation for Italy was considered more than dire than the situation in other "white" nations. Mussolini was particularly careful not to raise the issue of Italian emigration when talking to influential Argentine visitors. But he always considered the question of Italians in Argentina as an internal fascist question. This is possibly one reason for his supposedly diplomatic remarks about Argentine–Italian relations as going beyond a traditional "diplomatic rapport."[98] Like many other fascists, Mussolini saw Argentine interests as identical with Italy's definition of them. As he told an Argentine official in 1938, while laughing and happily slapping his back: "Bravo! The descendants of Italians in Argentina occupy official positions of first-rate and maximum importance." Mussolini felt a sense of contempt for a country so poorly populated that only 200,000 Italian peasants were working on a portion of land equal in size to the entire Italian peninsula.[99] However, he was adept enough as a propagandist to play down his notion that Argentina was up for grabs by Italy, remarking that "Italy knows and appreciates the national consciousness of the Argentine people."[100] It is difficult to accept that he actually believed this.

Paternalism at best, and neocolonialism at worst, informed Mussolini's "lively sympathy" for Argentina as a country that played a "host" to Italians.[101] As with many other topics, Mussolini boasted of knowing a great deal about Argentina, its provinces, and demographics, as well as other Argentine minutiae. In his private meeting with the Argentine official Miguel Rizzotti, he inquired about the presence of Britons, Germans, and Jews in Argentina and was gratified to hear that Italians outnumbered all these other groups combined. The Duce considered the Argentine territory to be a perfect setting for the collaboration between Argentines and "the sons of Italy" insofar as "all are brothers under the glorious name of Rome. Their common civilization descends from it."[102] The idea of Rome as being the strategic tower of light for Argentines to follow suggested a neoimperial concern. Mussolini attributed the fact that Italians and Argentines in Argentina interacted so well to the demographic debt Argentina owed Italy, and he believed Argentina was bound to follow Italian guidelines on international relations. In his recurrent concerns over the Anglo-Saxon presence in Latin America, and especially in Argentina, Mussolini came close to questioning the very idea that Argentina was a country of equal standing with Italy world power. This Mussolinian notion of Argentina as a malleable site directed by historical and contemporary Italian actors informed Italian propaganda. Mussolini believed that Latin Americans had chosen Rome as "the mother of your and our Latinity," and that Italy had a special relationship with South America because of the demographic presence there of Italians. He clearly ascribed to Argentina, a country with a majority of Italians in important positions, a special place in the world as "the leading nation among the South American nations. This is place that Argentina deserves."[103]

2

The Argentine Road to Fascism:
State, Culture, Politics, and Dictatorship

I n Argentina, the 1920s and 1930s witnessed a public political debate on fascism. As Argentine secret police reports graphically show, the battle between fascism and antifascism was carried out through a wide range of media that included not only newspapers and journals but also fliers, pins, stickers, and, most significantly, graffiti on walls throughout the country, from Buenos Aires to Córdoba. Argentine women and men could read a wide-ranging ideological program that nacionalistas propagated for the general public. On these walls, nacionalistas literally inscribed their presence in the public sphere: "Reactionaries . . . Yes!" "Trying to stop the triumphal march of fascist youth would be as stupid as trying to stop a train by standing on the tracks." "Fascism: order and discipline constitute its power."[1] The nacionalista graffiti and street posters referred to Argentina and mythical aspects of the dictatorship of General José F. Uriburu, to the persona of Mussolini, Italian fascism, and communist Russia. Social, labor, and gender issues also would appear.

But perhaps the central element in the graffiti was the relation between two different ideological devices that nacionalista ideology conflated. The first was the idea of an all-or-nothing national fight against an internal enemy. As one totalitarian poster from the streets of Buenos Aires told the Argentine public: "With us or against us . . . You must define yourself."[2] The second element was the emphasis on the particularities of Argentina's nacionalismo as an intrinsically Argentine adaptation of fascism that was not a wholesale imitation of Italian fascism as Mussolini understood it. One nacionalista graffito from the streets of Córdoba said: "Argentine fascism is inspired by the purest form of nacionalismo."[3] Interestingly, communist graffiti also promoted the idea that there was an all-or-nothing battle between Rome and Moscow. But in contrast to the nacionalistas, communists believed that nacionalistas were mere copies of Italian fascism and that nacionalismo bore no relation to Argentine political traditions.[4] Thus, the question of whether Argentine nacionalismo was peculiar or not to the Argentine context became part of Argentina's political and intellectual life and was central to Argentine nacionalismo's selective appropriation of Italian fascism.

Argentine nacionalismo was a fascist movement endowed with a fascist ideology of its own.[5] However, there is no historical consensus on the nature of the movement. Some historians of ideas have argued that an authentic fascism never existed in Argentina because, in their view, Argentine nacionalismo did not correspond to the original fascist matrix. These historians prefer to emphasize the nonfascist character of Argentine nacionalismo by presenting it as a mere copy or inferior version of its European counterparts.[6]

This approach can be criticized for its emphasis on mimesis and imitation. Its promoters seem to accept the traditional antifascist notion that rightist Latin American political movements are mere historical reflections of European developments. But it would be more useful to trace the particular contextual characteristics of fascism in Argentina—as well as in the rest of Latin America—than to try to derive it from a putative fascist ideal type. Current historiographical debates on fascism—usually ignored or misinterpreted by many historians of Latin America—actually show that a homogeneous form of European fascism never actually existed in history.[7] Hence it is problematic to deny the existence of a Latin American fascism just because it does not match the features of a preconceived, ahistorical notion of fascism. In Argentina, fascism was a "school," a point of political reference, not a model.[8] The Argentine nacionalistas understood themselves as members of a larger family of ideological and political fascist groups, both European and non-European. In many ways this fact makes explicit the need for a better understanding of fascism in terms of subjective experiences and perceptions, as well in terms of varied networks of ideological and political kinship. Emphasizing the relationship between experience and intellectual history would imply a return to a historical approach that pays attention to the ways in which fascism and extreme right-wing ideologies were perceived, appropriated, and acted out by different historical actors in Argentina and beyond.

This chapter provides the historical background to this Argentine appropriation of fascism from the vantage point of a set of institutional, political, literary, and nacionalista contexts during the 1920s and early 1930s. It provides the reader with a pathway to fascism that includes an introduction to Argentine history and its nationalist trajectory, the history of its international relations with fascist Italy, the reception of fascism in the press and among intellectuals, and, finally, the origins of dictatorial and mythical nacionalismo, particularly the myth of Argentina's first modern dictator, General José Félix Uriburu. The ever-changing construction of a mythical narrative concerning Uriburu's practice and ideology was based on the presentation of motives and theories that were supposedly identified with the figure of the dead general. This was one of the pillars of nacionalista ideology as Argentine fascists saw it. In chapter 4 we will see the theoretical aspects of this ideology, which generally transcended the myth of Uriburu and presented "clericofascism" as the Argentine expression of a fascist international matrix; the nacionalistas, as we will see, perceived their political "theory" as the ultimate Argentine and Latin American expression of a transnational family of extreme right-wing political movements and ideologies of the "new order."

Studying Uriburu as a symbol helps to construct a more complete picture of nacionalista activities and collective experiences during the period between the two world wars. Most historians who have studied the nacionalistas see them as a static and uniform phenomenon with a closed "doctrinal" corpus. But by concentrating on the "theoretical texts" of some of the nacionalista intellectuals, these historians tend to underestimate the fluidity of nacionalista theory and its character as a complement to a "movement."[9] In contrast, I see the nacionalista movement as a theoretically concerned political collective led by a group of political militants and leaders who maintained a strong identification with an ever-changing catalogue of symbols and liturgies. In this catalogue, the myth of Uriburu held a central place during the different contexts of the 1930s.

Although highly disparate, these Argentine contexts informed nacionalista theory and practice. State policies vis-à-vis fascist Italy affected nacionalistas, and nacionalistas in turn affected these policies. Nacionalistas were engaged in public debates with the multiple contextual fields of profascist and antifascist receptions of fascism. These contexts were frames of reference and counterreference for Argentine fascists, for what they did and did not like in politics. The contexts provided the fascists with structures of meaning for the understanding of the Argentine political tradition of nationalism that made fascism an Argentine possibility, framing its intellectual and political encounters with Italian fascism across the Atlantic. This was, in short, the context of the Argentine road to fascism.

Nacionalismo and the Origins of Argentina

The idea that a given politics could express the "will of the nation" was not peculiar to the Argentine Right; in fact, it defines Argentine history. Inspired by this totalizing notion, the territory of what was later to become the Republic of Argentina broke its ties with the Spanish empire in 1810 and declared its formal independence in 1816.[10] Influenced by historical events like the American and French revolutions, and more poignantly by the Napoleonic invasion of Spain, the creoles (*criollos*) of the viceroyalty of the River Plate tried to institutionalize in different and erratic ways their long-standing aim of political and economic autonomy. They soon equated this aim with the general will of the nation.

More surprising than the Hispanic American revolutions in general, and the declaration of Argentine independence in particular, is the length of time it took for these autonomist aspirations to transform themselves to new national entities. To be sure, the Spaniards' monopoly of imports and exports, and the fact that they held all important public posts, largely explain the creoles' desire to challenge the Spanish empire. However, other features of the Spanish administration also kept the creoles comfortable with Spanish rule for a while: for example, the centralization of the empire, especially the Bourbon reforms, which led to the formation of a new viceroyalty with its capital in Buenos Aires, and some other liberal measures that the empire promoted with respect to the importation of foreign goods. Moreover, Argentine creoles had more autonomy than creole elites in other parts of the Spanish empire such as New Spain (Mexico) or Peru.

Why then did the creoles revolt against the empire in 1810? Were they inspired by the ideas of the Enlightenment or even protoromantic nationalism? The nineteenth century was, after all, the century of inclusive nationalism. This is not an easy question, but it would be difficult to answer it in exclusively cultural or intellectual terms; economic and short-term political considerations were equally at stake when the creoles revolted. Creole resentment against political and economic privilege was fleshed out in the context of economic processes that, in the region of the River Plate, were more

advanced than political ideas. The Argentine "founding fathers" found themselves in a very difficult position. Some radicals among them were pushing
for independence, but mainstream leaders like Cornelio Saavedra and other
members of the elite wanted to keep things in order until the return of the
Bourbons to the Spanish throne (an event that was unlikely to occur). All of
them recognized the social effects of economic processes and looked for a
new "colonial pact" with a different European metropolis (England) based
on relative political autonomy and economic liberalization.[11]

In an early stage of the "revolution," creoles presented themselves as
direct representatives of King Ferdinand vii of Spain, who had been imprisoned by Napoleon Bonaparte; once they had arrived at the River Plate
in order to assume complete control over the colony in his name, they
rejected the Spanish emissaries of the imprisoned monarch. The creoles
realized, after some months in power, that keeping their autonomy was as
important to them as continuing their allegiance to King Ferdinand vii, even
if this allegiance was in name only. Ferdinand regarded the creoles as traitors, and when he returned to the Spanish throne in 1814, independence
seemed to be the only option for the Argentine politicians, both liberal and
conservative. They announced it to the world in 1816. Achieving political
independence proved to be easier than maintaining the centralization of
power and the social order that Spanish domination had previously imposed. The construction and dissemination of the idea of a single national
identity proved especially difficult in the face of a diverse postcolonial con-
stellation of fractured identities and political imperatives across the continental Southern Cone.

After the defeat of the Spaniards in the battle of Ayacucho in Peru in
1824—a defeat that secured independence also for other countries in South
America and in which the "Argentines" played a pivotal role—the United
Provinces of the River Plate (i.e., the future Argentina) found themselves
immersed in an unforeseen factionalism among their elites. All factions
proclaimed themselves to be the true expression of the future. Factionalism
and an extreme barbarization of politics dominated the Argentine landscape
for almost half a century, and all politics were equated with the supposed
"will of the nation." In this sense, Domingo Faustino Sarmiento's writings
are symptomatic of a reality that its author wanted to correct but could not
escape. As Sarmiento copiously noted, fratricidal warfare and assassinations
were the dominant pattern in Argentine politics up to 1852. However, even

Sarmiento claimed that his politics were the only true politics, describing his political adversaries as traitors to the nation.

Before 1852, Juan Manuel de Rosas, a Buenos Aires landowner and "federal caudillo," controlled the country by informal means.[12] Rosas, as a kind of *primus inter pares* among a set of different warlords and caudillos, controlled external relations. But with the exception of foreign relations, the regions that formed the United Provinces of the River Plate were highly autonomous, with their own economic borders and currency. In this regard the Argentine situation is comparable to Germany's before and briefly after the signing of the German *Zollverein* of 1834. Like Germany, and Italy, the Argentine nation was an idea that evolved with processes of state formation.[13]

This brand of territorial division was a mark of other Latin American territories, too; Central America and Mexico being cases in point. Rafael Carrera in Central America and General Antonio López de Santa Anna in Mexico attempted to establish political hegemony in their respective territories, but in doing so impeded more modern forms of nationalism, republicanism, and liberal administration. In Argentina, the trend toward institutionalization and centralization was facilitated by a military alliance between imperial Brazil, the Argentine caudillos and intellectuals, and varied Uruguayan factions, who opposed Rosas's interference in Uruguayan politics. This alliance eventually convinced the Argentine dictator to seek exile in Southampton, England, after he was defeated by the alliance in the battle of Caseros in 1852.[14] *war & consolidation*

In the fight against Rosas, both the Argentines and the Brazilian empire learned the benefits of displacing internal factionalism by engaging in an outside war. The war of the triple alliance (1865–1870), that is of Argentina, Brazil, and Uruguay against Paraguay, decimated Paraguay but was central to the consolidation of Argentine nationalism. When the war finally concluded in 1870, after five years of combat, the Argentine army emerged as a powerful actor, if not the most evident proof of the existence of the Argentine central state. Thus, after the war the Argentine army could be seen as a centralizing power that had its origins in Buenos Aires but that effectively imposed order throughout the country, eliminating the last pockets of resistance among those trying to hold on to their former autonomy. The provincial warlords and, more important, the provincial elites who were behind them realized that the modernization of the state, and a general recognition of its territories as a single nation, was unavoidable.

The 1880s saw the constitution of an alliance between Buenos Aires and the provincial elites. This was an alliance in which the Argentine state, with Buenos Aires as its capital, promised the provinces a share of the export-import taxes, and more generally a greater input in the economic processes that Buenos Aires had already centralized. Thus the consolidation of the state, and nationalism, came from the city of Buenos Aires. Yet it was the suppression by the army of a revolt in Buenos Aires against the hegemony of the new national state (and its related redistribution of wealth among the provincial elites) that sealed the peace of the next decades. The defeat of the Buenos Aires rebels showed Argentines that the centralized state was now powerful enough to defeat its own and first creator, Buenos Aires.

The period of "national organization" that characterized the 1880s saw the emergence of political positivism as an almost official ideology. Like Porfirio Díaz in Mexico, or perhaps even like the different governments of Rafael Núñez and Rafael Reyes in Colombia, the new hegemonic pact created by the Argentine elites was represented as the triumph of progress and stability over barbarism. This presentation was an institutional articulation of the Argentine idea of the nation. Influenced by the historical writings of Juan Bautista Alberdi, Sarmiento, and the president and historian Bartolomé Mitre, this new positivism presented Argentine nationalism as an inclusive enterprise.[15]

Positivist ideologues saw the nation as a national living organism in the process of evolving, and in political terms they presented outsiders as "healthy" additions to the body of citizens, who would energize the collective body. This idea would later be developed and distorted by the Argentine fascists, who used the notion of the "outsider" to fuel a national xenophobia. The fascists would consider some outsiders as aliens to the Argentine collective body, redefining Argentine nationalism in exclusive terms, in contrast to the inclusiveness of the period of nationalist positivism, when all inhabitants of the world were formally invited, as stated in the Argentine constitution, to live in Argentina.

Before those events, during the period of "national consolidation," Argentina transformed itself into one of the richest countries in the world, a central partner of the British Empire, and an envied example of stability in the Americas. From the 1880s until 1916, conservative positivist politicians dominated the political and economic scenes; but despite appearances, the cost of this domination turned out to be extensive and even traumatic. The period witnessed genocidal campaigns by the army against the Argentine native populations in Patagonia, Chaco, and the north of the country. At the time these campaigns were dubbed "the conquest of the desert." It signaled a recurrent pattern in Argentine politics: to use the army to achieve political and even murderous ends for the sake of the nation. This was Argentine nation building at its most symptomatic.

At the end of the nineteenth century, Argentina was once again radically changed. European immigration—promoted by the government to obtain cheap labor for the mechanized processing of agricultural exports—had transformed the country in cultural, political, and ethnic terms. At the beginning of the century, half of the inhabitants of Buenos Aires were European, mostly Italian and Spaniards, but they also included Eastern European Jews, Germans, French, and British. According to the historian José Luis Romero, the result was an "alluvial society" created by the super-imposition of different immigration sediments that successfully left their "particularities" behind and began to think of themselves as Argentines. The Argentine "melting" did not recognize ethnic particularities; in fact, it de-nied them: to become an Argentine meant forgetting one's origins. This was the definition of Argentine inclusive nationalism. The extensive anti-Semitism of the early decades of the century might be partially explained through this nationalist lens: many well-to-do Argentines saw Argentines of Jewish origin as not wanting enough to be Argentine insofar as they re-mained attached to their "particularities." Anti-Semitism was the catalyst in the transition from radical inclusivism to radical nacionalista exclusivity, and it shows the connection between these two forms of Argentine national-ism. Things were actually messier than the alluvial image suggests, but Ar-gentines generally preferred to think of their national identity in inclusive terms—a radical inclusiveness that entailed the exclusion of other possible identities within the nation. In other words, Argentines imagined an inclu-sive homogenous nation by denying the "otherness" of varied groups of Argentine citizens.

The emergence of a powerful middle class, the most important in the Americas at the time after that of the United States, signaled new political preferences and ambitions for the nation that the old aristocratic regime could not channel. The emergence of the Radical Party in the 1890s and its subsequent victory in the elections of 1916 came to be seen as the triumph of a new modern Argentina. Many historians present this image as a truism, but it would be more interesting to distinguish between rhetorical and political praxis when dealing with the Radical Party. To be sure, many members of the new party belonged to the traditional aristocratic and business elites and, indeed, the middle classes identified themselves with the party. But the reality of traditional politics—the continuous repression of workers, traditional corruption, traditional economic policies, and traditional political deals (the so-called *trenzas*)—coexisted alongside the party's reformist rhetoric. In other words, the emergence of the Radical Party represented a mediated break and not a radical break with the past tradition of nation building.

Moreover, the electoral reform of 1912 that enlarged the franchise by mandating universal and secret male suffrage was not the result of a revolution but of a political decision from above. Historians still debate the reasons behind conservative president Roque Sáenz Peña's reformist decision, which ceded power to the Radical Party and destroyed conservatism for years to come. The belated effect of this electoral reform was that it eventually left the Argentine establishment without a legitimate political representative, and the first coup d'état in Argentine history in 1930 can be partially explained as a repercussion of this decision.

Between 1916 and 1930, Argentina had democratically elected Radical Party administrations. This was a new type of political regime for Argentina. In 1916 Hipólito Yrigoyen was elected president, and in 1922, Marcelo T. de Alvear, another Radical Party leader, succeeded Yrigoyen.[16] Soon Yrigoyen and Alvear clashed over the leadership of the party, and in 1928 Yrigoyen was elected as Alvear's successor in the presidency. Yrigoyen's second term saw increased opposition from conservative sectors from his own party as well as from aristocratic groups, socialists, and the majority of the military. Two different generals, José Félix Uriburu and Agustín P. Justo, represented this opposition. Whereas Uriburu was a fascist sympathizer, Justo was a convinced anti-Yrigoyen radical who, in practical terms, identified with the traditional electoral politics of pre-1912 Argentina.[17] In September 1930, an alliance of civilian groups, including anti-Yrigoyen radicals, independent or reformist socialists, aristocratic conservatives, and nacionalista fascist groups, participated in a swift military coup, which although supported by the Justo group in the army, was carried out by General Uriburu and his followers.

The military coup of 1930 occurred just a decade after the rise of Italian fascism. A young officer who participated in the coup at the time, Juan Domingo Perón, presented Uriburu "as a perfect gentleman," a "pure" individual with the will to fight against Yrigoyen. Moreover, Captain Perón added that the coup had the support of "our people that so far have not lost the 'sacred fire' that made them great for 120 years of history."[18] Like many of his contemporaries, Perón saw the coup as the political product of a sacred Argentine will. In other words, it was a continuation of the historical idea of the nation as having an absolute and exclusive political expression. Uriburu shared this view of nationalism and its explanation of the coup, but he actually lacked the resolve to define the new regime's political orientation. As a result the apparent "people's fire" was soon extinguished by their subsequent repudiation of the dictatorship. In 1932, Uriburu left power, after his failure to enact a fascist-inspired reform of the constitution, and General Justo became the Argentine president after rigged elections. The Justo regime inaugurated a new wave of fraudulent conservative politics. A nacionalista called its reign the "infamous decade," and the conservative administrations lasted until the nacionalista military coup of 1943 that installed a new military dictatorship—a junta soon to be led by Juan Domingo Perón.[19]

Fascism and the Argentine State

Notwithstanding the differences among radical, conservative, and military administrations, fascist Italy and Argentina maintained excellent relations throughout the period 1922–1943.[20] Ángel Gallardo, the Argentine ambassador in Rome at the time of the fascist rise to power, was instrumental in presenting a highly positive version of fascism that would shape Argentine policies for years to come.[21] On November 2, 1922, he wrote an extremely profascist version of the origins of the Mussolini regime. For Gallardo, fascism was a necessary "nacionalista reaction against the communist and antimilitarist movement." He also argued that fascism was "beneficial for Italy." The following year, during the Alvear administration, Gallardo went on to become the minister in charge of foreign affairs.[22]

President Alvear himself stressed the special relationship between Italy and Argentina. For him, "loving" Italy defined Argentine nationality, as he told the Corriere della Sera in 1926: "I would not be an Argentine if I didn't love Italy. My love for Italy is second only to my love for my own fatherland."[23] President Alvear's appreciation had some rhetorical implications, but it nonetheless extended beyond Italy to include fascism and its leader; in 1928 he told the fascist senator Giovanni Indri that Mussolini had "saved Italy."[24] These presidential statements about Italy in general, and fascism in particular, resonated in a country where almost one-half of the population was of Italian origin and many still had Italian citizenship. The Radical administrations may have been especially interested in a long list of fascist trends that differed from previous Italian democratic administrations, such as fascist antiparliamentarian politics and authoritarian electoral maneuvering.[25] All in all, Argentine diplomats and senior officials from the period of the Radical administrations were only mildly critical of the authoritarian dimensions of fascism, which they attributed to the specific Italian context.[26] However, neither Yrigoyen nor Alvear was a fascist. Yrigoyen was a taciturn reformist politician, who emphasized the harmonizing role of the state and was mildly critical of Argentine cosmopolitanism and opposed to the U.S. role in the western hemisphere.[27] Alvear was a Francophile aristocratic politician identified with the class interests of the conservative sectors in the 1920s who later became a popular front antifascist in the 1930s.[28] While Italian fascists considered Yrigoyen an archetypical "demagogical" "caudillo," they regarded Alvear as a conservative politician.[29]

The pattern of friendly relations did not change with the Uriburu dictatorship of 1930–1932.[30] Uriburu told the *Corriere della Sera* in 1930: "Indestructible links unite Argentina to Italy." Italy, Uriburu stressed, was one of the first countries to officially recognize the Argentine dictatorship.[31] Uriburu was less excited than Gallardo had been about the Italianization of Argentine historical figures.[32] As we will see, he admired fascism but saw it as the Italian expression of a more universal extreme right-wing ideology. We shall return to the first modern Argentine dictatorship toward the end of this chapter.

After Uriburu's government fell, the conservative administrations of Presidents Justo (1932–1938) and Roberto Ortiz (1938–1940) maintained a more critical posture toward Italy, as directed by their foreign ministers Carlos Saavedra Lamas, José María Cantilo, and Julio Argentino Roca Jr. In 1932 and 1933 secret reports of the Argentine ambassadors in Italy were briefly critical of some specific prowar attitudes of Mussolini and his admirers, but they also praised Mussolini, his thinking, and his corporatist reforms. From mid-1933 to 1934, the reports returned to the same positive statements that had been the hallmark of the Radical administrations.[33]

The top priority of Saavedra, who would win a Nobel Peace Prize in 1936 for his mediation in the Paraguay-Bolivia War, was to mediate in world events, and, as some observers remarked, to further his bid for the presidency.[34] In this context, the Italian invasion of Ethiopia in 1935 provided a recipe for bilateral conflict. Argentina first wanted to mediate between the Duce and the Ethiopian emperor, Haile Selassie, and Selassie officially asked for a meeting at the League of Nations to discuss the situation. Although the Italians were initially receptive to Latin American nations like Argentina or Chile that had member seats in the council of the League of Nations, no solution was reached within the framework of the League. After the failure of these negotiations, Argentina, following the dictate of the League of Nations, supported economic sanctions against Italy, but, as Mussolini himself recognized, Argentina never applied them in practice.[35] Tensions were increased by Italian covert propaganda operations in Argentina that tried to turn Argentine public opinion against the official policy of its government. The Justo administration took note of the Italian opposition to the Argentine mediations, which Saavedra Lamas had to consider when dealing with this problem.[36]

The nacionalista press, which as we will see in the next chapter received financial assistance from Italian fascists, supported Italy and harshly criticized Saavedra Lamas for his self-interested foreign policy.[37] As the records of the Argentine Foreign Affairs Ministry show, the nacionalistas were correct in their criticism of Saavedra Lamas's careerist motivations, but they also had personal reasons for supporting the fascist adventure. Important intellectuals signed petitions and urged the government to support the Italian imperialistic campaign. A group of Argentines in favor of urging the Argentine government to adopt a pro-Italian position formed an association called the Argentine Friends of Italy. The association continued its work throughout the period, and was more than a pro-Italian lobby group. It justified its attachment to fascist Italy because they were "a Latin nation, whose original strain is Roman . . . because 40% of the Argentine population has Italian blood." The association displayed a strain of zealous nacionalista exclusiveness (only Catholics and "Latins" could belong) and was almost a political organization with a single political premise: to defend the Italian empire, and later the Italian war, as if they were a part of Argentine policy.[38]

In addition to the Argentine Friends of Italy, the defense of the fascist empire and Italian interests at large received support in the Argentine Senate, where the nacionalista senator Matías Sánchez Sorondo successfully lobbied for an official challenge against a minister in Congress who was supported by the Socialist senator Alfredo Palacios. Mussolini personally backed Sánchez Sorondo in his quest for a change of policy. The Argentine nacionalista press and Italian fascist propagandists praised Sánchez Sorondo highly when he argued that the Argentine relationship with the fascist state should be a priority.[39]

The Justo administration saw this bond between nacionalista politics and Italian fascist propaganda as a sign of Italian interference in Argentine internal politics. Moreover, during these years the nacionalistas were actively conspiring to overthrow the Justo administration with the help of nacionalista military officers, including highly ranked general and admirals.[40] The Italians did not seem to care about this source of tension with the Argentine administration. Tellingly, in a meeting with an Argentine diplomatic representative, the Italian official Fulvio Suvich criticized the Argentine government for not showing solidarity with Italy. He even argued that the Justo administration was not following Argentine "popular trends" that were opposed to sanctions. Suvich reflected the official thinking of fascism at large. The fascist press, which seldom opined on foreign policy without the approval of the fascist hierarchy, repeated the same arguments. Fascists invoked the traditional ties between Argentina, a country where half the "surnames" were of Italian origins, and Italy, the center of "Latinity." Argentina, these fascists argued, was the only Latin American country with specific ties to Italy that required a constant "obligation of gratitude." While presenting the Argentine official position almost as a betrayal, the fascist press carefully differentiated between the "official" Argentina and the "most real one," that of the Argentine people who allegedly favored fascism and opposed the sanctions. For some provincial fascist papers, British imperialism was behind Argentina's "hostile" posture toward Italy. In addition, the most important Italian fascist papers heavily criticized Saavedra Lamas and Argentine "ambiguity" as well. But these mainstream papers also perceptively noted that the Argentine posture was complex and was related both to Pan-American concerns and to internal politics. In other words, they were able to read between the lines and recognize that Argentina problematically aimed to please different internal political constituencies and a variety of Latin American countries, as well as the United Kingdom and Italy.[41] The same interpretation was apparent in Italian diplomatic and propaganda reports.[42]

Some mainstream fascists understood the reasons behind Argentine "ambiguity." However, they shared with the Argentine administration a misunderstanding of the British position vis-à-vis Italian imperial ambitions. Although the British had initially invoked principles and opposed the Italian expansion in Africa, ultimately they wanted to please the fascist dictator in order to prevent an Italian alliance with Hitler. They were concerned with the outcome of sanctions that crippled the Italian economy (in one year Italy lost half of its foreign currency reserves) and gave Hitler a reason to reach out to the previously critical Mussolini. The British sought a new strategy, and as they candidly informed Count Galeazzo Ciano, Mussolini's son-in-law and the Italian minister of foreign affairs at the time, they wanted a discreet lifting of the sanctions against fascism after a reasonable period.[43] This was the first step of the much discussed policy of appeasement that led to the Munich accord. Less known are the activities of the Argentine government in trying to mediate between fascism and the United Kingdom. As I will show, no one except Saavedra Lamas was pleased with the Argentine attempt to play a prominent role in world issues.

This strategy of mediation presented many risks. The Argentine conservative administration had other interests besides its relations with Italy. It particularly wanted to avoid injuring Argentine relations with England. But, contrary to what Count Ciano and many other fascists believed, Britain played no role in Argentina's pressure on the League to explicitly deal with the Italian question. In other words, Britain was not pulling the strings: Argentina acted on her own initiative.[44] In fact, the Argentines put forward the traditional Latin American idea that Argentina represented a hemispheric counterbalance to the United States. According to this view, Argentina should care about "smaller" nations and represent them on the world scene. Argentine diplomacy found in the sanctions against Italian imperialism an opportunity to reassert a leadership role in Latin America. It focused on catering to popular opinion in Latin American countries such as Colombia, Chile, Mexico, and Uruguay.[45] The Argentine conservative administration also had an eye on the upcoming Buenos Aires meeting of Pan-American states that President Roosevelt and other dignitaries would personally attend some months later in 1936.[46]

Principles and national prestige were also involved in the Argentine management of the Ethiopian situation. Saavedra Lamas argued in a secret note to his ambassador in Italy that one could not sacrifice, for the sake of pleasing the Duce, the longstanding Pan-American tradition against the use of imperial preemptive force against other nations that would result in illegal territorial acquisitions—such as those of the United States in Central America or the British and French in Venezuela. The Argentine strategy, Saavedra Lamas argued here, should be neutral. However, he added, it would be helpful to Argentina if the Italians were made to understand that Argentina was secretly sympathetic to them.[47]

But if Saavedra Lamas really wanted to buttress democracy and equality in the world by enhancing the normative principles of traditional Latin American criticisms of imperialism, the use of preemptive force, and de facto territorial acquisitions, it is highly doubtful he achieved his goals. The Argentine actions helped Italy legitimize its imperial actions. In other words, Saavedra's efforts at promoting world peace backfired. The Italians believed that he was acting on behalf of the British, the Argentine nacionalistas believed the same, and many Latin Americans believed that the Argentines were working on behalf of the Italians. Rumors spread in Mexico that Saavedra Lamas was working for the Duce.[48] In terms of the practical consequences of Saavedra Lamas's policy, they were right, but Saavedra probably did not know it at the time. Saavedra Lamas traded Latin American principle for geopolitical realism, and in his failure to defend these "Argentine principles" he ultimately benefited Mussolini.[49] In the end, for the Argentine conservative administration the tensions that the sanctions provoked did not prove to be excessively destabilizing, and the Italian fascists, despite their grievances, continued their cordial relations with Argentina, including military and commercial exchanges.[50]

During the next three years, the Argentine Foreign Service was not as worried by the Italian involvement in the Spanish Civil War (1936–1939) as it had been by the invasion of Ethiopia one year before. Without being overtly critical, the ambassador of Argentina in Italy reported on the evolving strength of the Italian–German alliance and the enactment of the Italian racial laws in 1938. By 1939, the Argentine ambassador stressed in "objective" terms the positive character of the fascist reform of the state. As Italy moved closer to entering the war on the side of the Axis powers, however, the Argentine diplomatic reports became more descriptive and somewhat ambiguous about Mussolini's "enigmatic" intentions.[51] At this time both the French and the American governments asked secretly for an Argentine mediation with the Duce. They based their requests on the large Italian and Catholic background of the Argentine population. Argentina had "the prestige" to talk with the Duce and also the power to persuade other Latin American nations to follow its lead. The Argentines were gratified by this French and American recognition but not so sure about the benefits for the country and rejected the possibility of Argentine mediation. The foreign minister of the time, José María Cantilo, an admirer of Mussolini and a former ambassador in fascist Italy, justified this rejection by pointing to the failure of similar American and Vatican attempts to convince Mussolini. More important, Cantilo noted that Argentina's past attempts to mediate with Mussolini put Argentina in a difficult position with the Duce, and formally democratic Argentina wanted to avoid being seen by Mussolini as helping the Western democracies.[52]

The Second World War and the presidency of Ramón Castillo, a right-leaning politician who befriended many nacionalistas, brought about a change in the relationship between Italy and Argentina. Italy had asked Argentina to represent her interests in Canada and in major Latin American countries that were now at war against fascist Italy.[53] Castillo's foreign minister, Enrique Ruiz Guiñazú, was a career diplomat who was closer to nacionalismo than the previous foreign ministers.[54] Although this new strategy did not imply an abandonment of official neutrality, the combination of Castillo and Ruiz Guiñazú effected a decisive turn toward support for fascist Italy.

Italian fascists were the first to recognize that Argentina's neutrality increasingly implied de facto support for the cause of the Axis. Mussolini appreciated this fact, as we see from his secret conversation with the nacionalista Juan Carlos Goyeneche in 1943.[55]

Nevertheless, Argentina tried to maintain good relations with both the Allied powers and the Axis. The Argentine government had good economic reasons to embrace neutrality. The Allied powers did not, however, believe that these reasons were the prime mover of the Argentine attitude, and they often regarded Argentine neutrality as covert support for the Axis.[56] The new Argentine military regime of 1943 seemed to confirm the fears of the Allies: the regime was embedded in nacionalista ideology and was a staunch supporter of Argentine neutrality rather than the Allied cause. Argentina did not change its position for most of the war: it was the last country in the world to go to war against the Axis, only weeks before Hitler killed himself.[57]

Fascism and Argentine Society

Like the Argentine state, Argentine society remained extremely receptive to fascism between the years of 1919 and 1945. Before the Uriburu regime (1930–1932), many "democratic" Argentines expressed their praise for Mussolini in literary journals and mainstream newspapers. In these early appraisals, Argentines presented fascist principles as most important for a "nacionalista party," but they also constantly affirmed that the success of Italian fascism could not be easily projected onto Argentina, given the legitimate democratic traditions of their country. In addition to the fascist nacionalistas, several other segments of Argentine society expressed admiration for fascism, often appropriating or reformulating it to present to the Argentine population. The first was a significant segment of the literary world that easily, sometimes too easily, equated fascism with its literary manifestations, particularly futurism.[58] In Argentina the literary image of fascism was buttressed by the presence in the country of Italian fascist writers such as Folco Testena and Lamberti Sorrentino, the latter a supporter of the Italian poet Gabriele D'Annunzio in his ill-fated battle for Fiume after the First World War. Both Sorrentino and Testena were members of the original radical fascism of 1919. It took Mussolini several years to quieten down this version of fascism, which frequently expressed open contempt for Catholicism. The Argentine nacionalistas shared Mussolini's dislike of this radical brand of anticlerical fascism, and when these Italian fascists decided to write for Argentine publications, they published in avant-garde and left-leaning literary venues rather than in the nacionalista political and cultural press.[59]

Some liberals, as well as people in the socialist and communist parties, were strongly opposed to the Mussolini regime and considered it a subject for serious political study. However, most of their analyses of fascism focused on the literary and aesthetic dimensions of fascism.[60]

This focus on the literary face of fascism was particularly active during the 1920s. Increasingly during the 1930s literary figures started to regroup, either in the nacionalista movement or in the antifascist camp. An anecdote from that period is revealing (I referred to the event briefly in the introduction). Borges and Bioy Casares met in the early 1940s at the Chinese restaurant La Pagoda on Florida Street in Buenos Aires with the poet Ulises Petit de Murat and critical theorist Ezequiel Martínez Estrada (a noted disciple of the then radical fascist writer Leopoldo Lugones) in order to coordinate the signing of a statement condemning the Axis powers. The ambivalence on this occasion of Martinez Estrada, who later in his life embraced the Cuban revolution and emigrated to Cuba, irritated Petit de Murat. Martínez Estrada wondered if the fascist powers represented the wave of the future and the purity of its youthful character. Moreover, he wondered if fascism was not the vehicle for renovation against the old and decadent world of the past. In other words, he was close to believing that Argentine literary circles should in fact support fascism rather than condemn it. Bioy Casares, who told the story, thought that Martínez Estrada was lost to fascism, but Petit de Murat cut him short and stated that for "us" the "matter is simple": "On one side there are the decent people and on the other side there are the sons of bitches." In characterizing fascism as a moral failure, Petit de Murat and those who thought like him were rejecting the spirit of mutual tolerance that existed through the 1920s among profascists and antifascists in Argentina. Martínez Estrada, probably mindful of his prospects as a literary figure in the increasingly antifascist literary world, was convinced on the spot to join the side of the Allies in the Argentine public sphere.[61]

This anecdote demonstrates the near impossibility in the 1930s and 1940s of taking a neutral or friendly stance toward fascism without being called a fascist. Whereas in the 1920s fascism was a subject of discussion among Argentine writers and literary critics, in the 1930s the reception of fascism transcended the literary field, or to put it differently, most Argentine writers progressively conceived their views on fascism as political rather than merely literary. Particularly after the dictatorship of Uriburu, those identifying with the politics of nacionalismo felt compelled to identify themselves with Italian fascism as well.[62] But many other Argentine writers joined the antifascist camp, including Jorge Luis Borges, Victoria Ocampo, Alberto Gerchunoff, María Rosa Oliver, Tomás Amadeo, Adolfo Bioy Casares, Ulises Petit de Murat, Ernesto Sabato, Julio Cortázar, and Roberto Arlt. The question of what exactly antifascism consisted of is beyond the scope of my analysis, but it has been carefully studied, in Argentine historiography and critical theory.[63] In the context of this book, suffice it to say that antifascists defined fascism by their opposition to fascism rather than by offering an explicit viable alternative to fascism.

Antifascism was an extremely diverse frame of reference, thought, and action for those opposed to the regime and its transnational counterparts. It involved the often joint actions of a diverse group of Italian émigrés with various Argentine liberals, socialists, anarchists, and progressive writers and intellectuals. The Italian émigrés were highly active during the period 1922–1945. Argentina became a center of antifascism—Mussolini himself noted their activities in the early years of the regime. The killing of Giacomo Matteotti in 1924 and the ensuing commentary and commemorations provided a joint field of action for Italian socialists and the Argentine socialist party. Opposition to the invasion of Ethiopia, to Italy's positions in the Spanish Civil War, and to its conduct in the Second World War provided other opportunities for Italian–Argentine antifascist collaboration. The antifascist paper *L'Italia del Popolo* and the Argentine socialist paper *La Vanguardia*, published in Buenos Aires, continually criticized fascism and implored the Argentine government to break diplomatic relations with Italy, generating numerous complaints from the Italian ambassador in Argentina.[64] There was also a separate trend of Italo-Argentine antifascist collaboration among those with anarchist leanings. Argentine and Italian anarchists like Severino Di Giovanni (who later would be executed by the Uriburu dictatorship) took part in terrorist actions against Italian fascists and Italian consulates in Argentina. These activities extended from Buenos Aires to Patagonia. In 1928, for example, at the Italian consulate in Buenos Aires, anarchists killed six fascist employees and injured thirty-seven people.[65]

The most efficient and longstanding organ of Argentine antifascist propaganda was *Crítica*, the most popular newspaper in Argentina. This paper criticized fascism throughout its existence. Its ironic and humorous approach was a thorn to both Argentine nacionalistas and the Italian fascist embassy.[66] *Crítica* argued, for example, that Argentina, as a country heavily settled by Italians, should not identify with Mussolini because he was a "traitor" to Italian history and because he had an "abnormal physique." Argentines, the paper insisted, shared an "invincible feeling of repugnance" toward fascist deeds.[67] The muckraking *Crítica* was not alone in denouncing Italian fascism. Other popular antifascist papers included *Jornada, Tribuna* (Rosario), *Nueva Palabra, La República, Córdoba, Ahora, Última Edición, Fastras, El Diario de Buenos Aires, Últimas Noticias, Argentina Libre,* and *Alerta,* among many others. All of these papers, and a significant number of radio broadcasters, belonged to the antifascist camp and were instrumental in fighting fascism.[68]

Antifascism provided a solid moral and political ground to act against what antifascists saw as an irreconcilable enemy. The antifascist perspective was necessary for political action against the fascist regime, but the establishment of binaries such as the "decent people versus sons of bitches" precluded a more nuanced assessment of the fascist phenomenon in Argentina. A typical product of this way of thinking was the idea that the nacionalistas derived all their ideological positions from outside sources.

Another dimension of the reception of fascism was a fascination with Benito Mussolini on the part of the conservative mainstream press. Newspapers like *La Nación, La Prensa,* and *La Razón* not surprisingly dealt with the everyday realities of fascism. All these papers were also obsessed with the figure of the Duce and his popularity even after they turned against his regime in the Second World War. *La Nación* (except in pieces written by Lugones and other figures of the literary world) and *La Prensa* were consistent in voicing moderate albeit increasing criticism throughout the period. In contrast, *La Razón*, a conservative anticommunist paper, allowed itself to be bought by the fascist regime (as we will see in the next chapter) until mid-1943, when it suddenly and opportunistically changed its editorial position to a rabid anti-Mussolini posture.[69] This does not mean that *La Razón* had been, prior to that change, a fascist paper across the board. It also published dissenting antifascist articles on fascism and European politics by the progressive socialist intellectual and antifascist historian José Luis Romero. Historians of fascism rarely have the opportunity to use as a primary source a fellow historian—indeed, the founding father of contemporary Argentine historiography—as a window through to which to observe the reality of the period. Like Antonio Gramsci in Italy, Romero was perhaps one of the most perceptive Argentine observers of fascism and nacionalismo in his period. For Romero a "similar nacionalista ideology" informed the regimes of Italy, Germany, and Japan. In perceiving the transnational character of fascist ideology, Romero was able to understand, before his antifascist peers did, the imperialist and warmongering elements of fascism that would lead to the Second World War at the international level and to nacionalismo and Peronism at the local, Argentine level.[70] But the socialist Romero was for *La Razón* what the fascist Lugones was for the more moderate *La Nación*: a remarkable exception who illustrated the limited fluidity of texts and thoughts in these papers during the 1930s.[71]

If the Argentine literati avoided a more complete image of fascism because of their understandable emphasis on the literary dimensions of the fascist phenomenon in the 1920s and then adopted either antifascist or profascist postures in the 1930s, the conservative press was generally more descriptive and closer to the reality of Italian fascist developments. The antifascist camp, with its simplified notion of fascism, was more "creative" and less attached to the external world than the conservative papers in its reception of fascism. For the antifascists, fascism had arrived in the country with the Uriburu dictatorship. Most nacionalistas seemed to agree with the antifascist view without buying the argument that they were imitating a foreign ideology. For them, fascism was the Italian version of the Italian extreme Right, and nacionalismo was the exclusive Argentine expression of global fascism.

Nacionalismo and Dictatorship

In the twentieth century, the class nature of the extreme Right radically changed. Although many of the leaders of Argentine fascism were members of the elite, the social structure of the Argentine extreme Right changed along with the widening of the country's political constituencies; by the mid-1930s and early 1940s nacionalismo became a massive multiclass movement of the far Right. Whereas in the previous centuries the Right was often reactionary, in the twentieth century the far Right accepted change as a way to modernize the nation while including premodern ideologies and traditions (i.e., Catholic, Hispanic, and Latin revivals) and combining them with newer ideological formations, particularly fascism, anti-Semitism and "proletarian" anti-imperialism.

The ideological system of the far Right made sense to its believers. In order to analyze the extreme Right in historical terms, one would have to confront its textual sources with the political, cultural, and intellectual Argentine contexts that shape the former. Contingency and "national solutions" are at the center of this cross-national project of historical understanding.[72] In short, the origins of fascism and nacionalismo predate the 1920s and are the result of "cumulative" layers of different European and Latin American traditions. As in Europe, nacionalismo in Argentina had links with previous nationalist trends that were not exclusionary but liberal, secularist, and inclusive.[73]

Who were the Argentine fascists? The typical antifascist answer, repeated by historians in the 1970s and 1980s, is that the Argentine fascists were a minority of upper-class intellectuals disgruntled with liberal Argentina and full of admiration for Mussolini and Hitler. Like every stereotype, this image conveys some truth, but is nonetheless exaggerated. Nacionalistas admired, but did not copy, European fascisms, and many among them did indeed belong to the upper echelons of Argentine society. But recent historiography presents a more nuanced picture of the social composition of nacionalismo. Initially, in the 1920s, most nacionalistas belonged to the upper classes but increasingly throughout the 1930s, the social composition of nacionalismo changed, and by the end of the 1930s it had a widespread middle-class following, including many descendants of European immigrants. Whereas in 1933 the German embassy calculated that there were approximately 100,000 nacionalistas in Buenos Aires, a U.S. official in 1940 estimated 300,000 for the country at large. There were no national censuses in Argentina during the 1930s. But in 1914, Argentina had a population of 7.8 million, which increased to 15.8 million in 1947. If we follow many studies and tentatively adopt the figure of 10 million inhabitants for the 1930s, and if we tentatively accept the German assessment of 100,000, the nacionalistas constituted around 1 percent of the Argentine population. In this sense, there were fewer Argentine fascists than Romanian fascists; the fascist party of Romania numbered around 300,000 members or 1.5 percent of the Romanian population. The proportion of Argentine fascists in the population was in fact close to the percentage of Nazis in Germany before they took over that country, and somewhat higher than the percentage of Italian fascists in Italy before the founding of the fascist regime there. The Nazis constituted 1.3 percent of the German population in January 1933, while the Italian fascists were 0.7 percent of Italy's population in 1922.[74] In any case, the numbers tell us that Argentine fascism represented a small political force (probably similar in size to the Argentine socialist party of that time), but its ideological influence expanded beyond its sheer numbers. Nacionalistas were able to change the political culture of the country for many years to come. As we will see, mainstream members of the Catholic Church and important nacionalista members of the military helped them achieve this phenomenal task. This book addresses how a political minority created a full-fledged ideology that displaced mighty Argentine secularism to the margins of political society. Transatlantic fascist ideology played no small role here as it was constantly reformulated on both shores of the ocean.

The idea of fascism as a radical form of nationalism was not peculiarly Argentine, but in Argentina it was related to the larger history of the Argentine Right, especially its inability to resist secularization processes before the 1920s. The rise of fascism implied a renunciation of the defining aspect of modern Argentina: liberalism. In nineteenth-century Argentina, liberalism had been mainly an economic position, although it also had presented a successful secular displacement of religion that included secular national education and state control of births, marriages, and death. Liberal politicians belonged to the upper classes and were identified with economic liberalism. They were not anti-Catholic but were more generically anticlerical. By the end of the nineteenth century and the early twentieth century, conservative groups had started to criticize the hegemonic cosmopolitanism and liberalism that had been cornerstones of the nation. New worries related to the main issue of the day, "the social question," and particularly its labor ramifications (unionizations and general strikes, as well as President

Yrigoyen's *obrerismo*), and widespread immigration and economic uncertainty prompted the creation of political groups outside the traditional political channels.

These groups increasingly identified with "social Catholicism," and the first two decades of the century witnessed the first active participation of the church in Argentine social politics. This new role of the church was exemplified by the "gran colecta nacional" of 1919, aimed at procuring housing on a massive scale for the working class, as well as by the constitution of the Popular Catholic Union of Argentina, a Catholic national party. With them, the church seemed to amplify its traditional caritative role with respect to the state. Many conservatives supported this role for the church. And yet the majority of political conservatives who were increasingly connected to the church were not fascists but supporters of the old conservative regime. After 1930 conservatives were able to "return" to the old regime that "defended" liberal democracy while denying its practical consequences.

Unlike them, the extreme right nacionalismo that emerged in the 1920s and early 1930s denied liberal Argentina as a theory and as a practice. Although political conservatives often considered the fascists as allies, they diverged from the far Right on issues such as the role of the military, totalitarian corporativism and social welfare, anti-imperialism, and the global role of Argentina in the presence of the British and American empires. Conservatives were still identified with nineteenth-century liberalism, whereas Argentine fascists absolutely rejected its legacy and present role.[75] It is ironic that although conservatives and radicals represented the votes of the majority of the population and, thus, that Argentina could be said to be essentially a modern liberal nation, the nacionalistas, along with the military and the church, would eventually be successful in their all-out attack on the legacy of liberalism in Argentina. This result is certainly shocking for a country that was "born liberal." For all its visibility and persistence, nacionalismo had represented a marginal presence in formal electoral politics. As many Italian fascists observed, Argentina was one of the most liberal countries in Latin America.[76] José Moya has argued that by the outbreak of the First World War Buenos Aires was the largest metropolis in the Atlantic region, second only to New York City. At the time, Argentina was the eighth richest country in the world. It also had the largest anarchist movement in the world after France and Catalonia, a liberal system of education, and an overwhelmingly secular society.[77]

Why did Argentina (with Uruguay), the most secular country in the western hemisphere, develop the most extreme rightists and the strongest Catholic movement in the new world? Why were this movement's ideology and the politics of the sacred that came with it eventually successful? Why did Argentine liberalism, which was endorsed by large political majorities, not resist the ideology of a powerful minority represented by the military, nacionalismo, and the mainstream Catholic Church? The answers to these questions are in part related to the authoritarian dimensions of Argentine liberalism, which made it prone to be displaced (as exemplified, for example, by the Patagonian genocide and the extensive use of the army to resolve internal disputes), as well its lack of concern for the role of the state on social issues. As we will see, these were issues that were central to the clericofascist minority, that is, those fascists who believed in a strong role for the church in fascist Argentina. Other elements that explain the collapse of liberalism include the manifestations of progressive politics and the fears they engendered among members of the elite, the church, and the military (for example, in 1904 Argentina elected the first socialist representative in Congress in the western hemisphere and had the largest labor movement in Latin America). Yet another explanation is the relative lack of response of traditional liberals to social unrest and mobilization from below, as well as the growing concerns about sociomoral issues and rapid urbanization. A crisis in the primary export economy and gradually increasing industrialization also played important roles in downgrading the legacy of liberal Argentina. And last but not least, the military's increasing role in politics was pivotal in the creation of illiberal Argentina. All these situations explain why Argentine liberalism found itself in crisis in the 1930s. Eventually, two Argentinas would coexist as multiple actors of the period imagined them: an Argentina with a democratic ethos embedded in civil society, and an "Argentina nacionalista," marked by its rejection of democratic life.[78]

The attack against liberalism was also an outcome of liberalism's own success. It was the actual success of modernization, and the complex and messy social and economic realities that emerged with it, that prompted a reaction against liberal Argentina and its order. In addition this attack was made possible by liberal failures in reconciling the interests of capital with wide political representation.[79] It was, in short, what Tulio Halperín Donghi has called "the melancholic history of an impossible republic."[80] The traditional liberal sources of stability and order became sources of contempt. In this context, militarism came to fruition and was reinforced by a crisis in the political party system, namely, the failure of old liberals to create a successful mass party of the Right. These elements provided a window of opportunity for the nonliberal Right and its politics of militarism, corporativism, and sacralization. This was apparent with the creation of the most important antecedent to fascist nacionalismo in Argentina, a paramilitary formation called the Liga Patriótica Argentina (LPA).[81]

By 1919, the Argentine landowning elites had lost political power and participated along with the military, the Catholic Church, and anti-Yrigoyen members of the Radical Party in the creation of the "White Guards" and vigilantes during the general strike of January 1919—the so-called tragic week, with its deadly military repression—formed an important precedent to the LPA. These developments led also to a conflation of communism and Judaism, resulting in a pogrom in El Once, the Jewish neighborhood of Buenos Aires.[82] At its peak, the Liga Patriótica Argentina had a membership of 11,000 drawn from a broad range of social classes. The organization combined an ideological mix of antilabor themes with a conservative reactionary critique of pre-Yrigoyen Argentina. Its nationalism, influenced by positivism, wanted to correct the shortcomings of the liberal nation but did not question it as a whole. The organization represented the radicalization of the center Right during a period of civil and labor unrest. When the more conservative president Alvear succeeded Yrigoyen in 1922, much of the agenda of the LPA was coopted by Alvear and his administration.

After 1922 (with the emergence of the administration of President Alvear) the LPA entered a steep decline and its legacy seemed to wane. But its temporary success in creating a violent national bloc of the upper and middle classes, the military, and the church modeled a path for radical intellectuals like Leopoldo Lugones, Juan Carulla, and Enrique Osés, priests like Gustavo Franceschi and Virgilio Filippo, and military men like José F. Uriburu. Carulla, a close friend of Uriburu, asked him to lead a military uprising against Alvear in 1927. He was preceded by Leopoldo Lugones, who had called for a military coup in various public forums. Lugones had been a founding a member of the Argentine socialist party and later the major writer of liberal Argentina (circa 1910). He had established a new form of nationalism that was not based, as the LPA had been, on an ideology that united the liberal and conservative Argentinas. As a socialist and then liberal, Lugones had presented nacionalismo as an inclusive enterprise: Argentina was open, as he expressed in his centennial poetry, to every foreigner willing to become assimilated to its past, present, and future, whatever his or her religious background or political views. But this idea of inclusiveness and openness to anyone willing to become Argentine gradually changed, and Lugones came to personify the transition from this liberal idea of the nation to a fascist one that would exclude those deemed to be "unworthy" of Argentina.

Lugones gave a series of popular lectures in 1923 that he later published as a book entitled *Action*. In these lectures, he claimed that in order to save itself, the nation should "look for Argentine swords" (i.e., the military) as a political solution to the threat of national disaster.[83] In Congress, Lugones's words prompted the Radical representative Romeo Saccone to accuse Lugones of being a fascist and to be the bearer of a wrongly understood nationalism.[84] In fact, this moment signaled the first step in the appropriation of the word "nacionalismo" by the Argentine extreme Right. This word for Lugones exemplified his own idea of a politics beyond politics that only a military dictatorship could accomplish.

The following year, Lugones became a member of the Argentine high-level official delegation to Ayacucho, Peru. The Peruvian government had organized festivities to commemorate the battle of Ayacucho (1824), in which a united South American army had defeated the Spaniards, establishing the independence of Peru and guaranteeing the political independence of half of the Southern Cone.[85]

In Peru, in his speech to all the Latin American delegations, Lugones decided to emphasize Argentine nationalism. It is symptomatic that he did so at a site and on an occasion of Latin American transnational unity. Lugones insisted that he personified Argentina, a country of both "progress" and "power." He added, more specifically, that he represented the Argentine military tradition and "Argentine intelligence." In his speech Lugones warned that he would make a daring statement in "these times of libertarian paradoxes and daring but failed ideologies."[86] Lugones augured the imminent arrival of the "hour of the sword" for "the well-being of the world." ("Ha sonado otra vez, para bien del mundo, la hora de la espada.") The hour of the sword, Lugones openly proposed, would overcome democracy, and its "natural consequences, demagoguery or socialism." Democracy had undermined the Argentine and Latin American concept of hierarchy, but the sword would bring a new order that would "complement our only achievement so far: independence."[87]

Lugones then reminded his Peruvian and other Latin American listeners that the new regime of the future could not be located in the pre-European past or in distant eastern models.[88] As independence was accomplished by the sword, Lugones argued, the sword once again would energize Argentina, and Latin America, with power and life: "Life itself is a state of power."[89]

This speech provoked a scandal in Argentina, which was mostly liberal at the time, and made Lugones a pariah in mainstream Argentine and Latin American politics and culture.[90] But the speech was also the founding moment of Argentine nacionalismo. It signaled Lugones as the icon of illiberal politics in Latin America. It is thus no surprise that Uriburu asked Lugones to write the "revolutionary proclamation" of the military coup in 1930. Lugones subsequently became its most important intellectual.

Like Lugones, most nacionalistas participated in the coup but the primary role belonged to the military. The Uriburu regime (1930–1932), with its contradictions and nonreflective and ultimately conservative turn, nonetheless helped to shape a nacionalista movement in which the church and the military had a central role, a role that was notably absent in the Italian original fascist matrix.[91] Gathering support from the moderate sectors of the military and varied groups of center parties, General Justo outmaneuvered Uriburu and eventually obliged him to resign from the presidency. But Uriburu's failed project to reform the constitution in corporatist authoritarian terms, including the elimination of secret universal suffrage, was widely supported by significant groups in the Argentine body politic. The government of Uriburu saw the rise of an organic link between the church, the Argentine fascists, and their fellow travelers on the conservative Right.[92]

Was Uriburu a fascist? Uriburu certainly had close links with nacionalistas like Lugones and Carulla among many others. He had been very interested in fascist institutional developments, particularly the Carta del Lavoro and fascist corporatism.[93] However, when confronted with the question of whether Argentina should adopt a fascist regime, he seemed to believe that nacionalismo was the appropriate Argentine response, not fascism. In an interview with an Italian fascist paper he disingenuously argued with respect to the coup, "Our insurrection did not need external influences nor had it been fomented by external political influences."[94] In 1931, Uriburu created the Legión Cívica Argentina (LCA), a nacionalista paramilitary organization that soon had a following of 50,000 in Buenos Aires alone. According to some Italian fascist reports, the LCA had a significant number of active military officers as members and also had great socioeconomic appeal among Italian immigrants in working-class neighborhoods such as La Boca, Barracas, or Avellaneda.[95]

Addressing LCA's members in 1931, Uriburu claimed that the "revolution" had a program and that it also had enemies who opposed it. He believed that these two elements were powerful enough to cause the nacionalistas to unify in a single movement.[96] One year later, when he resigned from the position that he had held for less than two years as the country's leader, Uriburu felt no hesitation in explaining his thinking on nacionalista ideology in particular and the "new political ideas" in general. In defending the ill-defined ideological nature of his regime, he argued that the "revolution" lacked an appropriate time frame to impose a nacionalista ideology. It would have been "naive and absurd" to impose these ideas when the country was "burning from within." He stated that he did not believe in the "pseudodemocracy" that he had toppled to become the country's leader. But he also argued that he was not "the exotic importer" of political systems: "We prefer to talk about republican principles and not of democracy. Democracy with a capital D no longer has any meaning for us."[97] Uriburu proposed a new "organic" democracy that clearly resembled what Lugones had presented as "functional democracy." Uriburu did not believe in "political parties," and like Lugones, he had in mind the fascist system of corporations, but he argued that this should not be a "copy" but rather an adaptation to "our own modalities."[98] Uriburu believed that fascism was an example and not a template: "Corporatism is not a discovery of fascism but the modernized adaptation of a system whose longstanding historical results justify a new resurgence."[99] As noted by Italian fascists, this was the first time that Uriburu made explicit reference to fascism in public.[100]

The Argentine dictator denied the charge that he was "reactionary" because this accusation adopted the "language and the ideas of the French Revolution." For Uriburu the Jews were behind the accusation that he was imitating fascism. He nevertheless stated, "It is a question of loyalty for us to declare . . . that if we had to forcefully decide between Italian fascism and the shameful Russian communism of the so-called parties of the Left, our choice would not be in doubt. Fortunately nobody imposes this dilemma upon us."[101]

Nacionalistas saw the coup d'état by General Uriburu on September 6, 1930, as a foundational moment for Argentine fascism. However, it was after the fall of the Uriburu regime in 1932 that the creative forces of Argentine fascism were unleashed. From that moment on, the "dilemma" that Uriburu had tried to skirt could no longer be avoided. Much like the antifascists, the nacionalistas also started to see the movement as the Argentine version of fascism. They recognized in the Uriburu coup the most important moment of their history, a moment that they could relate to other European events of similar importance.

Nacionalismo was not a political party; at first, especially during the 1920s, it was an ideology as elaborated by Lugones and others and only later, in the 1930s, did it become a movement. It was the conjunction of groups that shared a common political attitude and "philosophy." In short, it represented a *forma mentis* of the fascist type.

The death of General Uriburu in 1932 shortly after he was forced to resign left a political vacuum, which was filled by a myth. This myth made it possible, among other things, to finally choose fascism as a clear rendition of nacionalismo. What was created was a mythic version of Uriburu that could be used to confirm the fascist character of the late dictator's ideology. In other words, the majority of nacionalistas believed that the dictator's physical absence did not affect nacionalista ideology and practice. For example, some months after the death of Uriburu, Colonel Juan B. Molina, formerly a profascist senior member of Uriburu's dictatorship, received a letter signed by Alberto Uriburu, the general's only son. Commenting on the political vacuum left by his father, the son wrote: "Our disgrace, which is deeply felt all over the country, has nonetheless revived the spirit of September 6th [the day of Uriburu's coup], and our general, as Dr. Ramos said, is no longer the commanding leader [*Jefe*] but a living symbol."[102]

Was Uriburu a "living symbol" for the nacionalistas, as Alberto Uriburu and the nacionalista leader Dr. Juan P. Ramos believed? Uriburu in life had failed to reform the Argentine constitution in protofascist terms, but after his death, during the 1930s, he became very useful to the Argentine fascists who created a myth of Uriburu that reinforced their ideological commitments and political strategies.

The invented image of this Argentine nationalist dictator functioned as a "mobilizing myth" that led Argentine fascists to create their own version of the aesthetics of violence—one that vindicated torture, street fighting, assassination, and the fascists' preferred ways to treat the perceived internal enemy, namely, Jews and leftists. Following the putatively eternal mandate of their mythical leader, Argentine fascists established specified realms of memory and a specific version of Argentine history that emphasized both the past importance of their movement and their powerful connections with fascist counterparts in Italy. This myth mobilized not only men. Women as well played an active role in constructing and celebrating the cult of Uriburu. In the end however, the myth was not sufficient to successfully produce the political preeminence of these fascist groups; its failure led the fascists to rethink their role as leaders of a bloc formed by themselves, the military, and the church.[103]

From the very beginning, the myth of Uriburu served a political function for all the political groups that constituted the nacionalista universe in the 1930s. All these groups—the Liga Republicana (1929–1936), the Legión Cívica Argentina and Legión de Mayo (1931–1936), the Asociación Nacionalista Argentina/Afirmación de una Nueva Argentina (1932–1936), the Amigos de Crisol and the Comisión Popular Argentina contra el Comunismo (1936–1943), the Guardia Argentina and the Partido Fascista Argentino (1932–1935)—provided platforms for political statements and undertook overlapping political activities. Despite some minimal distinctions, these groups were hardly distinguishable in ideological terms or even in terms of membership, insofar as many nacionalistas seemed to be members of several.[104] This situation was not particularly surprising to contemporaries on the left and right, who saw nacionalismo as it saw itself, that is, as an ideological whole, related to fascism as a transnational phenomenon and to the persona of Uriburu on the national level.

In this sense, the case of Afirmación de Una Nueva Argentina (Aduna) is paradigmatic. This nationalist association was founded in May 1933, and in its brief existence was similar to previous attempts to unify nationalism and fascism in Argentina. Aduna was intended to be an umbrella organization for the different nacionalista and extreme right-wing paramilitary organizations that formed the core of Argentine fascism.[105] The need for a unified command and for a leader who could bridge the gap between these organizations was apparent to all of these groups. Thus, nacionalistas chose the fascist theoretician Juan P. Ramos to be the jefe or leader of Aduna. Crucial to his election as jefe were Ramos's personal and theoretical knowledge of fascist Italy and his close friendship with Uriburu.[106] Even more important was Ramos's central role, along with Carlos Ibarguren, Matías Sánchez Sorondo, and Leopoldo Lugones, in defining the "theory" and ideology of the Uriburu regime.

Ramos presented himself as an ideal *uriburista* leader. For most of his followers this was his most important credential. The majority of nacionalistas believed that the leader and the ideology of the movement was Uriburista, that is, that it enacted the "political ideas of General Uriburu."[107]

But what were these ideas? Uriburu lacked a strong theoretical formation and left his regime to be defined by contradictory actions and seemingly heterogeneous premises.[108] This was not an important problem for the nacionalistas. For them, the ideas of Uriburu were obvious and coherent. They saw their task as that of making those ideas explicit to others. This was, of course, an exercise in intellectual appropriation.

The relationship between nacionalista practice and ideology was greatly informed by the creation and reception of the myth of Uriburu. Argentine fascists generally presented Uriburista ideology as fascist and as a radical transcendence of traditional democratic politics. In defining this ideology they went beyond the politics and theoretical stances of the Uriburu regime itself, for example, its refusal to solve the "dilemma" that Uriburu had defined of whether to fully identify with fascism or not. This was possible for two reasons: first, Argentine fascists often ignored the everyday reality of politics; second, Uriburu was not there to express his opinion about his myth.

In this context, the leadership of Ramos was often presented as a contemporary personification of the supposed truths articulated in the myth of Uriburu. According to Ramos, the ideology of the movement had not reached the level of a doctrine; he considered it at best a doctrine in the making. The ideology of Argentine nacionalistas, he believed, would evolve from a shared feeling among all nacionalistas. This feeling was related to the legacy and virtual leadership of Uriburu. Theory would have to be constructed with the recognition of the myth as a foundational matrix of nacionalismo combined with the experience of Italian fascism as Ramos understood it. For Ramos, Uriburu's actions not only revealed his personal genius but also represented the ideology of the movement.[109]

Aduna, like all other nacionalista organizations, defined its political theory and practice according to the image of Uriburu as articulated in his myth. As the leader of nacionalismo, Ramos positioned himself under the "guidance" of Uriburu and presented his role as that of a medium, as it were, as Uriburu's earthly deputy.[110] In a presentation at the Coliseo Theater in Buenos Aires in 1933, which a Nazi journalist described as "the highest point of the celebrations to commemorate General Uriburu,"[111] Ramos argued that the image of Uriburu and his "revolution" were the essence "in thought and power" of contemporary nacionalismo. For Ramos, as well as for many other nacionalistas, the myth of Uriburu represented the political program of the present as well as the promise of a successful political future for his followers.[112]

For them, both feelings and ideology constituted the core of the nacionalista experience with respect to Uriburu as a person and as a "living symbol." In other words, feelings and ideas were part of the myth of
Uriburu, and the gap between nacionalista thought and practice was to be
bridged by the myth of Uriburu itself. The idea that the doctrinal apparatus
was closed before it was formulated in explicit terms may have been nothing
more than a wish. Ideology as a closed canonical body of thought never
came to fruition in nacionalismo or in Italian fascism, notwithstanding the
high expectations invested in the task. However, the conception of ideology
as a "thing" that had to be connected to political reality or, to put it differently, as a feeling and as an experience, was central to early nacionalista
ideology, as was the case for the entire history of Italian fascism. The presentation of Uriburu as the embodiment of ideology prevented possible disap-
pointments over programmatic concerns from being voiced insofar as it
presented Uriburu's persona as the "incarnation," the final version of nacionalista ideology even before its enactment. Praising Uriburu became a
sort of doctrine that was shared by everyone within the movement. Though
they had just happened, the events of September 6, 1930, and the death of
Uriburu less than two years later (1932) were sometimes considered both
inside and outside of history at the same time. They constituted a traumatic
experience that was paradoxically perceived as a liberation from the present.
Mysticism and classicism constituted the core of a life that many remembered by taking part in an intensely painful aesthetic experience.[113] And the
conception of history as a narrative, and presumably as a science that could
incorporate "the more recent events," was central to the nacionalista presentation of Uriburu's deeds as great historical events.[114] This mythical conception of the leader shaped nacionalista elective affinities vis-à-vis Italian
fascism. In this context, sublimated notions of torture and violence constituted seminal points of convergence between European fascism and Argentine nacionalismo. To this subject we now turn.

Myth, Torture, and Violence

Torture constituted a central aspect of the Argentine experience during the
Uriburu dictatorship. Understandably, most nacionalistas did not include
torture as one of its legacies. However, the vigorous and documented denunciations of torture in Crítica and on the floor of the Senate by the
socialist senator Alfredo Palacios, and the supposedly humorous responses

published in nacionalista paper *Bandera Argentina*, are central to a discussion of the myth and the importance that political violence played in it. The nacionalista politician Leopoldo Lugones Jr., son of the famous nacionalista figure, served as chief of the political police during the dictatorship, and was the instigator of the then-novel practice of torturing political prisoners. After 1932, Lugones Jr. took it upon himself to defend the dubious human rights record of the dictatorship and assumed the task of denying the implications and nature of his own acts.[115]

In fact, denial took center stage. Uriburu himself had claimed that he had nothing to do with torture and even refused to admit that it was ever used as a method of interrogation.[116] *Crítica* described Lugones Jr. as the man responsible for illegal repressive actions during the dictatorship. Lugones Jr. continually appeared in the front pages of this popular newspaper as the ultimate personification of sadistic behavior and criminality; a psychiatrist consulted by *Crítica* characterized Lugones Jr. as an "instinctive pervert." *Crítica* presented Lugones Jr. as a symbol for Uriburu and his regime.[117] Indeed, Lugones Jr. has an infamous legacy. He invented the torture methods of the "picana" and the "tacho." The "picana" is a device for torturing prisoners with electric shocks, usually in the vagina, testicles, mouth, anus, or nipples; the "picana" is the foremost symbol of torture in current Argentine culture, and it may be Lugones Jr.'s most gruesome legacy. The "tacho" is the direct antecedent of the water boarding or "submarine" used by the last Argentine military dictatorship in the 1970s and later adopted by other South American and Central American repressive regimes and more recently in Abu Ghraib, Iraq.[118] Most of the people tortured during the Uriburu dictatorship pointed to Lugones Jr. as the man responsible for their torture, although some victims personally implicated Uriburu's chief of staff, Lieutenant Colonel Juan Bautista Molina, who tortured people while telling them that he was doing it in Uriburu's name.[119]

For Lugones Jr., the accusations of torture were just politically motivated attacks by the enemies of Uriburu, of nacionalismo, and of the nation: "The socialists (all of them foreigners), the Jews, criminals, traditional politicians, pimps, and *Crítica*."[120] In 1933, Lugones Jr. cited his supposed absence from the site of torture as a proof that torture never happened. He argued that the accusations against him and Uriburu were invented by political prisoners and masterminded by Natalio Botana (the owner of *Crítica*) and the socialist senator Palacios.[121] The supposed presence of Jews in the "conspiracy of silence" that Lugones Jr. excoriated was highlighted when he referred with dubious delight to the interrogation of one Jewish victim who apparently could not hold his bowels during the interrogations. The equation of Judaism with dirtiness was, of course, symptomatic of a more general trend in Argentine anti-Semitism.[122] Lugones Jr. presented the denunciations of torture made after 1932 as an "infectious phenomenon."[123] His pseudobiological metaphor is not a casual one but points directly to a process increasingly present in nacionalismo: the dehumanization of the "internal enemy." According to Lugones Jr., antifascists such as Enrique Dickman or Botana did not belong to the national community and were not even human.[124] In 1934 he said: "I insist on highlighting the fact that I do not attack Botana for being Botana, in the same way that I do not smash a cockroach for its condition but because of the danger of infection."[125]

Like Italian fascists, Argentine nacionalistas wanted to impose a culture of terror. Violence and torture, Hannah Arendt has shown, are the ultimate attributes of totalitarianism.[126] Building this totalitarian nation was central to nacionalismo. Torture was certainly the first practical step in a process in which street fighting and eventually political assassination were considered to be appropriate, indeed sacred, means of political action. An evident difference between torture and street violence was that the latter was not subsequently denied but was presented as heroic action. In this sense, the nacionalistas shared with their Italian counterparts a belief in the regenerative character of violence and its totalitarian aims.

All of these practices presumed that truth could be obtained through violent acts. Violence, when rightly applied, was not seen as a moral problem but as commendable in aesthetic or even religious terms. As Ernesto Palacio argued, in a context of "civil war," "violence is a sacred thing." Palacio believed that in "this new era of violence" "violence is a very good thing. If we have to kill each other among brothers, violence would have to be exercised for the sake of national reorganization."[127]

The practice of violence helped nacionalistas to compensate for the absence of Uriburu (after his death in 1932) and make his spirit felt. These practices expressed an ethos of action as well as a tangible symbol of how Uriburu represented a unifying device for nacionalismo. During the street fighting, and even during the sessions of torture, nacionalistas commonly shouted, "Viva Uriburu!" as if Uriburu's discursive presence would legitimate the applied violence and nacionalista self-perceived heroism.[128]

Violent practice on the part of armed nacionalista groups was widespread during the 1930s and 1940s. In Córdoba, the members of the Partido Fascista

Argentino consistently attacked, along with their allies of the Asociación Nacionalista Argentina and the Liga Patriótica Argentina, cinemas that projected movies they judged to be offensive, and they harassed with guns and clubs both leftists and Radical Party meetings. For example, after commemorating the anniversary of the September revolution in 1933, they engaged in a scuffle with a socialist representative, José Guevara. Some days later, Guevara was delivering a speech at an antifascist rally and some nacionalistas shot him dead from behind, notwithstanding his police protection.[129] According to *Crisol*, Guevara was to blame for having previously accused the nacionalistas of being degenerate and for having questioned Uriburu's heroism.[130]

The commemorations of Uriburu's legacy triggered numerous acts of violence and killings, as in Córdoba and later in the Parque de los Patricios, Temperley, and Florida Avenue at the center of Buenos Aires, and elsewhere.[131] These violent acts, undertaken in Uriburu's name, not only helped to reaffirm the belief in the veracity of Uriburu's dictum. They also personified the feared internal enemy in the bodies of their victims. For many nacionalistas, violence helped to redefine the supposed existence of the internal enemy (socialists, Jews, radicals, and others). Rendered tangible, the internal enemy was seen to be as real as the figure of Uriburu was in their minds. Nacionalistas presented the internal enemy as an alien and threatening figure that had to be fought with nacionalista violence. For *Bandera Argentina*, nacionalista violence had "a superior ideological content" insofar as its enactment on sacred dates could express in visual and psychical terms the alleged reality of the presence of Uriburu.[132] For Carlos M. Silveyra of the Comisión Popular Argentina contra el Comunismo, as he explained to a military audience at the prestigious Círculo Militar, nacionalista practice should not only deal with propaganda "but also had to include executive" action, by which he meant physical violence against the enemy, including assassination.[133]

Nonetheless assassination was not the most frequent nacionalista practice; street violence was. In *Bandera Argentina*, for example, the ascription of value to street violence was often associated with religion and the Uriburu myth: "We are extremists with respect to God, the Fatherland, the army and General Uriburu and the Revolution of September. Indeed we are crude extremists without restraints."[134] For most nacionalistas, violence, when associated with Uriburu myth and its totalitarian aims, needed to be radicalized, "taken to the extreme again and again." "Those who are not with us, those who are not with nacionalismo, are against nacionalismo," *Bandera Argentina* declared.[135]

The actions of Uriburu had been violent in both institutional and individual terms. Uriburu's death signaled a return of the politically repressed.[136] Emilio César Castro, a member of the nacionalista group Agrupación Uriburu, argued, "We are today where we were yesterday." For him this situation permitted the continuation of the violent means Uriburu had used: "To a people [*pueblo*] like ours, we don't have to ask questions, we have to place before their eyes what is needed. It's not possible to satisfy the needs of the republic through peaceful means."[137] For nacionalista leader Lieutenant Colonel Emilio Kinkelin, despite Uriburu's radical break with Argentine history, violence in the Uriburu regime had been "moderate," and the current task of nacionalismo was to actually amplify its violence.[138] According to the nacionalista general Francisco Medina, the violence of the Uriburu regime had motivated its "characterization as a tyranny and dictatorship." Medina was proud of this description and claimed that violence, and even torture, had been applied in order to reestablish the health of the national organism: "We should not be ashamed of these terms, for many are dignified by the gratitude of the fatherland in the same way as one would thank a drastic torturer for the reestablishment of a healthy being."[139]

The act of remembering Uriburu combined aesthetic elation with the feeling of "the heart shrinking in pain and promise." As *Crisol* argued and many believed, Uriburu led from his grave.[140] The mythical remembrance of Uriburu and his legacy created in the believer a feeling of exaltation that was first posed in discursive terms and then promoted the practice of nacionalista violence. Violent rhetoric prefigured violent actions. Its legitimization through the lens of the Uriburu myth could only promise more violence. As Enrique Osés, the nacionalista leader and editor of *Crisol*, argued, the only response to those enemies who "daily mocked" Uriburu's revolution had to be violence: "The time of the sticks [*la hora de los palos*] has arrived. We are sorry for them that they had such a small capacity for punishment."[141] Violence and "blood" would be the chief characteristics of the "second revolution," as *Crisol* argued: "The second heroic act [*gesta*] will be accomplished with blood, with an excess of blood."[142]

The majority of nacionalistas shared the need to look for political visions in the Uriburista legacy. This legacy was partly real and partly fictional, but for most nacionalistas it constituted an almost objective reality. Less evident for them was the way in which the adoption of this myth ought to be connected to actual politics. In other words, the mythical narrative that they continually enacted and represented to the believers amounted to the ultimate political promise: the possibility of building a fascist regime in Argentina. However, the mythical narrative did not necessarily present a model for the implementation of that regime. Many of the nacionalistas remembered that Uriburu had promised a quick return to lead the movement after what he thought was going to be a brief European detour. His unexpected death left his followers with a vacuum that mythical thinking helped to fill. In this context, fascism provided a model from which nacionalistas believed they could create a political reality.

The creation of Aduna, the umbrella nacionalista organization, was often seen as an objective projection of nacionalismo. As the leader of Aduna, Juan P. Ramos, put it: "Adunism presents and defines all that is common to all the Argentina nacionalista groups. . . . Adunism is a doctrine born out of the ideals of General Uriburu. Adunism is based on the principles that Italian fascism had elaborated for more than ten years. Adunism put into effect the harmonious adaptation of fascism to the necessities and the modalities of Argentina national life."[143]

Nacionalista fascist ideology, in a narrow sense, was blocked from receiving fascist ideology as Mussolini delivered it. But in a broader sense, fascism, as the nacionalistas understood it, created a common bond that transcended national borders and crossed the Atlantic looking for "analogical" demonstrations of the inner truth of their own political sense of the world. Potential conflicts were buried under a layer of mythical artifacts. In their adherence to the myth of Uriburu, a dead military figure, the nacionalistas offered a variation on the Italian fascist conception of the leader. All in all, nacionalista practice expressed the concept of the primacy of politics, which was central to Italian fascist theory. There were other European influences, such as the Nazi, the French Maurrasian, the Portuguese, and the Spanish, that we will examine in the next chapters, but fascism was the most important influence for nacionalistas insofar as it informed the intellectual genealogy of nacionalismo and evolved with it.

All in all, the nacionalistas believed that nacionalismo could be "the national adaptation of fascism." Most nacionalistas questioned Mussolini's famous assertion about fascism not being for export and argued that the principles of fascism were not "static" but "dynamic." The export of fascism to Argentina was seen not as an Italian decision but as an autonomous Argentine choice.[144]

⊰ 3 ⊱

Fascism Discovers the Americas

During the early years of fascism, especially in the 1920s, the fascists who traveled back and forth across the Atlantic were supposed to ground and solidify Mussolini's vision for Argentina and Latin America. They did not.

The first attempt by Italian fascists to ignite an "intellectual and spiritual fascist action" was the "export" of fascist intellectuals who were to establish direct contact with the "life and consciousness" of Latin countries. Many Italian fascists complained that fascist "doctrine" was not sufficiently diffused in the external world. The mainstream consensus was that the diffusion of fascism would be best served by sending fascist figures abroad. In other words, fascist travelers would furnish proper notions of fascism to the natives; they would be a mobile firsthand source for fascism and the "fascist sense of conquest."[1] Giuseppe Bottai (minister of culture in Mussolini's fascist administration) visited Spain; Italo Balbo (the minister of aviation) flew to Brazil; and Enrico Corradini (the most important fascist nationalist intellectual) went to Romania; the long list of fascist ideologues who visited or stayed in Argentina was symptomatic of the interest that Argentina generated within Italian fascism.

Fascist travelers to Argentina were considered the embodiment of Mussolini's dicta. They included premier fascist journalists; propaganda bosses and confidants of Mussolini such as Franco Ciarlantini, Ottavio Dinale, and Margherita Sarfatti; and diplomats such as Count Ciano and Raffaele Guariglia. Other travelers—I will name some notable examples—were scientists (Carlo Foa), fascist theorists (Gino Arias), heroes of aviation (Francesco De Pinedo and Del Prete), politicians (Alessandro Pavolini, Senator Indri, Buffarini Guidi, and the president of the Senate, Luigi Federzoni), first-rate writers (Mario Puccini, Filippo Marinetti, Massimo Bontempelli, Giuseppe Ungaretti), and intellectual observers and second-rate journalists and correspondents who stayed in Argentina for extended periods of time (Sandro Volta, Paolo Girosi, Ettore De Zuani, Folco Testena, Lamberti Sorrentino, and Mario Intagglietta, among others).

To be sure, many embarked on political trips to Argentina. But the official trip of the Italian Senate president, Luigi Federzoni, represented the most important political visit ever made by a fascist to Argentina, and it warrants comment.[2] Federzoni met with Argentine mainstream politicians, top Argentine officials, and members of Argentine fascism and nacionalismo.[3] Important for the expansion of fascism abroad, his trip was also aimed at influencing Argentine society at large.[4] Federzoni not only appeared at strictly Argentine fascist and nacionalista gatherings in 1937 but also addressed "the Italians of Argentina." For Federzoni there were "no differences of interest between Italy and Argentina" and no possible conflicts. However, he reminded those Argentines who wanted to receive more Italian immigrants that that wish was a "mistake" because "Mussolini's Rome" would not allow more Italians to live beyond the borders of the Italian empire. Italy was, he said, a "universal interest" for Latin America and Argentina because it represented "the defense" against communism. Mussolini, he emphasized, was the builder of a "new political and social civilization for Italy and for the world." It is highly doubtful that the Argentine audience appreciated this kind of Italian paternalism. Federzoni was probably more in tune with his Argentine audience when he presented Mussolini and fascism as defenders of the Latin and Christian legacy.[5]

The Federzoni mission was certainly important for the institutional relation of the two countries and for the personal connection between fascism and Argentine nacionalismo. But as far as the fascist need for supremacy over its kindred movements was concerned, Federzoni's visit could not sell its product. Even less successful were the visits by other prominent fascist ideologues.

The first prominent fascist visitor to the country was one of Mussolini's closest confidants, Ottavio Dinale. In 1923, Dinale complained that Italy, unlike other countries, lacked specific studies of Argentina. Many writers, including Franco Ciarlantini, contributed to changing this situation. In 1926, there were reports that Mussolini would send special agents to Latin America to propagate fascism among Italian immigrants living there. In a secret conversation, an Italian diplomat admitted to his Argentine counterpart that these agents had a direct link with the Duce and could not be controlled by the Italian Foreign Service. The Italian diplomat told his Argentine confidant that Mussolini had already sent these personal emissaries to Chile in 1926, and he supposed that another special envoy would soon be sent to Argentina.[6] In 1927, Franco Ciarlantini arrived in Argentina as an official representative of the Duce for the inauguration of a book fair, and more generally to propagate fascism and establish political and intellectual contacts. Was Ciarlantini one of these special emissaries to Latin America? There is no doubt that Ciarlantini was a personal emissary of the Duce and to my knowledge no other Italian agents visited Argentina during that year. He had been the propaganda boss of the Italian fascist party, and could have become an ideal defender of fascism abroad.[7] From the point of view of Argentine–Italian relations, Ciarlantini was pivotal in diffusing fascist ideas concerning Argentina for fascist consumption in Italy, but his influence in Argentina was minimal.[8]

Ciarlantini wanted to be the epitome of the worldwide fascist traveler. He believed that traveling, as opposed to staying in one place, provided a kind of understanding through momentum and excitement that he could use to spread fascism. If nothing else, Ciarlantini represented the "imaginary Mussolini" that he later wrote about. The Duce in a sense was himself traveling with Ciarlantini, because for Ciarlantini his persona was the source of the dynamic, continual reshaping of fascist ideology.[9]

Ciarlantini saw Argentina as a half-civilized country. He argued that Italian cultural and political models should be established throughout Argentina, complementing the continuing Italian immigration to the country. More than other fascist travelers, Ciarlantini admired and "loved" Argentina, his personal involvement drawing on the contradiction between his admiration for Argentine women, for the tango, and the limitless Pampas, on the one hand, and the fascist need to supervise the so-called smaller and uncivilized nations, on the other. It was clear to Ciarlantini that Argentina faced a dilemma related to its modernization. The country had to choose between the Italian model and the Anglo-Saxon one. He was confident that Argentina was ready to choose the former insofar as it was "the center of Latinity in South America." Moreover, "Only Argentina could provide Italy with an entry into South America." Thus, for Ciarlantini, Argentina was the most important country in Latin America as far as Italy's "racial interest" was concerned; Argentines, an already racially Latin community, should be made into "Italophiles."

Mussolini had said "enough [basta] with emigration." Fascism should limit emigration, but it should also take advantage of the existing Italian presence in Latin America and, specifically, in Argentina. Ciarlantini acutely perceived this contradiction in Italy's relations with Argentina. Fascism wanted to stop Italian emigration, yet Argentina needed it. The solution, he argued, was propaganda. Argentines should be convinced of their central Latin American role in the "the battle of Latinity" that Mussolini was fighting, and Italy had to "secure" this role for Argentina.[10]

In most of their transatlantic traveling, fascists established contacts with Argentine figures. But these travelers and correspondents were more consequential in reaffirming fascist preconceptions about Argentina and Latin America among Italians; they were less effective in exporting fascism to Latin American natives.[11]

These travelers usually presented Argentina as both an empty and exotic living space and a democratic country that was vulnerable to communist infiltration, American and British imperialism, and, later, "antifascist-Masonic Judaism" or more generally "international Judaism."[12] As fascists such as Sandro Volta put it, Argentina was "the most evolved" Latin American country, but even Argentines could not escape the Latin American characteristic of being "primitive" and "civilized" at the same time. To fascists this dyad was not a contradiction but the result of a rapid unchecked process of modernization, since they believed that Argentina's economic development had occurred effortlessly. In fact, the country's economy was often seen as being wealthier than the economies of the "totalitarian" countries. Argentina represented, in fascist eyes, what fascism stood against: the legacy of liberalism, internationalism, and the Enlightenment. This emphasis on Argentine individualism, cosmopolitanism, and urbanism was part of the fascist negative stereotype of Argentina.[13]

But the "problems" of Argentina were not only ideological or related to economic theory. For most fascists, Argentina was still a country in the making. They argued that Argentina still faced a central task: to define its national being and its national race.[14] For fascists like Ettore De Zuani, Franco Ciarlantini, or the senator Innocenzo Cappa, Argentines had to choose between Europe and "Latinity" or an American style that they identified with U.S. Pan-Americanism.[15] As the fascist Paolo Girosi argued, Argentina had a "fluctuating soul" that was difficult to understand or influence by means of propaganda. This "soul," he argued, was characterized by a collective feeling that Argentines shared a multiple or "universal ethnicity" and that the country had a special national identity: "Argentines want to be Argentines with almost jealous exclusivity." This combination of multiculturalism with national identity constituted for Girosi "Argentineness." Argentineness, Girosi noted, was extensively shared and even "intensified" among the sons and daughters of immigrants.[16] The fascists saw Argentine identity as artificial, or as something perpetually in the making; this view was an implicit criticism of *ius solis* as the best expression of Argentine confidence in the normative aspects of nation building.[17] Ius solis opposed the supposedly concrete nature of Italian bonds of race and blood that Mussolini himself often highlighted.[18]

Other fascists, such as the famous writer Massimo Bontempelli and Franco Ciarlantini, preferred to describe Argentina in metaphysical terms. For Bontempelli, Argentina was a place of "wonder." He believed that Argentina's "light" was the reason behind "that longstanding mysterious attraction experienced between Argentina and Italy." In Argentina, Bontempelli argued, "the protagonist was neither time nor history but space." Bontempelli identified this "obsessive sense of space" with the Argentine Pampas. If for the Nazis, the American Far West seemed to be a model for both imperialism and exoticism, an ultimate marriage of Germanic civilizing forces, for the Italian fascists the Pampas represented a site for metaphysical engagement and a spiritual source that could solidify the "mysterious attraction" between fascism and Argentina.[19] The Pampas was the ultimate site of exoticism and otherness: "The Pampas, being infinite, has nothing of the primordial or savage. The Pampas is abstract, metaphysical and perhaps Apollonian. The Pampas is probably made up of pure spirit. I would not be surprised if a mathematician ever writes a tract demonstrating that the Pampas is the fourth dimension."[20]

But the Pampas could also represent a force that hastened Italian assimilation into Argentina. For Ciarlantini, it was not only the powerful influence of the Argentine state via education that provoked a "violent assimilation" that quickly Argentinized Italians, but also the power of the Pampas and "the evil of infinity." According to Ciarlantini, the "unbelievable" fact that Italians displayed the same un-Italian "melancholy" of Argentines was symptomatic of the "metamorphosis" of Italians into Argentines. In the Pampas, "the distressing infinity of the horizon" shaped the Argentine character in ways that were incompatible with the fascists' stress on the power of individual will. "The Pampas," Bontempelli similarly wrote, "is a great leveler of behavior; it binds the race in the same sense in which the individual is subjected to the infinite."[21]

For many fascists, Argentina represented the "paradise of men" (in Cesare Rivelli's phrase), a place where the unequal relation of men and women was expressed and reinforced by the tango and the "female sex is put in a condition of absolute and deplorable inferiority." This criticism of Argentina had no elements of a progressive stance on gender equality. Fascist readers were told that Argentine men did not treat women with the "gentle" manners of a "paternal" and "dominating" male; Buenos Aires in its "perverse" ways was influenced, rather, by Paris, "the most corrupt city in the world."[22]

The idea that Argentina was an exotic site of contestation, contamination, and dissolution of Italian identity pervaded the fascist press during the entire period. The Argentine diplomatic corps continually complained about these images, but the Argentine population at large rarely noticed them and when they did, did not care about them. Nor did the Italian immigrants, who, in great majority, did not care for fascism and remained in Argentina for good.

The tension between this exotic vision of a New World that ought to be colonized and ruled by Italians, and the negative idea of Argentina as a breeding ground for liberalism and antifascism informed the fascist imperial imagination. Why would Italians want to go to Latin America, or more precisely Argentina, if things were going better for them in Italy due to Mussolini and fascism? Latin American exoticism was, it was felt, at best a context for adventurers and fascist travelers. The answer to this question is that Argentina, unlike most of Latin America, in fact provided Italians with a better quality of life than Italy.

Italians were a higher percentage of the population of Argentina than they were of any other country outside of Italy.[23] To be sure, the country's importance to Italian foreign policy was second only to Europe and the United States, but relations with Argentina were important enough for fascism to enact and shape a specific Argentine foreign policy. The presence of Italians and their descendants made the Argentine reality very close to being considered internal. In short, Argentina was not only the concern of the Italian diplomatic corps, but also of the Fascist Party. This dual interest informed fascist relations with Argentina throughout the fascist regime.

There was always a paternalistic Italocentric sense that shaped fascist propaganda for Latin America and that was partly influenced by the negative perceptions mentioned above. Italian fascists perceived Argentina as infected with liberalism. But the fact that almost half of its population was of Italian origin could not be easily downplayed in explaining the positive aspects of Argentine reality, particularly its wealth. Thus, the fascist vision of Argentine politics was often contradictory. For fascists like Mario De Bagni, only the Italians that "Argentine law considers to be Argentines" were responsible "for Argentina's hegemonic position among the Hispanic nations of South America."[24]

Early on, fascism saw a laudable enterprise in Argentina's traditional hemispheric contestation of U.S.-backed Pan-Americanism. Italian fascists argued that Argentina represented Latin America's link to Europe rather than to the United States.[25] This positive reading of Argentina's uneasy relation with the United States would later be invoked to argue a common ground with fascist proletarian imperialism. However, the support that Argentina's independent stance supposedly gave to that fascist priority did not extend to fascist priorities with regard to Argentina's internal politics, which for the fascists remained mired in caudillismo, populism, and democratic trends. The only positive aspect within this context was a vague but repeated reference to the Italian ancestry of Argentine or Latin American politicians. The non-Italian gaucho was presented as a noble figure, in Argentina as in Uruguay and Brazil, but he was a "mythical character," they argued. Against this "myth" they pointed out that it was the descendants of Italian emigrants who accounted for the "whiteness" of the Argentine population.

The fascist political discussions of Argentine politics reproduced Italian internal debates of radical "leftist" fascism versus a more conservative nationalist and gradualist version of fascism. Although there was discussion about whether the Agustín P. Justo government was liberal or conservative, Justo himself was generally praised as being of Italian origins. President Marcelo T. de Alvear was seen as friendly to Italy but also conservative and aristocratic; Yrigoyen was presented as a "great Latin American caudillo" but also, in the words of Senator Bevione and Sandro Volta, as the "most corrupt political man," a "demagogue" with Masonic connections and a bias against "Italian interests." On the other hand, some fascists (Lamberti Sorrentino, for example) described Yrigoyen as a populist representative of the "people" against the "selfish class of the rich." Fascist visions of Argentine politics were hampered by this preconception that it was an attractive, primitive, and exotic country that was also modern and liberal. Thus it was difficult for the fascists to make sense of the differences between varied

Argentine radical and conservative administrations, or even to make political sense of the Uriburu dictatorship.[26] Argentine politics, and by extension
South American politics as well, were generally presented as the result of an
extremely "baroque" sense of political agency that exaggerated political
deeds and had a very expansive notion of the concept of "revolution." This
perception was influenced by stereotypical views of the role of conquista-
dores in Argentine history and of the form of leadership that emerged from
it, caudillismo. The fascists defined the caudillo as "a despotic capo" who
was able to control every political faction. These preconceptions rendered
ideology useless as a category of analysis for Argentina and Latin America.[27]

The fascist perception of Argentina vacillated between two very different
ideas. First, there was the idea that since Argentine nationality was "artificial," Argentines of Italian origin should return to the fatherland. Second,
this national identity was an Italian "creation," so Argentines of Italian
origin would have to play a hegemonic role in ruling the country; this
hegemony would benefit only Italy. The tension between these two views
was never resolved but informed a general fascist appreciation of Argentina.[28] In fact, a single fascist interpreter often presented them both in a
single argument. Thus, for Ottavio Dinnale it was due to Italians "scattered
throughout the world," in places like Argentina, that "Italy can be sure
about its national and imperial future."[29]

Reinforcing the Fascist Party abroad and solidifying links with Latin American states like Argentina were two contradictory goals of fascist propaganda
that were never unified. The existence of these two goals illustrates the fascist
conflation of internal and external policy. It was never clear whether Italy
should actually ask Argentina to give back its "Italian" citizens or whether it
should make Argentina follow the fascist path and become a Latin cultural
satellite of Rome. In fact, fascism wanted both to happen. This combination
of two different, seemingly exclusive aims informed fascist relations with
Argentina, and even more specifically, the fascist understanding of Argentine
history.

The Mother of All Argentines

In the first years of the Italian fascist regime, Mussolini was both the prime
minister and the minister of foreign relations. From 1922 to 1925, relations
with Argentina were strictly formulaic and friendly. In early 1923, Mussolini
somewhat deceptively argued that "there [was] no originality in foreign

policy," and that he was not going to be "original" at Italy's expense.[30] However, in his first years as leader, Mussolini botched a state visit to Britain and made an aggressive foray into Greece, two events that contradicted his argument that he wanted to abjure originality in international relations. In December 1922 he visited London, where he argued with journalists and argued about who should have the best suite in Claridge's, the hotel where he was staying. More seriously, he ordered an armed landing on the Greek island of Corfu, using what has been called a "ridiculous" pretext.[31] But these were two European events. From the point of view of a fascist Latin American policy, Mussolini was relatively disengaged and unoriginal, his attention occupied by more restricted concerns in European foreign policy and internal politics.[32] Thus, in the period between 1922 and 1925 there was almost no specific propaganda for Argentina and Latin America.[33]

In 1925, the second phase of fascism saw the first articulated efforts of fascist propaganda aimed at Argentina. In addition to proselytizing among Italian immigrants in Argentina, a venture that began with early fascism and did not cease until 1945, the fascists made plans for Argentine society at large.[34] Italian propagandists in Italy designed these plans with little regard for Argentine reality or traditional Italian diplomacy. They were surprisingly ambitious but hardly successful. Between 1922 and 1931, the fascist regime wanted to convince Argentines that their history, or part of it at least, was a direct outcome of Italian historical agency.

This period witnessed the first articulation of fascist understandings of Argentina as a country historically constituted by Italians. This view generated an Italian rewriting of Argentine history that had few repercussions outside Italy. Fascist Latin American policy stressed Latin America's origins with the voyages of Christopher Columbus, and hence the Italian origin of Latin America. The fascist interpretation of Argentine history presented two main claims: first, that the founding fathers, or at least some of them, were Italians, and second, that Argentina was demographically almost purely Italian. Like any mythical framework, this account had some basis in reality. To be sure, some Argentine historical figures had Italian surnames, and almost half of the country was of Italian origin from recent and ongoing immigration.[35] But few Argentines would have agreed with the idea that everything good in Argentina was due to Italian agency. To fascist historians, this Argentine failure to acknowledge the supposed preeminent role played by Italy in Argentine history was characteristic of Argentines' "chauvinistic ingratitude," exemplifying their annoying tendency to "forget" and "deny history." In his canonical historization of the Argentine past published in the most prominent Italian fascist journal in 1922, the fascist historian Franco De Felice wrote "impartially" that Argentine history could be divided into three periods: the colonial period (1535–1810), the period of independence and civil wars when Argentina "did not take part in civilization" (1810–1894), and the period beginning in 1894 and lasting to the then present day, a period marked by the appearance of "our superior race," which brought Argentina civilization and economic wealth. In short, Argentina was, for this preeminent Italian historian, an Italian creation.[36]

For many fascists, De Felice did not go far enough. In addition to their historical reclamation of the Argentine past from 1894 onward, they argued that De Felice's second period (1810–1894) was also influenced by Italian actors. It was not only that Giuseppe Garibaldi had effectively fought against the Argentine dictator Rosas, or that the nineteenth-century president Bartolome Mitre had been an Italianist.[37] Juan Manuel Belgrano, the creator of the Argentine flag during the Argentine war of independence—and with General San Martín the most important founding father of the nation—was, in fascist eyes, also an "Italian." The first concrete expression of this historical impression was the inauguration of monuments to the "Italian" General Belgrano in Italy in 1925–1927, and again to Belgrano and General Mitre in 1931–1932.[38]

This notion that Argentina was Italian was not an original fascist idea. In the late nineteenth century, at the very moment when Argentine and Italian nationalities were being constructed, some Italian imperialists argued that, instead of seeking African colonies, Italy should focus on establishing a colony in Argentina, a country that, according to them, was already colonized by Italian immigrants. This suggestion provoked uproar in Argentine fin-de-siècle politics, beginning with the xenophobic anti-Italian articles of former president Domingo Faustino Sarmiento in 1881, and actually boosted the formation of Argentine nationalism. These polemics resurfaced years later, when the fascist presentation of Argentine history as a product of Italian agency reignited a national debate in Argentina.

The debate quickly had implications for actual politics. At first, the Italian celebration of Belgrano went unnoticed in Argentina until the Argentine foreign minister of that time, Ángel Gallardo, accepted an invitation to take part in the event and promised to send some warships from the Argentine navy in 1927. Gallardo was an early admirer of fascism and did not seem to care as the Argentine mainstream press did about the "Italianization" of "the

Argentine hero." For the liberal Argentine paper *La Prensa*, Italy would gain "nothing with this 'Italianization,' " as it was part of a fascist will "to turn everything Italian."[39] For Gallardo, as he told the Italian king and his Italian audiences, Belgrano was "the prototype of the Italian-Argentine." Gallardo reminded his Italian audience that he was also of Italian stock and argued that Argentina regarded Italy as "her mother."[40] For the fascist press, Belgrano was "the Argentine Garibaldi." He had been the son of an Italian father and "Indian mother." The Italian press shared Gallardo's appreciation of a racial link of blood: "The great Argentine historical figure synthesizes the intimate bond of blood between the two countries." For Carlo Curzio, for example, the "common Latin root" actually made the two countries "share the same spirituality" and Belgrano was a "symbol" of their mutual bonds.[41] The Italian press did not, or rather could not, avoid presenting Belgrano as a defender of liberalism and a son of the French Revolution, but also concluded that with the Argentine war of independence, "the theorist of freedom transform[ed] himself into a soldier."[42] The analogy with Mussolini's conversion from socialist to protofascist soldier in the trenches was clear to Italian readers. Fascist propaganda, as on many other occasions, was merely expanding on some points that had originated with Mussolini.

Mussolini did not dwell on the question of his putative similarities with the man he believed "gave the sacred legacy of the White and Blue flag to the Argentine people." Instead, he argued, "General Belgrano is one of the purest creators of your [Argentine] independence, of your greatness, and we are proud that he descended from an Italian family."[43]

For Mussolini, Argentina and Italy shared "indissoluble links." The Duce argued that the "occasion" of the commemoration of Belgrano "represents the most spontaneous manifestation of the feelings that vibrate on both sides of the Atlantic." For Mussolini the feelings were an emanation of the "common origins and blood" that Argentina and Italy shared and, more generally, a manifestation of prerational, overpowering feelings that fascism, as the logical outcome of Italian history, conveyed. The notion of a shared "spontaneity" signaled in Mussolini's discourse a fascist preference for experience or feelings as opposed to the artificiality of rationality. In Belgrano, the Italian leader valued a man of letters who refashioned himself as a soldier, as the fascist press put it. In all probability Mussolini did not care about Belgrano.[44] For him, Belgrano represented the occasion to affirm the symbolic hegemonic presence of Italy in Argentina through its historical and present contributions of "blood" and "culture." Some years later, in a different context, Mussolini would highlight once again the importance of Italy's contribution to the shaping of the Argentine nation, including the role played by "Manuele Belgrano, son of Ligurians and the hero of Argentine independence." This statement captures the essence of the fascist refashioning of Argentine history as intrinsically connected to Italians. Mussolini noted, in his gross simplification of Argentine history: "It is possible to synthesize the history of the Argentine people as an awesome dual fight for independence and against an unfavorable nature for the prosperity of its people. In both fights, side by side with your great builders of modern Argentina, we find men of our race [stirpe]."[45]

The idea of revisioning Argentine history through an Italian lens began to wane after 1927, but it was definitely not abandoned. It simply became a less-traveled byway of fascist propaganda. By the 1930s, little attention was paid to the monumentalizing of Italy's presence in Argentina.[46] Argentines paid even less attention to the publication of a series of books on the history of Italians in Argentina, which followed earlier patterns of Italian propaganda.[47] The central argument of these books was not only that "Italians" played key roles in the country's founding moments, but that Italians were the majority of the "pioneers" who fashioned all that was good in modern Argentina.[48]

Flying for Fascism, 1927–1937

The negative reactions that this "historiographical" propaganda received after 1930 functioned as a reality check with respect to the fascist conception of Argentine propaganda. Clearly, it was not enough to use Belgrano as proof of Italian power and ascendancy over the Atlantic. Thus, propaganda efforts turned elsewhere or, to put it another way, turned to the skies above. The Duce in this period ascribed more importance to the flights over the Atlantic than to transatlantic history as a means of propaganda. Mussolini was himself an amateur pilot who relished describing himself as "Mussolini, the aviator." He was fascinated with flying, as were many of his fellow fascists, believing that aviation was a powerful means of propaganda as well as proof of his own propensity to "living dangerously." In 1923, when he was already the Italian premier, Mussolini personally flew from Rome to Udine on a flight that he described as "warlike." Fascists regarded flying as the best expression of the necessary wars of the future. Moreover, they considered flying a sublime expression of the fascist quest for radical transcendence over ordinary behavior.[49] For instance, Mussolini argued that his short flight showed "that it is possible to rule the nation without losing the habit of risk and boldness. Life has to be risked and revised on a day-to-day basis by showing that one is ready to throw it away when it is necessary." Italian pilots, he argued, were "among the best in the world." Like its pilots, Mussolini claimed, Italy should develop an "aviatory consciousness."[50] For fascism, flying signified a superior form of meaning through exhilarating spectacle. Transoceanic flights were presented as the ultimate air enterprise. They were the concrete expression of a "new civilization." Flying across the Atlantic Ocean represented a "dream," an exhilarating practice that was done primarily for the "fascist revolution."[51]

Fascism organized solo or squad excursions to far-flung lands that objectified the Duce's vision. As the *Corriere della Sera* put it, these flights represented the "strong and audacious wings of Mussolini's Italy."[52] Although their primary aim was internal propaganda, the flights had two other highly regarded features. First, they represented, in fascists' eyes, a self-reassuring objectification of the sublime in an act that would have political consequences. As an act of fascist spectacle, flying fascism could literally put the movement above the ground. The sky was a "natural" fascist realm. As a fascist expert on the question put it: "This new Italy, this young Italy, this fascist and Mussolinian Italy . . . wants to fly. Fascism has the foreboding that the civilization that it's building will talk and will be affirmed in the solar pathways. No current, whether it is called America, England, France or Germany . . . will be able to forbid to us the dominion of the skies and thereby the primacy of the new civilization, the fascist empire."[53] Second, there was the hope that flights would facilitate the penetration of fascist propaganda around the world. The second aim was harder to accomplish than the first, which was merely to confirm an already defined ideological motif.

The most famous of the Italian aviators were General Francesco De Pinedo and Italo Balbo. Balbo was the fascist leader who founded fascism in Ferrara. Alone or together, these two men were the most famous representatives of fascism's longings for the skies. Balbo, a veteran of the First World War who had studied social science, had a successful career in fascism, having played a central role in the March on Rome as a "quadrumviro." He became minister of aviation in 1929. He was later appointed governor of Libya, where he would die in Tobruk, when his plane was shot down by Italian antiaircraft guns in 1940.[54] At the time of his death, Balbo was one of the few fascist leaders standing against the Duce's anti-Semitic laws. Yet in spite of this many considered him a probable successor to Mussolini. The air-related accomplishments of Balbo played a large role in his successful career and prestige within fascism.

In 1929, Balbo and De Pinedo successfully flew with a squad of thirty-six planes to the eastern Mediterranean and the Soviet Union. Some years later, Balbo would cross the Atlantic nonstop from Italy to Africa and then Brazil (1930–1931), and to Canada and the United States (1933).[55] General De Pinedo was the most prominent fascist to inaugurate long-distance fascist flights from Rome to Australia and Japan in 1925, and to Brazil and Argentina in 1927. His achievements played a role in his contest with Balbo for the role of the preeminent fascist flier.[56] However, at the time of De Pinedo's flight, Balbo wrote, "De Pinedo does not talk, De Pinedo does not write, De Pinedo flies."[57]

Crossing the Atlantic became an important task for fascism. Reaching Buenos Aires from Italy by air represented such an important achievement that the Italian poet Gabriele D'Annunzio announced his goal of flying to Buenos Aires, thus "establishing the first air connection between the Italian people and the compatriots living in the rich land of Argentina." D'Annunzio planned to fly to Buenos Aires with a squad of two planes accompanied by the pilot Eugenio Casagrande, who later attempted on his own the flight to Buenos Aires in 1928. But D'Annunzio's intention was personal and hence not a product of state-sanctioned fascist propaganda, and he ended up not making the flight.[58] The spectacular travels of De Pinedo, first in East and Southeast Asia in 1925, and then across the Atlantic to Brazil and Argentina in 1927, were much more significant.[59]

In 1927, the American Charles Lindbergh set a world record by flying nonstop from New York to Paris. The fact that Lindbergh is still remembered as a hero today in spite of his own fascist tendencies points to the historical importance of air adventures in the history of the West.[60] The fascists, and particularly Mussolini, recognized the historical and present importance of aerial accomplishments. De Pinedo's "Italian wings" were seen as the perfect means of propaganda. Many fascists thought that De Pinedo's adventures were ideal demonstrations of the greatness of fascism, as well as a successful way to silence antifascist criticism. In a typical cartoon, for example, the philosopher Benedetto Croce, who had recently turned critical of fascism, was depicted as being surrounded (and metaphorically silenced) by De Pinedo and his plane.[61] Mussolini had presented

De Pinedo as a new Ulysses in 1925, and said that the aviator was "the Italian of the new generation that fascism wants to create." For the Duce the aviator was "a precursor of our infallible tomorrow."[62]

The act of crossing the Atlantic—as Columbus had done—was deemed extremely important to fascism.[63] De Pinedo's plane for the trip to Latin America was appropriately named the *Santa Maria* and was called the "caravel of the sky." Many fascists believed that crossing the Atlantic with Italian planes had "a high political and moral meaning." It blended the best expression of the fascist personality, "the tenacious will of De Pinedo" with the "resistance of Italian machines." In short, De Pinedo's air propaganda embodied all the sense of adventure and meaning that Mussolini had ascribed to flying. De Pinedo went to Argentina and then flew back to Rome by way of Chicago.[64] When he arrived in Rome, he was received as a fascist hero who, as Arnaldo Mussolini put it, "has always obeyed the orders of the commander of the fatherland." For Mussolini's brother, De Pinedo had broadcast, like Columbus before him, Italy's prestige abroad and particularly in the Americas. This held true even more in Buenos Aires, "a quasi-Italian city" where the "descendants of Italians call themselves Argentines, but who can deny that they are from the purest and strongest Italian race?"[65] That De Pinedo reached Argentina from the air was for Mussolini an occasion to reassert the racial links between Italy and Argentina, insofar as De Pinedo's flights were an "affirmation" of "the vitality of our Latin race."[66] As Mussolini later said, "General De Pinedo's flight has opened a new and grandiose path between Italy and Argentina."[67] In Argentina, President Alvear interrupted his vacation to meet the Italian aviator. If we are to believe the fascists' account, the Argentine public was more enthusiastic about De Pinedo than the Italians were back in Italy.

After De Pinedo's transatlantic adventure, the flights to Argentina continued, but none of them had the momentum and significance of De Pinedo's inaugural trip. The pilot Del Prete, who had traveled with De Pinedo, repeated the Brazilian and Argentine transatlantic flights in 1928.[68] During the years 1937 and 1938, there were at least four fascist attempts to establish transatlantic air connections to Rio de Janeiro and Buenos Aires, including the breaking of the world record for the longest nonstop flight, by the Italian pilot Mario Stoppani. Stoppani could not make it to Buenos Aires and was forced to land in Brazil, but his feat still broke the record set by Lindbergh. For the Argentine press, Stoppani's breaking of Lindbergh's record showed that Italian aeronautics were the best in the world.[69] This was an aim of the

1937–1938 resurgence of fascist propaganda for internal consumption, but it was also part of a more articulated export program that was absent in the years of De Pinedo's transatlantic adventure. Performance and the quest for "living dangerously" were, once again, a challenge to the fascist imagination. During this period "fascist wings" even crossed the dangerous Andean Mountains in a new quest for reaching the fascist edge. However, these feats began to lose significance in the years leading up to the Second World War, and by the time Bruno Mussolini, the Duce's son, crossed the Atlantic and went to Brazil in 1938, the period of transatlantic fascist flights was coming to a close.[70]

The fascist flights over the Atlantic can be seen as a metaphor for how the fascists understood the spread of Italian fascism to the Americas. No one in Argentina was converted to fascism by witnessing the Italians' aerial accomplishments. Only someone already having fascist sympathies could actually have believed that the flights justified fascist ideology. If fascism had to be sold abroad, it would require more than wings and adrenaline. Bribes, lies, and deceit were used to fill this gap. But radio, cinema, cartoons, and books were also used to sell fascism in Argentina and Latin America in general. In other words, fascist propaganda needed a totalitarian project that dealt with all aspects of fascism.

Fascism for Export: The Forking Paths of Italian Propaganda, 1934–1943

In 1934, Mussolini wrote to his South American embassies that the time was "favorable" to expand fascist propaganda in their respective countries. He was confident that "supremacy" in propaganda could be achieved in the short run.[71] Was fascist propaganda worthy of the Duce's confidence? If nothing else, fascist propagandists took the Duce's desires very seriously. This period, which lasted roughly from 1934 to the end of fascism in 1943, witnessed a new emphasis on fascist propaganda in Latin America, which grew stronger in presence but varied in its message. Given what Mussolini thought about Argentina and its supposed leading role in the Latin American contestation of Anglo-Saxon Pan-Americanism, it is no surprise that Argentina was given a special place in this new phase of fascist Latin American propaganda. The fascists decided to diversify their propaganda and its means of distribution. The diversification of the means and tropes was concurrent with previous tendencies, but disclosed a new goal, which was not as conceptually ambitious as the previous ones (reformulating history or the aerial neo-Columbian rediscovering of the Americas). However, from the point of view of its intensity, this new phase was certainly the most effective.

Unlike previous efforts, this new phase contained a critique of previous propaganda initiatives; it did, however, also incorporate earlier initiatives that could be modified or fleshed out. The new strategy had the benefit of being simpler: it would use money to buy groups, lobbyists, and publications and also export domestic topics of fascism as they were formulated in Italy for Italians. Put simply, this new strategy would sell fascism to "small nations" around the world. It was influenced by fascism's negative stereotypes of Latin America in general, and of Argentina in particular, as they had been expressed by the Italian fascist media. Fascist propaganda abroad was an outcome of major changes within the fascist structure of propaganda, which aimed at topical homogenization and administrative centralization.[72]

In this period, Mussolini created a Ministry of Propaganda and appointed as minister his son-in-law Count Galeazzo Ciano, who had been undersecretary of propaganda. First headed by Ciano, later by the former nationalist Dino Alfieri, and then by the future republican fascist Alessandro Pavolini, the ministry was for fascism an example of "modernity" and the "Duce's directive and formative thinking." The aim of the ministry was to unify internal fascist thinking and to boost the "understanding and the knowledge of fascism abroad and in Italy."[73] Ciano wanted to define a program for fascist world propaganda at large. He warned that fascist propaganda was not a form of "aggressive proselytism," and said that it would not interfere with internal situations of foreign countries; he claimed that the scope of propaganda was worldwide fascist "clarification."[74] Ciano had begun his diplomatic career in Rio de Janeiro and Buenos Aires and had maintained links with his Argentine acquaintances, often reminding them of his personal connections with the country. Moreover, Ciano was personally interested in Argentine politics.[75] Later, when he became foreign minister, Ciano wrote to the successive propaganda ministers advising them on Latin American policy and advocating "continuity" with previous Latin American policies (i.e., his own strategy).[76] Most of the propaganda bureaucrats followed Ciano's strategy of topical clarification, especially the continual stress on the need to boost Latin American propaganda.

Latin Americans, and Argentines in particular, were the objects of the new propaganda. This propaganda was not aimed at convincing them of their ultimate subjection to Italian needs, but rather established this subjection as the corollary to fascist might and power as shown in fascist propaganda. In this sense, fascist external propaganda, with the aid of topical consistency and money, spoke to those already convinced of the benefits of fascism. In addition, as we will see, fascist cash particularly seemed to help convince Argentine mainstream media publications like *La Razón* or *Caras y Caretas* of the benefits of fascism, just as it had convinced the press in France and other European countries.

Fascist propaganda aimed at boosting the reputation of fascism abroad and did not, with the notable exception of the events related to the invasion of Ethiopia, interject itself into Argentina's domestic developments. It wanted to present fascism as a political model, but the way it went about it meant that it was generally regarded in Argentina as an example of an external system, not as the template of a new political civilization that might fit their own country. In one sense, the new strategy of fascist imperialist propaganda implied a decline (and often a dissolution) of the previous strategy, which was to have a special policy aimed at Argentina or Latin America. The previous "historiographical" attempts had failed to turn Argentines into Italian fascists, but they had been designed to suit Argentine specificity. The historical strategy was intended to escape the notion of fascism as an exemplar and rather present itself and Italy as maternal figures to be followed and obeyed. The new imperialist propaganda did not abandon this tendency to regard Latin American countries as mere proxies of Latin civilization; in fact, they reinforced it. In short, fascism was not interested in understanding the Argentines and Latin Americans at large, but instead adopted a strategy of economic and neoimperial persuasion.

Ironically, it was during this period that internal fascist reports presented an analytic assessment of Argentina that reflected more closely the real characteristics of the country. How is this to be explained? For although these reports were often perceptive with respect to Argentine trends, they also adopted the same stereotypical and neoimperial lens that informed the Italian fascist press and Mussolini's thought.

Thus, Argentina was always presented in the fascist imagination as an exemplar of failed democracy in South America and the barbaric site for Latin American political and cultural practices.[77] If Argentina was also the land of millions of Italian colonists, the fascists wondered, how was it possible to make sense of the huge Italian population that despite its putatively strong racial will enjoyed and even took advantage of these liberal practices?

How could the "Italians of Argentina," Mussolini wondered, not have been more interested in forcing Argentina to follow fascist imperial policy? According to Raffaele Guariglia, Mussolini was actually "very irritated with the Italians of Argentina."[78] For the fascist propagandists, the explanation lay in the process of "assimilation," that same pervasive Argentine tendency denounced by the fascist press. Actually, in their secret reports fascist officials were candid about Argentina's "lack of history, political past, a social and racial nucleus" and about the "vacuous content" and "artificial means" of Argentine nation building.[79] This was a peculiar thought for fascist myth makers and propaganda experts to embrace. They were critical of Argentine vacuity, not because they saw it as the historiographical construction of a tradition, but because it conflicted with their own mythical view of the South Atlantic as yet another Italic ocean, ready to be conquered. Mussolini ascribed a special role to Italians in Argentina. However, it was widely accepted that these "Italians" were "progressively denationalized," and as one fascist official put it, the Ministry of Propaganda early on had adopted the principle that it was "useless to defend the passport of Italians; the soul has to be defended instead."[80]

Although Italian propagandists never ceased to see the Italian population of Argentina as a primary concern, they placed greater emphasis on connections with those Argentines who were willing to listen to Mussolini and buy into his ideology. One major affinity between fascism and nacionalista groups was the relation between fascist "proletarian imperialism" and Argentine anti-imperialism. Perceptively, the fascist regime saw in the question of the Malvinas / Falklands—the almost deserted South Atlantic islands that Great Britain refused to abandon as a British colony—an opportunity to be exploited.[81] Mussolini often made explicit his imperialist intent to protect Latin America against European colonialism and North American Pan-Americanism. However, the Argentine fascists and nacionalistas did not seem to care about this offered imperial protection because, as we will see, . they simply did not accept these aspects of fascist ideology. They considered fascism an example of a broader nacionalista trend and not a prefabricated model waiting to be assembled.

Even the foremost consumers of fascist propaganda seemed not to be interested in accepting what was offered. But this situation was not the only problem for the Italians. Guariglia reported to Ciano that there were few Argentines interested in taking up the Italian offers. Italian propaganda put great ideological emphasis (and cash) on solidifying the support of the

Argentine military, the church, the nacionalistas, and conservative politicians such as Senator Matías Sánchez Sorondo and Manuel Fresco, the governor of the Province of Buenos Aires. The idea that Italy supported Argentine national concerns was central in the communications between these groups, and it was displayed in both fascist propaganda and that of her allies.[82] The nacionalistas, "the Argentine movements of the fascist type," had a "slow development" due mainly to the desperate political context in which they had to operate; nevertheless, fascist internal reports argued, the nacionalistas provided Argentine society with a needed "toning up and polemic action." Guariglia told Ciano in 1938 that the Italian embassy in Buenos Aires had a close relation with these groups and recognized the need to give them money.[83] For fascism, the church had "a preeminent and higher moral position in Argentina" and links with it had to be nurtured.[84] Many of these actors were often invited to Italy to see fascism for themselves.[85]

Although the nurturing of links with the nacionalistas, the church, and the army had lasting effects in Argentine politics, they did not really affect the position of the Argentine state until the military coup of 1943, when these actors took power. But fascism as a state formation and Mussolini as a living being were not there to witness the effects of these actions and their legacy after 1945. Fascism's lasting influence was on military and nacionalista understandings of Argentina's role in the world. It was also a premier ideological factor in the intellectual origins of Peronism.[86]

In the short run, fascism focused a great deal of attention on ways of penetrating Argentine society at large. In Argentina, this strategy, like previous ones, was confused with the question of the Italian origins of the nation. Thus, although there was no specific Italian-language propaganda for those Italians who formally belonged to the community, it was noted that many Argentines of Italian origins could read, see, and hear fascism in both Italian and Spanish.

This strategy included a surge of subsidies to nacionalista and fascist Argentine groups, as well as attempts to buy favorable spots in the mainstream media. In addition, new propaganda media like the cinema and radio were stressed in order to convince Argentines of the need for importing fascism, accepting and supporting the legitimacy of fascist deeds internationally, and hopefully convincing some Argentines that they were actually Italian. This last ambition was, not surprisingly, the least successful. Fascism could not even convince the majority of Italian immigrants to become fascists, and Argentina remained a center of antifascism throughout the entire history of fascist presence.[87]

But what about the fascist attempts to deal with radio and cinema and to reach out to the Argentine mainstream media? What about fascist attempts to convince political groups that fascism was a superior political ideology? These are, of course, different questions and require different answers. For analytical purposes, it is possible to treat the different campaigns in fascist propaganda by focusing on the different media at which they aimed.

The use of the radio and the cinema was quite extensive. The propaganda related to them was simpler than that in printed media insofar as it was generally related to one voice and one image. The notion of oneness relates to the process of "Mussolinization" of the "fascist common denominator" that we saw in chapter 1. In fascist propaganda in Argentina, this notion was objectified, not only in some of the Spanish titles of the films about Mussolini that were reproduced but also in his speeches. These speeches could be heard in Italian on an Argentine radio station that was called "fascist radio" by the Left. Fascist radio was a major achievement of fascist propaganda in Argentina and, unlike propaganda broadcasts by French, British, and German leaders, the "voice of the Duce" could be understood in his own language by a majority of Argentines and Italians living in Argentina. Thanks to the central position of Argentina, Ambassador Guariglia thought that fascist radio broadcasting from Argentina would be able to reach Latin America at large. Among the stations that put Mussolini's voice on the air were Radio Rivadavia, Radio Excelsior, Radio Splendid, Radio Prieto, Radio Stentor, Radio La Voz del Aire, Radio Fenix, and other mainstream radio stations in the Argentine interior.[88] Mussolini was informed about radio transmissions in Argentina as soon as they were launched.

Films featuring Mussolini were quite successful in Argentina, but the fascist propagandists complained that they were expensive to distribute and promote. Fascist concerns about the Anglo-Saxon presence in Latin America were evident in the Argentine film industry, and this opening provided opportunities for fascist propaganda entrepreneurs like Raffaele Mancini, who founded the Italian–Argentine cinematographic alliance in the early 1930s. (The alliance was an agency for the Latin American distribution of fascist movies.) Mancini was an active fascist in Argentine Italian circles and had the support of Argentine fascist "experts" like Lamberti Sorrentino or Guido Buffarini.[89] In 1933, Mancini wrote a report for Mussolini arguing that the time had come for the "intensification of Italian propaganda" in Latin America. Mancini's timing was perfect, for Mussolini at that moment was thinking along the same lines.[90] Several fascist films were shown, but the most important and successful was One Man, One People. Mancini paid the Palace Theater located on Corrientes Avenue in Buenos Aires (the Argentine version of Broadway) to show the film, and the film generated widespread media and public attention. On some occasions fascist propaganda presented Mussolini's persona as an almost overpowering talking head. It seemed that the labor of fascist propaganda was finally coming to fruition. The Mussolini myth was presented in explicit terms to the Argentine public. The film's trailers emphasized the Mussolinian quality of the title in every way possible, and Mussolini's face appeared also in programs distributed to filmgoers.[91]

The idea that fascism was identified with the person of Mussolini was noted in reviews in the Argentine press. For mainstream papers like La Prensa, La Nación, or La Razón the film was required viewing because of its "historical" value and the interesting role Mussolini played in it. Noticias Gráficas also gave the film, and Mussolini as an "actor," positive reviews. According to La Fronda and the centrist paper El Mundo, the audiences applauded Mussolini at different points in the movie. Even the socialist paper La Vanguardia valued the film's technical aspects and highlighted the central role played by Mussolini. In short, every Argentine paper was talking about it. This was one of the few moments when Italian propaganda achieved the goal of situating fascism at the center of Argentine political and cultural discussions.[92]

Despite the success of radio and cinema, and despite propaganda minister Ciano's presentation of radio and cinema as the ideal means for fascist propaganda abroad, most fascist propaganda efforts emphasized the printed word.[93] Fascist propaganda dealt with important publishers and subsidized canonical works by Mussolini, Virginio Gayda, Ciarlantini, and others. More often than not, these books were widely read and distributed, and mainstream publishers like Tor and Ediciones Modernas Luz were eager to receive fascist cash for these titles. Fascist works were also published in Italy and distributed in Spain and Latin America, but the fascists believed that it was better to have a legitimate Argentine publishing house issue these works if they were to be widely distributed in Latin America. On some occasions, as with the translation of Gayda's What Does Italy Want?, a prestigious nacionalista writer like Carlos Ibarguren was secured to write the introduction.[94] Many books in Italian by Mussolini, Gino Arias, Bottai, Gentile, Spirito, Missiroli, De Michelis, De Begnac, and others were sent to specific organizations and individuals. "Clandestine materials" (i.e., pamphlets and fliers) and Italian fascist journals were also selectively distributed among fascist sympathizers, the conservative press, seventy selected libraries, members of congress, and army officers, among other sectors of Argentine society. The propaganda activities of free agents and spies—widely denounced by Argentine and Italian antifascists—were not as important as print propaganda but were nonetheless used.[95] All these activities proceeded concurrently, but fascist propaganda placed greatest emphasis on influencing newspapers and other periodicals.

The fascist concern with the press was mainly related to the news that the Argentine press reproduced from international news agencies such as Havas (based in France), United Press (United States), and Reuters (United Kingdom). Nazi propaganda was also a matter of concern. The Nazis had created a news agency (Transocean) to provide Nazi propaganda to Latin America by presenting it as "objective" news. The Italians did the same by creating an Italian fascist news service for South America called Roma Press. The name, Roma Press, alludes to the historic legacy of Rome, which fascists wanted to imply they shared with Latin Americans. The idea of having a specific agency for South America located in Buenos Aires did not originate with the Ministry of Propaganda. The founder of Roma Press, the self-described "agency of fascist propaganda," was the Italian Tommaso Milani. Milani was a fascist entrepreneur who had the support of important members of the Italian community in Argentina and the fascist regime in Italy. In his first proposal to the fascist government, Milani defined the reasons behind his project: the absence of any institution of its type in Latin America, the absence of any organ for fascist propaganda, the need to create an "atmosphere of increasing sympathy towards fascism and fascist Italy," and the need to respond to the rising tide of Nazi propaganda. Minister Ciano appreciated the agency's "vast work of propaganda" as well as its aims and Italian connections, rewarding Roma Press with a subsidy from Italy. For Ciano, the "masked" Nazi propaganda argument seemed to have been the most important reason for supporting Roma Press. With the support of Ciano, the agency could continue to supply free news articles and wires to a variety of Argentine papers, including both central conservative papers such as *La Razón* and major provincial papers. Roma Press also distributed news, at no charge, to Chilean, Bolivian, and Paraguayan newspapers and ran a daily radio broadcast on Radio Excelsior in Argentina. Roma Press distributed not only fascist news but also soccer news that was thought to bolster Italian prestige abroad. The effort of Milani was quite remarkable, particularly in the Argentine interior, where the most important papers published reports by Roma Press. Nonetheless, Roma Press was mistrusted by the Italian embassy in Buenos Aires, and this opposition eventually undermined the press's position. The agency disappeared with little fanfare after some years.[96] One criticism that Ambassador Arlotta voiced to Ciano in a secret report was that Roma Press catered principally to nacionalista and profascist papers, and this tendency, given their lack of a "mass following," could end up being "counterproductive." It is difficult, however, to believe that Arlotta actually believed his own statement, since he continued to give support to these papers himself after the waning of Roma Press. The problem that the Italian fascist embassy had with the "exuberant" Milani was the fact that he undertook propaganda activities that the embassy regarded as exclusively its own.[97]

During the 1930s, but particularly from 1934 to 1941, the Italian embassy in Buenos Aires handled Italian propaganda on the ground. Diplomatic officials decided which newspapers should be influenced and subsidized. The propaganda ministry (Ministry of Popular Culture) in Rome, however, made the final decisions on which outlets to support. The level of resources invested in Argentina points to the extent of fascist interest in the country. As Roma Press had done before, institutional fascist propaganda supported and subsidized mainstream Catholic papers like *El Pueblo* and *Los Principios* (Córdoba).[98] The propaganda ministry also offered free wires and subscriptions to fascist journals, distributed Mussolini's and Ciano's memorabilia, and, more important, gave money to nacionalista papers such as *Bandera Argentina, Crisol, El Pampero,* and *La Fronda.*[99] For fascist propaganda experts, the money given to nacionalistas was not an incentive but a reward for their continuing support of Italian fascism. According to these officials, fascism had a "comradeship" with Argentine nacionalismo. And these papers were supported for their "constant and clear position with respect to the war against Bolshevism (and) the Jewish-Masonic international." Thus, for the fascist propagandists, the Argentine nacionalistas and their press were on the same side as the Italian fascists in the "world ideological battle."[100]

Fascist propaganda also maintained connections with mainstream provincial papers, and money was not the only factor involved in this collaboration. Nacionalista, Catholic, and conservative provincials had supported fascism before money or free news wires and propaganda texts were used to solidify their association with fascism. All these papers generally spoke with what fascist observers called a "fascist intonation," or at least a consistent "sympathy" for fascism. It was often the nacionalista, Catholic, and conservative provincial papers that asked for fascist propaganda to be sent to the embassy in the first place, or that wrote directly to the ministry or to the Duce himself. Most, if not all, of the fascist articles and cartoons published by these media had been created in Italy and were distributed at no cost to the papers.[101]

The most difficult task for fascist propagandists was to reach out to the mainstream press. Whereas in pro-British papers like *La Nación*, fascism could hope only for the presence of sympathetic writers like Leopoldo Lugones, in other mainstream media outlets fascist officials found that cash triggered an enthusiastic reception of Mussolini's fascism. Fascist propaganda subsidized the mainstream journal *Caras y Caretas* and the newspapers *Noticias Gráficas* and *La Razón*.[102]

The case of *La Razón* deserves special mention. This paper became pro-fascist of its own volition, having established contacts with fascist Italy in the 1920s. In 1926 Mussolini himself had saluted the sympathetic tenor of the paper.[103] Not being satisfied with only having "Platonic relations" with the paper, the fascist propaganda minister Alfieri decided in 1937 to pay for an entire supplement of the paper devoted to the Italian empire. Although fascist "subsidies" to *La Razón* had begun the previous year, Alfieri had many reasons to do this. Italian propaganda officials clearly perceived that the empire was a great factor in Argentines' appreciation of fascism.[104] The competition of German propaganda was another incentive to produce the special issue. As the Italian expert of propaganda abroad put it, the "financial means of the German embassy allows the Germans to secure the sympathies of not only *La Razón* but also of almost all small nacionalista and Catholics organs."[105] Actually, the Germans were not as pervasive in the Catholic press as the fascists feared, but in *La Razón* they had clearly found a non-Platonic acquaintance. In the early days of May 1937, *La Razón* published a special "German supplement" entitled "Germany Rises Again." In typical totalitarian fashion, the issue dealt with all aspects of Nazi Germany altered to fit Argentine preoccupations, including anticommunism, anti-Semitism, sports, women, labor, military problems, and economics. The supplement included pictures, illustrations, and an anti-Semitic cartoon by the Argentine cartoonist Muñiz that provided a possible opening to Nazi anti-Semitic persecution. In addition, Argentine readers were presented with special messages to the Argentine people from the German foreign minister von Ribbentrop, from the German ambassador von Thermann, and from Hitler himself. The Führer specifically wrote: "Through the pages of *La Razón* I am sending my cordial regards to the Argentine people and the Germans of Argentina."[106]

As Hitler's "cordial regards" indicate, the German supplement was mild in its attempt to impress the Argentine public. It presented Nazism as an example and not as a model system for all countries. In this sense, it was the opposite of the fascist supplement of *La Razón* that appeared at the end of the same month. Instead of the totalitarian Nazi presentation, the Italian propaganda minister, Alfieri, chose another strategy. He personally supervised this supplement by asking all the major Italian fascist figures to write short pieces for it. The supplement, as Mussolini was told, was supposed to reach out to the Latin American public at large and not only to Argentines.[107] The special supplement would be thematic and focus on the single topic, promoted by Mussolini, of the bonds between Italy and Argentina. It thus signaled a departure from the strategy of totalitarian fascist propaganda that previous years had witnessed. But the emphasis on this topic was not new in Italian Argentine propaganda, and the supplement also addressed other issues, such as gender relations, business, and tourism.[108]

One might wonder how the specific nature of Argentina's relation with Italy as asserted by the fascists could appeal to the Latin American public at large. The fascist answer probably lies in the Mussolinean conception of Argentina's special leading role for Latin America.

The idea that the major voices of fascism should establish a direct dialogue with Argentines, and by implication with Latin American readers as well, presented a difficult task for the fascist propagandists.[109] It was not easy for Alfieri to convince his eminent fascist contributors of the wisdom of this idea, but he persisted and, with the exception of the intractable party boss Achille Starace, he convinced them all. Although the supplement was successful, it had been a very expensive initiative, and one that, as one secret report argued, the ministry could not afford to repeat. Thus, after the publication of this supplement, the ministry decided not to publish another the following year but to continue with multifaceted propaganda that emphasized the same theme, that is, Italian fascist imperialism.[110]

Mussolini's own short message in *La Razón* made explicit reference to the "Latin" bonds between Argentines and Italians. Reinforcing his vision were texts written by some of the major fascist figures of the day, which provided a window on the mainstream fascist understanding of Argentina in particular, and Latin America in general, as extensions of Italy's Latin empire. This view informed the texts of Italo Balbo, Admiral Costanzo Ciano (the father of Galeazzo Ciano, Mussolini's son-in-law), G. Bottai, L. Federzoni, Piero Parini (the leader of the fascists abroad), Marshall De Bono, Marshall Badoglio, and Senator Marconi, among others.

For Ambassador Guariglia, Italy was neither a "feudal empire" nor a capitalistic one, but an empire of Italian workers. All these fascists agreed on the essential part played by Italian workers in the making of Argentina. The Italian empire, in addition to the preexisting Latin bonds, could in their view strengthen their links with Argentina and Latin America. The conflation of the idea that Argentina was an independent country, having a certain autonomy of its own, with the notion that Argentina needed to follow Italy due to the presence of Italians, was acted out in these texts. For example, Federzoni reiterated his view that for Latin Americans, and especially for Argentines, "Rome, the eternal source of the Latin spirit and universal civilization," was a "*communis patria.*" Argentines, he argued, were nurtured by "the same spirit and culture" and also by the work of Italians. The inventor Marconi shared these notions and presented Argentines and Italians as the "dignified offspring of the old mother Rome." Parini, the "minister of Italians abroad," took Marconi's metaphor to its limit, comparing the "racial qualities" of the millions of Italians abroad with the ancient Greeks living in the Greek diaspora in Italy, linking Italians abroad to the Italian empire.[111] Marshall De Bono, one of the founders of fascism and the "conqueror" of Ethiopia, synthesized the fascist vision of Latin America as a land of both independent peoples and Italian colonies:

The Latin republics of America are the living expression of Romanness [*Romanidad*] in the new continent. The race [*estirpe*] not only does not die but also does not change with transmigration. The pioneers, before thinking of harvesting the fruits of the new lands where they put their feet instinctively, take care to establish the bases of the race. It is the Latin man, the Latin society that has given to a large part of the New Continent its current physiognomy and has implanted its civility. If a Roman citizen of the time of Augustus were to be reborn in Uruguay, Paraguay, Argentina, or Brazil, or for that matter in any other American state, this Roman citizen would feel the same beating of heart, the same geniality of mind, the reblossoming of intelligence, as in the lands of the Empire.

Emilio De Bono goes on to sum up the basic imperialistic tenets of fascist Latin American propaganda:

> Over the course of the centuries, Italy was always present throughout the entire Latin land of America. . . . Fascist Italy, elevated to the rank of imperial Italy, is sending today her caring and inaugural salute to her sisters of America, and essentially to Argentina, a country that due to her cultural development combined the characteristics of all these sisters. Italy does this with the security that they will see, in the new empire, the Roman empire, which is even today a guarantee of civilization, glory, justice, and world progress.[112]

De Bono's contribution to the supplement contains paternalistic touches that may have annoyed many Latin Americans, particularly the notion that Argentina was some kind of amalgam of the other Latin American republics and the assumption that everybody could relate to fascist imperialism. For the Argentine nacionalistas, however, De Bono's article spoke to the obvious limitations of an Italian imperialism that hoped to secure a relationship between "sisters" across the Atlantic. De Bono's text also bears witness to the fascist understanding of propaganda in an age of empire. In this as in other respects, the Argentine nacionalistas read between lines and saw what they wanted, particularly the connections between Mussolini's Roman empire and a Latin American anti-imperialism that was mostly directed against the United States and Great Britain.

The new legitimacy ascribed to propaganda in 1934 coincided with the period in which Italian fascism reached its peak of consensus.[113] It canonized its views on universal fascism and significantly reformulated its understanding of imperialism. From the spiritual and paternal imperialism of the Roman / Latin legacy, Mussolini switched to active imperialism with the invasion of Ethiopia. This new "imperialism of proletarian nations" (Italy being the prototype) was successfully conflated with the new Latin American version of anti-imperialism that, for example, the Argentine nacionalistas were so keen to adopt. The major success of the fascist notion of imperialism was, ironically, an outcome of its own failure to generate fear among those it expected to adopt fascism. In other words, the Latin American perception of the fascist notion of empire as a milder and unthreatening form of imperialism could, in their view, be easily equated with old and new patterns of Latin American anti-imperialism. Thus, the new fascist imperialism was palatable to an important segment of the Argentine public. In nacionalista eyes, Italian proletarian imperialism was directed toward Africa, and thus Argentina could find in Italy an extraregional ally in the Argentine nacionalista fight to overcome the neocolonial status of Latin America.

The Argentine Appropriation of Fascism

So far, we have seen that Italian fascists were overwhelmingly engaged in a monologue with respect to Argentina. This monologue had manifold populist dimensions that appealed to Argentines, including transnational flights and diversified means of mass propaganda. Italian propaganda had a popular target and a clear political aim:[114] that eventually, Argentina should become fascist. Argentine fascists were the natural carriers of this idea. But if the Italians were intent on selling fascism, the Argentine fascists were not interested in becoming mere customers. As we will see nacionalismo wanted to establish a direct dialogue with Mussolini. Moreover, nacionalistas actually inverted the rules of engagement. If the Italians considered their nacionalista cousins to be Argentine fascists, the Argentines regarded the Italians as "Italian nacionalistas."

The history of the Argentine response to the connection between Italian fascism and the South Atlantic cannot be seen as one of passive reception. Passive receptivity was, of course, what the Italians desired; Mussolini expected the Argentines to listen and be silent. This last section of this chapter explains why that did not happen.

The Italians' appreciation of the possibilities of fascism in Latin America was limited yet optimistic. On the one hand, fascist ideology insisted on the universal aspects of fascism that would make it fit any given country and particularly a "Latin" one such as Argentina. Fascist reports on nacionalistas were generally positive, albeit paternalistic. The Italian propagandists thought that nacionalismo should be modeled on Italian fascism. On the other hand, although secret Italian reports stressed that nacionalismo was "in accord with the totalitarian political line," they also criticized the nacionalismo's lack of preparation, its political failures, and lack of ideological consistency. In sum, Italian fascists reluctantly recognized that Argentine nacionalismo was different from fascism. They often called it "Catholic nacionalismo," while noting that it was *"filofascista."*[115] This ambivalence allowed Italian fascist commentators to admit, albeit reluctantly, that nacionalismo was a distinctly Latin American fascist ideology while acknowledging its more generic converging features. As a confidential fascist report put it: "Nacionalista ideals coincide with the fascist and National-Socialist ones."[116]

Many Italian fascist intellectuals were impatient with Latin American fascisms and particularly with Argentine nacionalismo, even calling it a "pseudofascism," an "insufficient imitation," and a "deformation of fascism."[117] As we see, the fascist relationship with the nacionalista movement was not devoid of contestation; nevertheless, generally the attitude was positive. The feeling was apparently mutual. As one Italian secret report put it when referring to a nacionalista group, "Young nacionalistas are enthusiastic for our regime and for Italy."[118] The report was correct. Most nacionalistas indeed shared a strong enthusiasm for fascism. The first successful nacionalista journal, La Nueva República (1927–1931), praised fascist Italy enthusiastically, especially its "principles of order."[119] To be sure, until the first serious Italian fascist articulation of a canonic self-interpretation in the early 1930s, fascist ideology had been somewhat vague, a situation that could be blamed on the original Italian matrix and not on its interpreters. But in the mid-thirties, well after the ideology had been clearly defined in Italy, Argentines continued to understand fascism in their own terms. Italian fascists complained about this misunderstanding in the Italian fascist press as well as in secret reports.[120] Whereas in the Italian fascist press the observers were more vocal in their criticism of the disconnect between Italian fascism and Argentine nacionalismo, the confidential reports written by fascist propagandists occasionally took a more hopeful line, presenting Argentine "Catholic nacionalismo" as an exception to what they saw as the general Argentine trend of "revolutionary dynamism that characterizes the local nacionalista groups."[121] As we saw earlier, Mussolini and his followers saw Argentina as either an Italian ethnic territory that ought to be conquered or as a neo-Italian postcolonial state ready to follow imperial Italy in the world. From the Italian fascist perspective, nacionalismo should adopt fascism as presented in Italian propaganda.

There were some exceptions, but almost no one within nacionalismo saw Italian fascism as a model to be adopted. In addition nacionalistas harbored doubts about the aspects of Italian fascist propaganda that focused on the Italian origins of Argentina as epitomized by "Italian characters" like Christopher Columbus or Manuel Belgrano.[122] Indeed, even those who paid attention to this propaganda were not convinced by it. Rather, they were highly critical and often offended by these paternalistic efforts at assimilation.[123] Understandably, most nacionalistas preferred to stress the assimilation of Italians in Argentina—for the Italian fascists in Italy this was, as we have seen, a matter of serious preoccupation—and they understood their links with Italy in terms of a trio of vague concepts: "latinidad," "estirpe," and "catolicismo."[124] Certainly, nacionalistas were very impressed by the Italian fascists' flights to South America, and Argentina in particular. However, these flights were never as important to them as the efforts related to the fascist international, and they were not as impressed by the technological accomplishments of these flights as the Italians wished them to be. The power of Italian authoritarian technology was exemplified for many in Ethiopia.[125] More important than an advanced fascist technology was the political aspect of fascist war. The war in Ethiopia was for the nacionalistas, as it had been for antifascists, a moment of explicit cooperation between Italian fascists in Argentina and the Argentine nacionalistas. This war anticipated the massive nacionalista engagement in debates that would occur in Argentina about the Spanish Civil War and the Second World War. Nacionalistas saw a "world antifascist conspiracy" and Italy had to be defended against it.[126] Mussolini's idea of fascism as an imperialism of "proletarian nations" was widely accepted because it offered many connections between fascist imperialism and the emerging nacionalista anti-imperialism. The Argentines also were convinced by the Italian equation of imperialism with the idea of a civilizing mission, as well as the idea of the need for an Italian "vital space," especially if this space was in Africa and far from Latin America.[127]

Conceptual encounters notwithstanding, the real strength of fascism within nacionalismo was related to the persona of Mussolini and his mythical image as the ultimate leader. Certainly, there was limited success if one judges fascism in Argentina to be a derivative phenomenon. But the influence of fascism was lateral and extensive, distorted and ultimately appropriated and reformulated, as we will see in chapter 4.

Most nacionalistas embraced the hyperbole surrounding Mussolini and presented him as template for the leader, "characterized by the rough sobriety of a macho man," as the nacionalistas from Tucumán put it, "the savior of modern civilization," and "the man that today rules the Western world."[128] Even General Uriburu, also considered as the prototype of the "macho man," was equated with the Duce.[129] But if nacionalismo appropriated Mussolini, this appropriation rested on a more complex mythical framework: namely, the homegrown myth of Uriburu. According to the nacionalistas, Uriburu admired fascism as a "doctrine." All the candidates for Jefe after Uriburu left office also had to be presented as the "Argentine

Mussolini." General Fasola Castaño, a nacionalista leader during the 1930s, was among the unlikely candidates to be the new Argentine Uriburu and Duce. Juan P. Ramos of the organization Aduna, Leopoldo Lugones of Guardia Argentina, and many others also fit this pattern.[130] The myth of Mussolini never achieved in nacionalismo the importance of the myth of Uriburu that I analyzed in chapter 2, but the Duce was certainly the most valued external figure of fascism, far exceeding Hitler, Pétain, or Franco. Moreover, nacionalistas often wrote to Mussolini asking for a signed photograph or autograph, as well as "doctrinal materials."[131]

Armando Lavalle, the jefe of the nacionalista association Legión Patriótica for instance, took advantage of his letter of request for fascist materials to ask for an "autograph signed on one of your pictures." Lavalle told the Duce in 1935: "I want to let you know that we are identified with the fascist regime as a whole. The basic principles of fascism are the basis of Argentine nacionalismo. We adapt fascism to our milieu and to our needs in order to achieve the total extirpation of the professional politicians."[132] In his letter to the Duce, Alfredo Villegas Oromí for the Legión de Mayo repeated a similar argument about the need for the Argentine adaptation of fascism and noted that he had an "immense wish to study and understand fascism."[133] But there was more than "adaptation" in the nacionalista reception of fascism. For Lavalle and Villegas Oromí, as for many other nacionalistas, the "New Argentina" that nacionalismo promised would have to be identified with "immortal Rome" and "the will of God." While the Italian propaganda official did send a signed photograph and fascist materials to the leader of the Legión Patriótica, it is highly improbable that for Mussolini the will of God and his vicar on earth, the pope, would have been a more important than his own will. As we will see in chapter 4, the nacionalista syncretism that conflated the Rome of the popes with the Rome of fascism posited the Mussolini myth as yet another artifact of their nacionalista views. They received fascist ideological positions and fascist material, and more generally the "basic principles of fascism" as fascist propaganda presented them. But for Argentine nacionalistas these "principles" included the conception of fascism as the political executioner of the sacred. To be sure, this position was also shared by a few Italian clericofascists in Italy, but in Argentina this was the opinion of the majority.[134]

It is symptomatic of the nacionalistas' selective reading that for most Argentine nacionalistas Mussolini was primarily regarded as the "mediator between the people and the will of God, represented in the power of an empire."[135]

Mussolini, the nacionalista writer Alfredo Tarruella argued, no longer belonged to Italians: "His ideas transcend national borders in order to be beneficial for all nations."[136] The "ideas" that the nacionalistas had in mind were more an affect, a collective "feeling," than the result of systematic close reading of the Duce's speeches. Catholicism encompassed this collective feeling, as the nacionalistas understood it. Unlike the Italian interpreters of the Duce, the nacionalistas did not feel compelled to make sense of a discursive whole. The transnationality of Mussolini's "ideas" was not necessarily linked to their systemic articulation. In Italy this open interpretation was a difficult and often forbidden task. For the nacionalistas, Mussolini's vagueness was a reason to fill the blanks with Argentine nacionalista motifs that would have been alien to Mussolini himself. An example is the dialogue with Mussolini that many proposed: in Argentina, this "dialogue" was often quite different from the dialogue that took place between Mussolini and his fascists in Italy. In Italy, fascists "listened" to the Duce, even when they were interpreting his remarks; in Argentina, nacionalistas "talked" to the Duce— literally, as when the nacionalistas Ramos Mexía,[137] Goyeneche, Richard Lavalle,[138] Manuel Fresco,[139] and Matías Sánchez Sorondo[140] met with Mussolini throughout the 1930s.

It is highly improbable that the Duce was actually listening to his Argentine interlocutors, but the idea of "talking to the Duce" as opposed to listening to him is symptomatic of the Argentine reformulation of fascist ideology as an Italian form of nacionalista ideology. Even more important than the personal connections with Mussolini was the more abstract fictional dialogue in which the Argentines expressed their opinions to the Duce. "What would you say to the Duce?" was the title of an inquiry organized by the nacionalista paper *Bandera Argentina*. The paper gave its readers a form to be filled out with their opinions and promised all forms would be sent to Mussolini to be reviewed. (Whether this promise was actually fulfilled is doubtful.)[141]

In their criticisms of antifascism, many nacionalistas accused antifascists of having an "obsession" with fascism.[142] This claim was a projection, for they were also obsessed with Italian fascism. In their obsession, the nacionalistas stood apart from other Argentines in their creative yet mischievous understanding of fascism's ideological core. One might even contend that they were the only group that paradoxically was more ludic in their approach and less interested in accurately perceiving fascism as it was evolving in Mussolini's Italy.

The process that nacionalistas followed in their encounter with fascism was often a nonderivative reformulation of fascism, many times a divergent form that had few links with the fascist matrix, notwithstanding their sharing of a transnational claim to be part of the same ideology. In other words, their ascription to fascist ideology was not the result of a passive reception.

For most nacionalistas, fascism and Nazism were, as Ernesto Palacio put it, "analogical movements." This did not mean they considered them to be identical, however; rather, nacionalistas shared an "affinity" with their European counterparts.[143]

In order to minimize the charge of imitation, some nacionalistas argued that nacionalismo was neither fascist nor Nazi. José María Rosa from Asociación Nacionalista Argentina/Aduna argued in a speech in Mendoza that nacionalismo should not "import" fascism, but should create a separate Argentine movement. Some nacionalistas anathematized Rosa, perhaps because he was too candid (for nacionalista standards) about the need to be detached from the Italian matrix.[144] There were important minorities like the Partido Fascista Argentino, which believed that Argentine fascism should not be different from Italian fascism. Italian fascism itself was of course very supportive of this idea and maintained the closest connection with the Argentine Fascist Party. In 1935, in the Amsterdam meeting of the Fascist International, General Eugenio Coselschi, the Italian ideologue of universal fascism, announced the official registration of the Argentine Fascist Party in the Fascist Universal Front.[145] The majority of the founders of this Argentine party were Argentines of Italian background. An Italian fascist secret report states that most of these founders "recognized as its [Argentine fascism's] spiritual leader the Duce, Benito Mussolini."[146]

Some Argentines living in Italy founded Argentine fascist sections in Rome and Milan, and some Italian agents of propaganda in Argentina were members of the Argentine Fascist Party.[147] The Argentine fascist section in Milan was active in distributing Argentine fascist propaganda in Europe in French, Italian, and Spanish. In Italy the boss of the Milan Section was a divorced young Argentine woman in her mid-twenties, Mercedes Carrasi del Villar (who had been married to the Italian Federico Carrasi del Villar). Carrasi del Villar presented the Argentine Fascist Party to Mussolini as having the primary objective of "establishing links of intimate spiritual understanding" between Italy and Argentina. The ultimate aim of Argentine fascism, she argued, was that of "developing" in Argentina "an 'assimilation-ist' knowledge of the achievements of Mussolinian fascism." With the assimilation of fascism, she argued, Argentina would become the "most progressive Latin State in the Americas."[148] The Italian sections in Italy and the constant trips of Argentine fascists to Italy to meet fascist officials consolidated a direct link between Italian fascism and the Argentine fascists. No other Argentine nacionalista organization sought this kind of close political bond.[149]

At one point in the 1930s the Argentine Fascist Party became a mass organization, particularly in Córdoba. Typically, the Argentine fascists argued that fascism was "the only solution to the chaos we are living."[150] In fact, there were Argentine fascists who appropriated Mussolini's fascism as they believed he saw it. Some of them were even particularly adamant in rejecting the myth of Uriburu insofar as they considered it to be in conflict with the myth of the Duce.[151] However, a majority of the "assimilationist" Argentine fascists borrowed Uriburian concepts and tended to identify fascism with the Uriburu dictatorship and the trilogy of "God, fatherland, and home."[152] Thus, even for the Argentine Fascist Party, Italian fascism was one example among many of "universal nacionalismo."[153]

How then did the nacionalistas understand nacionalismo? In other words, what did nacionalismo mean for them within the mutually interacting frameworks of Italian fascism and Argentine developments?

The first thing that has to be said about the term "nacionalismo" is that the nacionalistas won a battle for its ownership early on. Even in internal documents of the Argentine state the nacionalistas were recognized as nacionalistas.[154] From the inception of nacionalismo onward there have been only a few instances in which Argentine society put the name of the nacionalistas in question. This is remarkable because as late as the 1920s many radical, liberal, conservative, and leftist intellectuals used the term "nacionalismo" to identify their own national politics.[155] By the early 1930s, however, the word "nacionalismo" within the Argentine context almost exclusively referred to the radical extreme Right. In other words, in Argentina, "nacionalismo" meant fascism.

The nacionalistas presented fascism as yet another expression of their strong Uriburista ideology and, like their beloved dictator, they too stressed the disadvantages of a direct identification with European models: "It is not possible to search for the roots of September in foreign political movements.

Neither Hitler nor Mussolini told Uriburu what he should do."[156] In the first place, nacionalismo, as we have seen, identified the myth of Uriburu with the experience of his dictatorship and a set of practices. However, there were many other instances in which it was obvious to nacionalistas that they needed to define a more systematic ideology. As many nacionalistas argued, this ideology was encompassed by fascism. But fascism was, for the nacionalistas, what they wanted it to be. In other words, if fascism was an Italian version of transnational nacionalismo, nacionalismo as an inherently Argentine ideology would have to be defined.

As we have seen, for Uriburu, nacionalismo meant the political expression of the needs of the "patria" without the "traditional" political practices. Thus, nacionalismo was first and foremost antidemocratic. The definition of nacionalismo as being in opposition to a certain political entity was accompanied by a more "positive" self-understanding of it. Like his father before him, Leopoldo Lugones Jr. understood nacionalismo as having supreme values of its own, most certainly, its opposition to individualism and liberalism. Rather than defining nacionalismo, Lugones Jr. expressed that it was "a synthesis of the patria."[157] If nacionalismo was an embodiment of the patria, the patria or what actually constituted it needed to be made explicit. But for many nacionalistas, it was equally important to create a political movement that would unite all the significant sectors of the nation under a single leadership.

For Juan Carulla, nacionalismo was a political movement, and as such was political and not "apolitical," as the Lugones, father and son, implied. Rather than being outside of politics, Carulla argued, nacionalismo was within politics insofar as it transcended it. In other words, the political expression of nacionalismo had superior interests that overrode the particular interests of political sectors. The nacionalistas understood their political movement as a unique front of church, army, and civilians that represented the nation as a whole. To be sure, this was not much different from the self-understanding of other political sectors, such as the Radical Party. Following a contentious tradition that went back to nineteenth-century factionalism, the Radical Party of the 1930s presented its political competitors as "traitors." Likewise, for the nacionalistas, other political groups were not merely political competitors but internal enemies of the nation.[158] The identification of the nacionalista interest with those of the nation led them to conflate their political needs with those of the state. Obviously, the conquest of the state was for them a necessity that overrode other ideological considerations. This was a central tenet of nacionalista discourse, but ironically it did preclude more practical discussions about the nature of the state, the political system, and so forth.

Juan Carulla believed that nacionalista ideology would be oriented by reality, and by reality he meant political needs that guided the movement to its final aim.[159] In defining that aim, Carulla equated the welfare of all Argentines and the reification of the state. The eclipse of individual autonomy implied in this view was paradoxically considered a result of the over-determination of individual will, that is, the will of a finite group of individuals.[160] For nacionalistas like Enrique Osés, nacionalismo was above all an antiliberal reaction. Osés saw fascism and nacionalismo as entailing anti-liberalism, anti-Judaism, and anticommunism. Probably to avoid internal debate, Osés put forward the dubious argument that the negative thrust of nacionalista ideology, namely, the "critique" of these "isms," disclosed the ideological program of Argentine fascism: "We are 'anti' because we are an opposition. We are antipolitical, antidemocratic, anti-imperialist, antimonopolist, antiliberal." Osés claimed that Argentine nacionalismo was "positioned in neither the right, nor the center, nor the left." However, for Osés, as well as for all the members of the nacionalista movement, there were also positive strategies shaping the original patterns of nacionalista ideology. Osés argued that in political and ideological terms Argentine nacionalismo was more "advantaged" than "other nacionalismos" such as Italian fascism, German Nazism, and the fascisms of Spain and Portugal.

Unlike European fascism, Osés argued, Argentine nacionalismo was original and more consistent in its totalitarianism. "Our rebellion is not against a regime, a series of economic errors, a historical treason or social injustices," he wrote. "No. Our rebellion is against a regime, that is to say, it is against a *habitus*." This "habitus" that Osés opposed to nacionalismo was for him a "totality" that was at the same time "politically, economically, financially, spiritually, religiously, domestically, totally anti-Argentine." If nothing else, Osés presented the nacionalista habitus as opposed to an anti-Argentine one, which must be destroyed. "It is our duty to extirpate it forever from our fatherland," he wrote. While he saw the anti-Argentine habitus as evil, he considered the nacionalista one as based firmly in the "Christian system of faith." For Osés, Argentine nacionalismo advanced "an authoritarian regulation of individual duties according to the most Argentine and Christian concept of human personality. This is, and let's repeat it, the essential content of nacionalismo."[161]

Osés also claimed that nacionalismo should be a theory in the making, given that ideological discussion should be related to political realities. To be sure, this idea of nacionalismo as an "ideology" in constant reformulation was central to Italian fascism as well. However, the Argentines were more engaged in theoretical discussions than their Italian counterparts. Whereas for Mussolini such discussions were necessarily part of a broader theoretical legitimization for his ever-changing strategic view of day-to-day politics, for the Argentines theory sometimes foreclosed politics. In this sense the Argentine nacionalistas blurred the distinction between a reality-based perception of politics and the theological-theoretical drives of their clericofascist imagination. The main strategy of nacionalismo was to impose theory on reality and not the other way around, as had happened many times in Mussolini's Italy, to the dismay of the Duce's more radical colleagues. The nacionalistas continually complained about their own excessive focus on theory, but nonetheless constantly theorized in their publications.[162] The practical primacy of theory over politics was central to the nacionalistas' own understanding of their political self. In short, whereas the nacionalistas repeatedly claimed that politics was the ideal, and only, way to establish "Christian fascism," they found "high theory" to be an essential political task. In Italian fascism, theory was often perceived as threatening political developments. As we will see in the next chapters, for the Argentine nacionalistas, theorizing was in a sense the ultimate form of politics, one presupposed in their commitment to God. The nacionalistas believed that the incorporation of God into politics made nacionalismo a more complete version of fascism.

Many nacionalistas simply denied the fact that Italian fascism was not as interested or embedded in Catholicism as they thought it was. The tendency to equate nacionalismo and Catholicism was a seminal element of this strategy, and it became, along with the myth of Uriburu and a radical brand of clericofascist anti-Semitism, a crucial part of nacionalista doctrine.[163] The idea that nacionalismo represented in Argentina what fascism represented in Italy was seldom questioned, and for almost no one did this imply a contradiction with respect to the central dimension of nacionalismo: the equation of nacionalismo and Catholicism.

It was the famous nacionalista theoretician and writer Leopoldo Lugones Sr. who at the end of his long career personified this tendency. Lugones was first a radical atheist and anarchist, a founding member of Argentine socialism, and later the creator of the most important myth of liberal Argentina, the myth of the gaucho. By the end of his life, he had become a convinced fascist who converted to Catholicism before finally committing suicide in 1938. For the fascist Lugones, Hitler and Mussolini represented transnational nacionalismo.[164] He saw antifascism as often stimulated by "antipapism" and he equated the interests of the Vatican with those of Italian fascism.[165] Somehow, for him, the fascist conquest of Ethiopia implied a continuation of the Catholic ideal by imperial means. In the 1920s, he had equated Einsteinian relativism with particularistic tendencies in philosophy, history, and politics, and he remained consistently opposed to universalistic tendencies. The fatherland was for him not an "abstract" concept but a palpable reality. However, he did believe that the union of fascism and Catholicism transcended abstraction and national borders.[166]

The fact that Lugones arrived at this conclusion at the end of his political career made him more "European" in his model than the majority of his fellow nacionalistas. The famous Spanish *falangista* intellectual José María Pemán formulated this Latin American and, more specifically, Argentine characteristic in a very perceptive manner when he argued:

It is the case that the Latin American processes of reaction followed an inverse path to that of Europeans. Here [in Europe] it is the nacionalista and imperialistic consciousness that initiates the processes, and [European fascists] look for a way to accommodate Catholic principles and the church. There [in Latin America] the Catholic groups initiate the process and they start looking for collaboration with fascist instruments and styles. Here it is force and violence that, with a decorative intention, later call upon Catholic principles. There, these Catholic principles call upon force in order to defend themselves.[167]

It is to these "Catholic principles" that we now turn.

ᚒ 4 ᚕ

A "Christianized Fascism"

For Argentine fascists and nacionalistas, fascism was not a theory but a mold for Catholic thinking. For instance, one of the most significant nacionalista intellectuals, César Pico, argued that fascism was a "reaction against the calamities ascribed to liberal democracy, socialism, and capitalism. It's a reaction that, although instinctive in its origins, is searching for a doctrine that could justify it." In his mind, and in the minds of most of his colleagues, Catholicism represented the ideal theoretical apparatus for fascism. He argued that, although fascism could be totalitarian in the Nazi sense, that was not the case with Italian or Spanish fascism or with "the Latin American nacionalista movements." For Pico, Catholic doctrine needed to be the doctrine of fascism insofar as he considered fascism devoid of theory. In short, nacionalismo should be "a Christianized fascism."[1]

This chapter and the following one analyze how Argentine fascists understood themselves. They deal with the contradictions and debates within Argentine fascism, particularly over the conflation of Catholicism and fascism, as the Argentine fascists searched for a doctrine and a program. Whereas this chapter highlights the central role that Catholicism played in the definition of nacionalismo and its practice, chapter 5 focuses on how this role was equally affected and constantly reformulated by notions of global fascism, totalitarianism, imperialism, and Hispanic and Argentine neocolonialism, Nazism, and anti-Semitism. The aim here is to show how these notions framed the theory and ideology of nacionalismo, placing it at the crossroads of Europe and Latin America and between the secular and the sacred.

Most nacionalistas saw and accepted fascism as a form of radical nationalism and as a way of saving Argentina. But there were important complexities and qualifications in the relation between nacionalismo and fascism,
especially for certain key nacionalistas and Catholics such as Father Gustavo Franceschi. Most nacionalistas conflated Catholicism and fascism and
thought their movement had a central place in God's designs for Argentina. I
pay special attention to different nacionalista efforts to create a political
doctrine that accounted for this view. Nacionalismo conceived itself as the
political expression of God. Without a fascist leader or regime, which fascist
Italy had, Argentine fascists had greater autonomy to conceive an ideological canon and define their political culture in doctrinal terms. "What is
Argentine fascism?" nacionalistas continuously asked themselves during the
period 1922–1945. How does the "universal fascist" movement fit into Argentine history and political traditions? What relationship should the nacionalista movement have with the Catholic Church? Though the nacionalistas
were constantly accused of simply imitating Italian fascism, they often denied this accusation. They did not believe that they were simply buying an
ideological commodity that the Italians were selling.

Some historians have minimized the fascist tendencies of most Catholic
and nacionalista intellectuals.[2] But this argument does not square with the
sources. In the following pages, I analyze the development of a radical
synergy between fascism and Catholicism as perceived by Argentine nacionalistas and reactionary priests during this critical moment in Argentine
history. Deep changes occurred in Argentine political culture during this
period, characterized by the construction and affects of the myth of Uriburu
within the nacionalista movement and, more generally, by the restoration of
conservatism in Argentina, the subsequent rise of a corporatist military dictatorship, and its ultimate if unexpected offspring: the Peronist movement.

Italian fascists and German Nazis generally appreciated the central role
of the Catholic Church within Argentine fascist and nacionalista circles.[3]
Whether or not they explicitly connected Catholicism and the nacionalista
movement, most Argentine fascists took it for granted that the two were
linked. The combination of a potent strain of anti-Catholicism with a strategic pro-Catholic politics—present in many Italian fascists such as Mussolini,
Ciano, Bottai, and others—was absent in Argentine nacionalismo.[4] Without
generally acknowledging this difference with the Duce's fascist ideology, the
nacionalista movement deviated significantly from Italian fascism in this

way. This inconsistency did not pose a problem to the majority of nacionalistas, who thought of themselves as belonging to a general fascist matrix that they shared with Italians.

As for the Argentine Left, it believed that the church had always been linked to the reactionary Right. During the 1930s, for example, the Communist Party distributed leaflets in the streets of several Argentine cities that took for granted the connections nacionalistas made between the church and fascism.[5] In the antifascist Congress of Paris in 1937, the Argentine Glikin presented a report in which he argued, "The Argentine clergy . . . defends Hitler and Mussolini across the board, and more generally is an ardent supporter of the totalitarian regimes and authoritarian governments."[6] In the same manner, the Argentine Jewish newspapers continually insisted on the extremist nature of the Catholic Church in Argentina, and antifascists like the famous poet Raúl González Tuñón agreed with fascists like the Spaniard Pemán over the existence of an Argentine brand of Catholicfascism.[7] For González Tuñón, Argentine nacionalismo was first and foremost a "clerical fascism," but it was also an Argentine imitation of the European fascist matrix. The nacionalistas, he argued, saw Italian fascism, as well as Nazism, as instruments of the will of God and they wanted to construct that fascism in Argentina.[8]

The period between 1920 and 1945 witnessed the rise of a form of Catholicism that worked intimately with nacionalista ideals. Some Catholics opposed the equation of Catholicism with fascism, but they remained a small minority, grouped around the journal *Orden Cristiano*. These progressive Catholics criticized the mainstream Catholicism of the time by observing its move toward the radical Right, repeatedly denouncing nacionalismo as a form of totalitarianism. For these more progressive Catholics, nacionalismo succeeded in subordinating the mainstream church to its political goals.[9] But was this case? Was the Argentine church a pawn to nacionalismo? This was certainly not the way nacionalistas themselves conceived their relation with Catholicism. They considered themselves the political expression of the sacred will, just as the antifascist Glikin had described them in Paris.

Fascism and Catholicism were not the same thing, and these characterizations that Argentine fascists and antifascists left on record should not be read uncritically. There was less harmony between fascism and Catholicism than these documents imply. Contrary to what antifascists such as González Tuñón, the progressive Catholics of *Orden Cristiano*, or members of the Argentine communist party claimed, the relationships among clericofascists were not devoid of conflict. In fact, it might be better to understand the relationship between fascism and Catholicism in Argentina more as a conflation than as an equation. If, as González Tuñón noted, the nacionalistas considered Mussolini to be a willful instrument of sacred designs, they did not blindly accept Italian fascism in toto. Rather, they interpreted selected aspects of it through their understanding of Catholicism, then defined universal fascism as the political expression of the institutional church. To Mussolini, of course, this Argentine understanding of fascism would have been an aberration, as it would have submerged him within the fascist transnational movement. But for Spanish fascists like Pemán, Argentine fascism represented the correct fascist path. Pemán's idea that fascism was the defender or even enforcer of "Catholic principles" dovetailed with the nacionalistas' own views. As the Italian historian Loris Zanatta has shown, from an institutional perspective, the period under study witnessed the implementation of a strategy aimed at the "Catholicization of nacionalismo" by the elite of the Argentine church.[10] The difference between how the Argentine fascists represented Italian fascist views of institutional religion and what Italian fascists actually thought about institutional religion was seldom acknowledged in Argentina.

Generic Nacionalismo as the Political Expression of God

Nacionalistas developed several variations on the relationship between fascism and Catholicism. In fact, the notion of a "Christianized fascism" was to a great extent a product of the Argentine context. Nacionalistas believed that a coupling of fascism with Catholicism gave their movement more meaning than a secular fascism like the one touted by the early Lugones or even Italian fascism itself. This trend led to a phenomenon that some historians have termed clerical fascism.[11] In countries such as Argentina, the Catholic Church participated significantly in this strain of fascist thinking. In Italy, the church constituted only one factor in the development of the fascist regime; if the church did not help fascism actively, neither did it hinder fascism by putting up a resistance. Argentine historiography on fascism has generally downplayed the relationship between Catholicism and the nacionalistas by presenting them as "using" the church in strategic ways.[12] I, in contrast, see the relationship as synergistic. I view notions such as "Christianized fascism" or "clericofascism" as hermeneutic tools to understand nacionalista theory, but I also use them as experiential categories to analyze the practical dimensions of the conflation of fascism and Catholicism.[13] A central aim of this chapter is to show the primacy of this dynamic conflation within nacionalista ideology.

For Enrique Osés—who had for a short period edited *Criterio* (the most important Catholic journal of this period) and then published *Crisol*, one of the most popular nacionalista newspapers—one could not be a good nacionalista outside of Catholicism.[14] Osés believed that nacionalismo was neither right nor left, but was rather an integration of "order, hierarchy, and religious faith" with social justice.[15] Fascism, as the Argentine nacionalistas understood it, represented this same basic trilogy of "God, patria, and home." The use of the trilogy to depict fascist theory and practice was quite extensive.[16] The most important Argentine Jewish newspaper at the time, *Mundo Israelita*, commented that the use of the trilogy represented a conscious attempt to take part in a transnational fascist movement, "the black international."[17]

To be sure, many Argentines, then and now, identified this trilogy with a conservative position. But for most nacionalistas, this formula referred to an essentialized concept of what the patria was.[18] In the writings of Lugones or in nacionalista publications such as *Clarinada, Crisol, Bandera Argentina, Aduna, Nuevo Orden, Nueva Política*, and others, one found Italian fascism, German Nazism, and Spanish fascism all described as national forms of nacionalismo. The Argentines believed that true fascism was inherently Catholic, or to put it differently, that Argentine clericofascism expressed the generic traits of the universal radical Right.[19]

Most nacionalista and Catholic publications agreed with Osés that the essence of the country was to be found in Catholicism.[20] They argued that the elimination of secularism and the overpowering presence of the Christian, and specifically Catholic view of God should play a central part in nacionalista politics, including the belief in the reinstitution of mandatory Catholic education and more generally the reestablishment of preindependence colonial links between the church and the state.[21] Italian fascism had imposed mandatory religious education in the first year of its regime, but for most Argentine nacionalistas that was only a first step toward the union of nacionalista and Catholic politics. As the leader of the Argentine Fascist Party and former student of Ernst Cassirer, Nimio de Anquín put it, nacionalismo wanted to realize "the future kingdom [of God]." He asserted that nacionalismo "is an entirely Christian ideal, and though formulated for the temporal order, it is in perfect coincidence with the celestial city."[22] For the extreme nacionalistas of *Clarinada*—a publication that most historians present as Nazi-leaning—there were no differences among nacionalismo, fascism, and Catholicism. All these "isms" expressed an essentialized Argentina.[23] *Clarinada* argued that only "communist Jews" claimed the opposite and because they were anti-Christian they were anti-Argentine as well, "a danger to our Christian civilization."[24] Argentina, the publication advocated, had to be governed by "native" and "Catholic" Argentines, and those who opposed nacionalismo were "enemies of God and the patria."[25] In one of its gruesome covers *Clarinada* depicted the words that typified nacionalismo as an expression of Argentine Christian civilization: "Patria, Prayers, and Family." These words were framed in the national emblem and below it were corpses of "Jews."[26] In another telling cartoon on the cover of *Clarinada*, an Argentine grenadier stood steadfast against a threatening "Jewish shadow." An anonymous nacionalista woman, inspired by this image, wrote a poem that interpreted the cartoon as showing "a specter" that was threatening the "patria."[27] Excerpts of the encyclical *Divini Redemptoris*, in which Pope Pius XI argued that communism was intrinsically perverse, were continually reproduced in the pages of *Clarinada*, where one could read that this "perversity" was going to destroy the Catholic fatherland.[28] For these nacionalistas, the "communist" threat to the fatherland implied an equal threat to Christianity at large, as they considered Argentina to be the latter's best expression.[29]

The extremists from *Clarinada* were not unique in their reading of the papal encyclical.[30] It is important to highlight the significance of this encyclical in defining Argentine politics as an all-or-nothing battle between communism and Catholicism.[31] Communism expanded in Argentina during the 1930s, and the Justo administration worried about it.[32] But the fight against communism provided a master narrative for the clericofascist camp. *Criterio* had a permanent section on "communism" in its pages, and Catholic nacionalista writers such as A. H. Varela (also known as Hildebrando) shared the podium with Fathers Dionisio Napal and Virgilio Filippo as the premier clericofascist experts on communism.[33] For *Clarinada*, nacionalismo, with its explicit call for the extermination of Jews and communists, would install the "kingdom of Christ" in the fatherland, proposing "Christ as the only salvation from chaos." "Nacionalismo and Catholicism are united in a single idea: saving the patria morally and materially." This "union" was not a secular choice of nacionalismo but a decision made by God, as "God is using the nacionalistas to implant his kingdom on earth."[34] The editor of *Clarinada*,

Carlos Silveyra, believed there was a clear relation between nacionalista practice and Catholic theory, namely, that the will of God was expressed through nacionalista practice, making God's will the most important dimension of nacionalista politics.[35]

For other nacionalistas, such as the Argentine Fascist Party leader, Nimio de Anquín, the theoretical link between nacionalismo and Catholicism was a political practice in itself, indeed the most challenging and important aspect of nacionalismo.[36] Others argued for the primacy of theorizing fascist Catholic politics if nacionalismo ever wanted to dominate Argentine political life. Alberto Ezcurra Medrano, an important nacionalista intellectual, propounded this position. He conflated, as Osés did, nacionalismo with Catholicism, presenting them as a unique doctrinal blend that encompassed political and sacred truths. In a bourgeois world "bestialized by apostasy" and unable to "take advantage of the benefits of the Catholic reaction," Ezcurra argued, nacionalista politics should reestablish the primacy of religion over traditional politics. Ezcurra felt that this "restoration" was a "reaction of the will" against liberalism and the "modern satanocracy." For him, this willful, and essentially Argentine, revolution against liberalism could only be legitimate through Catholicism. Thus, the nacionalista movement was for him a profane political expression of the sacred.[37]

The Clericofascists

By the time Ezcurra made his assertions about the nacionalista relation with the sacred, these notions were shared "truths" within the nacionalista movement at large. It would be difficult, and indeed redundant, to establish who influenced whom, but nacionalista "civilians" and radical Catholic priests constituted the intellectual mainstream of Argentine Catholicism during the period under study. Argentine Catholicism presented a wide spectrum of radical Right and conservative expressions that nonetheless coincided in excluding more liberal or moderate variants of Catholicism from Argentine cultural and political life. For most Argentine Catholic intellectuals, the nacionalista extreme Right was at the center of their political identifications.

That nacionalismo and Catholicism were closely connected was a matter of course in the 1930s and 1940s, but this relationship had begun in the 1920s with the creation of the Cursos de Cultura Católica, right-wing publishing houses and journals that included the premier Catholic journal *Criterio* and the nacionalista publication *La Nueva República*. Originally, these two journals shared a similar style, ideology, and even staff writers. The nacionalista Ernesto Palacio defined them as "concurring groups."[38]

The Cursos and *Criterio* were theoretical breeding grounds for fascism in Argentina. The direct antecedent to the current Argentine Catholic University, the Cursos were an intellectual center with seminars and lectures that became a laboratory of Catholic antiliberal thinking and a meeting point for many young nacionalistas. At the Cursos, fascist ideas were systematically conflated with Catholic theory and then presented as inherently Catholic. Particularly in 1929, the year of the Italian concordat, fascism was considered to be the appropriate Catholic form of government in an increasingly secular and Protestant-leaning world. The nacionalista movement conflated fascism and Catholicism consciously from the beginning. In this section, I argue that Catholic institutions like the Cursos and *Criterio* worked as spatial objectifications of a more extensively shared conflation of the secular and the sacred within nacionalista ideology and practice. Most nacionalistas conceived the Cursos and *Criterio* as the voice of nacionalista criticism, theory, and self-expression.

Tomás D. Casares, "a typical exponent of Catholic nacionalismo," opened the 1933 semester of the Cursos by arguing in his welcoming address that Catholicism and the Cursos were intrinsically linked to nacionalismo.[39] For Casares (who later was chief justice of the Argentine Supreme Court under the Peronist regime), the imminent catastrophe that would come from a secular "asphyxiating vacuum" could only be averted by an active Catholic spirituality that he identified with patriotism.[40] Others agreed. Nacionalista Catholics like Ezcurra understood Catholic spirituality as the force behind the spirituality of the nacionalista movement at large. He believed, as did Carulla, Osés, and many others, that "nacionalismo should never forget its place within the terrible drama of Christianity. It should never forget its glorious quality as a reaction against apostasy."[41] Casares shared this concern and apparently thought that the obligation to care about "national problems" was met through his collaboration with publications such as *La Nueva República* or *Bandera Argentina*. He rhetorically asked: "Can we contemplate like spectators, without feeling guilty in our conscience, the intense need for a reaction that is rising in all the dimensions of Argentine life?"[42]

The existence of the nacionalista movement per se and the intellectual forays and theoretical ruminations of a diverse group of Catholic priests signaled "the intense need for a reaction." This belief was not the result of a clear assessment of the possibilities of fascism in Argentina, but teleologi-cally it constituted for most nacionalistas the most compelling "evidence" of the importance of that "reaction" (along with the legacy of Uriburu and the transnational intellectual encounters with European fascism that I dis-cussed in earlier chapters). The influence of this group of clericofascists was immense, particularly in theoretical terms. Although *Clarinada* warned its readers, in typical fascist fashion, about the dangers of an excess of "theory," the journal established a canon of "Catholic" works, advising readers, "If you are Argentine and Catholic you must read these books." The canonic texts that the journal promoted included the writings of the clericofascists Father Filippo and Father Julio Meinvielle, and the list itself is a telling example of the conflation of nacionalismo, Italian fascism, and Catholic nacionalista theory.[43]

Priests such as Gustavo Franceschi, Leonardo Castellani, Julio Meinvielle, Gabriel Riesco, and Virgilio Filippo, among others, shared, with variations, the apocalyptic vision of politics that the "secular" nacionalistas put for-ward. All these priests wrote for nacionalista publications and identified themselves with the movement in political terms, as the best expression of Catholic politics. All of them saw nacionalismo as a field for pastoral action, but they also tried to influence the movement's realpolitik. They presented their arguments in a wide range of venues, including sermons, radio broad-casts, nacionalista and Catholic papers, and cheap and widely distributed books and pamphlets. And more significantly, they wrote for the two most important Catholic publications in Argentina: the journal *Criterio* and the Catholic newspaper *El Pueblo*.

A "Nacionalista Awakening"

Criterio had praised Uriburu as a leader and had followed "uriburista" politi-cal guidelines during the Uriburu regime.[44] Uriburu himself had been a fervent Catholic and an avid reader of *Criterio* from its inception, and had maintained close contacts with its board.[45] Uriburu even told one writer from *Criterio*, "I always read *Criterio*; I read its doctrinal articles and its political pieces. I am within the current of ideas that you postulate and defend."[46] *Criterio* never embraced Italian fascism the way it embraced Ar-gentine nacionalismo. For Father Gustavo Franceschi, *Criterio's* most fa-mous editor, 1932, the year of Uriburu's death, was going to witness a "nacionalista awakening" in the face of "the anxious reality of the communist danger." For Franceschi, after 1930 (the year of the "revolution") nacionalismo became a mass phenomenon, although not yet a total one. It symbolized a change in the mentality of Argentina.[47] For mainstream priests like Franceschi, and for most nacionalistas, a clear political aim of Argentine Catholicism was to reconnect Argentina with its presecularizing "traditions," which stemmed from colonial times.[48]

Franceschi, like many other nacionalistas, equated patriotism and the generic word "nacionalismo" with the nacionalista movement in Argentina.[49] For him, Argentine nacionalismo had to avoid "exaggerated nationalism" and its two dangerous elements, "sentimentality" and exaggerated "statism." These elements were present in Europe in the right-wing Action Française, in German National Socialism (Nazism), and in some elements of Italian fascism.[50] For Franceschi and for other radical right-wing Catholics in the early 1930s, fascism, unlike Nazism, or Maurrasianism, was indeed redeemable through Catholicism.[51]

For Franceschi, Hitler was a bad "imitator" of Italian fascism.[52] Italian fascism was different. As many Italian fascists observed, Franceschi was a central figure within the Argentine church who could be "useful to the aims of our [Italian fascist] propaganda in Argentina."[53] Franceschi reciprocated this view, as someone who was not a fascist agent but an Argentine nacionalista interested in Italian fascism. In 1929, at the time of the signing of the Lateran treaties, Franceschi was chosen to give a speech at the special Te Deum ceremony in the Buenos Aires cathedral in the presence of the papal nuncio, the Italian fascist ambassador, and the archbishop of Buenos Aires.[54] Franceschi visited fascist Italy many times during his career, and had secretly expressed to fascist officials "his interest in visiting fascist social organizations."[55] For Franceschi, fascism was imbued with a moral dimension poised to reclaim the Christian tradition of Rome during times of indecision and materialism. Mussolini, Franceschi argued, had recognized and obeyed the voices of the Italian race and the Roman Catholic tradition.[56] Franceschi expressed his "sincere admiration" for the Duce and inscribed the latter in the tradition of "Augusto Cortes" [sic] and Napoleon as examples of the "energetic," "imperative" archetype of the "Latin jefe."[57] The "obscure but powerful feeling" that fascism generated among Italians was more important than theoretical discussions or fascist doctrine itself. All in all, Franceschi preferred other versions of nacionalismo over its "totalitarian" ones.[58] For Franceschi, as well as for other Catholic nacionalistas such as Manuel Gálvez or the Aduna leader, Juan P. Ramos, the political choice was between

Rome or Moscow.[59] But the Rome that Franceschi and Gálvez had in mind was ultimately the Rome of Christ and not the Rome of Mussolini.[60] Most nacionalistas, however, never made this distinction. For Franceschi, fascism in Italy embodied only "partial truths" because of its secularizing tendencies and its "totalitarian" view of the state.[61] Argentina, however, though related to Europe, differed from it because of its Catholicism, which made the country an "organic whole" that had a "race of its own."[62] Argentina needed to eliminate "laicism," by restoring obligatory Catholic education in state schools and enforcing Catholic views on issues such as abortion and euthanasia. Franceschi stressed the need to create a "corporative state" that could adapt to the "idiosyncrasies" of Argentina, while also relate to European fascist experiences.[63] In this sense, he agreed with the Spanish fascist Pemán on the specific character of Latin American forms of fascisms/nacionalismos, particularly the Argentine one. Franceschi argued that though European nacionalismos had their origin in the Great War, the Versailles Treaty, and traditional European antagonisms, in Latin America it was a different story. Argentina, embedded in Latin America, had been placed, in Franceschi's view, in a more dangerous historical juncture:

> We are facing a different situation: the external enemy . . . would not be in itself the cause of an Argentine nacionalista movement: the probability of an aggression on the borders is practically nil. But this is not the case with respect to the internal enemy, and its importance amply justifies in our country the sudden shock of patriotism called nacionalismo.[64]

For Franceschi, Argentina needed the nacionalista movement as a preeminent Catholic mode of defense against an internal enemy. Mexico and Brazil represented cases of internal insurgency that were to be avoided.[65]

Nacionalista ideology, Father Franceschi argued, should be essentially Argentine, and "cannot be constituted by a fully imported ideology." Fascism itself, although influenced by Sorel, Nietzsche, and Hegel, was "genuinely Italian." Franceschi did have important reservations about fascism and even about nacionalismo. But for many, and in certain ways for Franceschi himself, the need to support the nacionalista formation was a mandatory Catholic task related to the well-being of "the Argentine nation in the future." Argentine Catholicism played, or had to play, a central role in the life of the nacionalista movement. The collapse of the distinction between religion and politics signaled an end to the traditional Catholic absence from

Argentine politics. Thus, in Argentina a political movement, nacionalismo, was presented as a Catholic instrument of the will of God.[66] *Criterio's* official endorsement of the nacionalista movement Aduna should be read in this context.[67]

For Franceschi, as an Argentine ideology, nacionalismo should be part of a "Catholic social doctrine" and "Argentine social federalism." Argentina had to incorporate God into its "collective life." This was "an essential condition" of nacionalismo; otherwise, the Argentine priest suggested to his fellow nacionalistas, "we will not be doing good nacionalismo."[68] Most nacionalistas accepted this "essential condition" and generally understood the need for social change through the lens provided by "social Catholicism." The radicalization of their social demands during the 1930s was influenced both by the fascist experience of the corporatist reform in Italy and the social politics of the church. Nacionalistas often presented the encyclicals *Rerum Novarum* (1891) and *Quadragesimo Anno* (1931) as part of the nacionalista political and social vision. Most nacionalistas claimed that a process of industrialization, ample redistribution of land tenure, nationalization of the railways, and very strong presence of the state should accompany their social reforms.[69]

Franceschi agreed with all these proposals for social and economic change. He believed that good nacionalismo was inherently Catholic, and like fascism it was neither Right nor Left but opposed to "bourgeois," "conservative," and materialist interpretations.[70] Franceschi stressed the need for a radical change from the Argentine liberal nation to a Catholic one.[71]

The "New Christian Order"

Franceschi equated patriotism with a strong Catholic political authority. Almost by extension, Franceschi's vision became the quasi-official stance of Argentine Catholicism and was often expressed in the pages of its most important newspaper, *El Pueblo*.[72] This newspaper was itself the quasi-official mouthpiece of the Argentine Catholic hierarchy. In 1940, Cardinal Luigi Maglione, the Vatican secretary of state, called the newspaper "the Argentine Catholic paper" and defined it as "particularly 'benemérito' to the church." For Maglione, this newspaper was in "harmony" with the directives of the Vatican and he even told his Argentine readers that Pius XII himself knew "quite well the work of the newspaper."[73]

El Pueblo uncritically repeated traditional and pseudobiological anti-

Semitic discourse and even published the "Protocols of the Elders of Zion" (the most famous anti-Semitic piece of propaganda) during the early 1930s.[74] More than anything, *El Pueblo* railed against liberal Argentina, publishing pieces against liberal democracy and, more generally, the cosmopolitan aspects of Argentine society that Franceschi so passionately despised. There were some strategic changes in Franceschi's politics over time (he shifted from nacionalismo and anti-Semitism to Christian democracy and a belated support for the state of Israel in the 1950s),[75] but the thought of Luis Barrantes Molina, *El Pueblo's* most important editorialist, showed almost no variation over the years. For Barrantes, democracy was a system that had failed in Europe and should be abolished in countries like Spain. However, in Argentina, and Latin America at large, Barrantes argued, democracy could be "accepted" by the church provided important modifications were made, namely, that liberalism be quashed. "Democracy" without liberalism, Barrantes believed, could coexist easily with the "current reconstructive dictatorships" of Mussolini, Salazar, Franco, and Pétain. All these "jefes," who "had always respected the Catholic conscience of those they govern," represented for Barrantes the "action of providence" and "a necessary reaction" against "anarchy, immorality, and disorder." For him, these regimes represented the "new Christian order" as God wanted it.[76]

Barrantes was not alone in using the word "democracy" to describe fascism and nacionalismo. Mussolini himself and many Argentine nacionalistas often identified fascism with a nonliberal form of democracy. With the approval of Franceschi, Juan P. Ramos, the leader of the Aduna movement, called this new polity a "functional democracy."[77] But unlike Mussolini, the three Argentine nacionalistas Ramos, Franceschi, and Barrantes understood functional democracy as religious regency of the state. The "new Christian order" that Barrantes advocated coincided with that of other nacionalistas in conflating the ideas of nation and state with clericofascist notions of Catholic politics and radical patriotism.[78]

Barrantes criticized progressive Catholic approaches to fascism, like that advanced by the former Popular Party leader, the Italian priest Luigi Sturzo. For Sturzo, fascism was a form of totalitarianism that was incompatible with Christianity.[79] Barrantes disagreed with Sturzo, arguing that it was too early to define fascism, due to the theoretical difficulty of settling the question of fascism and how it related to Catholicism. As a constantly "changing concept," fascism was always in the making.[80] For the time being, Barrantes argued, Catholics should favor fascism and other forms of the "new order."

He reminded his readers that even Cardinal Pacelli, before becoming Pius XII, had praised fascism during his 1934 visit to Buenos Aires, and the Duce, Barrantes argued, was not totalitarian and respected the church, more so, in fact, than did most Latin American states.[81] Barrantes castigated the "infectious viruses" of liberalism, communism, and Nazism as forms of atheism that, along with Protestantism and Judaism, were promoting a civil war against the church and the Argentine nation.[82]

Similarly, Franceschi seldom identified totalitarianism with fascism and he never identified it with nacionalismo; instead, he reserved the term "totalitarianism" for Hitlerism, communism, and even liberalism.[83] He believed that the "Christian restoration" called for the "dictatorship of the sword."[84] Writing within a formal democracy, he did not dwell on the question of when this "dictatorship" should arrive, and he often stressed that it should not be "permanent." But he nonetheless stressed its necessity. Franceschi had no qualms about this, as he presented nacionalismo as the Catholic option.[85] The nacionalismo that Franceschi devised could ally itself with fascism on equal terms, but it should indirectly provide its own political direction. Though, as we have seen, Franceschi had certain doubts about fascism, a phenomenon that he saw as incomplete.

God Is Argentine

For Franceschi and Barrantes, Argentine nacionalismo had to detach itself from totalitarianism in order for the church to accept it. But for radical nacionalistas such as Enrique Osés, Father Julio Meinvielle, Carlos Silveyra, and his relative Eugenia Silveyra de Oyuela, Argentine nacionalismo comprised an acceptable form of totalitarianism that was inherently fascist, Argentine, and Catholic.

Eugenia Silveyra de Oyuela, one of the most important nacionalista women during this period, did not believe that totalitarianism contradicted Catholic dogma.[86] In 1937, she claimed that fascism was "subordinate" to "God's law," and therefore that the church did not need to condemn it. This was particularly true in the case of the Spanish Civil War, which she believed was fought for God.[87] Eugenia Silveyra, unlike Franceschi, believed that nacionalismo had to be totalitarian in order to achieve its Catholic program. In an obvious sense, the differences between the two were semantic, as *totalitarismo* (in the Italian sense of the word) was never part of the Argentine clericofascist conception of politics. But the official view of the institutional church, and of Franceschi in particular, preferred to deny rather than identify the nacionalista appropriation of the term. Fascist totalitarianism— as Mussolini understood it—was never "subordinate" to the church or God; it was subordinate only to the explicit and implicit aspects of Italian fascist theory and practice. Unlike the Argentine totalitarianism put forward by Osés, Carlos Silveyra, and Eugenia Silveyra de Oyuela, Italian fascist totalitarianism would have never accepted a theoretical and political discussion with a priest such as Franceschi. But in Argentina, such discussion could and did occur. The nacionalista recognition of the central role of the church in defining nacionalista theory did not warrant, in Franceschi's mind, the need to moderate his mild criticisms of nacionalismo. He believed, and said so on some occasions, that the secular nacionalista invocation of "Catholic dogma" was itself problematic. Thus, on a semantic level, these nacionalista positions contradicted Franceschi's understanding of totalitarianism. On a deeper level, however, all of them explicitly called for a subordinate role of nacionalismo with respect to Catholicism. In this sense, Franceschi agreed with Eugenia Silveyra and her fellow nacionalistas. But the nacionalista predilection to deploy Catholic dogma for political purposes troubled Franceschi, as it put into question the very notion of a theoretical and political nacionalista subordination to the church.

Many nacionalistas interpreted Franceschi's misgivings on fascism as a direct criticism of the unitary conception of clericofascism, and disputed that his statements represented the true opinion of the church.[88] Cesar Pico, for example, argued that Franceschi fought "the fascist regimes which constitute the only effective historical attempt to rectify democracy." Franceschi answered this "attack" by dismissing Pico—a layman—as incompetent to offer a critique on doctrinal questions and Catholic orthodoxy. Franceschi presented his opinion of totalitarianism as if expressing the view of the Catholic hierarchy, and stated that Pico did not. Pico's own misgivings about Franceschi may have stemmed from Franceschi's control of *Criterio*. Regardless, Pico's rebuttal highlighted his belief that when it came to politics and theory, the "laicos" could stand on equal terms with the "priests."[89] But the debate between Pico and Franceschi presents a rare view of a conflict that those in the nacionalista movement seldom acknowledged, since denying tension and contradiction was central to the clericofascist equation.

However, both Pico and Franceschi understood liberal democracy as being in opposition to Catholicism, and Franceschi's take on fascism did not imply a real difference with the nacionalista majority that viewed fascism as the Italian brand of an international nacionalista movement. Indeed, one week after his debate with Pico, Franceschi reiterated his explicit support for the nacionalista movement.[90] But he never identified Catholicism with Italian fascism, as he did with nacionalismo. Without noticing the change, or silencing it for strategic reasons, most nacionalistas equated Catholicism, fascism, and nacionalismo. Franceschi, however, never agreed with this equation, nor did he ever cross the line that would have made it impossible for him to retreat politically from nacionalismo. His position mirrored that of the Argentine bishops who regularly expressed anxiety about the conflation of nacionalismo and religion among the rank and file of mainstream Catholicism.[91]

Father Julio Meinvielle, a parish priest and influential nacionalista intellectual, enthusiastically embraced this conflation, but he often shared Franceschi's doubts about Mussolini and fascism.[92] Although many nacionalistas believed that there was nothing "irreligious," erratic, or anti-Catholic in fascism and Nazism, Meinvielle believed that a "Christian nacionalismo" would be free of these "errors." He opposed "Jews," communism, and Protestantism to this type of nacionalismo. Meinvielle considered history to be made up of epiphenomena of one large, transhistorical theme, namely, the battle between pagans, Jews, and Christians. He argued that fascism should counter the three "anti-Christian revolutions" of history—the Protestant, the French, and the Bolshevik revolutions. But fascism as a form of nacionalismo, he warned, could be either "Christian or pagan."[93]

Meinvielle categorized different groups according to their religiopolitical characteristics. Nacionalistas were placed within transnational developments, which he defined in pseudobiblical terms; Nazis were the personification of the pagans; and Russians, Chinese, and Mexicans were either Jews or personified them. Italian fascists were more difficult to categorize; their version of fascism was an open question that had to be addressed by nacionalista theorists such as himself.[94]

Early in his career Meinvielle was ambivalent about presenting fascism as an acceptable form of nacionalismo, but he later became more sympathetic. In 1932, he argued that, from a theoretical point of view, fascism was problematic, but in practice it could be considered "Catholic."[95] By the mid-1930s, Meinvielle had already decided that fascism had adopted a Catholic ideology, and that Argentines should generally adopt the Italian model. In his view, Italian fascism advanced economic and political reforms that accorded with traditional principles of the church. Though he believed fascism had statist and pagan tendencies, he ultimately concluded that fascism was a Christian political movement. He explicitly told his followers that his own version of Italian fascism was influenced by the fascist thinking of the Italian Gino Arias, one of the most important Catholic intellectuals of Mussolini's entourage, and a man who had an enormous influence in Argentina.[96] Arias's teachings "confirmed" to Meinvielle that fascism traveled down the correct "traditional" road, which avoided the "totalitarian," "pantheistic," and statist direction that many critics ascribed to it. Fascism, Meinvielle argued, was no longer "Machiavellian" and now coincided with Catholicism.

There was a great deal of interpretative independence and wishful thinking in Meinvielle's "reception" of fascism and his appreciation of Arias in particular. Arias never said, as Meinvielle claimed, that fascism was subordinated to the Vatican and the "universal primacy" of the pope. Meinvielle believed what he wanted to believe about fascism. By the mid-1930s, fascist violence was altogether "acceptable" for him.[97] In a universal apocalyptic context, he downplayed "theory" and the "wishes of the church" and called upon the use of "fascist violence" to counter "proletarian violence," a situation he believed expressed God's will more than any "theories."[98] Fascist "material violence" had to be combined with the "spiritual violence of the church." The radicalization of fascism did not imply for Meinvielle, as it did for Franceschi, a further detachment from its "excesses"—in fact, the opposite was true. However, like Franceschi, he warned Italian fascists, and by extension their Argentine associates, that the focus on politics obscured a more legitimate primacy: the primacy of the sacred over politics. In practical terms, this primacy of the sacred meant that fascists needed to subordinate themselves to theories of ordained intellectuals like himself, or as he put it, the "humble and soft primacy of the supernatural, of priesthood." Only with the subordination of fascist politics to the earthly representatives of God could fascism become acceptable.

Meinvielle was not alone in believing this, as this conception represented the essence of clericofascist ideology in Argentina.[99] In this view, fascism was "the affirmation of political authority" that the church wanted for the transitional period between bourgeois society and the kingdom of Christ.[100] Thus, fascism helped God in "purifying" the masses of bourgeois values and liberalism in order to bring about the "re-Christianization of the world."[101] But if Meinvielle showed some ambivalence toward the totalitarian problems of Italian fascism, Argentine nacionalismo was without fault. In Argentina, Meinvielle warned his readers, "pure democracy . . . is not acceptable" and only a "corporatist and authoritarian regime" could provide "justice" and the "common good."[102] Nacionalismo, as Meinvielle saw it, should aim for this corporatist dictatorship.[103] In addition, nacionalismo should recognize the limits of its own autonomy, "bearing in mind" the celestial origins of the "hierarchical organization of man."[104] Meinvielle believed that "authentic nacionalismo" would return Argentina to its Catholic, hierarchical roots, and nacionalistas should never forget this point. "Authentic nacionalismo" was not a deviation from the Catholic norm but had its origins in the sacred. Unlike the "totalitarian" forms of nacionalismo, "authentic nacionalismo" would not make its leader "divine" but would give him prestige as a facilitator of the temporal destinies of the people. It would recognize the importance of the nation and the state without ascribing divine qualities to them, "rejecting foreigners not because they were foreigners" but because they were "against the just national interests." Authentic nacionalismo, or nacionalismo in a "Christian mode" "would not hate the Jews because they are Jews . . . but, recognizing the destructive aims of the Jews among Christians, will limit their influence." Finally, authentic nacionalismo would not be totalitarian but would "totalize" life-giving cohesion to the state and to the nation. In short, for Meinvielle, the main aim of nacionalismo was to be, unlike fascism, a conscious and submissive instrument of God.[105]

Meinvielle's take on this question was both phenomenological (he wanted to describe the Argentine reality of nacionalismo) and ideological (as he wanted to provide a theoretical cover for nacionalista violent practices and authoritarian politics). "Authentic nacionalismo" had its origins in an "overabundance of Christian life," which could purify political institutions. Of course, Meinvielle did not suggest that nacionalismo and the Catholic Church should be equal partners. He reminded his fellow nacionalistas that Catholicism could live without nacionalismo but that nacionalismo could not "survive without Catholicism."[106]

Other clericofascists like Fathers Virgilio Filippo and Gabriel Riesco shared Meinvielle's notion of nacionalismo as living in and through the church. Like many others, Filippo thought Catholicism constituted an essentialized Argentina, standing against "mentally ill" foreigners (Jews, Masons, and communists) who conspired to destroy "tradition," as he often wrote in his poetry.[107] Filippo equated Catholicism and Argentine politics less with a problematic temporality (such as that of the era of Argentine liberalism) than with an essentialized Argentina based on the trilogy of family, religion, and fatherland. For Filippo, Argentina belonged to God, as the country was his creation.[108] He feared a perennial "plot against Argentina" and foresaw only dangerous, apocalyptic times in the country's near future.[109] He was terrified by the prospect of an Argentina ruled "without God."[110] If conspirators succeeded in their machinations, Argentina would become the anti-fatherland, the "kingdom of Satan."

Both Nazism and communism represented destructive forms of totalitarianism, and Filippo was clearly against them. In his mind, even the Nazis stood with Jews and communists against Argentina. Filippo was more reluctant than Meinvielle, or even Franceschi, to see the Nazis as an unwilling instrument of God, believing instead that they represented irreducible totalitarian enemies of the church.[111] Nonetheless, Filippo often complained that critics attacked Nazism more than communism as a form of totalitarianism.[112] With his fellow nacionalistas, Filippo understood Nazism as a miscarried and "extreme" form of nacionalismo, and not as a distinct version of fascism. He described Nazism in pathologizing terms, as a kind of insanity, an "unhealthy nacionalismo."[113] Nacionalismo, a "sane" political movement, unlike Nazism, would respect the lebensraum of the church. "Sane nacionalismo, yes. Insane, exaggerated, selfish, pejorative, and aggressive nacionalismo, no."[114]

Filippo agreed with Meinvielle that fascism was an instrument of God because, as he claimed, God had chosen Mussolini.[115] He pondered the papal encyclicals dedicated to Nazism, communism, and fascism, and concluded that, contrary to how it saw Nazism and communism, the church did not condemn fascism in its essence.[116] He appreciated the role fascism played in the world while insisting that it was not an equal partner with the church: fascism had to subordinate itself to the "integral" aims of the church.[117] Precisely because fascism often did not subordinate itself, Filippo never considered it as a full-fledged form of "sane nacionalismo."

For Filippo, Argentina played a special role in the world. Rather than follow others ("We would prefer death to being the someone else's satellites"), the country should lead fellow nations toward the nacionalista, Catholic way. Argentine priests were to carry the "national emblem" and stand with the Argentine people (pueblo) as the symbol of a Christian world, or as he put it, as the "international flagship of this enterprise of national sanctification of the name of God among the peoples [los pueblos]."[118] In order to do so, to become the flagship of the New Order, Argentina he declared, "needed" a "dictatorship."[119]

Father Riesco, another clericofascist intellectual and close acquaintance of

Filippo who invoked the writings of Franceschi and Castellani, claimed that defending liberalism, a "dead system," meant committing treason against the fatherland.[120] He believed that the "new Argentina" of a "Catholic national rebirth" that he proposed had been blessed by God.[121] Referring to the nacionalistas whose writings he constantly cited, Riesco argued that they understood the inherently Catholic character of the Argentine nation. Nacionalismo had a historical contribution to make in the construction of the "new Argentina." He even suggested that God is Argentine. According to Riesco, God had asked Argentine youth (i.e., the new generation of nacionalistas) to nurture "the Christian feeling, because Catholicism is consubstantial with our idea of nationality." In Riesco's mind, the cross and the sword were the main symbols of *argentinidad*, Argentiness, because they represented the political expression of Argentine Catholicism and its ultimate aim: a "Catholic state." The Catholic state would be the main tool for the "Argentinization of Argentina." This was a teleological exercise that he identified with exorcising Argentina of its constitutive liberalism (the liberalism that identified argentinidad with democracy) and instituting the clericofascist, antidemocratic, and corporatist tenets of nacionalismo.[122]

Debating Global Totalitarianism

F riends and enemies alike alternatively called nacionalismo "Catholic nacionalismo," "clericofascism," or, more bluntly, "Christianized fascism."
A self-ascribed Catholicism and its explicit adherence to a generic form of
fascism informed the nacionalistas' understanding of these terms. Father
Gustavo J. Franceschi's position conforms to them well. The difference
between Franceschi and most of the nacionalista camp was that Franceschi
did not accept Italian fascism as the solution, whereas nacionalistas, though
they did not agree wholesale with the Italian brand of fascism, could ideologically rationalize it as another form of generic nacionalismo.

Most nacionalistas linked fascism, nacionalismo, and Catholicism. This
linkage, of course, misrepresented Italian fascism, and Franceschi was one of
the few nacionalistas who noticed this. Only parts of Italian fascism, he constantly argued, could be incorporated into Argentine nacionalismo. Most
nacionalistas agreed with this assessment, but for different reasons (including financial and propaganda interests) they never made this explicit. For
many, it was obvious that nacionalismo, as an Argentine phenomenon, was
different from Italian fascism. Although César Pico represented this view, he
alone criticized Franceschi for his position. Most nacionalistas preferred to
turn a blind eye to Franceschi's misgivings about fascism and were happy to
include him in their political cadre. Probably because of his position as a
mouthpiece for the church hierarchy, however, many nacionalistas did not
identify with Franceschi but saw him distinctly as a fellow traveler. All in all,
few Catholics and nacionalista intellectuals could conceive of political alter-
natives outside of nacionalismo. This situation became painfully apparent

during discussions provoked by the visit to Argentina of French Catholic philosopher Jacques Maritain, the so-called Maritain debate.[1]

Jacques Maritain Meets the Clericofascists

The "Maritain debate" divided Argentine Catholicism between a minority who supported Jacques Maritain's move toward a Catholic form of democracy and the majority of clericofascist nacionalistas, who did not. The debate represented a real trauma for nacionalistas. Argentine clericofascists considered Maritain a father of theory and most of his works, unlike those of Italian or Portuguese rightist thinkers, were extensively available in Spanish translations.[2]

An important part of Maritain's earlier work focused on the relationship between religion and politics. Maritain's approach emphasized a form of "integral" Catholicism that Argentines found particularly attractive. It presented nacionalistas with an appealing conception of political autonomy while simultaneously critiquing modernity by highlighting alternative Catholic possibilities. This conception, many nacionalistas believed, avoided the "errors" of the French thinker and leader of the movement Action Française, Charles Maurras, and his "naturalist" form of nationalism.[3] Thus Maritain emphasized the "supremacy of the spiritual" over politics, or what he called the "metapolitical" authority of the church, although he also warned of the problems that a full identification of political parties and the church could bring, even if politics remained fully subordinate.[4] All told, however, Argentine clericofascists embraced Maritain's notions of "indirect power" and the metapolitical authority of the church, as these notions mirrored their own ideas about the relative autonomy of the nacionalista movement and its dependence upon guidance from the church.[5]

It was in this intellectual context that Maritain visited Argentina in 1936. It is symptomatic of the Argentine refusal to acknowledge the changing, "progressive" character of Maritain's work—which began in the mid-1930s—that a profile of Maritain originally written in 1923 was republished in Spanish by the Cursos de Cultura Católica as late as 1935.[6] Even when they knew about Maritain's recent thinking, nacionalista intellectuals like Father Leonardo Castellani, Federico Ibarguren, Enrique Osés, and César Pico presented the same static and old-fashioned view of Maritain when introducing the philosopher to different Argentine venues.[7]

However, to the dismay of the Argentines, the Maritain who arrived in

Argentina refused to abide by the version Argentine fascists presented of him.[8] Maritain's *Humanisme Intégral* was published in 1936, some days before he boarded the ship to Argentina, and by the time Maritain was giving talks in that country many nacionalistas had read it.[9] In this book, he extensively criticized fascism as a form of totalitarianism, elaborating on ideas he presented in lectures in Santander, Spain, which were eventually published in 1935 as *Problemas espirituales y temporales de una nueva cristiandad*, a book that was also widely read in Argentina.[10] In these lectures—and in his previous book *The Things That Are Not Caesar's*—Maritain had already warned against a strict political formation based solely on Catholicism.[11] Before his visit in July 1936, *Sur* (a mainstream literary journal) published Maritain's essay "A Letter on Independence," in which he claimed that he (unlike Franceschi) was willing to engage with leftist publications. Moreover, Maritain criticized in particular the Catholic predilection for "solutions of the Mussolinian type." By presenting fascism and communism as two anti-Catholic poles, Maritain defiantly made clear his opposition to the clericofascist conception of politics. For him, fascism could never be an instrument of God.[12]

During his two-month visit to Argentina, Maritain gave lectures at the Cursos de Cultura Católica that generated great expectations among nacionalistas, and the nacionalista press took part in the enthusiastic reception of the French philosopher.[13] But to the surprise of his Argentine admirers, he also accepted an invitation to give a lecture at the Hebraic Society. At a time when most Argentine Catholic intellectuals were engaged in an active anti-Semitic campaign, Maritain criticized anti-Semitism at the Cursos, especially excoriating its Catholic variant, as epitomized by the clericofascist newspaper *Crisol*. For Maritain, Catholicism could not be equated "with a spirit of blind hatred." The director of *Crisol*, Enrique Osés, reluctantly concluded that it was painful but necessary for Argentine Catholics to respond negatively to Maritain. *Crisol* argued that Maritain "neither represents the church nor Christian philosophy," and that Maritain's criticism of fascism and anti-Semitism amounted to an attack against "our church and the fatherland [patria]."[14]

Maritain, by 1936, was on the verge of becoming a full-fledged antifascist, making his visit to Argentina ripe for an Oedipal confrontation. His presence put in question the nacionalista tendency to read European events and theorists selectively. The nacionalistas answered Maritain's criticism with aggressive, critical dialogue that soon devolved into an all-or-nothing dispute over the Catholic legitimacy of Argentine nacionalismo.

Maritain also had social and intellectual exchanges with the *Sur* literary group that *Criterio*, one year later, would describe as "communist."[15] In this debate, Maritain proposed for Argentine politics an "effective union" between socialists and Catholics similar to that in Belgium. He probably hoped to establish a bridge between the Left and Right by speaking in their different venues. He also denounced both fascism and communism as forms of totalitarianism.[16]

As soon as the *Sur* debate ended, most nacionalistas who heard about it expressed anger and dismay.[17] Father Leonardo Castellani, the prominent nacionalista intellectual, a former student of Maritain in Paris in 1932, and a self-described disciple of the French thinker, was present at the debate, and although he did not want to confront his former master, he could not let Maritain's proposal for a democratic Catholic alliance go without comment.[18] Although Maritain had already stated his opposition to an Argentine "strong state" maintained through brute force and fascist means, Father Castellani countered that this remained the best option for Argentina. He implored Maritain to reconsider his position by taking into account the specificity of the Argentine context and the urgent need for authoritarian politics. In short, Castellani suggested that Catholics should embrace political movements—namely, nacionalismo—that expressed their interests. Maritain compared that suggestion with the errors of Maurrasianism, and he described Castellani's position as "miserable and misguiding." He argued that a "fascist style takeover of power" as put forward by Castellani could only "lead directly to civil war" and ultimately to what he defined as an un-Catholic position. In short, Maritain criticized the whole ideological framework of nacionalismo, explicitly the alliance between Argentine fascism and the church.[19]

Maritain had originally been invited to Buenos Aires as the French delegate for the reunion of the international PEN Club when a meeting was held in September 1936. At the meeting, Maritain sided with antifascist delegates in a proposal for the condemnation of anti-Semitism. He clearly opposed the position of prominent nacionalista members of the Argentine delegation such as Carlos Ibarguren and Manuel Gálvez, who preferred to abstain on such an issue.[20]

The PEN Club provided an unlikely forum for a discussion about fascism between fascists and antifascists from both sides of the Atlantic. This situation could not have happened in Italy after the early years of the Mussolini regime. Though some nacionalistas expressed exasperation about delegate

Emil Ludwig's project to write a biography of General San Martín—the founding farther of Argentine independence—most nacionalistas focused on the problems of the development of the Spanish civil war and Maritain's equation of fascism with totalitarianism.[21] The very idea that Maritain had willingly become a symbol of Argentine antifascism was astonishing for both his former clericofascist admirers and Argentina's progressive Catholic minority.[22]

The Catholic antifascist vision of a "new Christianity" contrasted with the "Christian new order" that nacionalistas like Meinvielle had advocated. Among the nacionalistas, Franceschi may have been the only one who remained in personal contact with Maritain. While openly disagreeing with Maritain on such delicate subjects as the sacred quality of the Spanish Civil War or the idea of fascism as an instrument of God, Franceschi never broke with Maritain but suggested that the French philosopher had recently adopted a "naive" attitude.[23] But for Meinvielle, the Maritain affair was a different story. Since Meinvielle was in charge of *Criterio* during Franceschi's long visit to the fascist front in the Spanish Civil War,[24] this publication became a center of critique and debate about Maritain.[25] For Meinvielle, Maritain was "the philosopher, the lawyer of the Spanish reds . . . and the friend of the Jews of the Hebraic Society and the PEN Club, the *'judaizantes'* and *'comunoides'* of *Sur* and the Buenos Aires yellow press." Meinvielle identified Maritain and his "friends" with the "mockery of Christ" and the opposition to the pope.[26] He argued that given his "naive" and "infantile attitudes" Maritain could not even perceive what "every normal woman" could.[27] The image of women as naive and distanced from politics expresses an extensively shared traditional idea of gender relations within nacionalismo. Women, with some notable exceptions such as Silveyra de Oyuela or Delfina Bunge de Gálvez, had an important but subaltern role in the movement. The Argentine church and its traditional politics of gender played no small role here. By using gendered descriptions of Maritain, Meinvielle highlighted an extensively shared fear about the uncanny role that women, or those that he identified with them, could play in politics and society.

For Meinvielle, the Spanish civil war was indeed a "holy war" and Franco "the mere instrument of God." "The nacionalista and Catholic Spain," Meinvielle argued, had to be defended with violent means. In short, for Meinvielle, Maritain had become an "antifascist."[28] As a regular reader of *Criterio*, Maritain wrote from France contesting Meinvielle's position as representing a "holy cause." He argued that the Argentine priest was "dishonest" and that he engaged in ad hominem critiques. "The methods of Mr. Meinvielle are not . . . examples of justice and moderation; they are apt to dishonor polemics."[29]

Most nacionalista critics focused on Maritain's denunciation of fascism as a form of totalitarianism, a focus which was developed during his stay in Argentina and increased after he left. Maritain made clear to clericofascists that their very existence contradicted the teachings of the church. In addition, he refused to see the Spanish conflict as a "holy war."[30] Argentina was not the only place where Maritain was excoriated for his stance on Spain. In Spain, the Spanish fascist Ramón Serrano Suñer, the soon-to-be foreign minister for the Franco regime, described Maritain as "a Jewish convert."[31] However, in Argentina the criticisms were fundamentally different. To Argentine fascists, Maritain's tendency to equate generic fascism with totalitarianism was misguided for religious reasons. As we have seen, most nacionalistas agreed that although the Argentine church had denounced "exaggerated" nacionalismo as a form of totalitarianism, Italian fascism was exempt from these denunciations because it was not "totalitarian." In fact, Mussolini himself had adopted totalitarianism as a motif of self-definition, but Argentines did not care about this fact and insisted that Maritain had "no right" to equate fascism with what they considered to be the real totalitarianisms: communism and liberalism. Fascism worked against those ideologies, as Meinvielle or Pico implied, and Catholics should end their "horror of fascism" and work with it against communism and liberalism.[32]

Although César Pico had introduced Maritain approvingly before his talks in the Cursos, he thereafter became his most ardent critic. Pico did not claim that the church should be friendly to totalitarian regimes, but simply argued that generic fascism was not a form of totalitarianism. Pico asserted that the Catholic influence in Italian fascism inhibited any possible totalitarian orientation, and he advocated a radical collaboration between fascism and Catholicism.[33] He affirmed that generic fascism would increasingly become similar to a Catholic form of fascism. Father Castellani agreed with Pico that Catholicism should be the theory of fascism, but the priest was less sure that generic fascism and nacionalismo had already achieved that aim. Although Castellani conceded that the word "nacionalismo" could have many general meanings, he defended his own definition of the term as "a sociological-historical phenomenon of the present world that appeared after the War of 1914 . . . that was first concretized in Italy and named fascism.

Nacionalismo aims . . . to be the solution to the contemporary political problem between the unquestionable insufficiency of the liberal solution and manifest falsity of the Marxist solution."[34]

Castellani equated his notion of political theory with Catholic doctrine and argued that fascism was an expression of generic nacionalismo. He wrote a letter in the form of a literary fantasy to Mussolini, in which he adopts the persona of Charles V of Spain, writing from purgatory. In this letter, the "Emperor" tells the Duce that purgatory awaits him as well, but he praises the Italian dictator for defending Catholicism and Latinity (latinidad) as he had done in his time.[35] The letter shows that Castellani shared with Italian fascists like Marshall De Bono an idea of transnational fascism as related to the Roman legacy. But the letter also represents his ambivalent Argentine posture about Italian fascism; this ambivalence expressed the tension between theory and practice within nacionalismo, specifically the view that fascism was acceptable on a practical but not theoretical level.[36]

As we had seen, many nacionalistas believed their movement already had a theory—a fascist Catholic one. However, for Castellani as well as Franceschi and other nacionalista members of the clergy, the nacionalista theoretical apparatus remained an exercise in the making. In this context, Castellani clearly identified the "sacred task and duty" of building an acceptable Catholic form of fascism with the intellectual exercise of "thinking the patria," namely, giving a Catholic doctrinal underpinning to nacionalismo. "Thinking the patria," Castellani argued, will bridge the gap between "pure theory" and "pure practice" within nacionalismo.[37]

Hispanidad, Spanish Fascism, and the "Argentine Empire"

Father Gabriel Riesco, a Spanish-born Argentine priest, went beyond the nacionalista mainstream when he asserted that "hispanidad" should work as an international template for Argentines, a notion later historians of Argentine nacionalismo have reified.[38] Riesco argued that Latin America lacked autonomy and always copied Europe. Thus, he sometimes criticized the nacionalistas for their excessive "localism" in conceiving politics and their refusal to accept the Spanish European template. By calling for a transnational ideology that could go "beyond nacionalismo," Riesco made explicit a hope to copy Franco's version of fascism.[39] Riesco was an exception. Although, there were mimetic tendencies in nacionalismo, they did not predominate among the nacionalista majority.

*Sp**ain***

The importance of Spanish fascism and the Spanish Civil War of 1936 should not be underemphasized. If Italian fascism dominated the international fascist scene before 1936, the appearance of Spanish fascism, a form of fascism that resembled Argentine nacionalismo, clearly affected the dynamic fluctuations of Argentine nacionalista ideology. Most nacionalistas saw the Spanish Civil War as a crusade in which fascism worked to "restore Christianity." Franceschi, for example, traveled to the Spanish front as an official representative of Argentine Catholicism and played a central role in the Argentine denial of the massacre at Guernica.[40] Unlike Riesco, most nacionalistas identified Spanish fascism as yet another form of nacionalismo. Moreover, between 1936 and 1945 Argentine nacionalistas presented hispanidad as a central dimension of nacionalismo.

Hispanidad was not born with nacionalismo but, like Argentina as a whole, it was born liberal.[41] For the earliest ancestors of nacionalismo (the still liberal cultural nationalists such as Manuel Gálvez or Ricardo Rojas, among many others), the essence of the Argentine "soul" was Hispanic and Creole. These ancestors presented the heavy Italian immigration as undermining this essentially Hispanic character of Argentina. Against a liberal tradition (ideally represented by Sarmiento) that equated civilization with non-Iberian European cultures, these intellectuals reclaimed the Hispanic roots of the country and at the same time denounced the cosmopolitanism of other European and North American influences. Cultural nationalists shared with Latin American thinkers such as the Uruguayan José Enrique Rodó a rejection of U.S. influence and a clear fear of the unmediated irruption of the masses in public life.[42]

If for many nineteenth-century liberals, Italian immigration had represented progressive trends and Spain represented backwardness and informal imperialism, the cultural nationalists of the early 1900s inverted the terms of the equation. For them Italians represented urbanism, political radicalism, and secularism, while Spanish immigrants such as the Basques were now equated with religious attitudes and the pastoralism of the Pampas. While reversing the hispanophobia of the past, the early twentieth-century predecessors of nacionalismo did not identify hispanidad with a noninclusive notion of the national self; the cultural nacionalistas of the beginning of the century were not, in short, protofascists. But in terms of what they opposed and condemned, they shared targets with Argentine fascists. They especially shared a rejection of positivism, anticlericalism, materialism, and "soulless cosmopolitanism."

Whereas the cultural nationalists had an anti-Italian bias, nacionalistas were able to fuse and present Italian and Spanish ethnic backgrounds as necessary elements of Argentina. Ironically, in this specific sense, the nacionalistas were more "inclusive," but only as far as Italians and Spaniards were concerned. In other words, nacionalistas were open to foreigners only to the extent that they considered both Spaniards and Italian as acceptable Latin races that could be digested by the body of the nation—"ultimate others" such as Jews were excluded from this equation.

All in all, nacionalistas were able to accept the hispanophilic elements of their predecessors while implicitly rejecting their anti-Italian trends. Nacionalistas considered both national groups as relatively equal partners within the context of the Latin fascist world. Thus, the centrality of Spain as a symbol of the country preceded the Spanish Civil War but once the war was under way, it became firmly established. Like their ideological ancestors, nacionalistas saw hispanidad as embedded in Catholicism, but unlike them, nacionalistas now linked this idea with an unprecedented hostility toward liberal democracy.[43]

After 1936, for nacionalistas, the idea of hispanidad was directly related to the Spanish Civil War, as Spanish fascists needed to rethink their imperial past in neoimperialistic terms. But the very term "hispanidad" (as it was used by fascists across the Atlantic) was born not in Europe but in Argentina. The Spanish-born Catholic priest Zacarías de Vizcarra, a significant clericofascist intellectual and a guide of Argentine nacionalismo in its early years, coined the term "hispanidad" in Buenos Aires in the pages of an Argentine Spanish journal. Vizcarra, who was a regular contributor to *Criterio*, stated that "hispanidad" worked better than "race" for thinking about the links between Latin America and Spain.[44] Vizcarra's original use of the term was quickly recognized by Spanish fascists. However, before the Spanish Civil War, the idea of hispanidad was mainly known through the influence of Ramiro de Maeztu's text *Defensa de la hispanidad* (1934). In this book, Maeztu put forward ideas that were shared among Argentines, such as the stress on the interpenetration of the temporal with the spiritual and its corollary, namely, the conflation of the Antichrist with an internal enemy (the "Antipatria").[45] Maeztu had been the Spanish ambassador in Buenos Aires in the late 1920s and had maintained close contacts with nacionalistas and Catholics ever since.[46] Before the publication of his defense of hispanidad, Maeztu anticipated his main points in articles that he wrote for *Criterio*. He also wrote for *Crisol*.[47] Although Maeztu made very clear that

Spain had a parental mission toward the territories of her former empire, *Criterio* symptomatically reviewed his book as though it spoke only of the Spanish past and ignored its supposed paternalism toward Latin America.[48]

The death of Maeztu at the hands of Spanish antifascists confirmed the nacionalista belief that the debate about hispanidad was not exclusively theoretical. For the entire nacionalista movement, the future of nacionalismo was at stake in Spain.[49] Spanish fascists agreed with this argument during their frequent visits to Argentina. With the exception of the strategically dialogical José María Pemán, most of the Spanish fascist hispanicists—especially the rightist priest García Morente and Spanish theorists and fascist personalities Antonio Tovar, Alfonso de Ascanio, Feliciano Cereceda, the Catholic priest Enrique Díaz de Robles, José Ibáñez Martín, and General José Millán Astray—displayed without nuance a religious and neoimperialistic notion of hispanidad that claimed Spain was destined to play the leading fascist transnational role in Latin America.[50] Neoimperialism had a crucial place in Spain's plans for the future, as the Spanish foreign minister Serrano Suñer told the Nazi paper *Völkischer Beobachter* in 1941: "The future of Spain and her empire is the foremost preoccupation of the Spanish leader."[51]

For Serrano Suñer, Spain had a natural "preoccupation" with the nations of Hispanic America and the "danger" of communism in the region.[52] But what kind of obligation and what sort of empire did the Spanish fascists have in mind? Most believed that Spain should reclaim the leading role in a Hispanic Latin American "spiritual empire." They pushed for a Spain that guided Latin America intellectually and politically. As the Spanish fascist General Millán Astray told the Argentine people in an open letter published in *La Razón*, Latin America was going to experience the same crisis that led to the nacionalista insurgency.[53] Thus, the Spanish solution could be their solution.

Most Argentine nacionalistas agreed. However, without acknowledging the differences between the Spanish notion of hispanidad as a neoimperialistic endeavor and their own notion of hispanidad as a Latin American postcolonial venture, most nacionalistas integrated the concept of hispanidad with an idea of Latin America that had Argentina as the legitimate heir of the empire.[54] For Pemán, the Spanish fascists had to "listen" to Latin America, and particularly Argentina, as it was the territorial manifestation of hispanidad.[55] Pemán personally praised the writings of Meinvielle and Pico on Maritain and fascism, arguing that Argentine nacionalismo was better qualified than European fascism because it lacked the latter's "suggestive or mimetic" character: "When there is no Ethiopia to conquer, no Tunisia to remember, and no Austria to absorb, it is cleaner and nobler to engage in a bit of fascism."[56] Pemán's understanding of Argentine fascism mirrored the way Argentine nacionalistas understood themselves, but Pemán tended to consider fascism as generic and nacionalismo as a particular national case, and not the other way around. He told nacionalistas that hispanidad represented the best way to equate fascism with the church, a system that he approvingly called "Christian totalitarianism."[57]

Rather than simply accepting Pemán's proposal for a "dialogue" and an ideological encounter of "transoceanic hispanidad," Argentine fascists appropriated his words and asserted an Argentine-centric notion of hispanidad.[58] The Spanish insurgence and the concept of hispanidad acted as catalysts for the nacionalista idea of an Argentine "imperialist vocation" or "Argentine empire."[59]

The Argentine idea of empire was encrypted in the supposed European dimensions of Argentina.[60] The idea that Argentina deserved a leading imperial place in Latin America, an idea that Mussolini also put forward, was related to this putative Europeanism of the country. This idea of Europe was rooted in hispanidad and "Christianized fascism." Argentina was supposed to represent the legacy of imperial Spain and the idea of a golden colonial past. Argentina—a Latin American country—was more European in the Hispanic sense than Spain. In this view, Latin America, and especially Argentina, was the repository of imperial European authenticity. The idea of an Argentine empire was a state of becoming. It implied an active realignment, the reformulation of the neocolonial pact. In other words, this imperial architecture that nacionalismo redefined Argentina's place in Latin America and the world. It was less rooted in national sovereignty and more in transnational "spiritual" or ideological hegemony.[61]

The redefinition of the neocolonial situation had to be rooted in this imperial past, which Argentine spiritual and racist values ideally represented. In a postcolonial world, Argentina, and not Spain, should fuse Latin American imperialism with anti-American and anti-British anti-imperialism. A typical example of this anti-imperialism was the nacionalista argument about the Malvinas/Falklands. Nacionalistas argued that the islands should be Argentine because Argentina was the heir of the Spanish empire. To be sure, other Argentine ideologies (from socialism to liberalism) shared this view, but for nacionalismo it was mainly an imperial and sacred question. Argentina defended against Britain the legacy of the Catholic Latin empire.[62] In short, Argentina stood against what Mussolini had called "plutocratic imperialism."[63] But in its position against Western imperialism, nacionalista ideology was not against the West per se. It was, rather, defending a particular fascist notion of Western anti-imperialist proletarian imperialism impregnated with Catholic fascist overtones. It was based on a typical, Latin American, ambiguous affiliation with European fascist notions of imperialism. Anti-Western anti-imperialism could not be a projection of "non-European values" but an Argentine imperial reassertion of the Western Christian tradition. Catholic nacionalistas such as Juan Carulla and César Pico considered Catholicism, patriotism, and the "defense of the West" as the appropriate nacionalista response to "the danger of Orientalism."[64]

For Pico, Latin America was always "late" with respect to Europe, particularly with respect to the threat of communism and the necessary reaction to it.[65] For many this had to change. For Carulla, Latin America had to be defended from a dangerous kind of internal intellectual development. This development was a "continental nationalism" that stressed "Asiatic communism" and the indigenous legacy of the Americas. Carulla believed that Argentine nacionalismo had to act against this "delirious" version of nacionalismo that denied the "Latin legacy" of Catholic Spain. In his view, Argentine nationalism had to be protected from the influence of ideas that he believed had their origin in revolutionary Mexico. Carulla argued that Argentina, as opposed to Mexico, had racial, religious, and cultural links with Europe that made it more European than Latin American: "We are Europeans in America," he said. Sharing Carulla's position, Father Franceschi argued, "There is no need to deny this: many of us Argentines feel closer to France or Italy, or Germany, depending on our backgrounds, than to Venezuela or Nicaragua."[66] Carulla argued that the choice for Argentina was clear: either it would end up like Mexico or any other Latin American country, or it should remain "European."[67]

The idea of "remaining European" was related to the notion of keeping hispanidad and Latin values as defining Argentina's uncanny place in Latin America and beyond. The notions of Argentina's leading anti-imperialist role in Latin America or the creation of the cult of nineteenth-century dictator Juan Manuel de Rosas were also affected by this Argentine conception of hispanidad. Much has been written about the myth of Rosas and its nacionalista historians. Here it would suffice to say that the first nacionalista vindication of Rosas in the 1930s was related to his presentation as a champion of both religion and anti-imperialism as encompassed by the idea of hispanidad.[68] It is in this context that some Argentines developed the far-fetched notion of an Argentine empire.

The idea of an Argentine empire preceded the events of the Spanish Civil War. The Uruguayan born writer Horacio Quiroga had warned against it, while Leopoldo Lugones and even the positivist intellectual José Ingenieros had earlier advocated it. But in the earlier thought of Lugones (the actual object of Quiroga's criticism), and in the later works of José Ingenieros, Argentine imperialism was not related to the notion of a crusade or presented as the defense of the Christian world. It was in the pages of *La Nueva República* that these ideas were first defended in the late 1920s, but the notion of Argentine Catholic imperialism had to wait for the events of the Spanish Civil War and the emergence of the idea of hispanidad to fully develop as a political trope for nacionalismo.

The fact that nacionalismo appropriated and reformulated the idea of hispanidad from "Europe" was part of the rationale behind the antifascist accusations of mimicry. For antifascism the close ideological encounters across the fascist Atlantic were occasions for European fascist negations of the multicultural reality of Argentina and Latin America. For example, the Argentine notion of hispanidad was presented ironically in the antifascist literary stories *Seis problemas para Don Isidro Parodi* (1941), written by Borges and Bioy Casares. In these stories, the character of the Italo-Argentine intellectual Mario Bonfanti, while working for his rich patron, the Italian immigrant *commendatore* San Giácomo, plagiarized versions of the works of Spanish fascist Pemán. Borges and Bioy Casares probably wanted to show the artificiality of an exclusivist notion of the Spanish legacy in melting-pot, half-Italian Argentina.[69]

In a more serious accusation, the literary journal *Sur* argued that nacionalistas were not really a "national" product insofar as they rejected the legacy of Argentine independence and wanted to return Argentina to its preindependence, colonial status vis-à-vis Spain.[70] This pointed stance was certainly not the view of most nacionalistas. Less interested in finding contradictions, the nacionalistas understood Spain as a peer interlocutor rather than the sort of template that Italian fascists wanted Argentines to understand Italy as offering them.[71] Ironically, this situation promoted some apprehension about certain Spanish fascist ideological motifs, but only to the extent that Argentine nacionalistas saw the presence of Catholicism in Spanish fascism as a confirmation of the coherence and success of their own Argentine road to fascism. As the Pemán case shows, this "transoceanic" interaction was not monological but almost polyphonic.[72] When Pemán, like Gino Arias before him, defended the Argentine form of Catholic fascism as an example for Europeans to follow, he told the Argentines what they wanted to hear.

Nazis

During the period 1933–1945, the German embassy distributed pro-German propaganda throughout Argentina, just as Italians distributed pro-Italian materials. The German effort failed miserably.[73] Most of the embassy's efforts were countered by successful antifascist campaigns and allied propaganda. U.S. officials joined Argentine antifascists in spreading rumors regarding an alleged Nazi plan to invade Patagonia and, more generally, alleged Nazi plans to conquer South America and ban Catholicism in the region, as President Roosevelt stated on October 28, 1941.[74] Equally important, Nazism was not copied by nacionalistas because they understood it as yet another example of international fascism.

For Argentine antifascists, the nacionalistas were Nazi-fascist automatons who received orders from Berlin and Rome.[75] As was always the case, nacionalista ideology was more complex and dynamic than the antifascists depicted. To radical extremists like Silveyra or Osés, Nazism was compatible with the Catholic core of Argentine nacionalismo. For Silveyra, both fascism and Nazism defended Christian civilization.[76] But neither Osés nor Silveyra believed that nacionalistas imitated the Nazis or Italian fascists. A great admirer of Hitler, Silveyra wrote a special dedication and sent a copy of his most famous nacionalista book to him. In this text, Silveyra told the Führer that he was interested in hearing "his valued opinion about this work" and symptomatically characterized Hitler as "the incarnation of the purest nacionalismo." The fact that Silveyra conveyed this to Hitler in a private text written only for Hitler proves that Silveyra's belief in generic nacionalismo was probably more genuine than strategic.[77] In Silveyra's mind, Nazism was an example of generic nacionalismo rather than an expression of anything original.

As we have seen with Father Filippo, nacionalistas took seriously the accusation that they were Nazis, because of its dangerous anti-Catholic implications. Borges, in his "Definition of the Germanophile," equated Nazism with nacionalismo and dismissed nacionalistas as un-Catholic, arguing that their "Jesuitical or Nietzschean" explanations were far from the "morality of Jesus."[78]

The writers of *Clarinada* had no qualms about accepting the term "germanófilo" for themselves but they never called themselves Nazis.[79] The obvious question remains: were nacionalistas mimicking the Nazis, as Borges, the Jewish press, and the entire antifascist movement contended?[80] Politically, ideologically, and even religiously, nacionalistas did not understand the question in these terms. They believed they had two choices: either denounce the pagan tendencies of the Nazis, or ignore them. Most nacionalistas chose the latter, whereas all the nacionalista priests and Catholic publications were almost compelled, as we have seen, to choose the former.[81]

Nacionalismo and the Creation of the Enemy

Argentine nacionalistas explained Nazi, Spanish, and Italian fascist experiences as examples of an international tendency of the radical Right, namely, as European versions of nacionalismo.[82] The Argentine reception of the moderate and conservative form of fascism that the Portuguese regime represented took the same line.[83] They did not regard these European fascisms as ideals to follow slavishly. Many nacionalistas in fact claimed that Argentine nacionalismo was more Hispanic than Spain itself because it better expressed Spain's imperial traditions.[84] As we have seen, they understood Italian fascism in the same way, believing themselves more fascist than the Italian fascists. The later Peronist alliance with Franco, and even perhaps the warm Peronist reception of Nazi and Italian fascist "refugees," owed something to this notion of Argentina as a primary, albeit adaptive, Catholic repository of transnational ideas of fascism. Notwithstanding the imperialistic claims of the Spanish regime, Spanish propaganda amounted little more than unsubsidized discursive overtures.[85] Nacionalistas never criticized Franco's regime, considering it an attempt to establish a "national Catholic state," such as Argentina might one day become, but which represented future possibilities more than a reality. (After 1945, many nacionalistas understood Peronism as the realization of this state.)[86]

Understanding nacionalismo as an instrument of God allowed nacionalistas such as Leopoldo Lugones to think that their politics transcended profane normative restrictions and realized its totalizing imperatives and wishes. Only sacred normativity mattered. Nacionalista politics then put forward a notion of what should be done, namely, create a "Christianized" fascist normativity for a secular world. This was less a political program than a religious, spiritual, and even aesthetic impetus. The theory and prac-

tice of Lugones represented at times a symptomatic expression of aestheti-
cism, yet, in his original articulation of Christianized fascism in political and
literary terms, fascism was equally influential and deserves a special analysis.
This last section of the chapter briefly deals with Lugones's ideological
machinations, and through Lugones it aims to establish a bridge between
the idea of Christianized fascism and the fascist conception of the enemy.

In his late Catholic period, Lugones wrote sacredly inspired poetry in
which he expressed his taste for pushing the aesthetic to the extreme. He
wrote, for example, a poem about the swaddling clothes of baby Jesus and
another about a sacred bell that saved a child.[87] These Christian pieces, when
combined with Lugones's late political writings, linked to his overall conception of nacionalista politics as Catholic.[88] For Lugones, the "reality" of these
Catholic politics showed that they were a religious and aesthetic choice that
transcended ethical concerns. God, he concluded, lay behind all beauty, and
beauty was essential to the harmonic nature of Lugones's politics.[89] The
"medieval synthesis" of Catholicism and classicism provided a template for
the contemporary authoritarian state that he championed. Aesthetics for Lugones not only dovetailed with politics, but at times seemed to constitute it.

Lugones highlighted the beauty of the Argentine past considered from
the points of view of war and the religiosity of Argentina's founding fathers. But he insisted that beauty, as an expression of God, transcended
history. In Lugones's mind, upholding sacred beauty meant, in practical
terms, upholding nacionalista politics and defending an authoritarian civilization. Against his sacred and aesthetic notion of the world, which constituted his politics, Lugones held up the usual suspects—rationalism, materialism, and sensualism—"isms" that he believed "inverted" a proper politics
and divinized materialism. He presented communist notions of expropriation and rebellion as acts of vandalism that were offensive not for ethical but
for religious and aesthetic reasons.[90] For Lugones, nacionalismo was destined to be an instrument of God in the final apocalyptic moment, the
ultimate fight between two enemies, "hierarchic civilization against communist barbarism."[91]

Lugones believed the enemy represented a reversed form of absolutism
that included "the denial of God, of the fatherland, of duty."[92] He insisted
that thinking should be an act of "faithful" intuition, in which the thinker as
an artist had to achieve a "state of beauty" to create beauty, as opposed to
the typical "supreme means" of individualist "analysis" that focuses on
"understanding."[93] The "Catholic synthesis" helped the nation achieve this

state of beauty. In 1910, Lugones, during his liberal phase, had argued that despite its national prosperity, Argentina lacked a proper spirituality.[94] Now he argued that Catholicism provided a "dogma" that could counteract the degeneration that accompanied rationalism, which he characterized as a "form of suicide that eliminates hope." The "progressive transgressions" of rationalism implied, for Lugones, a return to the "apotheosis of matter and instinct." Instinct was an aspect of the rationalist program, "a moral without dogma," that he, and the nacionalista movement, opposed.[95]

Like most nacionalistas, Lugones identified this secular, rational enemy with unrestrained lubricity and excessive sexuality, which poisoned politics and the state. But even worse, these traits tainted Argentine culture, which informed and influenced the national being: "The materialization of art progresses toward the same goal, and we are reaching the point of systematic absurdity—that is to say an ugliness lacking sexual purity [*fealdad impúdica*]—which includes the jazz of blacks, the infamous lubricity of tango and foxtrot, and nudism, which is the precursor of free love; all these things are for monkeys."[96]

In the last article he published before his suicide—an event, according to Jorge Luis Borges that was related to his extramarital affair with a young Argentine university student—Lugones elaborated on his notion of bestiality, or more generally, the inhumane nature of the internal enemy, identifying its program with a theoretical apparatus that included not only Hegel, Marx, and Lenin but also Darwin, Schopenhauer, and Nietzsche (with his "anarchic anti-Christianity and egocentric omnipotence"). But there was a more contemporary and equally dangerous outcome of these philosophical systems that Lugones identified as a central element of the rationalist project against God and Argentina:

> Thus, at last, it is Freud, for whom all human life develops as the moral subject and object between two determinations: physical love, of course that is to say carnal appetite, and hatred, that is to say the empire of instincts as principal motor of intelligence. Freud entitles these determinations under the significant labels of Eros and Ananké or fatality (*Civilization and Its Discontents*).[97]

For Lugones, Freud sidelined God and reduced him to a mere illusory product of the human mind. He found this idea outrageous in both aesthetic and ethical terms. He was particularly worried that psychoanalysis blurred the line between his standard notion of the Christian West and the "savage" non-Western societies, perhaps including the native inhabitants of Argentina and Latin America, whom he saw as the ultimate other—a radical other who by their mere existence defined the European racial qualities of Argentina. "God is [for Freud] no more than the idealization, in itself bipolarized, of the Totem or beast-pet that some savage tribes possess."[98]

Freud connected Darwin with politics, as standing against God and nation. Thus, according to Lugones, their new "religion" was "synthesized in the overpowering beast" of instinctual forces that psychoanalysis brought to the fore. He clearly saw psychoanalysis as a counterreligion, an "attempt at transcendental explanation" that, by embracing sexuality, the "Totem-God" and the "monkey-man," was essentially "anti-Christian." If nacionalismo, which for Lugones meant Argentina, needed a Christianized fascism, it was not surprising but rather "highly significant" that the theoretical subjects of the enemy, from Marx to Darwin to Freud, were "Jews and Protestants."[99]

This fundamentalist conflation of fascist notions of the enemy and anti-Semitism with radical critiques of science and psychoanalysis is a defining element of Argentine fascist ideology at large.[100] Nacionalismo, like Italian fascism, was against the legacy of the Enlightenment and associated its defenders with the notion of a radical abject. This notion was one of the lasting legacies of Christianized fascism. It was its rather dubious gift to Argentine history. In other words, it represents its most original contribution to what was destined to become a standard notion for the fascists, the neofascists, and ultimately the military of the last Argentine dictatorship in the decades that followed. The place of nacionalista ideology in the construction of Peronism is the other indirect, and sometimes direct, legacy of nacionalismo. The epilogue of this book provides a critical reflection about these two legacies of nacionalismo, but before that, let me provide a necessary moment of transnational recapitulation.

Trasnational Fascism: A Recapitulation

In 1934 Italy was both host and victor of the soccer World Cup. Some antifascists still contend that Mussolini manipulated some referees, particularly one Swiss referee, during the tournament. When Italy reached the final against Czechoslovakia, Mussolini attended the game with great expectations. Some days before, he had declared his "passion" for the sport. The championship match at the Fascist National Stadium was intense and messy. During the second half, the Czechs scored on a shot from an almost impossible angle. But then Orsi scored for Italy, tying the game just nine minutes before the end. The story is well known. In overtime, the famous Italian player Giuseppe Meazza passed the ball to Enrique Guaita, who passed it to Angelo Schiavio, who scored the goal that secured the championship, in an act that he later described as one of "desperation." In the concluding ceremony, Mussolini personally handed the players the trophy as well as a special fascist medal as they made the fascist salute, right arms pointed to the sky. The victory, *Il Corriere della Sera* asserted, was "a grandiose work of propaganda."

Four of the eleven members of the starting team, Enrique Guaita (the top scorer of the World Cup), Raimundo Orsi (second top scorer), Luis Monti, and Attilio De Maria, were in fact born in Argentina and two of them (Monti and De Maria) had played for Argentina in the previous World Cup of 1930. But this fact went without notice in the fascist press. These Argentine players had gone to Italy as adults to play professional soccer, and just before the World Cup they were granted Italian citizenship and became fascist heroes.[101] For Italian fascism, these players were Italians through and through. No trace of "Argentineness" was ever mentioned in the fascist press. Even today some Argentine antifascists would claim that without these "Argentine players" Italy would not have won the World Cup.

This anecdote is symptomatic of a broader phenomenon described in this book. It shows the complexity of the construction and interpretation of the Italian–Argentine connection. Mussolini not only saw Argentina as a site of potential conquest, but also as a nation lacking autonomy. Argentina, due to its Italian "blood," had to follow Italy in its imperial designs. In a specific fascist sense, Argentines were, or could only be, Italians. However, for most Argentines, Italy was, at best, one component of the blood running through the veins of the nation. For Italians, these veins were just an expansion of the Italian organism, or as Mussolini claimed its "arterial links." Fascist Italy, the "mother" of all Argentines, considered itself entitled to use Argentina in the same maternal way it had used its Argentine scorers during the World Cup. This conception was at the center of the Italian project for spreading fascism in Argentina, particularly through nacionalismo. They did this in direct competition with the Germans, who were also intent on propagandizing their version of fascism. In this study of previously unresearched Italian fascist archives I have shown how the Italian ministry of propaganda subsidized the same nacionalista venues and activities subsidized by the Nazis.[102]

Mussolini once said that fascism as a radical form of Italian nationalism was not for export. However, fascism was exported outside Italy from its very beginning. More generally, the Duce did not see a contradiction between fascist radical nationalism and transnational fascism. Fascist imperialism provided the ideological binder. He presented fascism as a universal phenomenon ready to be adopted worldwide by "smaller nations" such as Argentina, as he once told an Argentine fascist at a secret meeting.[103] As Antonio Gramsci perceived early on, fascism was a movement of "international scale."[104] Whereas Gramsci saw fascism as an instinctual form of imperialism, Mussolini often saw this imperialism as a form of derivative propaganda. He often thought of Argentina as a special case, as a "family member," but also considered it another small nation. To some extent, this seemingly contradictory notion was inspired by the equally contradictory prefascist nationalist tradition of Italian imperialism. In this view Argentina was not only a "colony" but also an example of Italian entrepreneurship. In the liberal period both countries had decided to take shelter under the Pax Britannica, which imposed limits to their expansion, providing them not only with a sense of being "small" great powers but also with restricted regional aims that were often legitimized through shared Roman roots as well as shared citizens. But as far as Mussolini was concerned, these aims were now a thing of the past. Mussolini's geopolitical ambitions were far from regional, and he no longer considered that exporting Italians was beneficial for the Italian organism. Propaganda was now a vessel for a new transregional fascist imperialism that included Argentina as a special case in the export of fascism.

Italians, as I have shown in this book, were selling fascism across the Atlantic, but the Argentines were not buying it wholesale. In response to the Italian proposal that Argentina adopt universal fascism, the Argentines put forward "universal nacionalismo."[105] This was a model of adaptation that was based on longstanding Argentine traditions of "reading" Europe from the distant "European" perspective of the Southern Cone. It is not possible to understand Argentine nacionalismo without Italian fascism. But this is only half of the story.

Nacionalistas took what they wanted from the original fascist matrix. They believed that this Argentine adaptation of fascism made it better than, or superior to, European fascism. God himself guaranteed the superiority of the Argentine version of fascism. This idea was not restricted to Argentines.

It was shared, as we have seen, by some European fascists, such as the Spaniard José María Pemán. Whereas Italian fascism mainly saw itself as a political religion or a "faith," as Mussolini put it, the Argentines saw their movement as the political expression of God. It is this conflation of fascism and Catholicism that made the Argentine variant different from other forms of fascism. Not even Spain's or Romania's, the most "religious" European forms of fascism, presented such a radical fascist conflation with the sacred as did Argentine clericofascism.[106] Both the Spaniard José Antonio Primo de Rivera and the Romanian "Captain" Codreanu had a more Maurrasian notion of religion as an instrument of fascist politics.

Although Primo de Rivera argued that "every historical process is, in the end, a religious process," only point twenty-five of the twenty-seven points of Falange's program of 1934 made reference to religion. Moreover, the program clearly stated that church and state should be separated.[107]

Romanian fascism was related to the sacred, but its proponents presented God as a protector "who cares for us" rather than as the ultimate political decider. Their leader, Corneliu Codreanu, did not present himself as a medium of the sacred but claimed autonomy from God when it came to making political decisions, a separation that Argentine nacionalistas never claimed. The archangel Saint Michael protected the Romanian fascist movement but did not direct its politics.[108]

In short, although the Romanian and Spanish fascists engaged fascism with the sacred, neither Primo de Rivera nor Codreanu ever said that they represented a "Christianized" fascism, as Argentine nacionalistas claimed. For instance, one Argentine fascist, Nimio de Anquin, defined nacionalismo as an entirely "Catholic idea" specially connected to God. One of the most famous of the Argentine fascists, Father Virgilio Filippo, insisted that Argentine nacionalismo, rather than Italian fascism, represented a template for the radical Right, not only in Latin America but throughout the entire world. Most nacionalistas, like Filippo, inverted the terms of the equation and presented fascism as a generic form of nacionalismo.[109]

The nacionalista idea of "Christianized fascism" presents the case of Argentine fascism as the more radical fascist conflation of politics and the sacred. The notion that God was the real chief, the political decider, would have been anathema to Mussolini. For Mussolini, if there was one God for fascism, it was himself.

Both Argentine antifascists and fascists projected a harmonious image of the conflation of fascism and Catholicism, which the contemporary historian must present in both contextual and critical terms. Whereas antifascists saw clericofascism as a matter of fact that confirmed traditional antireactionary stereotypes, for nacionalistas the conflation of the clerical and the fascist implied a denial of actual differences. In addition, for nacionalistas this clericofascist conflation was informed by the blurring of distinctions or hierarchies between laymen and clergy. Most important, this conflation ultimately provided a legitimatizing device for the nacionalista movement in the army and among the population as a whole.

For the Argentines the fascist experience was part of the Italian and, more broadly, European fascist subordination of empirical knowledge to ideological conviction. But in the Argentine case the refusal to have the reality principle at work even included Italian fascism itself. In other words, nacionalistas were not significantly concerned with the Italian fascist experience as Italy perceived and represented it. In Italy the fascist master narrative and its Mussolinian core could only be "changed" by the leader. In Argentina this narrative was appropriated, criticized, and reformulated by everyone in the nacionalista movement. For both Italian fascism and Argentine nacionalismo the realm of politics was reinterpreted as the expression of a sacred whole (the ever-changing doctrine). But in the Argentine case, the fascist sacred was literalized by the inclusion of the institutional church within the ideology of the nacionalista formation. The strong Italian tension between "fascist secularism" and the "sacred"—which often included an aggressive and secularizing reframing of religion by Mussolini and others— was not avoided in Argentina. But it was, rather, encrypted within the ideology of the nacionalista movement. Both the Argentine and the Italian movements included a dynamic theoretical, and sometimes practical, quest for the sublime heights of radical transcendence (the fascist flights that I have previously analyzed are a case in point). However, the Argentines understood their quest, and their movement at large, as the earthly political expression of God. God was, so to speak, the Duce of nacionalismo.

For the fascist *forma mentis*, politics involved the primacy of meaning over the external world. In the Italian case, the primacy of politics was the outcome of a meaningful concept of fascism that presented doctrine not as an allegory to be deciphered but as reality itself presented in doctrinal terms. Day-to-day politics was frequently understood within this framework, which blurred the more enlightened opposition between belief and knowledge. This was the actual meaning of the act of "listening to the Duce." Being a "listener" involved the conscious and unconscious devaluation of empirical experience and reality checks. Across the Atlantic fascist theory emptied "experience" and rendered it mythological and extraordinary. But for the Argentine nacionalistas, Italian fascism itself was an allegory that had to be deciphered in conjunction with the teachings of the church. The nacionalistas, in particular, interpreted Argentine reality in accordance with the views of nacionalista priests. Whereas in Italian fascism "theory" was personified in the dicta of the Duce, in Argentina fascist theory became Catholic theory. Clerical fascism constituted the mainstream of Argentine Catholicism in the 1930s and 1940s.[110] Nothing the Argentine nacionalistas claimed can be understood without taking into account this relation between the secular and the sacred in Argentina. All politics were for them theological in their ultimate sense.[111]

In Argentina, the full or totalizing stress on historical change through the agency of one individual (Mussolini) was displaced into a set of core myths: the myth of Uriburu, the myth of an integral Catholic Argentine society, and the myth of a Catholic nacionalista army, the conjunction of the sword and the cross that cared for all three. All these myths were grounded in reality, but their practical articulations were less embedded in it. An extreme individualistic fusion of empirical political practice with an exaggerated sense of a sacred individual legacy and crusade-like mission made it almost impossible for the nacionalista movement to have a single leader. It also liberated nacionalistas from the strong Italian emphasis on emulation and gave them much more intellectual autonomy. On the other hand, as many nacionalistas repeatedly claimed, the movement always risked becoming a field for abstract theoretical debate and impotent political strategies. Typical stagnant discussions were frequently related to the nature of electoral politics and the problematic relationship of nacionalismo to the conservative party.[112]

But in other areas the nacionalista brand of theoretical politics proved extremely influential. Nacionalismo was engaged in international debates on an equal footing with their European counterparts. Some of the most important Italian and Spanish fascist intellectuals (Ramiro De Maeztu, José María Pemán, Gino Arias, or Massimo Bontempelli, for example) wrote special articles for Argentine publications, as did some of the most renowned French intellectuals, such as Jacques Maritain or Pierre Drieu la Rochelle, who put forward their own ideas about fascism and antifascism in Argentina. Drieu la Rochelle, for example, wrote a regular column for the most important Argentine paper, La Nación, saying in one issue that fascism was a "historical necessity" and a new "civilization." Moreover, for the

French intellectual, fascism was a transnational phenomenon with specific national currents. "The fascist international," Drieu la Rochelle argued, "is acting around the globe [and is] the international of nationalisms."[113] This was certainly political music for nacionalista ears. Even Mussolini, as we have seen, frequently boasted to Argentines about his own position in the "international" dimensions of fascist ideology. The Argentines engaged these intellectuals in longstanding debates, but by and large they never adopted their arguments. The nacionalista conflation of fascist imperialism with hispanidad and Latin American anti-imperialism proved quite original and influential. Hispanidad was born in Argentina, not in Spain.[114] A nacionalista intellectual created the anthem of the Malvinas/Falklands that Argentines sang during the war in 1982 and that children still sing in every Argentine public school today.[115] Moreover, the nacionalista Catholic notion of anti-imperialism underlies the genealogy of the totalitarian ideological dimensions of the 1982 war in the South Atlantic. The ideologues of the last Argentine dictatorship (1976–1983) presented Argentina as an absolutely Catholic, nondemocratic, authoritarian nation. As one mainstream priest and ideologue of the juntas put it in 1982, this Catholic vision personified the "Christian state." The war, he argued, represented the ultimate means of national reaffirmation. The war was supported by God insofar as the divine had established the sovereignty of the nation. God gave Argentina its territories including the Malvinas/Falklands and God supported the war against "colonialism." Defending the sovereignty that God provided was an "act of self-defense." This was confirmed by "a religious and supernatural vision— the only one in the end absolutely real with respect to the actual context that the country is living through and its current and future placement among other nations." This view was explicitly informed by the nacionalista idea of national politics as being "at the service God" and against liberalism and Marxism. It also reproduced the idea of Argentine primacy in Latin America's battle against plutocratic imperialism. This explanation, provided by a priest at the University of Buenos Aires, is symptomatic of the central link between nacionalista theory and the ideology and practice of the last military junta.[116]

The influence of nacionalista ideology defines Argentine collective memory. It is the nacionalista revisionist view of history that still prevails among a majority of the Argentine population[117] and, although largely occluded by historians, the nacionalistas' social, totalitarian, corporativist policies first articulated topics that were later appropriated by Peronist populism.[118] The nacionalista and clericofascist push for neutrality during the Second World War strongly influenced Argentine military leaders and significantly affected Argentina's official abandonment of Jewish victims of the Holocaust and its subsequent openness toward Nazi and other fascist "refugees."[119] The nacionalista denial of the killing of Patagonia's native population (the brothers Irazusta presented it as a Christian crusade)[120] played a role in the national denial of this ethnic cleansing—a denial that still informs Argentina today. Nacionalistas were a substantial force behind the degradation of Argentine Indians, and they clearly embraced Domingo Faustino Sarmiento's call for their extermination as a "sublime" endeavor.[121] From Salta to Buenos Aires to Patagonia, nacionalistas also participated in the longstanding Argentine debate about the national being, adding xenophobic illiberal colors to the Argentine prism. They were eager to shape an idea of Argentina as detached from liberalism and instead constitutive of a "republican" entity that the influential nacionalista José Luis Torres—who coined the now widely accepted term "infamous decade" to refer to the 1930s—defined as "a dictatorship of patriots."[122] Nacionalistas were the first political movement to politicize the issue of crime and security, even organizing demonstrations against crime in Plaza de Mayo during the 1930s.[123] And, last but not least, it was the nacionalista view of the enemy that shaped military policies for years to come.

Epilogue

Totalitarian solutions may well survive the fall of totalitarian regimes in the form of strong temptations which will come up whenever it seems impossible to alleviate political, social, or economic misery in a manner worthy of man.

—HANNAH ARENDT, 1959

Buscamos inspiración política en nuestra propia casa, fronteras para adentro.

—ALIANZA DE LA JUVENTUD NACIONALISTA, 1941

Si conservan los hijos de Israel esa índole de colonia tan invasora como inadaptable, una hora llegará en la que la población argentina los rechazará de su seno.

—GUSTAVO FRANCESCHI, 1933

Nacionalismo, Fascism, and Peronism

By the end of the fascist regime, Mussolini seemed to have arrived at a better understanding of Argentina's Catholic and profascist role in the "new order." Mussolini explicitly wanted to test the Argentines on their desire to fight North American "imperialistic" influence in South America and seemed to value, or at least recognize, the clericofascist character of Argentine nacionalismo.

In 1943, in his top-secret meeting with the nacionalista Juan Carlos Goyeneche, Mussolini made clear that there had been a change in his thinking.[1] Goyeneche was concerned about the prevalence of the view of fascism as an anticlerical movement and wanted Mussolini to explicitly state that it was not. That the Duce would finally recognize this as late as 1943 is indicative of the previously derivative dimensions of Italian fascist propaganda and its lack of concern for establishing bridges between Italian concerns and nacionalista realities in Argentina.

Mussolini also promised Goyeneche that Argentina was going to play "a role of vital importance in the World Order of the future insofar as Argentina would have to secure . . . a balance between Latin America and Anglo-Saxon America." The Duce argued that Italy "always had bonds of blood, culture and friendship with Argentina and is obliged to collaborate with the Argentine republic in her action aimed at getting rid of all false, foreign elements [*elementos extraños*] that could impede the development of this great South American nation and her deserved supremacy among the peoples of Latin origins." Even when Mussolini could no longer avoid recognizing that Nazi Germany had taken on a tutelary role over his own regime, he did not renounce the imperialist idea that Italy had a tutelary role with respect to Argentina and Latin America at large; he actually characterized the Latin American nations as "smaller states."[2] The notion of the small state or small nation recalled the first fascist articulation of empire, as a spiritual entity. In a sense, for Mussolini, Argentina had always been a minor player in his neo-Roman understanding of a Latin American politics driven by cultural and racial Latin and European patterns of behavior that British and American imperialism was trying to thwart. Rather than thinking that the Latin legacy was a cultural choice for Argentines, Italian fascists considered Argentina to be a repository for Italian blood.

By stressing Argentina's neocolonial role in leading the Latin bloc against American and British expansion, and by his belated recognition of the Catholic character of Argentine fascism, Mussolini finally seemed to have answered the question he raised during his conversation with Marshall Göring as we saw it in the first chapter of this book: why was it, Mussolini pondered, that "Italy's relations with Argentina were not particularly good"? Now, he was no longer perplexed about Argentina. Although still insisting on spiritual imperialism, he clearly understood the differences between two different transnational fascist projects. But it was too late for him, and soon the question had no significance for anyone. Some months after his meeting with Goyeneche, Mussolini would be toppled by his own fascists, including Count Ciano, who had been present at the grandiose meeting with Marshall Göring. The story is well known. Mussolini was soon "liberated" by German commandos, and Hitler established a Nazi puppet fascist republic in the north of Italy. Some days before he met his end at the hands of Italian partisans in 1945, Mussolini unrealistically thought of escaping to Argentina. But that was not to be. Instead, I would argue, the Argentine nacionalista alliance of church, nacionalista intellectuals, and the army were, in certain ways, to continue his projects. The following year, Juan Domingo Perón, a young Argentine colonel who would many times define himself as a "student of Mussolini," won the presidential election.

Perón famously argued that he would learn from Mussolini's "mistakes." Mussolini was no longer there to see his transatlantic legacy, but Peronism would be less a form of fascism and more an "ambiguous" cold war phenomenon, a sui generis radical reformulation of fascism.[3] Perón had lived in fascist Italy for a short period in 1940, and when interviewed by the fascist press then he had expressed his admiration for the fascist state, its doctrine, and the "unitary" direction that "the people and the army have received from their Duce." Like Mussolini, Perón stressed the "unity of blood" and the arterial bond between Italy and Argentina, "a bond that victoriously resists the action of time." Unlike Mussolini, Perón stressed the importance of the "adaptation" of models as opposed to their outright "adoption."[4] This transatlantic adaptation was perhaps Mussolini's most unexpected legacy— as many fascists and antifascists recognized after fascism was gone. Writing in June 1945, Hannah Arendt believed that the seeds of the fascist international were well planted in South America, "whose strong fascist movements are sufficiently well known."[5] On the fascist side, after the war, it was argued in a publication of Asvero Gravelli, one of the founders of the fascist international and the principal theoretician of transnational fascism, that Peronism was a "revolution" and its result was "a renewed Argentina."[6]

Was Peronism a natural continuation of fascism, as these fascists seemed to imply? Was Perón a fascist? There is no shadow of a doubt that fascism influenced Perón and populism. But equally significant to Perón's political development was what he learned from the "Christianized fascism" that Argentine nacionalismo promoted during the fascist years. Nacionalismo did not buy what the fascists were selling. Argentine nacionalismo reformulated fascism until it was almost unrecognizable while nevertheless adopting some specific aspects of fascist propaganda.

By the time Perón become the "first" Argentine, most nacionalistas noted that their politics were a failure, insofar as they felt that their theoretical discussions on economics, politics, and cultural and social life could not influence day-to-day politics. However, in this, as well as in other matters, the nacionalistas were wrong. The general public and, more important, the military and the church had been listening.

Hyperbole is an essential component of historical and political narratives alike. This work is not an exception. However, I am not overdoing hyperbole when I argue that to some extent the entire Argentine twentieth century became painted with nacionalista ideology. From Argentine imperialism to Argentine anti-imperialism, from the revisionist refashioning of Argentine history to the later refashioning of the Argentine economy and social life, nacionalistas played a significant formative role. Peronism was not only the channel for nacionalista currents. Some decades later, the last military junta (1976–1983) would be profoundly influenced by nacionalista ideology. In short, the nacionalistas' longstanding longing for theory often displaced them from actual politics to a more traditional, yet politically important role, in Argentine history: that of enlightened intellectuals whose main activity was programmatic nation building.[7] The figure of Leopoldo Lugones represents a belated sign of this process despite his originality. Lugones returned at the end of his life to the Catholic fold and indeed became a less contentious member of the movement. But the nacionalistas, through their practical failure as a political movement, became what Lugones wanted to avoid being: a guiding intellectual, close enough to power to influence it deeply but never achieving it in his own right.

During the 1930s and 1940s, nacionalistas fluctuated between different myths and their related politics. During the period from 1930 to 1936, the myth of Uriburu and the Argentine translation of Italian fascism legitimized the idea that nacionalismo, with the help of the military and some conservative fellow travelers, would be the dominant influence on a fascist bloc of power. From 1936 onward, this idea began to wane, and the myth of Uriburu was refashioned as the emblem of either the nacionalistas' choice of the profascist governor of Buenos Aires, Manuel Fresco, or their choice of a military dictatorship. The Fresco option was chosen by some nacionalistas, particularly the group around *Bandera Argentina* and later the Alianza de la Juventud Nacionalista. In the late 1930s and early 1940s, Fresco presented himself as a legitimate nacionalista option that included social reform, neutrality, and Catholicism.[8] But many nacionalistas strongly resisted Fresco and were also influenced by the example of the Spanish fascist military alliance.[9] The military option encompassed by the newly created myth of Lugones and his "hour of the sword" had been embraced by all nacionalistas from the beginning. But this was not an all-or-nothing choice. Nacionalistas did not discard all civilian options, and even Osés and his group played with the idea of supporting the conservative president Ramón Castillo and had secret meetings with him.[10] Elsewhere I have shown that by the end of the 1930s they tended to emphasize the military option, participating in secret gatherings and conspiracies throughout the decade.[11] However, in 1943 the military coup that brought Colonel Juan Domingo Perón to power caught them by surprise. Most of them supported the dictatorship and later the Peronist regime. Perón and other members of the secret association GOU (Group of United Officers) were the prime ideological and political movers behind the actions of the military dictatorship (1943–1946). The group's program was inspired by nacionalista ideology, and it was probably drafted by Perón himself.[12]

Perón had acknowledged the "flaws" and the mistakes of fascism, a movement that he admired. In addition, he had learnt from the strategic errors of General Uriburu in his "Revolution of September 6" of 1930. Having taken part in that event as a young captain, Perón saw the problems underlying Uriburu's protocorporativist revolution, which lacked enough popular support.

In its first year, the military dictatorship adopted the nacionalista clerico-fascist ideology contained in the GOU program. The dictatorship intervened in all realms of life: it imposed mandatory religious education in public schools, banned all political parties, significantly restricted the freedom of the press. But this clericofascist regime was not to last. Between 1944 and 1945, in a context of political instability and external pressures, including the threat of U.S. military intervention, Colonel Perón attempted to erase the nacionalista undertones of the regime with the aim of reconnecting Argentina with the United Nations and, domestically, reaching out to traditional political parties. Perón, who had become secretary of labor early on in the military dictatorship, was able to create a state program for social reform that ultimately gave him a mass following of workers and union leaders, who saw the advantages of Perón's social conceptions. Thus, from his post in the secretariat Perón established dynamic links with revolutionary and state syndicalism that ultimately established a new hegemonic pact for the nation. He put forward successful labor reforms that were an eclectic fusion of corporativism and social welfare.

By 1944, in addition to his secretarial position, Perón had become minister of war and vice president. Both the external and the internal antifascist front resisted Perón's efforts, labeling him a fascist, and they expected that liberal Argentina would strike back against Perón. But in his search for political survival, Perón reformulated fascism, appealing to the working class and maintaining a reluctant alliance with the army and the church. Transcending traditional nacionalista notions of adaptation, Perón succeeded in creating a new, postfascist ideology for the cold war era.

Perón created a popular party of his own and won the presidential elections of February 1946 with worker support and despite the opposition of the middle classes and the traditional establishment. Industrialist policies, social welfare, and authoritarian repression of dissidents, extreme anticommunist policies, and totalitarian cultural, religious, and cultural strategies constituted the main features of his presidency. The incorporation of workers and other subaltern sectors into the rhetorical and often nonrhetorical mainstream of Argentine politics was combined with the legalization of women's suffrage. Perón's wife, Eva Perón, had a unique role as a mediator between genders, bearing witness to the equally unique Peronist rethinking of traditional gender relations. In this aspect, as in many others, Peronism transcended fascism.

The increasing Peronization of society ironically planted the roots of the regime's failure to surpass traditional Argentine factionalism. The experience of the Peronist regime sharply divided Argentina's population, each of which could not accept the political presence of each other. Like Colombians during the period of La Violencia, Argentines could not avoid sectarian factionalism. To be sure, Perón had dominated the historical developments of Peronist and post-Peronist Argentina, but he represented the interest of many previously sidelined sectors that always supported him in the streets and elsewhere and voted for him in national elections. Peronism represented a turning point in Argentine politics. It was an abrupt change, complexly embedded in significant continuities, particularly with respect to 1912 and 1916 (that is, the conservative reform and the integrative politics of the Radical Party).

The widening of the political base under Perón to include the previously silenced sectors differs from the revolutionary political reforms that took place in Mexico, and with the reforms from above that characterized Colombia under López Pumarejo and Uruguay with its even more structural reforms, brought about by President Batlle y Ordóñez. But the similarities among these countries are striking. All but Argentina endured civil war as a central means for achieving political ends. Why Perón refused to engage in civil warfare after warplanes of the anti-Peronist Argentine navy bombarded Buenos Aires's main plaza and Peronist buildings remains an open question, one that may be partially explained in personal terms. However, as in the case of Laureano Gómez's regime in Colombia, Peronist rhetoric and the all-or-nothing approach promoted the development of an extremely factional atmosphere that resulted in a hegemonic deadlock. Perón's escape from Argentina in 1955 did not resolve it, as his critics desired, for it only continued by other means.

Peronism was an integralist movement that aimed to change the body politic by equating itself with the nation. In this sense Peronism put forward in *"trasformista"* fashion an older factional tradition. The subsequent Argentine crisis, from 1955 onward, may be partially explained by this fact.

The history of Argentina from 1810 to 1955 presents an early process of civil war and stagnation followed by accelerated economic and institutional modernization. The period saw the rise of aristocratic authoritarian positivism as the means to rule the country. This system effectively did so until a transformation from above, deeply influenced from below, allowed the Radical Party to expand in part the legitimacy of the political system. The period from 1930 to 1943 may be seen as moment of constant transformation. Between the two world wars Argentina saw the emergence of a powerful middle class that was not necessarily represented in the ballots. The popular front that Perón had defeated in the presidential elections of 1946 by a narrow margin represented the middle-class groups that saw in Peronism the Argentine postwar continuation of fascist politics. The majority of the working class elected Perón, and they voted for him by an act of volition. Peronist myths and rhetoric were appropriated by the workers movement, and Perón in turn obtained the direction of its politics. During Peronism, the Argentine nation remained in a kind of all-or-nothing standstill, which the following military regimes, as well as the elected regimes that followed them, tried but failed to overcome. The post-1955 ban on Peronism excluded from the political body of the nation a movement that represented as much as half of its citizens. Extreme factionalism remained a key political factor from the remaining half of the century as it did in the previous years.

The Peronist regime was a vehicle for the widening of Argentina's political base. It is ironic that two minority parties, the Argentine Socialist Party and the fascist nacionalistas, prompted the strongest debates and the greatest amount of political projects during the regime.[13] Moreover, both socialism and nacionalismo, along with Italian fascism, provided the ideological roots of Peronism. Peronista practice was essentially informed by these roots. Like Italian fascism, Peronism combined a non-Marxist reading of socialism with extreme right-wing nationalism.

Before Peronism, the working class had a limited political role, notwithstanding socialist and nacionalista efforts to represent it. With Peronism, its economic and social advances were finally acknowledged. Against the opposition of the upper and middle sectors, Perón realized that Peronism would be a freely inspired postfascism of the working classes. Peronism was itself not a form of fascism but the surprising outcome of a fascist *forma mentis* that Perón cautiously but relentlessly tried to put in practice.[14] Born out of the "fascist attempt" of 1943–1945, Peronism on the intellectual plane was a sui generis movement with a fascist unconscious. There were more important structural issues affecting Peronism, including major social and demographic changes, processes of state modernization, and recurrent Argentine economic and political patterns. Moreover, populism and the mythical aspects of Peronism, including the role of Eva Perón, are central intellectual dimensions.[15] But in its ideas of anti-imperialism, its totalitarian rituals, extreme nationalism, notions of social justice, and mythical views of history and state formation, Peronism was certainly inspired by Mussolini's fascism, as well as that of the nacionalistas.[16]

Contrary to what Jorge Luis Borges and most Argentine antifascists believed, Peronism was not fascism. As they had seen nacionalismo as an imitation of European fascisms, so also they saw Peronism. Borges wrote in his famous article "L'illusion comique" (1955) that Peronism was a mixture of "opprobrium and stupidity." More seriously, in cold war antitotalitarian fashion, he also argued that Peronism was comparable to communism.[17]

But Perón was a staunch anticommunist who had lived in fascist Italy, arriving at an understanding of fascism that he adapted for Latin America. This notion of fascism was even more heterodox than that of the theoretically inclined nacionalistas. In its laxity, Peronism radically departed from the fascist matrix while conserving it as a repressed remnant. To be sure, Peronism had other intellectual influences, including state syndicalism, non-Marxist socialism, and spiritism. But the transnational fascist intellectual contribution to its ideology should not be underestimated. Nacionalista proposals for imagining the nation have been part of the genealogy of the Argentine political and cultural landscape of the twentieth century, including in the era of Peronism. Beyond this problematic "contribution," equally influential were nacionalista ideas of the enemy as a radical abject, as a radical other who had to be destroyed.

The Fascist Theory of the Abject

The fascist matrix that inspired Europeans and Latin Americans alike included constitutive elements of the Western tradition: namely, traditional dichotomies such as friend and foe, insider and outsider, normativity and anomy, primitive and modern, leader and followers, potency or strong will and passivity, discipline and uncontrolled behavior, power and powerlessness, perpetrator and victim, patriotism and treason, civilization and barbarism or nation and anarchy, and war and peace, to name the most significant ones. Thinking in terms of dichotomies was not limited to fascism. Fascism in its radical pursuit of irrationality is unique. However, it also did not differ from the most dichotomist and victimizing dimensions of the modern intellectual tradition but simply pushed them to the extreme. These dichotomies provided believers with an experimental feeling of radical transgression of modern norms, an abjectification of the enemy that rendered this enemy tangible and available for sacrifice, national hyperchauvinism and the reification of war as a dream world of battle and adventure.[18] Fascism might even be said to embrace Thanatos as a source of power and a transfiguration of instinctual forces.[19] This embracing of the repressed bordered on the enactment of a fascist unconscious. In other words, there was no mediation between the violent fascist longing for radicality and what Dominick LaCapra, in referring to some dimensions of Nazi practice, has termed a return of the repressed that is itself a "constitutive other" of modernity and not simply a "regression to barbarism."[20]

There were many anti-Christian dimensions to the pseudoreligious sadism of fascism, well exemplified in the most esoteric aspects of Himmler's ss, in the "blood-sucking" practices of the Romanian Legion of the Archangel Michael, or in the imperial fascist esotericism of Julius Evola.[21] But mainstream fascism on both shores of the Atlantic was far from pagan, and it was not a Satanic cult. Fascism presented a force toward the death drive absurdly exemplified in fascist Spanish general Millán Astray's famous exclamation "Long live death!" ("Viva la muerte!"), also repeated in the Romanian fascist insurrection of 1941, and in the use of skeletons as icons of pseudomilitary formations. The longing for a radically abject other, the search for an ideal sacrificial enemy represented the most significant negative or "anti" element of the fascist basic matrix. Besides its ideological "negation" of socialism and Marxism, fascism involved the negation of the other as an object of dialogical political exchange. In 1924, Mussolini warned his fellow fascists about the dangers involved in blurring the line between friend and enemy. This basic distinction was central to fascist ideology. Before its more conceptual Nazi articulation by Carl Schmitt, it played an active role in Mussolini's thought. He too saw politics as an all-or-nothing contest between fascism and its enemies. For him there was no middle ground: "Gentlemen, it is necessary to be either in favor or against, either fascism or antifascism. Those who are not with us, are against us."[22] Even for those who were "against us," it was difficult to understand the fascist conception of the enemy as a radically abject being who ought to be destroyed. But these ideas were a reality for the fascists and their victims. In the Argentine case, fascism presented ritual elements that made it a "political religion," but it was also fused with the institutional church in creating a "Christianized" fascism." Fascism and religion, as this book demonstrates, were not mutually exclusive. Basically, the argument that fascism was anticlerical in nature simply fails to describe the fascist reality of the past. Fascism was characterized by religious forms (language and rituals) and also at times established strong links with institutional religions.[23] And the idea that fascism expressed the will of God was central to nacionalismo. One question that arises from the present inquiry is whether Argentine fascism, or fascism at large, is connected in any way with fundamentalist ideologies. But then, is it possible to believe, as United States President George W. Bush stated, that Osama Bin Laden's ideology is a form of Islamic fascism?[24] To be sure, Bin Laden and his acolytes stress the value of ideological global networks, the messianic power of violence, the normative aspects of total war, and even take part in a negative sublime involving a conception of the abject that was dear to the most extreme dimensions of fascism in its prime.[25] And like Argentine fascism, the Islamic terrorists believe they are instruments of God.

But fascism was a revolutionary movement of the radical Right that presented itself as looking toward the future. Fascism created not a reactionary destruction of the political but rather its sublimation as an expression of modern sacred preconceptions. Even the Argentine nacionalistas, although they looked to God as the Duce of their movement, conflated this belief with the idea that nacionalismo also expressed popular sovereignty. As Mussolini often said, and fascists worldwide agreed, "History does not travel backward." Fascism did not want to return to the period before the French Revolution. It recognized the French Revolution as an indisputable event and presented itself as its ultimate ideological and political overcoming.[26] As Hannah Arendt perceptively noted, fascism as a form of totalitarianism relied on a specific idea of progression.[27] Fascism appealed to the legacy of the anti-Enlightenment but always resorted to a form of political sovereignty that the enlightenment had refashioned in democratic terms. Fascism, as Enzo Traverso has shown, demonstrated the worst possibilities of modernity.[28] Fascism understood itself as the ultimate expression of the future and not as a reactionary movement looking to establish a new version of a golden age.

In his 1928 book, *The Contemporary Anxiety*, Father Franceschi claimed that dictatorships and authoritarian patterns, such as those of Primo de Rivera, the Ku Klux Klan, the Chilean dictatorship of Carlos Ibáñez del Campo, and Italian fascism were somewhat inevitable as products of a historical trend toward dictatorship.[29] Franceschi never embraced the Klan but saw in the regimes he cited the best political choices available. During the 1930s, like all nacionalistas, he called for an authoritarian political reform of the democratic system. Like his friend the nacionalista intellectual Carlos Ibarguren, Franceschi presented this need for reform with a preeminent role for nacionalismo.[30] For Franceschi this need was urgent due to the impelling and seemingly infectious presence of the internal enemy. Argentina was at "war" with the "internal danger."[31] The internal enemy, he argued, put "our nationality" at risk.[32] This apocalyptic vision of politics was at the center of nacionalista political culture. Argentine fascism had a dark legacy, especially in its vision of the abject. This specifically Argentine idea of the enemy not only conflated fascism and Catholicism; it also presented a unique blend of sacred and secular anti-Semitism. Marxism, Darwinism, and psychoanalysis were considered to be the theoretical apparatus of the enemy, but pseudo-biological ideas of Jewish sexuality and Argentine masculinity also played a role.[33]

Anti-Semitism held a central place in the Argentine fascist idea of the enemy. As opposed to Europe, with its standard notions of anti-Semitism (Hannah Arendt is its main expert in this regard), in Argentina there was not a clear distinction between "modern" anti-Semitism and "traditional" anti-Judaism.[34]

On a theoretical level this book has addressed, in a Latin American context, issues raised by current theories of secularization.[35] If these theories stress the complexities linked to the transfiguration of the sacred into the secular, I have looked at this process in reverse, in a Latin American reformulation of these theories: namely, how a secular political ideology with implicit religious dimensions becomes sacralized through the idea that a secular movement with secular aims is the political expression of God. If Argentine fascism implied, more generally, a conflation of fascism and Catholicism, Argentine anti-Semitism presented a conflation of religious and "scientific," pseudobiological anti-Semitism. Freud and psychoanalysis played a central role in this conflation.[36]

As a young poet just returned from Europe, Jorge Luis Borges wrote to a Spanish friend in 1921 about a major, if not impossible, literary project. He was to write a collective and fantastic novel with Macedonio Fernández and other literary friends. The novel, Borges said, would claim the existence of a Bolshevik plan to gain power by way of spreading a "general neurasthenia" among the Argentine people.[37] Borges, of course, never wrote this novel or, for that matter, any novel at all. For Borges, the idea of a psychological plan to dominate the minds of Argentines was a fantasy. In the minds of nacionalistas, however, it was reality.

Most Argentine fascists actually believed that Freud was part of the master plan against Argentine fascism and Catholicism—the central elements of Argentine nationality. Nacionalistas saw psychoanalysis as the superstructure of the Jewish conspiracy. It was a kind of double-negative dialectic, an inverted version of the Frankfurt school, which presented the Jewish conspiracy as a mix of Marx and Freud. In short, they perceived psychoanalysis as the theory of the enemy. It was a dialectical plan that would invert the terms of General Uriburu's own attempt to change "the psychology of the Argentine people." For nacionalista leader Juan Carulla, for example, nacionalismo had to develop its own psychological warfare. Moreover, it was this very attempt to aim at the psyche of Argentines that made nacionalismo's political aims and activities, "a sacred war."[38]

Not all nacionalistas were opposed to Freud. Some nacionalistas like Ernesto Palacio actually thought that Freudian psychoanalysis, like Italian fascism, could be appropriated and reformulated for the Argentine context.[39] Other nacionalista and Catholic intellectuals remained ambivalent about Freud.[40] Populist nacionalistas, such as the renowned anti-imperialist writer Raúl Scalabrini Ortiz, opposed Freudianism to the "true" characteristics of the Argentine macho.[41] However, like Father Filippo and the poet

Leopoldo Lugones, most nacionalistas considered psychoanalysis to be the abject, the enemy with which there is no possible transaction beyond its violent sacrifice for the sake of the nation. The aim of uprooting psycho-analysis was totalitarian. The goal was to exterminate it from the minds of Argentines not only during the day but also during the night. Nacionalistas such as Delfina Bunge de Gálvez analyzed dreams in clericofascist terms that presented psychoanalysis as opposed to God.[42] Another nacionalista writer, Ramón Doll, like Freud, analyzed his own dreams. But unlike Freud, Doll conceived his dreams as a legitimization of nacionalista politics.[43] The politi-cal nightlife of Argentines fed into the totalitarian campaign to control the Argentine psyche.

There were different interpretations of Freud as the enemy. For the most important Catholic publication in Argentina, *Criterio*, the question was sim-ple. Freud was a theoretical figure of Judaism and communism. For Leo-poldo Lugones—perhaps the most important Latin American writer at the time—psychoanalysis was a central element of the conflation of modern philosophy, the literary avant garde, African American creations like jazz, and Marxism and Darwinism.

The case of Filippo differs from *Criterio* and Lugones because Filippo actually synthesized all these critiques. Indeed, Filippo represents the ulti-mate symptom of the anti-Semitic conflation of fascism and Catholicism. But Filippo thought that he had to engage Freud theoretically. In other words, he felt he had to present his own Argentine fascist theory of the mind. This might have been the most bizarre aspect of the already bizarre intellectual and political tradition that this book studies. Filippo thought that to counteract Freud he had to provide his own theory of the workings of the unconscious. He proposed, for instance, his own theory of the ego (namely, that it was a binary conception involving a daily and nocturnal ego) to oppose what he saw as a diabolical Freudian trinity of the ego, id, and superego. Freudian psychoanalysis would create a mentally and sexually abnormal Argentina, he believed; it was a disease that had to be corrected and "extirpated." Against God, and against the nation, the notion of Freud as a Jewish communist agent became a symbol of the enemy of Argentine fascism at large.

Despite nacionalista efforts, the hated outsider to some extent became an insider. Historians of psychoanalysis have shown how in the years following Peronism psychoanalysis became a central dimension of Argentine life.[44] This book shows that the terrain was prepared in part by nacionalismo.

Thanks to nacionalismo's radical criticisms, psychoanalysis became an identity of the liberal Argentina defeated by the military and Peronism. In a totalitarian context, psychoanalysis showed its emancipatory potential and became a counterpoint to reactionary conceptions of the sacred, competing with the right for spaces previously occupied by the state and competing also with the church for spaces traditionally occupied by religion. Liberal Argentina, particularly its middle sectors, which were defeated by "fascism" in 1946, may have found in Freud the theorist of the politics of everyday life that nacionalistas had predicted he would be. As it is claimed Freudian psychoanalysis had done in Austria, Argentine psychoanalysis may have retreated to culture from politics, but this "retreat" posed a long-lasting resistance against the forces of authoritarianism. Standing against the return of the repressed, Argentine psychoanalysis was itself ultimately repressed. Its persecution by the military dictatorship shows that this idea of Freud as a target in an Argentine civil war was created to last.

As I have shown, the apocalyptic notion of a total battle was central to nacionalista ideology. For nacionalistas like Osés, the trinity of God, fatherland, and family provided a sense of radical closure in an equally radical context, that is, an apocalyptic one. He framed "nacionalista totalitarianism" in the context of "a war among brothers."[45] For Osés, as well as for many other nacionalistas, the prospect of civil war justified political excess and violence that could have been avoided in a more stable situation.

Before becoming a critic of the "nacionalismos extranjerizantes," a fighter for democracy, and an antifascist (and later anti-Peronist) critic of "totalitarian ideology," Eugenia Silveyra de Oyuela claimed in 1937 that Argentina needed totalitarianism. This need was, for her, self-evident because the "red hordes" had "invaded Argentina" and also because totalitarianism was not in contradiction with "Catholic dogma." Like Franceschi, Osés, Carulla, and every other nacionalista, she saw that a strong nacionalismo was needed to fight the internal enemy: "We have the invader living within ourselves; we are, in fact, in a state of defensive war, that is to say a licit war for Argentines who have to 'defend the rights of the threatened patria.' "[46]

In this view, the patria was threatened by the antipatria, the antifatherland that, according to nacionalista ideology, had to be exterminated. This was a vision promoted, they claimed, by God. This nacionalista idea of the internal enemy was related not only to the past or the present but, most important, to the future. *Crisol*, one of the central fascist papers in 1934, promised its readers: "'The day of final reckoning is close at hand; for the sake of the patria we will make all the undignified disappear."[47]

For an Argentine these words are very disturbing. The word *desaparecido* (disappeared) was the key term of the last military dictatorship (1976–1983). Like the Nazi term "evacuation," *desaparecer* was a euphemism for assassination. At the level of language and practice, on a spectrum from rhetorical subterfuge to murder, this may have been one of the longstanding contributions of Argentine "Christianized fascism." The creation of an original idea of the internal enemy that had to be eliminated for the sake of God and the nation is part of the traumatic genealogy of the Argentine dictatorship.

Notes

Introduction

1. The question of fascism and nacionalismo relates to such Argentine events as Peronism or the last military dictatorship and more generally to Latin American forms of populism and authoritarianism. On this issue, see Halperín Donghi, *Argentina en el callejón*, 29–55; Halperín Donghi, *La larga agonía de la Argentina peronista*; Novaro and Palermo, *La dictadura militar*, 81, 93, 108–109; Luis Alberto Romero, *La crisis argentina*, 67–69, 77–81; and Vezzetti, *Pasado y presente*, 72–73.

2. For an excellent study see Vezzetti, *Pasado y presente*. See also Luis Alberto Romero, "La democracia y la sombra del proceso"; Groppo and Flier, *La imposibilidad del olvido*; and Sarlo, *Tiempo pasado*. For a theoretical and historical argument about the Latin American split between civil society and the state, see Forment, *Democracy in Latin America*, especially 425–442; Cohen and Arato, *Civil Society and Political Theory*.

3. See Finchelstein, *La Argentina fascista*.

4. More recently the antifascist view of fascism has been highly contested in different countries. For the debate in Italy, see Zunino, *La Repubblica e il suo passato*; Collotti, *Fascismo e antifascismo*; Passerini, "Memories of Resistance, Resistances of Memory"; Focardi, *La guerra della memoria*.

5. For my criticism of both tendencies, see Finchelstein, *Fascismo, liturgia e imaginario*, 10–27. See also Traverso, *Le passé, mode d'emploi*, 114–119.

6. See the excellent analysis of this topic in Altamirano, *Peronismo y cultura de izquierda*, 27–38. See also Gorelik, "Buenos Aires y el país," and more recently

his *Miradas sobre Buenos Aires*. I have myself been accused by "Peronist intellectuals" of representing an intellectual conspiracy, a "pensamiento dependiente," that is not truly Argentine. In a recent article written for *Clarín*, the most important Argentine daily, the Peronist "philosopher" Silvio Maresca argues: "Tomemos entonces por un momento, aunque cueste, la nota de Finchelstein en serio y digamos un par de cosas. El error metodológico de Germani, Tulio Halperín Donghi y tantos otros es siempre el mismo: tratar de conceptualizar los fenómenos sociales y políticos argentinos a través de la aplicación de categorías que fueron forjadas para explicar otras realidades. Es el vicio típico del pensamiento dependiente, al cual son tan afectos nuestros intelectuales." See Maresca and Galasso, "Debate," 10–11. See also Finchelstein "Fascismo y peronismo." It is not difficult to perceive the anti-Semitic undertones of Maresca's piece. The idea of Argentine Judaism as not being truly Argentine is often mixed with Holocaust denial and the anti-Semitic presentation of Argentine Jews as international purveyors of "Nazi-fascism." This equation further radicalizes the notion that Argentine nacionalismo or the experiences of the last military dictatorship have no relation whatsoever to fascist violence and practices of scapegoating, victimization, genocide, and the Holocaust. For example, an Argentine neofascist and Holocaust denier recently argued in a letter to *Clarín* that my subject position could be equated with that of the fascists. This neofascist says: "Trate denodadamente, pero no pude entender la diferencia entre el señor Finchelstein y Hitler o Mussolini." See "Y contra Finchelstein," *Clarín*, Ñ, March 4, 2006, 5. See the concerned responses from other readers: "El camino del antisemitismo," *Clarín*, Ñ, March 11, 2006, 5. See also Finchelstein, "Irving, el negador de la historia," 14.

7. I analyze this statement within the broader context of Argentine antifascism in chapter 2. For another telling example, see also Archivo Cedinci, Fondo Solari, FS 24.91. For an excellent study of Argentine antifascism, see Bisso, *Acción Argentina* and *El antifascismo argentino*.

8. See Croce, *Scritti e discorsi politici*, 1.7 and 2.46, 357. See also De Felice, *Interpretations of Fascism*, 14–23; and Zunino, *Interpretazione e memoria del fascismo*.

9. On antifascism in Italy, see Paggi, "Antifascism and the Reshaping of the Democratic Consensus in Post-1945 Italy"; Pavone, *Alle origini della Repubblica* and "La Resistenza in Italia." For other recent Italian historical debates on the legacy of antifascism in Italy, see Finchelstein, "The Fascist Canon"; and Traverso, *Le passé, mode d'emploi*.

10. Traverso, *The Origins of Nazi Violence*, 44, 153. Traverso is influenced by Nor-

bert Elias's notion of the civilizing process but does not agree with the latter's notion of fascism as a parenthetical "regression" or impasse. A similar understanding comes from Benjamin Brower, *A Desert Named Peace*. For Traverso, fascism is a logical consequence of the civilizing process. I share Traverso's criticism of Elias, but like him I believe that many "counterrevolutionary" dimensions of fascism can be related to Elias's idea of fascism as standing against progressive processes of pacification of social space. For an analysis of Elias and the Holocaust, see Chartier, "Elias, proceso de la civilización y barbarie," 35, 197–204. For an analysis of modernity and the mediations of modernization, see Lomnitz, *Modernidad indiana*, 9–12. See also Mason, "Moderno, modernità, modernizzazione"; Corner, *Riformismo e fascismo*; Griffin, *Modernism and Fascism*.

11. For an analysis of subjectivity in these terms, see Steinberg, *Listening to Reason*, 4–9, 18. For an analysis of the problem of agency in recent social thought, see Sazbón, "El sujeto en las ciencias humanas" and "Conciencia histórica y memoria electiva." See also LaCapra, *History in Transit*, 35–71.

12. I borrow the term "in motion" from Luis Alberto Romero's seminal essay "Católicos en movimiento."

13. "Corporativism" is a term with a long history, from Roman times through the Middle Ages, reemerging in Catholic social theory in the late nineteenth century. In the Italian fascist context, corporativism was, as De Grand cogently states, no more than an "illusion." It was presented as a "third way" between communism and capitalism but these "corporativist" reforms were not successful, and not even put fully in practice; eventually corporativism proved irrelevant in fascist economic policy after the Depression. De Grand notes that in the fascist sense "corporativism can be defined as a system of institutional arrangements by which capital and labor are integrated into obligatory, hierarchical, and functional units (corporations), recognized by the state, which become organs of self-government for issues relating to the specific grouping as well as the basis for participation with other corporatively organized interests in policy decisions affecting the whole society (corporative parliament). The corporations may be the controlling element in the state or they may be, as in Italy, controlled by a political authority which exists independently of and outside the corporative system." De Grand, *Italian Fascism*, 79–80. See also Maier, *In Search of Stability* and *Recasting Bourgeois Europe*.

14. Gentile, *Fascismo*, ix, x.

15. In this regard see the editors' critical introduction in Cohen and O'Connor,

Comparison and History. For other approaches to transnational history and comparative issues, see Stoler and Cooper, "Between Metropole and Colony"; Truett and Young, "Making Transnational History"; de la Guardia and Pan-Montojo, "Reflexiones sobre una historia transnacional"; Sorba et al., "Sguardi transnazionali"; Rodgers et al., "Penser l'histoire croisée"; Budde, Conrad, and Janz, *Transnationale Geschichte*.

16. See Finchelstein, *Fascismo, liturgia e imaginario*.

17. On the recent trends in political history, see Rosanvallon, "Para una historia conceptual de lo político"; Altamirano, "De la historia política a la historia intelectual"; Cattaruzza, "La historia política en el fin de siglo"; Palti, "Temporalidad y refutabilidad de los conceptos políticos"; Piccato, "¿Modelo para armar?" and "Public Sphere in Latin America." See also Joseph, *Reclaiming the Political in Latin American History*; Orsina, *Fare storia politica*.

18. Altamirano, *Para un programa intelectual y otros ensayos*, 15–16.

19. I am not alone in my emphasis on the primacy of fascist ideology over cultural politics. The works of Gentile, Sternhell, and Zunino are central in this sense. See Gentile, *Le origini dell'ideologia fascista*; Sternhell, with Sznajder and Asheri, *The Birth of Fascist Ideology*; Sternhell, "How to Think about Fascism and Its Ideology"; Zunino, *L'ideologia fascista*. See also among others, Isnenghi, *Intellettuali militanti e intellettuali funzionari*; Zagarrio, "Fascismo e intellettuali"; Turi, *Il fascismo e il consenso degli intellettuali* and *Giovanni Gentile*; Carli, *Nazione e rivoluzione*; Ventrone, *La seduzione totalitaria*.

20. De Felice, *Interpretations of Fascism*, 77, 174–175. See also Nolte, *Three Faces of Fascism*, 17–47. For taxonomists like Roger Griffin, fascism was not important in Latin America because of the regional power of the military and the church. But the military played a central role in some fascist movements, such as the Spanish one. And more recently the excellent works of the Italian historians Emilio Gentile and Enzo Collotti have stressed the important role that religious rituals and the sacred played in fascism. For Gentile, fascism was itself a political religion. See Griffin, *The Nature of Fascism*, 196. The position of taxonomist Roger Eatwell vis-à-vis Latin American or other developments outside Europe is rather unclear; see his "Universal Fascism? Approaches and Definitions," in Larsen: *Fascism outside Europe*. In his book, Eatwell studies fascism as a European phenomenon; see Eatwell, *Fascism*. See also Gentile, *Le religioni della politica*; Collotti, *Fascismo, fascismi*. For specific studies of fascist cases of political religion, see Ioanid, "The Sacralised Politics of the Romanian Iron Guard"; Steigmann-Gall, "Nazism and the Revival of Political Religion Theory"; Musiedlak, "Religion and Political Culture in the Thought of Mus-

solini." For Argentina, see Finchelstein, *Fascismo, liturgia e imaginario*. For a critical assessment of the notion of political religion, see Eatwell, "Reflections on Fascism and Religion," 145–166.

21. For the notion of "imperial eyes," see Pratt, *Imperial Eyes*. The renowned historian of fascism Stanley Payne also embraces traditional stereotypes about Latin Americans as "copying" European models and presents at least seven reasons for fascism's lack of importance in Latin America: (1) minimal political mobilization, (2) nationalism without territorial ambitions, (3) the predominance of the military, (4) the impossibility of autarchy in dependant and underdeveloped countries, (5) elitist client / patron relations, (6) the multiracial nature of society, (7) the weakness of the Left before 1960. Whereas points 1, 2, 5, and 7 are simply wrong where major South American countries like Argentina, Chile, or Brazil are concerned, it would be possible to ascribe point 3 to Spanish, Romanian, Slovak, or Croatian fascism; points 4 and 5 to Italian fascism in the southern half of the Italian peninsula; and if we replace "race" with ethnicity, we could easily present Nazi Germany before the Holocaust as a multiethnic society with regard to 6. These points did not preclude fascism from being a reality on European soil. See Payne, *A History of Fascism*, 340, and his previous *Fascism*, 167–176. See also Hennessy, "Fascism and Populism in Latin America," 255–294.

22. See Sharp, *South America Uncensored*. See also Gunther, *Inside Latin America*; Chase, *Falange*; Josephs, *Latin America*.

23. See Stoler, "Intimidations of Empire," 6.

24. See Chakrabarty, *Provincializing Europe*. See also a perceptive exchange in Ghosh and Chakrabarty, "Reflections."

25. Halperín Donghi, "España e Hispanoamérica: miradas a través del Atlántico (1825–1975)," in his *El espejo de la historia*. See also José Luis Romero, *Situaciones e ideología en Latinoamérica*, 21–29; Carmagnani, *El otro Occidente*; and Sabato, "La reacción de América."

26. See Lomnitz, *Deep Mexico Silent Mexico*, xvii.

27. See Germani, *Política y sociedad en una época de transición*, 308–309 and 319–327; and his *Autoritarismo, fascismo y populismo nacional*. On Germani, see Blanco, *Razón y modernidad*; Neiburg, *Los intelectuales y la invención del peronismo*, 183–214; and Finchelstein, "Fascismo y peronismo." On fascism in Latin America, see the now classic essay by the Brazilian scholar Hélgio Trindade, "La cuestión del fascismo en América Latina," and his *O Nazi-fascismo na América Latina*. See also Bertonha, *Fascismo, nazismo, integralismo*; Molinari Morales, *El fascismo en el Perú*; and the essays in the pathbreaking collection edited by

Stein Ugelvik Larsen, *Fascism outside Europe*. See also Harootunian, "The Future of Fascism," 28–29; Deutsch, *Las Derechas*; Spektorowski, *Argentina's Revolution of the Right*; Zanatta, *Del estado liberal a la nación católica*; Daechsel, "Scientism and Its Discontents."

28. For example, in 1913 Italian, Spanish, and Portuguese salaries represented 33, 30, and 23 percent of U.S. salaries, but 60, 54, and 42 percent of Argentine salaries, respectively. See Carmagnani, *El otro Occidente*, 243. For a fascinating historical comparison of Italian immigration in Argentina and the United States, see Baily, *Immigrants in the Lands of Promise*. For a different Argentine case, see Moya, *Cousins and Strangers*.

29. Gentile, "L'emigrazione italiana in Argentina nella politica di espansione del nazionalismo e del fascismo"; Zanatta, "I fasci in Argentina negli anni Trenta"; Newton, "Ducini, prominenti, antifascisti" and "¿Patria? ¿Cuál patria?"; Fanesi, "El antifascismo italiano en Argentina"; Grillo, "El antifascismo italiano en Francia y Argentina." More recently, see Scarzanella, *Fascisti in Sud America*; and Bertagna, *La inmigración fascista en la Argentina*. See also the study by Prisley, *Los orígenes del fascismo argentino*.

30. On this, see the important work by Ronald Newton, *The "Nazi Menace" in Argentina*.

31. See Schieder, "Fatal Attraction."

32. Mussolini, "Italia ed Argentina," in Mussolini, *Discorsi del 1927*, 191–193. See also Archivio Centrale dello Stato, Italia, Ministero della Cultura Popolare, D.G. Serv., Propaganda, B6, Argentina, 4/131.

33. See Mack Smith, *Mussolini's Roman Empire*, v–ix.

34. More studies are needed on fascist propaganda in Latin America, but a cursory survey of fascist propaganda in Colombia, Bolivia, and Chile shows that the Argentine-related policies were followed in other Latin American countries but with a smaller degree of involvement. Colombia seemed to have witnessed a similar policy of fascist collaboration with right-wing newspapers that published free fascist propaganda (primarily fascist cartoons), such as *La Patria* (Manizales) and *El Fascista* and *Derechas* (both of Bogotá). However, unlike Argentina, in Colombia the Italian embassy "lacked a propaganda nucleus" and Italian fascists in Barranquilla, Cúcuta, Cali, Medellín, and Bogotá acted as a link between Italian propaganda and the "local elements." See Archivio Centrale dello Stato, Italia, Ministero della Cultura Popolare, D.G. Serv., Propaganda, Reports B67, prot. 310, pos. st. 1–4, T801, prot. 310, prot. 395, prot. 368, 275, prot. 204, 25890, prot. 684. A fascist report for 1936 argued that in Colombia it was dubious that propaganda was useful for fascism

because of the "primitive and limited life" of the "Colombian people." It is highly probable that the fascist prejudice against Colombians was related to their high level of illiteracy. More significant, the fascist reading of Colombian reality showed no concern whatsoever for the rhetorically sophisticated aspects of Colombian political culture and the proximity of the Colombian liberal governments to more progressive or populist forms of political engagement. For an analysis of Colombia's political culture, see Roldán, "The Local Limitations to a National Political Movement." Fascists generally displayed the same paternalism and negative vision of Latin America with respect to other countries that had Latin American citizens of non-Italian origin, and this attitude certainly helps to explain the scarce success of fascist propaganda in many other countries. See also Archivio Centrale dello Stato, Italia, Ministero della Cultura Popolare, D.G. Serv., Propaganda, Reports B28 68; ibid., D.G. Serv., Propaganda, N.U.P.I.E., B16 13.1, Colombia, pos. st. 1.5, T1522, T2299; ibid., D.G. Serv., Propaganda, B16 11.1, Cile, pos. st. 4, T2484; ibid., D.G. Serv., Propaganda, N.U.P.I.E., B16 7.1, Bolivia, pos. st. 4, T86, T563, T57. Fascist propaganda regarding Italian immigrants in Brazil has, on the other hand, been well documented by Brazilian historians and there is no need to deal with it here. I would nonetheless argue that fascist propaganda aimed at Brazil was based on a more negative, and probably racist, vision for the future of Brazil than is generally recognized and that it was more engaged with the Italian community in Brazil and less with Brazilian society at large. See Bertonha, *O fascismo e os imigrantes italianos no Brasil*; and dos Santos and Carneiro, *Os seguidores do Duce*. See also, on Peru, Ciccarelli, "Fascism and Politics in Peru during the Benavides Regime." For a more general, if restrictive, approach, see Albónico, *L'America Latina e l'Italia*. For a fine analysis of fascist propaganda in the United States, see Luconi, *La "diplomazia paralela."* For Britain, see Baldoli, *Exporting Fascism*. For Mexico, see Franco Savarino, "The Sentinel of the Bravo: Italian Fascism in Mexico, 1922–1935," in Sørensen and Mallett, *International Fascism*; and Savarino, "Juego de ilusiones."

35. I have recently explored this genealogy in my book *La Argentina fascista*, chap. 6.

1. Transnational Fascism

1. See United Kingdom, *Documents on German Foreign Policy*, doc. 211. See also Archivio Centrale dello Stato, Italia, Archivi Fascisti, Segreteria Particolare del Duce, Carteggio riservato, B4 F, B4 F, Bottai Giuseppe, Sf. 4, doc. 040014; ibid., Ministero della Cultura Popolare, D.G. Serv., gabinetto B158, June 1934.

2.   "Il nostro orgoglio e la nostra sicurezza di grande Nazione. Tra le incertezze di altri Popoli noi abbiamo: Un regime saldo; Il popolo concorde; La parola precisa e decisa del Duce, il quale vede, prevede e provvede, ed ha sempre ragione." Archivo del Ministerio de Relaciones Exteriores y Culto, Argentina, División Política, caja 2386, Italia, expediente 1, año 1933, N39, R.E. 1/33. See also *Giornale d'Italia*, March 11, 1933.

3.   United Kingdom, *Documents on German Foreign Policy*, doc. 211. For the previous meeting with Göring and other Nazi leaders during these years, see United States National Archives, *Papers of Count Ciano*, roll 1, frame 173, frame 105 (Frank), frame 238 (Von Neurath.)

4.   See Sternhell, *Les anti-Lumières*.

5.   The most famous expressions of the idea that fascism is shaped by anticommunism are by Ernst Nolte and A. J. Gregor. See Nolte, *Three Faces of Fascism*; Gregor, "Fascism, Marxism and Some Considerations Concerning Classification"; Furet and Nolte, *Fascism and Communism*. For an intelligent criticism of the "anticommunist paradigm" of Nolte, Furet, and others, see Traverso, "De l'anticommunisme." For Nolte, fascism is basically anti-Marxism (in his view, a combination of Marx and Nietzsche). The historian Zeev Sternhell stresses the antiliberal nature of fascism. Thus, for Sternhell, fascism has two essential components: (1) a brand of antiliberal and antibourgeois tribal nationalism based on social Darwinism and often biological determinism; and (2) a radical leftist antimaterialist revision of Marxism. See Sternhell, with Sznajder and Asheri, *The Birth of Fascist Ideology*, 9, 12; Sternhell, *Neither Right nor Left*, 27; Sternhell, *La droite révolutionnaire*, ix–lxxvi; Sternhell, "Fascist 'Ideology.' "

6.   See Traverso, *A feu et à sang*.

7.   See Mosse, *Masses and Man* and *The Nationalization of the Masses*. For Mosse's theory of fascism, see his *The Fascist Revolution*.

8.   See Schieder, "Fatal Attraction." See also Ben-Ghiat, "Italian Fascists and National Socialists"; De Grand, *Fascist Italy and Nazi Germany*; Knox, *Common Destiny* and *To the Threshold of Power*; Burrin, *Fascisme, nazisme, autoritarisme*; and Bessel, *Fascist Italy and Nazi Germany*.

9.   See Finchelstein, "Fascism Becomes Desire." See also Horkheimer and Adorno, *Dialectic of Enlightenment*; Zaretsky, *Secrets of the Soul*, 217–245.

10.   Paxton, *The Anatomy of Fascism*, 23.

11.   See Megaro, *Mussolini in the Making*, 153.

12.   Mussolini would later recall the explosion as "the most beautiful in my life." See Mack Smith, *Mussolini*, 28.

13.   This was for Zeev Sternhell the essence of fascism: a synthesis of organic

nationalism and anti-Marxist nonmaterialist socialism, a revolutionary ideology based on a simultaneous rejection of liberalism, Marxism, and democracy. By opposing liberalism and Marxism, fascism presented a project to society: "a socialism for the nation as a whole, a revolution for the nation as a whole, a nationalism that despised the bourgeois world, that believed in a civilization of monks and soldiers, came together to form an attractive, powerful and successful ideological synthesis" (Sternhell, "Fascism," 150).

14. Marinetti also warned about the dangers of both red and black Bolshevism. See "Il discorso di Marinetti," *Il Popolo d'Italia*, October 11, 1919. On the topic of futurism and early fascism, see Gentile, *Le origini dell'ideologia fascista*, 109–128.

15. See "La lista elettorale del blocco fascista a milano: i nostri candidati," *Il Popolo d'Italia*, October 26, 1919.

16. Bibliothèque de documentation internationale contemporaine, Dossier France, GF Delta, L'attitude des fascistes: Mussolini, May 25, 1921.

17. D'Annunzio had occupied the now Yugoslavian city of Fiume with radical squads of followers, in an effort to establish a protofascist experiment. Mussolini officially approved and supported D'Annunzio, but secretly opposed the poet's quest for leadership of the radical Right. See the following articles, all in *Il Popolo d'Italia*: "Il trionfale ingresso di Gabriele D'Annunzio a Fiume," September 14, 1919; Mussolini, "Gesto di rivolta," September 14, 1919; September 23, 1919, 1; "Fiume è la rivolta della 'Grande Proletaria,'" September 28, 1919; Mussolini, "Il discorso," September 28, 1919.

18. For some examples, all in *Il Popolo d'Italia*, see "Il programma," October 11, 1919; Agostino Lanzillo, "Ricostruzione: la premessa," October 8, 1919; "I postulati elettorali del blocco fascista," November 2, 1919; Mussolini, "Contro le ignobili speculazioni social-borghesi-nittiane," September 26, 1919; Mussolini, "I fantasmi idioti!" September 26, 1919. See also Mack Smith, *Mussolini*, 35.

19. Mussolini, "La significazione," *Il Popolo d'Italia*, October 25, 1919.

20. Bibliothèque de documentation internationale contemporaine, Dossier France. Mussolini, "Disciplina," *Il Popolo d'Italia*, July 24, 1921.

21. See De Felice, *Mussolini il duce*. See also Roberts, "Myth Style and Substance in the Totalitarian Dynamic in Fascist Italy"; Colarizi, *L'opinione degli Italiani sotto il regime*. See also Corner, "Italian Fascism"; Bosworth, *Mussolini's Italy*.

22. Levi, *Conversazioni e interviste*, 245.

23. "Another necessary component was, of course, the prohibition of any criticism or sarcasm. One of the first Mussolini speeches I remember was, I think,

the one about 'libro e moschetto, fascista perfetto' ('book and rifle make the perfect Fascist'). At the end of it, Il Duce brought out from under the windowsill a book and a rifle: a wonderful coup de theatre. I remember having heard about this at home from an anti-Fascist uncle who had seen it in the cinema. (If it was not that speech, it must have been another from the same time, shortly after 1930; this can be checked on film.) I recall my uncle aping Mussolini's gestures, his fists firmly on his hips, and at a certain point blowing his nose into his hand. I remember my aunt's interjection: 'Well, what do you expect? He's a bricklayer!' A few days later, I saw the newsreel of the speech, and recognized the grimaces described by my uncle—even the quick blowing of the nose. The image of Mussolini came to me filtered through the sarcastic discourse of adults (certain adults), which jarred with the chorus of praise. But that chorus was expressed in public, whereas the reservations were confined to private conversations, and never put a dent in the facade of unanimity of which the regime made a great show." See Calvino, "Il Duce's Portraits," 34. On the Mussolini cult and fascist public rituals at large, see Berezin, *Making the Fascist Self*; Falasca-Zamponi, *Fascist Spectacle*; and Gentile, *Il culto del littorio*.

24. On antifascism, see Traverso, *À feu et à sang*, 305–331; Rabinbach, "Legacies of Antifascism."

25. Archivio Centrale dello Stato, Collezione Mussolini, 94. These meetings were in Switzerland and Holland, and they were attended by representatives of Italy, Norway, Spain, France, Denmark, Belgium, Ireland, Switzerland, and Czechoslovakia, including Primo de Rivera and Quisling. The meetings were also supported by Argentine fascists. On fascist universalism, see Ledeen, *Universal Fascism*; Sabatini, *L'internazionale di Mussolini*; Cuzzi, *L'internazionale delle camicie nere*. See also Traverso, *À feu et à sang*, 73.

26. Archivio Centrale dello Stato, Rome, Italy, Archivio Asvero Gravelli, B4 F4, 1.

27. Hitler reiterated his arguments in his testament: "But nor have I left any doubt that if the nations of Europe are once more to be treated only as collections of stocks and shares of these international conspirators in money and finance, then those who carry the real guilt for the murderous struggle, this people will also be held responsible: the Jews!" Hitler's testament set down in Berlin, April 29, 1945, reprinted in Arad, Gutman, and Margaliot, *Documents on the Holocaust*, 134, 162. See also Herf, *The Jewish Enemy*; Koonz, *The Nazi Conscience*; and Kershaw, *Hitler, the Germans, and the Final Solution*.

28. In addition, Mussolini supported among others French, Croatian, and Norwegian fascists. He initially supported Austrian fascists against the Nazis, but increasingly approached the Nazis, after a long period of personal distaste for

Hitler's version of fascism. Whereas the Duce was a model for Hitler, Mussolini in the early 1930s considered Hitler a clownish and mediocre figure.

29. The Jewish question remained one of the few fields of relative autonomy for Italian fascism until 1943.

30. The title of the film is *Salò o le 120 Giornate di Sodoma* (1975). For a criticism of Pasolini in this sense, see Levi, *Conversazioni e interviste*, 251. A similar representation of fascism as reactionary can be found in Bertolucci's film *1900* (1976). For some actual "social" examples from the Social Republic, see "Mussolini ai fascisti di Torino," *Corriere della Sera*, February 4, 1945, 1; *La Stampa*, January 27, 1945, 1; *Il Secolo*, January 26, 1945, 1; *La Repubblica Fascista*, February 5, 1945, 1; *La Repubblica Fascista*, February 3, 1945, 1; Archivio Centrale dello Stato, Archivio Asvero Gravelli, scatola 2 76 / B 19.

31. See Hilberg, *The Destruction of the European Jews*, 660–679; Zuccotti, *The Italians and the Holocaust*; Picciotto Fargion, *Il libro della memoria*.

32. See Sternhell, *The Birth of Fascist Ideology*, 4–6; Friedlander, "Nazism" and *Memory, History, and the Extermination of the Jews of Europe*, 26.

33. R. J. B. Bosworth argues that the fascist regime "at a minimal count, with its repressive policies at home and its aggressive wars in its empire and in Europe, must bear responsibility for the premature death of a million people." See Bosworth, *Mussolini's Italy*, 4. For Spain, see Casanova et al., *Morir, matar, sobrevivir*; Casanova, "Civil Wars, Revolutions and Counterrevolutions in Finland, Spain, and Greece"; Del Boca, *I gas di Mussolini*. See also Rodogno, *Fascism's European Empire*. On fascist colonial policies, see also Pergher, "Impero immaginario, impero vissuto."

34. I borrow the concept of "laboratories of fascism" from Traverso, *The Origins of Nazi Violence*.

35. Paxton, *The Anatomy of Fascism*, 148–171.

36. See Arendt, "Ideology and Terror" and *The Origins of Totalitarianism*, 158–184; also Arendt, "The Seeds of a Fascist International," 147.

37. Mussolini, "La significazione," *Il Popolo d'Italia*, October 25, 1919; Mussolini, "Un programma," *Il Popolo d'Italia*, February 26, 1920. See also Grandi, *Le origini e la missione del fascismo*, 1, 52–57, 58–62, 66–71; "Lo spirito e il compito del fascismo," *L'Idea Nazionale*, May 24, 1924.

38. Gentile, *Le origini dell'ideologia fascista*, 4–6. See also the interesting study by Simonini, *Il linguaggio di Mussolini*.

39. For the best example of this trend, see Mack Smith, *Mussolini's Roman Empire*.

40. Gramsci, *Socialismo e fascismo*.

41. See the following articles, all by Mussolini in *Il Popolo d'Italia*: "Dopo l'adunata

ascista: verso l'azione," October 13, 1919; "Logica e demagogia," October 26, 1919; "I volti e le maschere," March 3, 1920; "Dopo un anno: il fascismo," March 26, 1920; "Fatti, non parole!" March 30, 1920; "Nella foresta degli 'ismi,'" March 31, 1920; "Panglossismo," April 11, 1920; "Verso la reazione!" April 29, 1920. See also Archivio Centrale dello Stato, Italia, Mostra della Rivoluzione Fascista, B91 F154, sala Dotrinna, SF 2, "tabelloni murali."

42. On this topic, see Adamson, "Avant-garde Modernism and Italian Fascism," and *Avant-Garde Florence*; Ben-Ghiat, *Fascist Modernities*.

43. Although I pay attention to antifascist conceptions of fascism, my emphasis does not rely much on Walter Benjamin's somewhat integralist aesthetic notion of fascism. For Benjamin, "the logical result of Fascism is the introduction of aesthetics into political life." See Benjamin, "The Work of Art in the Age of Mechanical Reproduction," in Benjamin, *Illuminations*, 241. On Benjamin's notions of fascism, see also Benjamin, "Theories of German Fascism." For contemporary arguments that aestheticize and decontextualize fascism and victimization in ways that Benjamin would have never dreamed of, see Žižek, *Did Somebody Say Totalitarianism?*, and Agamben, *Remnants of Auschwitz*. More recently Žižek argues: "There is no fascism avant la lettre, because it is the letter itself that composes the bundle (or, in Italian, fascio) of elements that is fascism proper." See Žižek, "Learning to Love Leni Riefenstahl." For a more nuanced approach by Žižek, which is nonetheless detached from recent historical debates, see his "The Two Totalitarianisms." For a criticism of these approaches see LaCapra, "Tropisms of Intellectual History," 523; Finchelstein "The Holocaust Canon," 16.

44. Spackman, *Fascist Virilities*; Schnapp, *Staging Fascism*; Falasca-Zamponi, *Fascist Spectacle* and "Fascism and Aesthetics"; Vander, "Estetica e fascismo." For an excellent assessment of the contributions of this trend, see Fogu, "Fascism and Philosophy."

45. See, for example, Volt, *Programma della destra fascista*, 49–51.

46. "Ma fuse e confuse nella sostanza." See Mussolini, "Blocco fascista anticagoiesco delle 'teste di ferro!'" *Il Popolo d'Italia*, October 24, 1919.

47. See Mussolini, "Sintesi della lotta politica" (1924), in *Opera omnia*, 21.46.

48. See Gramsci, "La guerra è la guerra," *L'Ordine Nuovo*, January 31, 1921, reprinted in *Socialismo e fascismo*, 55.

49. On fascist anti-Semitism, see Collotti, *Il fascismo e gli ebrei*; Sarfatti, *Gli ebrei nell'Italia fascista*; De Felice, *Storia degli ebrei italiani sotto il fascismo*; Michaelis, *Mussolini and the Jews*. See also Belardelli, "L'antisemitismo nell'ideologia

fascista." On fascist racism, see the excellent study by Gillette, *Racial Theories in Fascist Italy*.

50. Archivio Centrale dello Stato, Italia, Mostra della Rivoluzione Fascista, B93 F159 SF 1, "Il Sacrificio"; ibid., B93 F155 SF 1, sala Sanzioni Impero; ibid., Mostra della Rivoluzione Fascista, B91 F154, sala Dotrinna, SF 2, "tabelloni murali." See also ibid., Archivi Fascisti, Segreteria Particolare del Duce, Carteggio riservato, B48 F242/R, Salvemini, Prof. Gaetano, SF 1, and B48, L'Impero, December 2–3, 1925, 1. See also Borges, "Deutsches Requiem," in *El Aleph*; and Bataille, *Visions of Excess*. On the topic of fascism and the abject, see also Kristeva, *Powers of Horror*; and Stone, "The Changing Face of the Enemy in Fascist Italy."

51. On the centrality of the fascist vision of gender and masculinity, see Mosse, *Nationalism and Sexuality* and *The Image of Man*. See also De Grazia, *How Fascism Ruled Women*.

52. On the conceptual history of totalitarianism, see Traverso, *Il totalitarismo*; Rabinbach, "Moments of Totalitarianism"; Ben-Ghiat, "A Lesser Evil?"; Beltrametti, "L'autorappresentazione totalitaria del fascismo italiano"; Gentile, "Fascism and the Italian Road to Totalitarianism."

53. Mussolini, "La dottrina del fascismo," in *Opera omnia*, 34.119–121. See also Mussolini, *Fascism*, 27.

54. On this topic, see Arendt, "Ideology and Terror."

55. See, for example, Archivio Centrale dello Stato, Italia, Archivi Fascisti, Segreteria Particolare del Duce, Carteggio riservato, B50 251/RF, "Avanti!" Pietro Nenni, 1931; Bibliothèque de documentation internationale contemporaine, Dossier France, Daniel Guerin, F Delta 721, 51/1, Vingt ans d'histoire allemande; Gobetti, *On Liberal Revolution*, 226; "1935," *Cuaderno di Giustizia e libertá* 12 (1935).

56. Slavoj Žižek seems to shift from argument into hyperbole. For him, the rationalist background of communism explains the "emancipatory potential" of Stalinism. Žižek, *Did Somebody Say Totalitarianism?*, 131.

57. On the idea of listening to reason, see Steinberg, *Listening to Reason*. On the Nazi appropriation of Beethoven, see Dennis, *Beethoven in German Politics*. I want to thank Eli Zaretsky for sharing his thoughts about Lenin, Beethoven, and the Enlightenment with me.

58. Luc Besson's *The Professional* (1994) presents a similar situation, in which a person who listens to Beethoven performs gruesome killings. The killer in *American Psycho* (2000), who listens to Phil Collins while massacring people, may be seen as ironic downgrading of this aesthetic movement.

59. See Levi, *The Drowned and the Saved*, 105. On Levi's identification of Nazism with fascism, see Levi, *Conversazioni e interviste*, 245, 250.

60. See LaCapra, *History and Memory after Auschwitz*, 27–30; LaCapra, *Representing the Holocaust*, 100–110; and LaCapra, *Writing History, Writing Trauma*, 94.

61. For some examples, see Panunzio, *Diritto, forza e violenza*, 17; Suckert (Malaparte), *L'Europa vivente*, xlviii, 1–5, 22–25, 34, 111–119; Suckert, *Italia barbara*. For an early criticism of fascism's appreciation of violence "for its own sake," see Mondolfo, *Per la comprensione storica del fascismo*, i–iii, xv, xxxiv–xxxv, and Mondolfo, "Forza e violenza nella storia (aprendo la discussione)," in Panunzio, *Diritto, forza e violenza*, viii, xi, xiii, xv, xvii, xviii, xix.

62. Archivio Centrale dello Stato, Italia, Mostra della Rivoluzione Fascista, B93 F159, SF 1. Mussolini said: "I don't give a damn [*me ne frego*]—the proud motto of the fighting squads scrawled by a wounded man on his bandages, is not only an act of philosophic stoicism; it sums up a doctrine that is not merely political: it is evidence of a fighting spirit that accepts all risks. It signifies a new style of Italian life. The Fascist accepts and loves life; he rejects and despises suicide as cowardly. Life as he understands it means duty, elevation, conquest; life must be lofty and full; it must be lived for oneself but above all for others, both nearby and far off, present and future." Mussolini, "La dottrina del fascismo," in *Opera omnia*, 34.119–121.

63. Archivio Centrale dello Stato, Italia, Mostra della Rivoluzione Fascista, B93 F159, SF 1.

64. See, for example, ibid., Mostra della Rivoluzione Fascista, B93, F158; B91, F154, sala Dotrinna, SF 2, "tabelloni murali."

65. See Mussolini, "Vivere pericolosamente," (1924) in *Opera omnia*, 21.40.

66. See Mussolini, "La dottrina del fascismo" in ibid., 34.119–121; and Mussolini, *Fascism*, 30. For a more specific fascist self-understanding of the state as shown in the "permanent" fascist exhibition of 1942, see Archivio Centrale dello Stato, Italia, Mostra della Rivoluzione Fascista, B91, F154, sala Dotrinna, SF 2, "tabelloni murali," "Lo stato fascista," and "I codici di Mussolini." See also Carli, "Par la volonté du Chef et par l'oeuvre du Parti"; and Schnapp, *Anno X*.

67. See Stoler, "On Degrees of Imperial Sovereignty," 135.

68. *Dizionario Mussoliniano* (Milan: Hoepli, 1939), 45, 88.

69. For a study of this notion within other forms of contemporary imperialism that embrace the notion of a "war without an end," see Wood, *Empire of Capital*, 143–151. Wood does not mention that fascism may have been the first imperialism to embrace this notion of war, thus being a precedent to its contemporary followers. See also Maier, *Among Empires*.

70. Archivio Centrale dello Stato, Italia, Mostra della Rivoluzione Fascista, B93, F155, SF 1, Impero. See also ibid., Collezione Mussolini, 92, 47.

71. Mussolini, "La dottrina del fascismo," in *Opera omnia*, 34.119–121. See also Mussolini, *Fascism*, 30–31.

72. An equally pertinent joke would be the definition of an Argentine as "an Italian who happens to speak Spanish but thinks he / she is British."

73. In addition, in 1910 Mussolini gave a speech denouncing the persecution of anarchists in Argentina. In this speech Mussolini decried the Argentine residence law, which was similar to laws he enacted later as the leader of the fascist regime. Mussolini justified the assassination of Argentine police Chief Ramón L. Falcón by anarchists, calling Falcón "the odious butcher of workmen." Mussolini denounced Argentine martial law and defined Argentina as a "liberticide Republic." He concluded, "Our gesture . . . will serve to stir the still water of our local political life." Mussolini addressed a protest mass meeting of 150 persons in front of the Argentine consulate at Forlì. He was later sentenced to pay a fine of ten lire "for having promoted at Forlì a demonstration against the Argentine Republic without due notice." See Archivio Ministero degli Affari Esteri, Serie Z—Contenzioso, buste 47–51. I want to thank José Moya for this archival reference. See also Megaro, *Mussolini in the Making*, 199–200.

74. For some examples of this sort of fascist orientalism, see the following, all in *Il Popolo d'Italia*: "Il paradiso tropicale di Buddha," May 11, 1924; "Il pellegrinaggio della Mecca," August 14, 1924; "Al piedi dell'Everest," September 7, 1924; "Sugli altipiani misteriosi del Tibet," September 21, 1924; "Un venerdì sulla frontiera dell'Afganistan," December 21, 1924; "Misticismi e pervertimenti dell'India: i saggi di Bramha ed i pazzi del Kama-Sutra," December 28, 1924; "Una fumeria d'oppio a Singapore," January 18, 1925; "Eterno femminino d'Oriente," March 7, 1925. Also see "Fascino d'oriente," *Corriere della Sera*, September 6, 1927.

75. On orientalism, see the classic work by Said, *Orientalism*. For an analysis of fascist "oriental" policies, see De Felice, *Il fascismo e l'Oriente*.

76. See C. Poletti, "L'America latina," *Il Popolo d'Italia*, September 26, 1924. For examples of "orientalist" travelers' accounts, see the following, all in *Il Popolo d'Italia*: "Il periplo dell'America Latina," June 17, 1924; "Sulla rotta di Magellano," July 26, 1924; "Lima de los Reyes," September 14, 1924; "Guayaquil: verità e leggenda," October 4, 1924; "Dall'Araucani in fiore alla terra dei Patagoni," June 2, 1928. Other examples are "Dall'Atlantico al Pacifico sorvolando le Ande," *Corriere della Sera*, September 16, 1930; "Viaggio nelle Ande

Boliviane: la millenaria vita dell'immutabile indio," *Il Giornale d'Italia*, July 14, 1935; "Colori e silenzi d'un mercato indiano," *Il Giornale d'Italia*, July 28, 1935; "Il mistero impenetrabile dell Matto Grosso: il verde inferno della jungla brasiliana," *Il Giornale d'Italia*, August 27, 1935.

77. See Archivio Centrale dello Stato, Italia, Ministero della Cultura Popolare, D.G. Serv., B8, Argentina, 1938, I / 4 / 3, T1061, pos. 2-1-4; ibid., D.G. Serv., B7, Argentina, 1937, I / 4 / 37, T2339, pos. R.G.I-5; ibid., D.G. Serv., Propaganda, B12, Argentina, Varie 5, V8, 26959.

78. See Francesco Coppola, "I paesi d'emigrazione per la difessa dei comuni interessi," *L'Idea Nazionale*, May 11, 1923.

79. See Archivio Centrale dello Stato, Italia, Ministero della Cultura Popolare, D.G. Serv., B8, Argentina, 1938, I / 4 / 3, T1061, pos. 2-1-4.

80. "The illegal, arbitrary, tyrannical and despicable South American dictatorships are nothing else than the consequence of an unchecked democratic infatuation." Sandro Volta, "L'America Latina di Siegfried," *Critica Fascista*, May 15, 1934, 193–194. See also Battista Pellegrini, "Per la nostra espansione nel Sud America," *Il Popolo d'Italia*, July 1928; Carlo Curcio, "La politica internazionale e l'Italia: Nord e Sud in America," *Critica Fascista*, January 1, 1929, 6; Giuseppe De Luigi, "Il comunismo in America Latina," *Critica Fascista*, May 1, 1940, 221–223; Aldo Bizzarri, "America 'Latina'?" *Critica Fascista*, September 15, 1940, 372–373. See also the remarks of the Chilean Gennaro Prieto, "Necessità di scoprire nuovamente l'America," *Civiltà Fascista*, June, 1934, 505.

81. See Archivo del Ministerio de Relaciones Exteriores y Culto, Argentina, División Política, caja 2717, Italia, expediente 19, año 1928, N78, R.E.; Italy, Senato del Regno, *Discorso del capo del governo ministro degli affari esteri*, 6.8; Battista Pellegrini, "Per la nostra espansione nel Sud America," *Il Popolo d'Italia*, July 22, 1928.

82. See Archivio Centrale dello Stato, Italia, Archivi Fascisti, Segreteria Particolare del Duce, Carteggio riservato, B48 F242 / R, Salvemini, Prof. Gaetano, SF 1; Mussolini, "Rettifiche di tiro," in *Opera omnia*, 26.34.

83. See Archivio Centrale dello Stato, Italia, Ministero della Cultura Popolare, D.G. Serv., Propaganda, B8, Argentina, 1938, I / 4 / 3. It is interesting to note that Mussolini's father, Alessandro, had also complained about Italian emigration to South America and blamed "bourgeois Italy" for not caring about Italians leaving the country. See Megaro, *Mussolini in the Making*, 31. In his socialist years Mussolini put forward his peculiar idea that Italian emigrants abroad were better, more "tenacious, courageous, and sober" than "the work-

ers of other nations." See Mussolini, "Di qua e di là emigranti italiani," (1909) in *Opera omnia*, 2.238.

84. See Enrico Corradini, "L'emigrazione dopo la guerra," *L'Idea Nazionale*, January 4, 1923. On Mussolini as an immigrant, see his speech to the fascists abroad of December 1925. Archivo del Ministerio de Relaciones Exteriores y Culto, Argentina, División Política, caja 2386, Italia, expediente 1, año 1925, 2 / 11.

85. Mussolini, "L'espansione italiana nel mondo: Milano, 2 aprile 1923," in Mussolini, *La nuova politica dell'Italia*, 1.101; Mussolini, "La conferenza per l'emigrazione: Roma, 15 maggio 1924," in ibid. 3.95–98; "I lavori della conferenza dell'emigrazione," *Il Popolo d'Italia*, May 17, 1924; Mussolini, "Per la conferenza internazionale dell'emigrazione," in Mussolini, *Discorsi del 1925*, 257–259. See also Mussolini, "Risultati delle trattative con la repubblica del Brasile per il regolamento della nostra emigrazione," in *Opera omnia*, 21.209–216. See also Luigi Luiggi, "I desideri degli Italiani all'estero e specialmente in America," *Critica Fascista*, September 15, 1923, 139–140; Gino Arias, "La nuova politica dell'emigrazione," *Gerarchia*, January 1924, 27–32; Lastra, *Lavoratori nostri d'oltralpe*, 90–92.

86. On this topic see Santinon, *I fasci italiani all'ester*; de Caprariis, " 'Fascism for Export'?"; Gentile, "La politica estera del Partito fascista."

87. Mussolini, "Sulla politica estera: Senato del Regno, 11 dicembre 1924," in Mussolini, *La nuova politica dell'Italia*, 3.495–497, 505. See also Camillo Pellizzi, "Il fascismo e l'estero," *Il Popolo d'Italia*, November 2, 1923; Francesco Geraci, "La politica dell'emigrazione," *Il Popolo d'Italia*, September 11, 1924; "L'azione del fascismo all'estero nelle direttive fissate dall'on. Mussolini," *L'Idea Nazionale*, November 3, 1925; "Il fascismo e il sentimento nazionale degli emigrati," *Il Giornale d'Italia*, October 5, 1929.

88. For the concept of imagined communities see Anderson, *Imagined Communities*.

89. See Archivo del Ministerio de Relaciones Exteriores y Culto, División Política, caja 2293, Italia, Embajada Argentina en Italia, expediente 10, año 1924. For some example in the press, see "L'emigrazione in Argentina," *Il Messaggero*, February 28, 1924; "Gli italiani emigrati nell Argentina," *Il Giornale d'Italia*, February 29, 1924. See also Italy, Ministero degli Affari Esteri, *I documenti diplomatici italiani*, vol. 7, doc. 277, T496 / 42, 1929, Il capo del governo e ministro degli esteri, Mussolini, all'ambasciatore a Buenos Aires, Martin Franklin.

90. For some examples see Guido de Lucca, "L'Italia nel mondo: problemi del

rimpatrio degli Italiani," *Critica Fascista*, December 15, 1938, 60–61; "La voce del sangue: emigrazione e razza," *Il Giornale d'Italia*, December 18, 1938; *La Difesa della Razza*, December 5, 1938, 7; Francesco Costa, "Emigrazione e rimpatrio," *Universalità Fascista*, January 1939, 77–86.

91. Arnaldo Mussolini, "Italiani nel mondo," *Il Popolo d'Italia*, February 5, 1928, 1; "Italiani nel mondo," *L'Impero*, December 20, 1927.

92. The Italian fascist press often complained about Argentina's opposition to the Italian education of Argentine children of Italian origin. See "'Tecnici e operai italiani obbligati in Argentina a naturalizzarsi sotto minaccia di licenziamento," *Il Giornale d'Italia*, March 13, 1929; "Per l'insegnamento della lingua italiana," *Il Messaggero*, December 29, 1933; Mario Intaglietta, "Perquè si chiudono le scuole italiane di Buenos Aires," *Il Giornale d'Italia*, July 12, 1939; "L'accordo fra Italia e Argentina," *Il Giornale d'Italia*, August 24, 1938. On the history of indirect participation of foreigners in Argentine politics, see Sabato, *The Many and the Few*.

93. I deal with this topic in the next chapter.

94. See Franco De Felice, "Gli Italiani in Argentina," *Gerarchia*, September 22, 1922, 516–518. See also, for nationalist and protofascist argument of this sort, Corrado Zoli, "Un po' di Patria che si disperde," *L'Idea Nazionale*, October 29, 1921. See also Guariglia, *Ricordi*, 332.

95. Guariglia, *Ricordi*, 335.

96. See Archivio Centrale dello Stato, Italia, Archivi Fascisti, Segreteria Particolare del Duce, Carteggio riservato, B32 F, Gran Consiglio, SF 15, 1937, inserto A. See also *Il regime fascista per la grandezza d'Italia: discorso pronunciato il 26 maggio 1926 al Parlamento* (Rome: Libreria del Littorio, 1926), 11, 17–21. See also Agostino Lanzillo, "Mussolini e il problema demografico," *Critica Fascista*, December 1, 1928, 447–448; Curcio, *La politica demografica del fascismo*, 13–32.

97. He argued: "In the Argentine republic, a country ten times bigger than Italy and where eighty to one hundred million people could live at ease, the negative birth rate [*denatalità*] is creating a slaughter and . . . it is being forecast that in 1939, the population of Argentina would remain at the current twelve million inhabitants, but they will become twelve million old people [*dodici milioni di vecchi*]." Mussolini considered Malthusian economics to be wrong and actually complained that South America, like Africa, had "vast zones" of "virgin" territories. This was the kind of statement that Argentines could not appreciate. At the end of the article Mussolini warned that the typical laissez-faire attitude could be fatal, insofar as the survival of the "white race" was a

question of "life and death." Mussolini, "La razza bianca muore?" *Il Messaggero*, September 5, 1934. See also Virginio Gayda, "Difesa dei bianchi," *Il Giornale d'Italia*, February 29, 1940. For a detailed study of fascist "totalitarian" demography, see Ipsen, *Dictating Demography*.

98. Mussolini, "Italia e Argentina," in *Opera omnia*, 25.219. On some occasions Mussolini openly talked with Argentine visitors about his obsession with demography. See Archivio Centrale dello Stato, Italia, Ministero della Cultura Popolare, D.G. Serv., Propaganda, B5, Argentina, I / 4 / 3. See also "Política: una entrevista con el Doctor Fresco," *Córdoba*, May 13, 1935.

99. Archivio Centrale dello Stato, Italia, Ministero della Cultura Popolare, D.G. Serv., Propaganda, B8, Argentina, 1938, I / 4 / 1, T487.

100. Mussolini, "Italia e Argentina," in *Opera omnia*, 25.221.

101. Mussolini, "La funzione dello stato corporativo," in ibid., 22.28.

102. See Archivio Centrale dello Stato, Italia, Ministero della Cultura Popolare, D.G. Serv., Propaganda, B8, Argentina, 1938, I / 4 / 1, T487.

103. See Archivo del Ministerio de Relaciones Exteriores y Culto, Argentina, División Política, caja 22, Italia, "Entrevista concedida por el señor Mussolini al señor Juan Carlos Goyeneche," expediente 7, año 1943, folio 4. See also Archivio Centrale dello Stato, Italia, Ministero della Cultura Popolare, D.G. Serv., Propaganda, B8, Argentina, 1938, I / 4 / 1, T487; Mussolini, "Italia e Argentina" in *Opera omnia*, 26.212, 421.

2. The Argentine Road to Fascism

1. Archivo General de la Nación Argentina, Archivo Agustín P. Justo, caja 49, doc. 170, and caja 54, doc. 12. See also Archivio Centrale dello Stato, Italia, Ministero della Cultura Popolare, D.G. Serv., B4, Argentina, 1934, Movimento Fascista in Argentina, I 4 / 8.

2. Archivo General de la Nación Argentina, Archivo Agustín P. Justo, caja 49, doc. 166.

3. Ibid., caja 54, doc. 12.

4. Ibid. For other examples, see ibid., caja 49, doc. 105; caja 49, doc. 107; caja 36, doc. 3.

5. See Deutsch, *Las Derechas*; Buchrucker, *Nacionalismo y Peronismo*; Klein, "The Legión Cívica Argentina and the Radicalisation of Argentine Nacionalismo during the *Década Infame*"; Spektorowski, *Argentina's Revolution of the Right*. For a survey, see Emmanuel Kahan, "El nacionalismo autoritario argentino."

6. See Navarro Gerassi, *Los nacionalistas*; Zuleta Álvarez, *El nacionalismo argen-*

tino; "Enrique Zuleta Álvarez," in Herrero and Herrero, *Las ideas y sus histo-riadores*, 192; "Presencia de Irazusta en la Argentina Contemporánea," in Zuleta Álvarez, Saravi, and Díaz Araujo, *Homenaje a Julio Irazusta*, 11–26; Zuleta Álvarez, "Historia de una revista nacionalista Nueva Política," "El nacionalismo argentino y la historiografía contemporánea," and *España en América*; Mutsuki, *Julio Irazusta*; Rock, *Authoritarian Argentina*; Barbero and Devoto, *Los nacionalistas*; and Devoto, *Nacionalismo, fascismo y tradicionalismo en la Argentina moderna*.

7. See, for example, Gentile, *Fascismo*; Paxton, *The Anatomy of Fascism*. See also Tacchi, Lyttelton, and Rossi-Doria, "Discussioni"; Salgó, "Recenti studi sul fascismo"; and the essays by Gentile, Falasca-Zamponi, Sternhell, Stone, Tra-verso, and Finchelstein in *Constellations: An International Journal of Critical and Democratic Theory* 15.3 (2008).

8. For Sandra McGee Deutsch it is clear that fascism was a transnational reality in South America during the 1930s. Furthermore, she claims that fascist ideo-logical influence and, perhaps more important, fascist political practice was projected into the postwar history of the Southern Cone in general and Argentina in particular. Hence it helped to shape a varied range of authoritar-ian policies, including those of the most recent military dictatorships. Deutsch defines this historical connection as the most striking, if not overpowering, legacy of the extreme Right in Argentina, Brazil, and Chile. The Chilean *nacistas*, the Brazilian *integralistas*, and the Argentine nacionalistas were ver-nacular fascist movements imbued with autonomous agency and influenced by external elements, particularly by the universal message of fascism. The salient aspect of Deutsch's approach is the preeminence of the Argentine case in terms of political importance, violence, anti-Semitism, and longstanding historical influence. In other words, she argues that in the era of fascism Argentina represented the most extreme case in terms of right-wing ideology and practice (Deutsch, *Las Derechas*). For fascism as a point of political refer-ence, see Halperín Donghi, *Ensayos de historiografía*, 115. See also Halperín Donghi, *La Argentina y la tormenta del mundo*, 18, 31, 34–36, 40, 48–49, 208, and *La república imposible*, 222, 288–289.

9. See my criticism in Finchelstein, *Fascismo, liturgia e imaginario*, 26–27.

10. For an exaggerated version of this argument for the history of Europe, see Talmon, *The Origins of Totalitarian Democracy*.

11. For an analysis of this process, see the classic study by Halperín Donghi, *Revolución y guerra*. For other approaches, see also Chiaramonte, *Nación y*

estado en Iberoamérica; Adelman, *Republic of Capital*; Lynch, *The Spanish American Revolutions*; Guerra, *Modernidades e independencias*.

12. For a refreshing new account of the Rosas regime, see Di Meglio, *¡Mueran los salvajes unitarios!* See also Gelman, *Rosas, estanciero*; Myers, *Orden y virtud*.

13. This was the case in Latin America at large. For a nuanced approach to this topic with a focus on the Mexican case, see the essays in Joseph and Nugent, *Everyday Forms of State Formation*.

14. Independent Argentina inherited the longstanding competition between the Spanish and Portuguese empires for the Banda Oriental (Uruguay). The imperial excursion against Rosas in 1852 was not the first war between independent Argentina and the Portuguese. The appetite of the Brazilian empire to expand southward represented a very specific European threat. The creation of the Republic of Uruguay in 1830 established a cushion state between the Argentines and the Portuguese, and it might have belatedly helped the forging of an alliance between the two main powers that expelled Rosas from power.

15. See Halperín Donghi, *Una nación para el desierto argentino*. See also Halperín Donghi, "Mitre y la formulación de una historia nacional para la Argentina"; Terán, *Positivismo y nación en la Argentina* and *Vida intelectual en el Buenos Aires fin-de-siglo*.

16. For a history of radicalism, see Rock, *El radicalismo argentino*; and more recently Cattaruzza, *Historia y política en los años treinta*; Ana Virginia Persello, *El radicalismo en crisis* and *El partido radical*; Alonso, *Between Revolutions and the Ballot Box*.

17. On General Justo, see de Privitellio, *Agustín P. Justo*.

18. See Perón's report in Halperín Donghi, *La república imposible*, 355–360.

19. The term "década infame" was used by nacionalista journalist José Luis Torres to describe what he saw as the corrupt and decadent nature of conservative parliamentarian politics.

20. The Argentine position regarding the Salò Republic (1943–1945) was different from its relationship with previous Italian administrations, and Argentina did not have foreign relations with it, despite fascist attempts to get Argentine recognition. See Archivo del Ministerio de Relaciones Exteriores y Culto, Argentina, División Política, caja 22, Italia, expediente 4, año 1943; ibid., Guerra Europea, mueble 7, casilla 43, expediente 545, año 1943; ibid., Guerra Europea, mueble 7, casilla 43, expediente 557, año 1943; ibid., División Política, caja 25, Italia, expediente 6, año 1944.

21. In addition, it is shocking that the few works on the topic are semiofficial texts

that briefly deal with this aspect of Italian and Argentine foreign policy and do not explain, or recount, the most important aspects of this history, such as the central role played by Argentina during the invasion of Ethiopia. See Ruiz Moreno, *Historia de las relaciones exteriores argentinas*, 390–393. See also the extensive collection edited by Andrés Cisneros and Carlos Escudé, *Historia general de las relaciones exteriores de la República Argentina*, 9.190–198. The sections of the volume dealing with Argentina's relationship with the fascist government provide only limited information.

22. See Archivo del Ministerio de Relaciones Exteriores y Culto, Argentina, División Política, caja 46, Italia, Legación argentina en Roma, expediente 1, año 1922; see folios 19, 20–21, 26, and especially 28–29; also 31 and 36. In 1927 Gallardo, as Argentine foreign minister, made a state visit to Italy and declared the desirability of creating closer links with Italy. This bridging, he argued, was not a "myth" insofar as "the two peoples share the same blood, the same soul and the same thinking." "Il ministro degli Esteri Argentino," *Il Mattino* (Naples), October 10, 1927. During his visit Gallardo expressed, once again, his quasi-fetishistic attitude toward anything related to Mussolini when he showed his interviewer from United Press a bouquet of flowers in his hotel room, and told him, "I feel particularly honored by these flowers, because they are a present from Mr. Mussolini." See "Manifestaciones de Gallardo a los periodistas romanos," *La Prensa*, October 7, 1927. Gallardo even kept a picture of Mussolini on the desk of his studio until the end of his life in 1934. See Gallardo, *Memorias para mis hijos y nietos*, 328. For a profile of Gallardo as an eminent representative of Argentine Catholicism, see "Doctor Ángel Gallardo," *Criterio*, May 17, 1934, 57. Gallardo's own anticommunist vision of the nation and his own preoccupation about the "internal enemy" and "subversion," were of consequence for his shaping of Argentine policies with respect to fascism. Archivo del Ministerio de Relaciones Exteriores y Culto, Argentina, División Política, caja 2717, Italia, Embajada Argentina en Roma, expediente 11, año 1928. The fascist embassy in Buenos Aires had a very positive view of Gallardo, considering him, an "estimatore del fascismo" and a "friend of our country." See Archivio, Ministero degli Affari Esteri, Rome, Italy, telespresso 2272 / 53, August 7 and December 7, 1927.

23. Archivo del Ministerio de Relaciones Exteriores y Culto, Argentina, División Política, caja 2488, Italia, Consulado Argentino en Milan, expediente 14, año 1926. See also Arturo Calza, "Un colloquio col presidente della Repubblica Argentina: le sue simpatie per l'Italia," *Corriere della Sera*, June 1, 1926. Alvear had visited Italy some months before the *March on Rome*. See "L'arrivo del

presidente dell'Argentina," *Il Giornale d'Italia*, July 12, 1922; and "Roma al presidente dell'Argentina," *Il Giornale d'Italia*, July 13, 1922.

24. "Un'intervista con il sen. Indri sulla sua missione nell'America Latina," *Il Popolo d'Italia*, May 18, 1928.

25. Incidentally, in the same interview with the *Corriere*, President Alvear criticized parliamentarism. In 1922 Argentine diplomats praised the "order" brought by fascism and in 1923–1924 the dubious electoral law of 1923 that gave the fascists, with only one-quarter of the total vote, two-thirds of the seats in Parliament. Archivo del Ministerio de Relaciones Exteriores y Culto, Argentina, División Política, caja 2293, Italia, expediente 1, año 1924, N17, folios 1–18.

26. Argentine radical party officials and diplomats were critical of some specific Italian fascist policies regarding the Italian fascists abroad; one Argentine diplomat called them "focos anti-argentinos." These officials often commented on the special predisposition of Mussolini toward the citizens of Argentina. Moreover, diplomats were highly enthusiastic about fascism as a political regime and expressed their admiration for its leader. They highlighted the favorable attitude of fascism toward the church. Last but not least, the Argentine diplomats admired fascist corporatism and the hegemonic workings of the fascist party. See Archivo del Ministerio de Relaciones Exteriores y Culto, Argentina, División Política, caja 2197, Italia, Conmemoración de fechas históricas, expediente 11, año 1922; ibid., caja 46, Italia, Legación argentina en Roma, expediente 1, año 1923, folio 1; ibid., caja 2293, Italia, Política interna, expediente 1, año 1924, folios 1–4, 8–9, and especially 50–51. In his annual report of 1924 the Argentine ambassador, Pérez, "justified" fascist violence and valued the supposedly positive and unique historical contributions of fascism. See also Archivo del Ministerio de Relaciones Exteriores y Culto, Argentina, División Política, caja 2717, Italia, Embajada Argentina en Roma, expediente 11, año 1928; ibid., caja 2717, Italia, Legación argentina en Roma, expediente 21, año 1928, folios 1–2; ibid., caja 2830, Italia, Política interna, expediente 1, año 1929, folios 1–2, 4–10, and especially 11–14 and 16–17.

27. Yrigoyen was influenced by the harmonistic thought of the German romantic philosopher Karl Krause. See Rock, *El radicalismo argentino*, 63.

28. On Alvear, see Cattaruzza, *Marcelo T. de Alvear*.

29. See Archivio, Ministero degli Affari Esteri, Rome, Italy, telespresso 1484/345, May 27, 1927; ibid., telespresso 3167/451, July 17, 1930; ibid., telespresso 2943/1353, September 21, 1940. An Italian fascist report noted in 1939: "Alvear . . . che pure praticó, durante la sua presidenza, una politica moderata in generale, ed una politica di simpatia verso l'Italia, non ha esitato in fatti a scrivere: 'Chi

potrá sostenere oggi seriamente o sinceramente che i regimi totalitari, rappresentino un beneficio per l'humanitá?' " Ibid., telespresso 3039 / 1419, July 18, 1939.

30. See ibid., Situazione in Argentina, August 5, 1931; ibid., telespresso 523 / 148, March 7, 1932.

31. See "A colloquio col generale Uriburu," *Corriere della Sera*, September 12, 1930. Surprisingly, in the Argentine foreign archives there are only few records of the period between 1930 and 1932. However, tentatively it would be possible to argue that with respect to fascism, and from an institutional point of view, there was a clear continuity between the elected radical governments and the dictatorship of Uriburu. See Archivo del Ministerio de Relaciones Exteriores y Culto, Argentina, División Política, Memoria, Italia, Política interna, expediente 20, año 1929; ibid., División Política, caja 3033, Italia, Política interna, expediente 14, año 1931. See also "La prensa extranjera sigue comentando el triunfo de la revolución argentina," *La Razón*, September 8, 1930, 4; "Cinco estados reconocieron hoy al gobierno provisional de la república Argentina," *La Razón*, September 16, 1930, 1; "Irigoyen cede i poteri," *Corriere della Sera*, September 6, 1930; "La rivoluzione a Buenos Aires," *Corriere della Sera*, September 7, 1930; "Come è stato rovesciato il governo Irigoyen," *Corriere della Sera*, September 9, 1930; "In Argentina," *Corriere della Sera*, September 10, 1930; "Gli avvenimenti a Buenos Aires," *Corriere della Sera*, September 11, 1930.

32. The next chapter explores this issue in more detail. See Archivo del Ministerio de Relaciones Exteriores y Culto, Argentina, División Política, caja 3033, Italia, Política interna, expediente 20, año 1931; ibid., caja 3033, Italia, Embajada Argentina en Italia, expediente 3, año 1931. See also "Le impressioni dell' Ambasciatore argentino," *Il Giornale d'Italia*, January 10, 1925.

33. See Archivo del Ministerio de Relaciones Exteriores y Culto, Argentina, División Política, caja 3175, Italia, Política interna, expediente 5, año 1932, folios 1–4; ibid., caja 3298, Italia, Política interna, expediente 1, año 1933; ibid., caja 3298, Italia, Política interna, expediente 2, año 1933, N152 R.E., November 13, 1933, and 155 R.E., November 16, 1933; ibid., caja 3175, Italia, Política interna, expediente 5, año 1932. Cantilo, the Argentine ambassador in Italy in 1933, openly expressed his praise for Mussolini as "man of superior qualities" and said that "fascist doctrine" was of "interest to the entire world." For the liberal Argentine paper *La Prensa* this statement represented an inopportune profascist declaration against democracy in Argentina. To be sure, the newspaper asked the foreign minister to reprimand Cantilo, and so he did. But this episode shows the extent of sympathy for fascism among officials in the upper level of

the conservative administrations. Typically, Cantilo denied that he said what he said. The episode was not a liability for Cantilo, who some years later would become the Argentine foreign minister. See Archivo del Ministerio de Relaciones Exteriores y Culto, Argentina, División Política, caja 3298, Italia, Política interna, expediente 20, año 1933, telegramas cifrados 1659 and 1663. See also "El embajador Cantilo destacó las vinculaciones ítalo-argentinas," *La Nación*, November 10, 1933; "Presentó sus credenciales al Rey de Italia el nuevo embajador de la Argentina, Señor J. M. Cantilo," *La Prensa*, November 19, 1933; "Declaraciones imprudentes de un embajador," *La Prensa*, November 19, 1933; "Las declaraciones atribuidas al embajador en Roma," *La Prensa*, November 23, 1933.

34. "La lotta presidenziale iniziata in Argentina," *Il Regime Fascista*, January 24, 1937.

35. Archivo del Ministerio de Relaciones Exteriores y Culto, Argentina, Varios, caja 3, 1–1, expediente 65, año 1933, telegramas cifrados 1276, 682, 1289, 694, 1303, 696, 1305. See also "Gran movimiento a favor de la reforma del organismo ginebrino," *La Prensa*, May 23, 1935; "Los países Latinoamericanos," *La Prensa*, September 2, 1935; "Texto del memorándum presentado por Italia," *La Prensa*, September 5, 1935; *La Prensa*, September 7, 1935. See also Archivio Centrale dello Stato, Italia, Ministero della Cultura Popolare, D.G. Serv., Propaganda, B8, Argentina, 1938, I / 4 / 1.

36. He was particularly worried about the opposition to his policies expressed by the liberal paper *La Prensa*. See Archivo del Ministerio de Relaciones Exteriores y Culto, Argentina, División Política, caja 3, Conflicto Italo-Etiope, expediente 65, año 1933, Estrictamente confidencial, telegrama cifrado 682. See also "Las relaciones exteriores del país y los pedidos parlamentarios de informes," *La Prensa*, June 18, 1936. In addition, the fascist paper *Il Mattino d'Italia* of the Italian community of Argentina launched a campaign against Saavedra Lamas and even argued that Argentina was buttressing slavery in Africa and linked the latter policy with the Argentine killing of the native populations in Patagonia. See Archivo del Ministerio de Relaciones Exteriores y Culto, Argentina, Varios, caja 3.6 bis, expediente 65, año 1933, legajo 2, tomo 2, N121, R.E.; Archivo General de la Nación, Argentina, Archivo Agustín P. Justo, caja 104, docs. 114, 459.

37. See "La stampa argentina contraria alle discussioni segrete sulla politica internazionale," *Il Giornale d'Oriente*, June 18, 1936; and "Il Ministro Saavedra Lamas attaccato dalla stampa argentina," *Il Giornale d'Oriente*, June 19, 1936. See also "Nuestro país y la Liga de las naciones," *Crisol*, October 2, 1936, 1. See

also "1.a instancia: obra de Saavedra Lamas," *Crisol*, October 4, 1936; and "La pobre mentalidad materialista del canciller expuesta al desnudo," *Crisol*, October 14, 1936.

38. See *Agrupación Argentina Amigos de Italia*, July 9, 1941, 2. Many nacionalistas, including Juan P. Ramos and Carlos Ibarguren, and nacionalista fellow travelers such as Manuel Fresco, gave their support to this association; other supporters and contributors included high-ranking nacionalista military generals and even "liberals" such as Roberto J. Noble, who would later found the newspaper *Clarín*. See also Archivio Centrale dello Stato, Italia, Ministero della Cultura Popolare, D.G. Serv., Propaganda, B 9, Argentina, 5/1/1. See also de Vecchi, *La prensa argentina y el momento actual de Italia*. Most members of the association, including its two directors, the Argentines Arturo Rossi and Miguel Rizzotti, had Italian surnames and many of them were officers in the Argentine army. The most important member of the association, however, was the old conservative jurist Rodolfo Rivarola, who tried to show how the Argentine constitution almost compelled Argentina to support the Italian empire and opposed the sanctions. Rivarola's position paper (his presentation to the Argentine House of Representatives) was published by Arsenio Buffarini (the head of the Italian community in Argentina) and was promptly sent to Mussolini. Rivarola's academic and political stance legitimized the Italian campaign against Saavedra Lamas and his policy. The association had close links with Italian fascist propaganda and with the Italian ambassador, Guariglia. Moreover, when the association was in "embryonic" stage, the Italian embassy in Buenos Aires informed the Italian foreign ministry that the association was "a project" that deserved "special dedication." Archivio, Ministero degli Affari Esteri, Rome, Italy, telespresso 1287/459, April, 18, 1937. The members of the association participated with Italian propagandists in pro-Italian events and celebrated the proclamation of the Italian empire in a fully crowded Colón theater. For Ambassador Guariglia, as he told Count Galeazzo Ciano, the association was a good asset for propaganda and should be "helped financially" (Archivio Centrale dello Stato, Italia, Ministero della Cultura Popolare, D.G. Serv., Propaganda, B8, Argentina, 1938, 1/4/2, 307/ 131). The Italian fascist press praised Rivarola and the association highly. Mussolini himself referred to Rivarola, and Count Ciano personally sent him a letter thanking him for his "understanding and friendship towards fascist Italy" (ibid., Propaganda, B6, Argentina, 1/4/8); Rivarola, *La constitución Argentina contra las sanciones de Ginebra*. See also "La maggioranza del Parlamento Argentino contro le sanzioni: l'autorevole giudizio del prof. Rivarola,"

Il Secolo XIX (Genoa), June 17, 1936; "Con un acto público, que se realizó en el teatro Colón, celebróse ayer el triunfo de los italianos en Etiopia," *La Prensa,* May 11, 1936. See also Archivo del Ministerio de Relaciones Exteriores y Culto, Argentina, División Política, caja s/n, Italia, Política interna, expediente 5, año 1941.

39. Senator Sánchez Sorondo had been an early admirer of fascism, a critic of liberal Argentina "and its hate for God," a close friend of Leopoldo Lugones, and a former minister of the interior of General Uriburu. He put himself at the center stage of Argentine politics with his proposal for the banning of communism and his denunciations of "Jewish infiltration." During the conflict with Ethiopia, the senator was instrumental in defending Italian interests in the Senate. At that time he told the Italian press: "I profess a great admiration for Mussolini. He has a prodigious brain and an iron will. He presents in the highest grade possible the highest quality of the Latin soul: clarity and ductility." "L'ammirazione per Mussolini di un senatore argentino antisanzionista," *Il Giornale d'Italia,* May 14, 1936; Sánchez Sorondo, *Historia de seis años,* xiv, 461; Archivo General de la Nación, Argentina, Archivo Agustín P. Justo, caja 36, doc. 125; "Il Senato argentino chiede chiarimenti," *Corriere della Sera,* June 11, 1936; "Saavedra Lamas invitato a spiegarsi davanti al Senato argentino," *Il Secolo XIX* (Genoa), June 11, 1936; "Una manovra di Saavedra Lamas per evitare la condanna pubblica della sua politica societaria," *Il Secolo XIX* (Genoa), June 17, 1936; "Argentina e S.d.N Riunione del Senato," *Il Lavoro,* June 17, 1936. See also Archivo del Ministerio de Relaciones Exteriores y Culto, Argentina, Varios, caja 3.6 bis, expediente 65, año 1933, legajo 2, tomo 2, N121, R.E. In addition, see *La Prensa,* June 17, 1936, 9.

40. See Archivo General de la Nación Argentina, Archivo Agustín P. Justo, caja 49, docs. 203, 236; caja 104, docs. 26, 83, 109, 111, 127, 149, 459; caja 45, doc. 146; caja 104 bis, docs. 253, 278; caja 36, doc. 226.

41. See Ugo Sacerdote, "Una comunicazione dell'Argentina a Ginevra provoca vivo malumore tra i sanzionisti," *Il Giornale d'Italia,* February 2, 1936; "Atteggiamento coraggioso leale e amichevole," *Il Giornale d'Italia,* May 14, 1936; "Iniziative antisanzioniste," *Il Messaggero,* May 14, 1936; "Dell'occasione di avere un'opinione," *La Tribuna,* May 14, 1936; Ugo Sacerdote, "Il passo argentino nelle interpretazioni dei circoli ginevrini," *Il Giornale d'Italia,* June 12, 1936; "Argentina, Uruguay e Cile verso il ripudio definitivo," *Il Messaggero,* May 16, 1936; Ugo Sacerdote, "America Latina antisocietaria," *Il Messaggero,* May 14, 1936; "Quale sarebbe il vero scopo della mossa dell'Argentina," *Il Messaggero,* June 12, 1936; "Il segreto del ministro," *Corriere della Sera,* June 18,

1936; Filippo Anselmo, "Argentina e argentini di oggi: enigma o tattica?" *Il Secolo XIX* (Genoa), June 4 and 11, 1936; "Aspri attacchi all'iniziativa argentina per la convocazione della lega," *Gazzetta del Popolo*, June 9, 1936; Virginio Gayda, "Oggi si inizia a Buenos Aires la conferenza degli Stati americani," *Il Giornale d'Italia*, December 2, 1936. See Archivio del Ministerio de Relaciones Exteriores y Culto, Argentina, Varios, caja 3.6 bis, expediente 65, año 1933, legajo 2, tomo 2, N121, R.E.; and ibid., caja 3.6, expediente 65, año 1933, tomo 1, N102, R.E. 7. See also "La neutralidad y la conferencia americana de paz," *La Prensa*, June 18, 1936.

42. See Archivio Centrale dello Stato, Italia, Ministero della Cultura Popolare, D.G. Serv., Propaganda, B 8, Argentina, 1938, I / 4 / 1.

43. United States National Archives, Papers of Count Ciano, roll 1, frame 7.1, Colloquio con l'ambasciatore di Gran Bretagna, June 16, 1936.

44. Ibid.

45. See Archivo del Ministerio de Relaciones Exteriores y Culto, Argentina, Varios, caja 3.6, expediente 65. For the repercussion of the Argentine position in Colombia, see "La Argentina pide reunión extraordinaria de la liga," *El Espectador*, May 29, 1936; "La Argentina exige la inmediata reunión de la asamblea de la liga," *El Tiempo*, May 30, 1936; "La iniciativa Argentina ha provocado una grave crisis," *El Tiempo*, May 31, 1936; "Por iniciativa de la Argentina la asamblea se reunirá el día 23; Ruiz Guiñazú después de consultarlo con los latinoamericanos, entregó la nota Avenol," *El Tiempo*, June 3, 1936; "Solicitud Argentina para que se reúna la asamblea de la liga," *El Siglo*, June 5, 1936; "La actitud de la Argentina ha producido sensación en Ginebra," *El Siglo*, June 25, 1936; "Argentina tiene preocupados a los europeos," *El Siglo*, July 2, 1936; "Los más intrincados intereses están poniendo en juego en Ginebra," *El Siglo*, July 4, 1936. For Mexico, see "Argentina contraria a la anexión," *El Nacional*, May 28, 1936.

46. See Italpress, Rome, December 8, 1936, no. 95. Archivo del Ministerio de Relaciones Exteriores y Culto, Argentina, División Política, caja 3838, Italia, Política interna, expediente 4, año 1937. See also *Diario de la conferencia interamericana de consolidación de la paz* (Buenos Aires, 1936).

47. Archivo del Ministerio de Relaciones Exteriores y Culto, Argentina, Varios, caja 3.6 bis (a), expediente 65, año 1933, anexo 2, telegramas cifrados 603, 354, 366, 710, 374, 705, 375, 376.

48. "Creen ver la mano del Duce tras Argentina," *El Nacional* (Mexico), May 31, 1936.

49. Thus, in 1936 in the meeting of the League of Nations that Argentina had

requested in order to reinforce international pressure on Italy, Argentina radically switched its positions and, in the voice of its representative Enrique Ruiz Guiñazú, voted in favor of dropping the sanctions against Italy. The institutional relations between the two countries seem to have improved. In contrast to Argentina, Chile, Venezuela, and Panama abstained, and Mexico, voicing its opposition, did not attend the meeting.

50. Even during the most difficult moments in the relationship, the Argentine representatives in fascist Italy continued to express in their reports their unchecked admiration for the person of Mussolini. The Duce ultimately had to thank Argentina for speeding the process of Italian reconnection with the world in the aftermath of its imperialistic adventures (Archivo del Ministerio de Relaciones Exteriores y Culto, Argentina, Varios, caja 3.6, expediente 65, año 1933, tomo I, N102, R.E. 10). Nonetheless, the Italians never forgot the "anti-Italian" actions of the "ginevrino" Saavedra Lamas. In Italian secret reports, the grudges and resentment over Argentina's official position on Ethiopia persisted over the years. On the other hand, most Italian secret reports of the period probably believed their own propaganda when they noted that the "Argentine people" were against the sanctions. Mussolini himself particularly appreciated the position of Sánchez Sorondo, Rodolfo Rivarola, and the Association of Friends of Italy. See Archivio Centrale dello Stato, Italia, Ministero della Cultura Popolare, D.G. Serv., Propaganda, B8, Argentina, 1938, I/4/I, T487. See also United States National Archives, Personal Papers of Benito Mussolini, T586, job 321; Archivio, Ministero degli Affari Esteri, Italia, cuaderno 5, Segreto, Argentina, 106975, 106976, 106994, 106995; Archivio Centrale dello Stato, Italia, Ministero della Cultura Popolare, D.G. Serv., Propaganda, B8, Argentina, 1938, I/4/I, T1575/809. For military cooperation, mainly Argentine military officers receiving training in Italy and also Italian vessels visiting Buenos Aires and Patagonia during this period, see Archivo del Ministerio de Relaciones Exteriores y Culto, Argentina, División Política, caja 3033, Italia, Política interna, expediente 16, año 1931; ibid., caja 3175, Italia, Política interna, expediente 12, año 1932; ibid., caja 3298, Italia, Política interna, expediente 14, año 1933; ibid., caja 3538, Italia, Política interna, expediente 8, año 1935; ibid., caja 3538, Italia, Política interna, expediente 21, año 1935; ibid., caja 3981, Italia, Política interna, expediente 13, año 1938; ibid., mueble 7, casilla I, Guerra Europea, expediente 14, año 1939. See also "Una missione militare argentina in Europa," *Gazzetta di Venezia*, February 12, 1937.

51. Archivo del Ministerio de Relaciones Exteriores y Culto, Argentina, División Política, caja 3981, Italia, Política interna, expediente I, año 1938; ibid., caja

4263, Italia, Política interna, expediente 1, año 1939; ibid., caja 4336, Italia, Política interna, expediente 1, año 1940; ibid., mueble 7, casilla 17, Guerra Europea, expediente 175, año 1940. The Argentine ambassador at the Holy See was much more critical about Italian racism than Ambassador Malbrán. Malbrán expressed his doubts about the necessity of defending all Argentine Jews living in Italy. See ibid., caja 3981, Italia, Política interna, expediente 16, año 1938. For other examples of anti-Semitic attitudes among Argentine diplomats in Italy, see ibid., caja 3033, Italia, Política interna, expediente 17, año 1931.

52.   Ibid., mueble 7, casilla 1, Guerra Europea, expediente 9, año 1939. See also ibid., casilla 17, Guerra Europea, expediente 213, año 1940.

53.   These countries were Colombia, Honduras, Canada, Costa Rica, Nicaragua, Cuba, El Salvador, Guatemala, Panama, Haiti, Peru, Mexico, and Dominican Republic. See Ruiz Moreno, *Historia de las relaciones exteriores argentinas*, 392. In addition, in 1941 Italy sold Argentina an assortment of military vessels and military cooperation continued.

54.   The American top official, Summer Welles, accused Ruiz Guiñazú's son, Alejandro, of having sympathies for Mussolini, but the latter denied the accusation, saying that while he "admired" Mussolini he opposed the "implantation of fascism in Argentina": "No tengo inconveniente, por ejemplo, en confesar mi admiración por el genial estadista que es Mussolini. Y sin embargo me declaro contrario a la implantación del fascismo en Argentina." Thus, Alejandro Ruiz Guiñazú was in favor of an Argentine "national revolution." See Ruiz Guiñazú, *La Argentina ante si misma*, 8; see also 130, 148–150. In his visit to Madrid in 1941, Ruiz Guiñazú repeated to a fascist diplomat his "fervent admiration for the creative genius of the Duce" (Archivio, Ministero degli Affari Esteri, Rome, Italy, Madrid, May 2, 1941, Riservato, telespresso 3286/ 1000). Summer Welles was concerned about the influence of Ruiz Guiñazú's son Alejandro, a nacionalista ideologist who identified Argentina's "national revolution" with the reaction of universal fascism but who, according to his nacionalista position, did not equate nacionalismo with fascism. See Welles, *The Time for Decision*, 229–230. Some nacionalistas initially described Enrique Ruiz Guiñazú as the "prototype of the liberal diplomat." According to his famous daughter Magdalena, Ruiz Guiñazú was manipulated by Mario Amadeo, a nacionalista who was his principal advisor at the foreign ministry. I thank Tulio Halperín Donghi for indicating this to me. The Italian fascists did not have the same impression as Magdalena Ruiz Guiñazú. In a secret report of 1941, Giuseppe Valentini wrote to his superiors in Italy that Enrique Ruiz Guiñazú was "the only member of the executive branch . . . impartial" toward

the Axis. See "Nuestra neutralidad y el ministro Ruiz Guiñazú," *El Restaurador*, June 12, 1941, 3; Archivio Centrale dello Stato, Italia, Ministero della Cultura Popolare, D.G. Serv., Propaganda, B 12, Argentina, Varie, 5, V8. See also Archivo General de la Nación Argentina, Archivo Agustín P. Justo, caja 104, doc. 149. Guiñazú was not alone in his feelings for fascism. Ambassador Malbrán in Rome was an eager fascist sympathizer. To be sure, he was many times annoyed by the working of Mussolini's police state, but he also was inclined to wish for a victory for the Axis, which he described as "a beautiful dream." See Archivo del Ministerio de Relaciones Exteriores y Culto, Argentina, División Política, mueble 7, casilla 40, Guerra Europea, expediente 448, año 1942, folio 5. Unlike the previous foreign ministers, Ruiz Guiñazú was almost obsessed with the evolution of the Italian situation. See ibid., mueble 7, casilla 40, Guerra Europea, expediente 448, año 1942, telegramas cifrados 655, 307, and telegrama ordinario 1244.

55. See Archivio Centrale dello Stato, Italia, Ministero della Cultura Popolare, D.G. Serv., Propaganda, B 9, Argentina, 5/1/8; Archivo del Ministerio de Relaciones Exteriores y Culto, Argentina, División Política, caja 22, Italia, telegrama cifrado, N511, N34, Estrictamente reservado y muy confidencial, folio 1, June 4, 1943. See also ibid., mueble 7, casilla 40, Guerra Europea, expediente 448, año 1942, telegrama cifrado 460. See also ibid., mueble 7, casilla 37, Guerra Europea, expediente 365, año 1941.

56. Archivo General de la Nación Argentina, Archivo Agustín P. Justo, caja 104, doc. 114.

57. For an analysis of the military regime of 1943, see Halperín Donghi, *La democracia de masas*, 13–50.

58. See, for example, Rafael B. Esteban, review of Rafael Estenger, "Mussolini y la ideología fascista," *Síntesis* 4.38 (August 1930): 266. This trend can be seen in literary journals such as *Martin Fierro*, *La Vida Literaria*, and *Proa*, as well as in the literary supplements of *La Nación* and *La Razón*. Although in the 1920s some political stances were already clear and others were certainly not, most protonacionalistas and proto-antifascists were found in the same groups of the Buenos Aires "literary vanguard." The first reception of fascism related less to its authoritarian politics than to its aesthetics. These aesthetics were almost absolutely focused on the personas of Filippo Marinetti and, to a minor extent, D'Annunzio and other literary figures; "Contribución al estudio del romanticismo," *Proa* 2.8 (March 1925): 56; de Laferrere, *Literatura y política*, 50. The reduction of fascism to one of its literary currents was problematic, but it was not limited to the Argentines. Walter Benjamin, for example, tended to explain

fascism through Marinetti on some occasions. See, for example, Benjamin, "The Work of Art in the Age of Mechanical Reproduction," in *Illuminations*. On Benjamin and fascism, see Traverso, *La pensèe dispersèe*, 40–43, 103; Michael Steinberg, "The Collector as Allegorist: Goods, Gods and the Objects of History," in Steinberg, *Walter Benjamin and the Demands of History*.

59. See Lamberti Sorrentino, "Virgilio poeta de la romanidad," *Síntesis* 3.34 (March 1930): 48; Lamberti Sorrentino, "Gabriel D'Annunzio trabaja," *Síntesis* 2.16 (September 1928): 65; Folco Testena, "Consideraciones deshilvanadas de un periodista, sobre problemas que son o podrían ser trascendentales," *Síntesis* 3.35 (April 1930). On Lamberti Sorrentino, see also Franco Ciarlantini, *Viaggio in Argentina*, 94–95. Folco Testena even attempted an Italian translation of *Martin Fierro*; see "La versión italiana del Martin Fierro," *La Razón*, May 23, 1935. See also *Bibliografía Fascista*, March 1935, 211.

60. See, for example, the interesting analysis of fascism by Amadeo, *El fascismo y su jefe*, 34, 36. Amadeo claimed that he had met with Mussolini in 1923.

61. "De un lado está la gente decente, del otro los hijos de puta." Martínez Estrada responded: "Si es así firmo con ustedes encantado." See Bioy Casares, *Descanso de caminantes*, 132–133.

62. These nacionalistas included writers such as Leopoldo Lugones, Manuel Gálvez, Carlos Ibarguren, Juan P. Ramos, Ernesto Palacio, Bruno Jacovella, Armando Cascella, Alfredo Tarruella, and the brothers Irazusta.

63. On antifascism, see Bisso, *Acción Argentina* and *El antifascismo argentino*. See also Nállim, "Del antifascismo al antiperonismo."

64. Archivo del Ministerio de Relaciones Exteriores y Culto, Argentina, División Política, caja 2488, Italia, Política interna, expediente 16, año 1926; ibid., caja 2717, Italia, Política interna, expediente 14, año 1928; ibid., caja 3033, Italia, Política interna, expediente 20, año 1931; ibid., caja 3298, Italia, Política interna, expediente 7, año 1933; ibid., mueble 7, casilla 40, Guerra Europea, expediente 463, año 1942. See also "Nel secondo aniversario del martirio di Giacomo Matteotti," *L'Italia del Popolo*, June 27, 1926; "En memoria de Giácomo Matteotti," *La Vanguardia*, June 7, 1927; "El gran mitin antifascista de anoche," *La Vanguardia*, June 6, 1928; "L'assassino Dino Grandi," *L'Italia del Popolo*, December 13, 1931; "El embajador fascista," *La Vanguardia*, May 9, 1933; Nicolas Ciilla, "El 'jus murmurandi' en Italia," *La Vanguardia*, July 1, 1939. See also Archivo Cedinci, Fondo Solari, S18, 73 / 74; ibid., Fondo Repetto, 30, 101. See also "De la Torre e la politica," *L'Italia del Popolo*, December 13, 1931.

65. See Archivo del Ministerio de Relaciones Exteriores y Culto, Argentina, División Política, caja 2386, Italia, Política interna, expediente 10, año 1925; ibid.,

caja 2717, Italia, Política interna, expediente 14, año 1928; ibid., caja 3298, Italia, Política interna, expediente 8, año 1933; Archivio Centrale dello Stato, Italia, Ministero della Cultura Popolare, D.G. Serv., Propaganda, B7, Argentina, 1937, I / 4 / 1; ibid., B8, Argentina, 1938, I / 4 / 1.

66. For an analysis of the origins of *Crítica*, see Saitta, *Regueros de tinta*.

67. "Denso Rumor de protesta, airado gesto de indignación: eso ha provocado la noticia," *Crítica*, June 10, 1940. See also "Cesare Rossi está en vísperas de formular graves acusaciones," *Crítica*, March 6, 1926; "El juez Lamarque desestima la denuncia formulada contra 'Crítica' por el embajador de Italia," *Crítica*, October 8, 1928; "Que quedó de la Italia de Cavour," *Crítica*, December 7, 1929; "Raquel Mussolini," *Crítica*, August 13, 1938; "Amores contrariados," *Crítica*, May 5, 1939; *Crítica*, June 10, 1939; *Crítica*, July 3, 1939. For the Italian fascist criticism of *Crítica*, see Virginio Gayda, "Tre articoli di F. S. Nitti," *Il Giornale d'Italia*, August 24, 1929; and "Ancora una replica a Nitti: i fatti contro le parole," *Il Giornale d'Italia*, August 27, 1929. For Gayda, *Crítica* was a "mercenary" paper. See also Archivo General de la Nación, Argentina, Archivo Agustín P. Justo, caja 36, doc. 7.

68. See Archivo del Ministerio de Relaciones Exteriores y Culto, Argentina, División Política, caja 2717, Italia, Política interna, expediente 25, año 1928; ibid., caja 2830, Italia, Política interna, expediente 2, año 1929, telegrama ordinario 1272; ibid., caja 3033, Italia, Política interna, expediente 20, año 1931; ibid., caja 3838, Italia, Política interna, expediente 16, año 1937; ibid., caja 3981, Italia, Política interna, expediente 11, año 1938; ibid., caja 3981, Italia, Política interna, expediente 16, año 1938; ibid., caja 3981, Italia, Política interna, expediente 19, año 1938; ibid., caja 4263, Italia, Política interna, expediente 7, año 1939; ibid., caja 4336, Italia, Política interna, expediente 11, año 1940. For some examples, see "Un código fascista exalta abusivamente el poder del Estado"; the cartoon "El ejercicio metódico del terror," *Jornada*, November 18, 1931; Asdrubal Noble, "Charlas de café," *La República*, June 10, 1937; "Carta de Nueva Palabra," *Nueva Palabra*, July 3, 1939; *Ahora*, May 19, 1939; *Ahora*, June 9, 1939; *Ahora*, June 27, 1939; *Última Edición*, April 3, 1939; "Ascensión y decadencia de Mussolini," *El diario de Buenos Aires*, July 6, 1939; Ceferino Campos, "Giácomo Mateotti," *Tribuna* (Rosario), June 10, 1940; Toño Salazar, "La fuga relámpago," *Argentina Libre*, July 18, 1940; "Nobleza obliga," *Fastras*, July 31, 1940. See also Archivio Centrale dello Stato, Italia, Ministero della Cultura Popolare, D.G. Serv., Propaganda, B12, Argentina, Varie 5, V8, 905745 / 2236; Archivo del Ministerio de Relaciones Exteriores y Culto, Argentina, División Política, caja 3981, Italia, Embajada Argentina en Italia, expediente 20, año 1938.

69. For some examples in *La Nación* and *La Prensa*, see Olindo Malagodi, "Se determinan los límites de la acción fascista," *La Nación*, October 16, 1923; Fernando Rigny, "Mussolini," *La Nación*, October 27, 1923; "Terminó el congreso de la Alianza Antifascista," *La Nación*, April 9, 1928; "El pacto de Roma," *La Nación*, June 8, 1933; "Declaraciones imprudentes de un embajador," *La Prensa*, November 19, 1933; Enrique Villarreal, "Muchos elementos conservadores ingleses sostienen que sería errónea la prolongación de tales medidas," *La Prensa*, May 22, 1935; Ricardo Sáenz Hayes, "Benito Mussolini fue entrevistado por un enviado especial de 'La prensa,'" *La Prensa*, May 25, 1936; "Roma asistió a imponentes manifestaciones populares," *La Nación*, October 1, 1937; "Un mensaje italiano," *La Nación*, November 11, 1937; "Propaganda de mala voluntad," *La Prensa*, October 1939; "Actualidad," *La Prensa*, April 25, 1940; "Es deseo de muchos italianos que Italia no entre en la guerra," *La Nación*, May 20, 1940; "La actuación del ex-Duce," *La Nación*, April 30, 1945; "Se anunció ayer el fusilamiento de Benito Mussolini," *La Prensa*, April 30, 1945; "Artículos de Benito Mussolini," *La Nación*, July 19, 1945.

70. See articles by José Luis Romero in *La Razón*: "Europa vista desde Europa," March 13, 1936; "La idea de la guerra en Europa," April 10, 1936; "Sensación dramática de una víspera," April 17, 1936; "Europa vista desde Europa," April 20, 1936. Later on Romero would elaborate more in his pathbreaking work *El ciclo de la revolución contemporánea*. See also Romero, *La experiencia Argentina*, 127–128, 413–442.

71. *La Nación* presented in its high-quality literary supplement a variety of opinions on fascism from left to right, including the original pieces specially written for the paper by European intellectuals such as José Ortega y Gasset and Drieu La Rochelle. The eclecticism of this supplement contrasted with the increasingly conservative position of *La Nación* in its main pages throughout the fascist period.

72. See Romero, *El pensamiento político de la derecha latinoamericana*, 17, 59, 144–145, 149–150, 159, 161–177. See also Romero, *La vida histórica*. Though seemingly obvious, Romero's point nevertheless always tends to be overlooked by a large portion of historiographical works on the right that deal with fascism in Latin America in general and in Argentina in particular. For some examples of this more presentist trend, see important works by Middlebrook, *Conservative Parties, the Right, and Democracy in Latin America*; Chalmers, Campello, and Boron, *The Right and Democracy in Latin America*.

73. For the European case, see the classic study by Hobsbawm, *Nations and Nationalism since 1780*.

74. Deutsch, *Las Derechas*, 202, 315–339. As Deutsch states: "Even allowing for exaggeration, these estimates—which centered on Buenos Aires—suggested that nacionalismo had grown" (239). Individual nacionalista groups such as the Alianza de la Juventud Nacionalista had between thirty and fifty thousand adherents (233); Lvovich, *El nacionalismo de derecha*, 43–48. Other groups were also said to have a popular following. For example, an Argentine secret police informant reported that the single nacionalista group Una-Patria had around forty thousand members (Archivo General de la Nación, Argentina, Archivo Agustín P. Justo, caja 49, doc. 170). The Argentine nacionalista publication *El Momento Argentino* would exaggeratedly claim that it had a readership of 350,000. See *El Momento Argentino*, March 16, 1936.

75. For the relations between conservatives and fascists in Argentina, see Finchelstein, *Fascismo, liturgia e imaginario*, 34–40; and Deutsch, *Las Derechas*, 231–232.

76. See especially chapter 1 of this book.

77. See Moya, "The Positive Side of Stereotypes" and *Cousins and Strangers*, 376.

78. For an analysis of the idea of the Argentina nacionalista throughout the twentieth century, see Finchelstein, *La Argentina fascista*. For an excellent analysis of the Latin American democratic tradition, see Forment, *Democracy in Latin America*.

79. See Adelman, *Republic of Capital*, 289–291. Adelman argues: "In effect, the republic of capital was such a triumph that it made it difficult to imagine—never mind assimilate—alternative, countervailing and evolving republican sensibilities" (90). See also Moya, *Cousins and Strangers*, 365.

80. See Halperín Donghi, *La república imposible*, 290.

81. For the history of the Liga Patriótica Argentina, see Deutsch, *Counter Revolution in Argentina*, and Caterina, *La liga patriótica Argentina*.

82. For a more detailed account of this process, see Deutsch, *Las Derechas*, 78–106.

83. Personal library of Leopoldo Lugones. I thank Carmen Lugones for allowing me to read this material.

84. Lugones Jr., *Mi padre*, 322, 327–329.

85. General Agustín P. Justo led the Argentine delegation. Justo, the future president of Argentina and then minister of war, was at the time a personal friend of Lugones.

86. The word "libertarian" was in the Argentine context a synonym of anarchism.

87. "Así como ésta hizo lo único enteramente logrado que tenemos hasta ahora, y es la independencia, hará el orden necesario, implantará la jerarquía indispensable que la democracia ha malogrado hasta hoy, fatalmente derivada,

porque ésa es su consecuencia natural, hacia la demagogia o el socialismo."
Lugones, "La hora de la espada," in Lugones, *La patria fuerte*, 13–19.

88. "Pero sabemos demasiado lo que hicieron el colectivismo y la paz, del Perú de los Incas y la China de los mandarines. Pacifismo, colectivismo, democracia, son los sinónimos de la misma vacante que el destino ofrece al jefe predestinado, es decir al hombre que manda por su derecho de mejor, con o sin ley, porque ésta, como expresión de potencia, confúndese con su voluntad." Ibid., 18.

89. Ibid.

90. According to his nacionalista biographer Julio Irazusta, Lugones, who had been considered the icon of liberal Argentina, found himself alone after giving the speech. See Irazusta, *Genio y figura de Leopoldo Lugones*.

91. For a historical analysis of this period, see Halperín Donghi, *La república imposible*; Romero, *Breve historia contemporánea de la Argentina*.

92. See Zanatta, *Del estado liberal a la nación católica*.

93. Carulla, *Al filo del Medio Siglo*, 250.

94. "A colloquio col generale Uriburu," *Corriere della Sera*, September 12, 1930.

95. The Italian embassy informed its foreign minister: "La promessa di procurare ad ogni iscritto un impiego o comunque un'occupazione, rappresenta, specialmente in questo periodo di crisi, e di disoccupazione una attrattiva irresistibile per molti nostri connazionali, che pertanto . . . affluiscono in numero rilevante nelle file del nuovo partito." See Archivio, Ministero degli Affari Esteri, Rome, Italy, 1063 / 170, Riservato, March 17, 1931; ibid., telespresso 5067 / 528, August 15, 1936. See also Archivo General de la Nación, Argentina, Archivo Uriburu, legajo 20, sala 7, 2596; ibid., Archivo Agustín P. Justo, caja 49, doc. 232.

96. "Legionarios, como Jefe de la Revolución soy vuestro Jefe y os aseguro que, a pesar de las asechanzas de todo orden con que sordamente se intenta contrariarla, ella sostenida por vuestra acción patriótica y valiente, seguirá su marcha vencedora hasta la plena realización de su programa." See Archivo General de la Nación Argentina, Archivo Agustín P. Justo, caja 36, doc. 277, Reacción 1, quincena June 1935, no. 1.

97. See ibid., caja 36, doc. 277.

98. See ibid., Archivo Uriburu, legajo 20, sala 7, 2596, Carpeta recortes.

99. See ibid.

100. See Archivio, Ministero degli Affari Esteri, Rome, Italy, telespresso 523 / 148, March 7, 1932. The Italians did not agree with Uriburu. A fascist report stated: "Notwithstanding his arguments, Uriburu's [political reforms] were inspired

by the theory and practice of Italian fascism." The writer of the report informed the Italian foreign ministry that Uriburu's view of fascism "reduced fascism to a conservative phenomenon" and this was the reason behind the general's "failure" to reform Argentine politics.

101. Archivo General de la Nación, Argentina, Archivo Uriburu, legajo 20, sala 7 2596, Carpeta recortes.

102. Ibid., legajo 23, doc. 370, carta de Alberto Uriburu al teniente coronel Juan B. Molina, June 16, 1932. The Italian fascist embassy regarded Molina as "one of the most representative figures of nacionalismo." See Archivio, Ministero degli Affari Esteri, Rome, Italy, telespresso 3213 / 1496, August 1939.

103. Finchelstein, *Fascismo, liturgia e imaginario*, 131–144.

104. Deutsch argues, "Without ignoring distinctions, I focus on the immense overlap among them—one which Nacionalistas recognized. To some extent all professed Catholicism (except Lugones), corporatism, and Hispanism, and all criticized liberalism, electoral democracy, imperialism, feminism, leftism, cosmopolitanism, and Jews. Many moved from one group into another or belonged to several. Despite their petty jealousies and differences, the movements cooperated with each other, held common functions, and participated in joint forays against their enemies. Rather than divide Nacionalismo into mutually exclusive functions, it is best to see it as a coalition of shifting extreme rightist forces, some more radical than others. The importance lies in the whole, rather than in the individual groups" (*Las Derechas*, 207).

105. Among them the Asociación Nacionalista Argentina, the Legión Cívica Argentina, the Agrupación Uriburu, and the Partido Fascista Argentino.

106. Navarro Gerassi, *Los nacionalistas*, 100.

107. *Bandera Argentina*, September 19, 1933, 2. See also Archivo General de la Nación, Argentina, Archivo Agustín P. Justo, caja 45, doc. 146.

108. See Halperín Donghi, *La república imposible*, 25–56.

109. Juan P. Ramos, "La ideología de la Revolución de septiembre," *Bandera Argentina*, September 6, 1933, 3.

110. See "Discurso que podría ser programa: palabras del doctor Juan P. Ramos ante la tumba del General," *Bandera Argentina*, May 3, 1933, 1. See also Archivo General de la Nación, Argentina, Archivo Uriburu, legajo 23, sala 7, 2599, doc. 271.

111. "Der Gedenktag der Revolution," *Deutsche La Plata Zeitung*, September 7, 1933, 4; Archivo General de la Nación, Argentina, Archivo Agustín P. Justo, caja 45, doc. 146.

112. "Aus der grossen programmatischen Rede des Führers der Aduna Bewegung,

Dr. Juan P. Ramos am 6 September im Coliseo," *Deutsche La Plata Zeitung,* September 8, 1933, 5.

113. See "6 de septiembre de 1934," *La Fronda,* September 6, 1934, 3. See also "El fascio cordobés," *La Fronda,* April 26, 1933, 1; *Bandera Argentina,* April 28, 1933, 3; *Bandera Argentina,* April 2, 1933, 3; "¡Si volviera el general!" *La Fronda,* April 30, 1933, 1.

114. "El general Uriburu," *Los Principios,* April 28, 1935.

115. Archivo General de la Nación, Argentina, Archivo Agustín P. Justo, caja 46, docs. 107, 120, 121, 123.

116. Espigares Moreno, *Lo que me dijo el Gral,* 160, 161.

117. See Saítta, *Regueros de tinta,* 261.

118. "El tacho" is a method whereby the torturer "uses a wooden table, an oil drum filled with water, and a set of hooks linking the two, so that when the interrogators lift the table, the prisoner's head is submerged." The original Argentine version of the 1930s was described by one victim in the following manner: "Bruscamente se elevaba al atormentado, haciéndolo caer completamente atado y de bruces en un tacho inmundo, repleto de agua y de las asquerosas bazofias . . . y después de un nuevo interrogatorio y de otros golpes de puño, de cachiporras o de puntapiés, se le sumergía por segunda o tercera vez en ese . . . recipiente." See the gruesome testimonies of Lugones's victims in Llambias, Berraz, and Amadeo, *Los torturados.* Both the picana and the tacho were widely used by the last Argentine military dictatorship in its concentration camps and centers of torture, and they are still illegally used by the Argentine Federal Police and several provincial polices. See Justo, "Argentina" and *Nunca Más,* 26–54; Rodríguez Molas, *Historia de la tortura y el orden represivo en la Argentina,* 98. For the reference to the probable South American inspiration for the practice of torture by waterboarding in Iraq, see Danner, "Abu Ghraib," 46.

119. *Crítica,* February 22, 1932. Molina later became army general and the leader of the nacionalista group Alianza de la Juventud Nacionalista. Archivo General de la Nación, Argentina, Archivo Agustín P. Justo, caja 104, docs. 111, 149.

120. Ibid., caja 46, doc. 120.

121. Leopoldo Lugones Jr., "El origen de las supuestas torturas," *Bandera Argentina,* August 16, 1933, 1.

122. For this dimension of Argentine anti-Semitism, see chapter 5. See also Finchelstein, *La Argentina fascista,* chap. 3, and "The Anti-Freudian Politics of Argentine Fascism." For a general history of Argentine antisemitism, see Lvovich, *Nacionalismo y antisemitismo en la Argentina.*

Notes

123. Archivo General de la Nación, Argentina, Archivo Agustín P. Justo, caja 46, doc. 121.

124. Ibid.

125. "Tuvo lugar ayer en el Coliseo la segunda conferencia de Leopoldo Lugones (hijo)," *Bandera Argentina*, September 9, 1934. See also Archivo General de la Nación, Argentina, Archivo Agustín P. Justo, caja 49, doc. 167. Like his father, Lugones Jr. committed suicide, and one of his daughters (Piri) was "disappeared" during the last military dictatorship (1976–1983).

126. Arendt, "Ideology and Terror."

127. *La Nueva República*, October 13, 1931.

128. See Finchelstein, *Fascismo, liturgia e imaginario*, 72–73.

129. See Deutsch, *Las Derechas*, 211. On Guevara, see also Archivo Cedinci, FR 22.29 / 30 / 31.

130. See *Crisol*, September 30, 1933, 1, and October 1, 1933, 1. A secret report for President Justo blamed the provincial police for the lack of security. See Archivo General de la Nación Argentina, Archivo Agustín P. Justo, caja 49, doc. 182.

131. Archivo General de la Nación, Argentina, Archivo Agustín P. Justo, caja 54, doc. 12; ibid., caja 27, doc. 6. See also Federico Ibarguren, *Orígenes del nacionalismo argentino*, 194; Silveyra, *Historia y desarrollo del comunismo en nuestro país*, 26; and Carlos Ibarguren Jr., *Roberto de Laferrère*, 63.

132. "El socialismo ha visto algo este 6 de septiembre," *Bandera Argentina*, September 9, 1936, 1; Carulla, *Al filo del Medio Siglo*, 283.

133. Silveyra, *Historia y desarrollo del comunismo en nuestro país*, 26; Archivo General de la Nación Argentina, Archivo Agustín P. Justo, caja 45, doc. 115.

134. "La inaudita insolencia de 'La Vanguardia,'" *Bandera Argentina*, August 17, 1932, 1.

135. "El que no está con nosotros, el que no está con el nacionalismo está contra el nacionalismo." See ibid.

136. For an analysis of repression and fascist violence, see LaCapra, *Representing the Holocaust* and *History and Memory after Auschwitz*.

137. Emilio César Castro, "La fuerza al servicio del orden," *Bandera Argentina*, April 10, 1935, 3.

138. Emilio Kinkelin, "En el aniversario de la Revolución," *Bandera Argentina*, September 6, 1934, 20.

139. General Francisco Medina, "La dictadura de Uriburu," *Bandera Argentina*, April 28–29, 1935, 1.

140. "La segunda gesta y el Jefe," *Crisol*, April 28, 1936, 1.

141. *Crisol*, September 19, 1933, 1.

142. "La segunda gesta se hará con sangre, con demasiada sangre." See "La segunda gesta y el Jefe," *Crisol*, April 28, 1936, 1.

143. Juan P. Ramos, "Significación del adunismo," *Crisol*, February 1, 1934, 9.

144. See Archivo General de la Nación Argentina, Archivo Agustín P. Justo, caja 45, doc. 146. See also "La adaptación nacional del fascismo," *Crisol*, August 18, 1934; Luis F. Gallardo, *La mística del adunismo*, 13; *Nueva Idea* 1.1 (January 19, 1935).

3. Fascism Discovers the Americas

1. Ninno Sammartano, "Azione fascista nel mondo," *Critica Fascista*, February 15, 1928, 74–75. See also, in the same periodical, Francesco Geraci, "Il fascismo all'estero," November 1, 1923, 203–204; Ulrico Aillaud, "La propaganda corporativa all'estero," July 15, 1928, 262–263.

2. There were important nonfascist political visitors during this period, including Senator Vittorio Emanuele Orlando and Prince Umberto in 1924. See República Argentina, Ministerio de Relaciones Exteriores, *Memoria anual presentada al Honorable Congreso Nacional, 1923–1924* (Buenos Aires, 1925), 270–271, 612–621. See also Archivo del Ministerio de Relaciones Exteriores y Culto, Argentina, División Política, caja 3838, Italia, Embajada Argentina en Italia, expediente 17, año 1937, M.R.E. 73, confidencial. For the visits of Indri and Pavolini, see also "Un'intervista con il sen. Indri sulla sua misione nell'America Latina," *Il Popolo d'Italia*, May 18, 1928; "Conmemoró el aniversario del Imperio la Colonia Italiana, habló sobre la fecha celebrada el Sr. Pavolini," *La Razón*, May 9, 1937.

3. See Archivio, Ministero degli Affari Esteri, Rome, Italy, telespresso 2986 / 1050, July 19, 1937; Archivo General de la Nación Argentina, Archivo Roca Hijo, legajo 6, sala 7 3107, docs. 153, 154.

4. Archivio Centrale dello Stato, Italia, Ministero della Cultura Popolare, D.G. Serv., Propaganda, B7, Argentina, 1937, I / 4 / 52, 4.

5. See ibid., I / 4 / 1; "Llegó a Buenos Aires el Presidente del Senado Italiano S.E. Luis Federzoni," *Crónica* (Rosario) July 6, 1937; "El discurso de despedida del Presidente del Senado Italiano al abandonar el país," *La Acción* (Rosario), July 19, 1937. See also Federzoni, *Parole fasciste al Sud-America*, 11–13, 15–22.

6. Archivo del Ministerio de Relaciones Exteriores y Culto, Argentina, División Política, caja 2488, Italia, Embajada Argentina en Italia, expediente 5, año 1926, M.R.E. 73, confidencial.

7. Franco Ciarlantini was a member of the Fascist Grand Council. He was also the first publisher of the speeches of Mussolini, the owner of the publishing house Alpes, and an early member of Mussolini's Milanese group of fascists. He was also a biographer of Mussolini, the director of the fascist journal *Augustea*, a fascist soldier in Africa, a fascist leader in the party (as a propaganda boss he shaped fascist party propaganda), and most of all a member of the group of adulators that Mussolini liked to have around him. See United States National Archives, Personal papers of Benito Mussolini, T586, no. 430, reel 33, job 32, 015390. See also "Le direttive della propaganda fascista in un colloquio dell'on. Ciarlantini," *L'Idea Nazionale*, December 27, 1924; "La morte di Franco Ciarlantini," *Il Giornale d'Italia*, February 6, 1940; "La morte di Franco Ciarlantini," *Corriere della Sera*, February 6, 1940; See also Mussolini, "Nel quinto anniversario della fondazione dei fasci: Roma, 24 marzo 1924," in Mussolini, *La nuova politica dell'Italia*, 3.28.

8. Ciarlantini stayed for more than a month in Buenos Aires and later visited Córdoba, Rosario, and Bahía Blanca. He was not extremely active in connecting fascism with kindred movements. He was more interested in establishing close links with some Argentine intellectuals and literary figures, many of them future antifascists, like Ricardo Rojas or his "friend" Alberto Gerchunoff. Ciarlantini became immersed in the world of Argentine literature and actually dedicated a chapter of his book to its study, noting, for example, that no author in Argentina could match Leopoldo Lugones: "a writer of the first order [because] it is not possible to find in Old Europe more than a dozen like him." But Ciarlantini also predicted that Jorge Luis Borges was the Argentine author of the future.

9. Consequently, in a conference in Buenos Aires, Ciarlantini—by then a fascist representative—gave a lecture titled "Thinkers of Today's Italy." He talked about Croce and concluded by saying that the most important renewal of Italian thought came from the intellectual work of Mussolini himself. See Franco Ciarlantini, "Il grande successo a Buenos Aires della Mostra del Libro italiano," *Il Popolo d'Italia*, September 14, 1927; Franco Ciarlantini, "Vita argentina," *Il Popolo d'Italia*, November 6, 1927.

10. Ciarlantini, *Viaggio in Argentina*, 78, 82–87, 155, 161, 173, 179, 180–182, 188, 194, 235, 237, 258–259, 263, 279–281.

11. The Italian fascist Lamberti Sorrentino was right when he argued that Ciarlantini's was not a propaganda trip. However, Sorrentino conflated effects with intentions. See Lamberti Sorrentino, "Letras italianas," *Síntesis* 2.24 (May 1929): 355–356. Sorrentino's review of Ciarlantini was the only review that I

was able to find in an Argentine publication, and even then, it was not written by an Argentine: Sorrentino was Italian and a friend of Ciarlantini. On the fascist profile of Lamberti Sorrentino, see Archivio Centrale dello Stato, Italia, Ministero della Cultura Popolare, D.G. Serv., Propaganda, 16 B4, Argentina, 1934, I / 4 / 6.

12. For some symbolic examples of fascist exoticizing visions of Argentina, see three articles by Mirko Ardemagni in *Il Popolo d'Italia*, "Viaggio alla terra del fuoco: la desolazione del Sud," March 18, 1928; "I figli delle selve e i demoni della foresta," May 15, 1928; "L'arcipelago dei morti," May 16, 1928; and Ardemagni's book *Viaggio alla terra del fuoco e in Patagonia*; see also Arnaldo Fraccaroli, "Lettere argentine: la quotidiana strage," *Corriere della Sera*, August 8, 1930; and four other unsigned articles in the *Corriere*: "Il campo che vola," August 28, 1930; "Le quattro stagioni sono tre," September 12, 1930; "Scorribande nel cielo della Pampa," September 13, 1930; "Luz mala, che paura!" September 18, 1930. Also see Giorgio Quartara, *Un viaggio nel Sud-America*; Puccini, *L'Argentina e gli Argentini*; *Gerarchia* (December 1939): 823.

13. See F. B. Spina, "Limiti di sviluppo e limiti di immigrazione in Argentina," *Gerarchia* (February 1923): 778–785; Ciarlantini, *Viaggio in Argentina*, 235; "Le tragedie dell'economia liberale," *Il Giornale d'Italia*, August 20, 1933; Sandro Volta, "Lettera dall'Argentina: la scoperta dei sudamericani," *Critica Fascista*, January 15, 1934, 37–38; Sandro Volta, "Lettera dall'Argentina: le rivoluzioni sudamericane," *Critica Fascista*, April 1, 1934, 133; "Baruffe in seno al partito socialista argentina," *La Ultima Notizia* (Trieste), January 27, 1937; *La Vedetta d'Italia* (Fiume), January 28, 1937; Lamberti Sorrentino, "Gli assurdi dell'urbanesimo: anche le campagne dell'Argentina disertate," *Il Giornale d'Italia*, August 9, 1938; Ettore De Zuani, "Ebrei in Argentina," *La Difesa della Razza*, January 5, 1939, 26–29; Pietro Valli, "Aspetti dell'Argentina: le piaghe segrete di una grande Repubblica," *Il Giornale d'Italia*, July 16, 1939; Ettore De Zuani, "Lettera dall'America del Sud," *Critica Fascista*, July 1, 1940, 285–286; "Le capriole delle 'democrazie,'" *Il Regime Fascista*, January 16, 1941; "Le scandalose mene degli Stati Uniti in Argentina per aizzare i popoli alla guerra," *Il Messaggero*, October 14, 1941. See also Archivo del Ministerio de Relaciones Exteriores y Culto, Argentina, División Política, caja 4263, Italia, Embajada Argentina en Italia, expediente 13, año 1939.

14. Sandro Volta, "L'America Latina di Siegfried," *Critica Fascista*, May 15, 1934, 193.

15. See Innocenzo Cappa, "Per la cultura italiana nell'Argentina," *La Sera*, Janu-

Notes

ary 23, 1934; Ettore De Zuani, "Crisi dell'America Latina," *Critica Fascista*, April 15, 1940, 203–204. See also Ciarlantini, *Viaggio in Argentina*, 163, 172, 178.

16. Paolo Girosi, "L'Argentina alla ricerca di una propria cultura," *Il Messaggero*, June 30, 1939.

17. "Ius solis" is the legal principle according to which all persons born in the soil of a given country are regarded as its full citizens.

18. "L'Argentina e gli ebrei," *La Difesa della Razza*, March 1939, 47; Ettore De Zuani, "Crisi dell'America Latina," *Critica Fascista*, April 15, 1940, 204; Mussolini, "Italia ed Argentina," in Mussolini, *Discorsi del 1927*, 191–193. See also Archivio Centrale dello Stato, Italia, Ministero della Cultura Popolare, D.G. Serv., Propaganda, B6, Argentina, 4 / 131.

19. On Nazism and the Far West, see Traverso, *The Origins of Nazi Violence*, 70–71.

20. Massimo Bontempelli, "La Pampa o la cuarta dimensión," *Antología*, January 1945, 10–11. On Bontempelli's visit to Argentina, see Archivio, Ministero degli Affari Esteri, Rome, Italy, telegrama in arrivo, September 17, 1933.

21. Ciarlantini, *Viaggio in Argentina*, 159. See also ibid., 156–158, 206, 208.

22. Cesare Rivelli, "Colore Argentino: il paradiso degli uomini," *Il Piccolo*, May 5, 1931. For an excellent study of fascism and gender relations, see De Grazia, *How Fascism Ruled Women*.

23. Many official reports put the numbers of Italians in Argentina in the 1930s at around three million. See Archivio Centrale dello Stato, Italia, Ministero della Cultura Popolare, D.G. Serv., Propaganda, B4, Argentina, 1930–1933, I / 4. See also ibid., Argentina, 1934, I / 4 / 6. *La Difesa della Razza* claims that there were 4,398,138 Italians in the United States and 1,540,173 Italians in Argentina; France and Brazil had respectively 992,061 and 851,105 Italian immigrants, and Italy's African empire, 221,366. See *La Difesa della Razza*, December 5, 1938, 32–33. See also "Italianos y españoles forman la mayoría inmigratoria," *La Razón*, September 4, 1938.

24. See Mario De Bagni, "Italiani nell'Argentina," *La Difesa della Razza*, December 5, 1938, 44–45.

25. Mario Intaglietta, "Lo sforzo dell'Argentina per impedire l'allontanamento dell'America dall'Europa," *Il Giornale d'Italia*, December 11, 1936.

26. For example, Margherita Sarfatti, who was visiting Argentina when the Uriburu coup d'état took place in 1930, did not seem to be interested in the new dictatorship. See "Un saludo de Margarita Sarfatti para 'la Razón,'" *La Razón*, September 13, 1930. See also Prislei, *Los orígenes del fascismo argentino*, 49.

27. Ottavio Dinale, "Gli Italiani in Argentina," *Gerarchia*, August 1923, 1209–1210;

221

Viator (Senator Giuseppe Bevione), "I ludi cartacei del 1928," *Gerarchia*, February 1928, 89–90; Lamberti Sorrentino, "Lettere dal Rio de la Plata: il cozzo tra la vecchia e la nuova Argentina," *Il Giornale d'Italia*, January 1, 1929; "Lezioni all'Istituto fascista," *La Tribuna*, May 22, 1929; "Un colloquio con il presidente argentino," *Il Secolo XIX*, February 14, 1937; Sandro Volta, "Lettera dall'Argentina: le rivoluzioni sudamericane," *Critica Fascista*, April 1, 1934, 133. See also Archivo del Ministerio de Relaciones Exteriores y Culto, Argentina, División Política, caja 2717, Italia, Embajada Argentina en Italia, expediente 10, año 1928; ibid., caja 2830, Italia, Embajada Argentina en Italia, expediente 9, año 1929.

28. See Franco De Felice, "Gli Italiani in Argentina," *Gerarchia*, February 1923, 518–519; Attilio Dabini, "L'influenza italiana in Argentina," *Civiltà Fascista*, May 1935, 505.

29. See Ottavio Dinale, "Gli Italiani in Argentina," *Gerarchia*, August 1923, 1215.

30. Mussolini, "Sulla politica estera dell'Italia: Camera dei deputati, 10 febbraio 1923," in Mussolini, *La nuova politica dell'Italia*, 1.62–63.

31. See Mack Smith, *Mussolini's Roman Empire*, 4–6.

32. On fascist foreign policy as it was perceived by the fascists, see, for example, Orazio Laorca, "Il fascismo in Italia ed all'estero," *Il Popolo d'Italia*, January 7, 1925. See also Cassels, *Mussolini's Early Diplomacy*; Kallis, *Fascist Ideology*; Bosworth, "Mito e linguaggio nella politica estera italiana"; Knox, *Common Destiny*; and Collotti, *Fascismo e politica di potenza*. More specifically for Latin America, see Mugnaini, "L'Italia e l'America Latina."

33. There were a few instances of fascist dealings with Argentina, such as the establishment of a direct telegraphic connection between Italy and South America or the acknowledged importance of Argentina for Italy's economic needs. In his early years the Duce generated admiration among Argentine officials and may have been satisfied by this and by the Argentine delivery of food. See for example doc. 35, T7356 / 104, Il Ministro a Buenos Ayres, Colli al Presidente del consiglio e ministro degli esteri, Mussolini; and doc. 55, T2501, Il Presidente del consiglio e ministro degli esteri, Mussolini a de Alvear, 1922, both collected in Italy, Ministero degli Affari Esteri, *I documenti diplomatici italiani*, vol. 1; ibid., vol. 7, doc. 131, T2311 / 34, 1924. See also Archivo del Ministerio de Relaciones Exteriores y Culto, Argentina, División Política, caja 46, Italia, Legación Argentina en Roma, expediente 1, año 1922, telegrama cifrado 636. Mussolini told the Argentine ambassador in 1922 that "Italy needs Argentine wheat." On the telegraphic connection, see Mussolini, "Inaugurandosi il cavo fra Italia e l'America del sud," in Mussolini, *Discorsi del 1925*, 159–

160; and Mussolini, "Fra l'Italia e l'America del Sud," in *Opera omnia*, 21.409–410. In 1924, the relations with Argentina were significant enough for the Mussolini government to undertake a "great commission" that would buttress the development of "Italo-Argentine intellectual relations." Mussolini presided over the commission, and Giovanni Gentile served under him. Fascists and nonfascist celebrities participated in the commission, including the fascists Acerbo, Cappa, D'Annuncio, Marconi, Pirandello, and Sergi; scholars Einaudi, Pantaleoni, and Benedetto Croce; and conservative nonfascist politicians Salandra, Albertini, and Orlando. The inclusion of nonfascists or soon-to-be antifascists in the Argentine commission is a testimony to the broader "outreach" policies of Mussolini and other fascists toward their critics in the early years of fascism. This commission did not accomplish any important work, but that might not have been its primary aim, as the commission was a personal project of the Argentine ambassador Pérez, who suggested its creation to the Italians. The creation of this commission notwithstanding, it would be possible to argue that in the early years of fascism, external propaganda was not as aggressive and articulated as it later became. Before 1925, the fascist regime was not extensively preoccupied with Argentine issues, but had an eye on antifascist activities in Argentina and Italian emigration. Archivo del Ministerio de Relaciones Exteriores y Culto, Argentina, División Política, caja 2717, Italia, Embajada Argentina en Italia, expediente 11, año 1924, N19, confidencial; Ottavio Dinale, "Gli Italiani in Argentina," *Gerarchia*, August 1923, 1211. See also Archivio Centrale dello Stato, Italia, Archivi Fascisti, Segreteria Particolare del Duce, Carteggio riservato, B48 F242 / R Salvemini, Prof. Gaetano, SF 1. See also Italy, Ministero degli Affari Esteri, *I documenti diplomatici italiani*, vol. 3, doc. 276, T. Gab. 848 / 84, L'ambasciatore a Buenos Ayres, Aldrovandi al Presidente del consiglio e ministro degli esteri, Mussolini, 1924.

34. For Italian fascist politics with regard to the Italian community in Argentina, see Gentile, "L'emigrazione italiana in Argentina"; Zanatta, "I fasci in Argentina negli anni Trenta"; Newton, "Ducini, prominenti, antifascisti" and "¿Patria? ¿Cuál patria?" More recently, see Scarzanella, *Fascisti in Sud America*; and Prislei, *Los orígenes del fascismo argentino*.

35. For a general history of Italian immigration, see Devoto, *Historia de los italianos en la Argentina* and *Historia de la inmigración argentina*.

36. Franco De Felice, "Gli Italiani in Argentina," *Gerarchia*, September 1922, 509, 511, 513.

37. That Mitre, the nineteenth-century president who as a historian was the creator of Argentine official history, was presented by the fascists as an impor-

tant figure for Italians is somewhat ironic, but, more important, symptomatic of the vacuity of the Italian efforts to present Argentina as an Italian country. On Mitre and nationalism, see Halperín Donghi, "Mitre y la formulación de una historia nacional." On Italian imperialism and the construction of Argentine nationality, see Bertoni, *Patriotas, cosmopolitas y nacionalistas*, 23–34. For the Italian side of the question, see Dore, *La democrazia italiana e l'emigrazione italiana in Argentina*.

38. "Per l'insegnamento della lingua italiana," *Il Messaggero*, December 29, 1933.

39. "Nada ganará nuestra buena amiga de allende el océano, con la pretensión de italianizar a un prócer argentino. . . . Italia no es tan pequeña como para honrar a los próceres de otros países solo porque hayan llevado en sus venas sangre de italianos." See also "La literatura oficial y la estatua de Belgrano," *La Prensa*, October 14, 1927; and "Exageración inconveniente," *La Nación*, June 6, 1927. See also Ramón de Franch, "Parece que la estada del ministro Gallardo en Roma no tendrá otro significado que el que emane de los agasajos que se le tributen," *La Prensa*, October 6, 1927.

40. Gallardo argued: "Podemos considerar a Belgrano como el prototipo del ítalo-argentino. Su solo nombre, Belgrano, parece predestinado providencialmente a una misión gloriosa. Realmente, fue un gran semilla de una estirpe egregia, de la cultura itálica, que en poco más de un siglo llegó a tan pródigo florecimiento en las comarcas de allende el Atlántico." Archivo del Ministerio de Relaciones Exteriores y Culto, Argentina, División Política, caja 2386, Italia, Embajada Argentina en Italia, expediente 6, legajo 1, año 1925; ibid., legajo 2, año 1925; ibid., legajo 3, año 1925. See also "La prima pietra del monumento al generale Manuel Belgrano," *Il Cittadino*, April 28, 1925; "L'ospite illustre," *Il Messaggero*, September 30, 1927; *Il Messaggero*, October 6, 1927; "Il ministro Gallardo," *Il Messaggero*, October 11, 1927; "Il Re presenzierà oggi a Genova alla inaugurazione al Generale Belgrano," *Il Messaggero*, October 12, 1927; "Fondeó ayer en Genova la fragata Sarmiento," *La Nación*, October 6, 1927; "Mussolini ofreció un banquete al canciller de la Argentina," *La Nación*, October 7, 1927.

41. Carlo Curcio, "Italia e Argentina," *Critica Fascista*, October 15, 1927, 397.

42. "Il generale Belgrano," *Il Messaggero*, October 6, 1927; "Il significato della visita," *Il Messaggero*, October 2, 1927. See also Ludovico Giordano, "Giudiziosa intitolazione," *La Riviera: settimanale della Liguria di Ponente*, February 2, 1935, 1. See also G. Agénore Magno, "Una grande figura dell'indipendenza argentina: Manuel Belgrano," *La Nuova Antologia*, November–December 1927, 77–104.

43. See "Il discorso dell'on. Mussolini," *Il Messaggero*, October 7, 1927. See also "L'amicizia Italo-Argentina," *Il Popolo d'Italia*, October 18, 1927.

44. Some fascist papers even claimed that the whole idea of the monument to Belgrano had its origins in a speech that Gallardo gave when he left his post as Argentine ambassador some years earlier. This does not mean that the Duce or a closer aide picked up the idea from Gallardo. There are no archival sources to confirm this claim made by the newspapers *Tribuna* and *Il Giornale d'Italia*. I am inclined to think that the idea may have originated in the Italian community in Buenos Aires and then been transmitted to Gallardo.

45. Mussolini, "Italia e Argentina," in *Opera omnia*, 25.219. See also Ricardo Sáenz Hayes, "Benito Mussolini fue entrevistado por un enviado especial de 'La prensa,'" *La Prensa*, May 25, 1936.

46. These included monuments to Belgrano and Mitre in Rome in 1932 or the naming a street for Belgrano in Imperia in 1935. One of the Italians in Argentina who supported this account was Arsenio Guidi Buffarini, the president of the General Federation of Italian Societies in Argentina. On Buffarini, see Devoto, *Historia de los italianos en la Argentina*, 350–351. Buffarini was perhaps the most important fascist in the Italian community in Argentina. He took part in Gallardo's visit to Italy in 1927 and wanted to reproduce a similar event in 1931–1932. The Uriburu dictatorship was not as interested as its predecessors in meeting with Buffarini or in his historical project. Buffarini was the uncle of Guido Buffarini Guidi, the then fascist leader of Pisa and later interior minister of Salò. The elder Buffarini had close links through his nephew with important figures of fascism and with the Duce himself. His influence should not be underestimated when considering the earlier articulations of Italian propaganda in Argentina and their failure. See Archivo del Ministerio de Relaciones Exteriores y Culto, Argentina, División Política, caja 3033, Italia, Embajada Argentina en Italia, expediente 3, año 1931; ibid., caja 3538, Italia, Embajada Argentina en Italia, expediente 4, año 1935.

47. These histories presented Belgrano as the "most important figure" of Argentine independence. They also claim that an Italian priest was the "civilizer [*civilizzatore*] of Patagonia," not the Argentine general Roca of official accounts. See Mario Intaglietta, "L'eroica vita di monsignor Cagliero civilizzatore della Patagonia," *Il Giornale d'Italia*, July 8, 1938; Lori Mangano, "Italiani nel mondo," *Italia Fascista*, May–June 1942, 15.

48. See Sergi, *Historia de los italianos en la Argentina*; Cuneo, *Storia dell' emigrazione italiana in Argentina*; Mario Intaglietta, "Italiani in Argentina," *Il Giornale*

d'Italia, March 13, 1940. For a similar statement from an earlier period, see "Collaborazione Italo-argentina," *Il Giornale d'Italia*, August 13, 1929.

49. The act of flying was deeply aestheticized in fascist art. Futurist painters, for example, identified their art as "air painting" (*aeropittura*). Marinetti defined air painting "as the celebration of flight." For the futurists, this form of art aimed to present a modernist perspective in the form of an aerial view that captured the essence of fascism, its power and aim for combat. On this aspect of fascism, see the excellent work by Stone, *The Patron State*. See also Andreoli, Caprara, and Fontanella, *Volare!* For an analysis of the sublime in Nazi ideology and practice, see three works by LaCapra: *Representing the Holocaust*, 105–110; *History and Memory after Auschwitz*, 32–33; and *Writing History, Writing Trauma*, 93–94.

50. Mussolini, "Per l'aviazione italiana: Roma, 6 novembre 1923," in Mussolini, *La nuova politica dell'Italia*, 1.67–71. See also Mussolini, "Saluto agli aviatori italiani. Milano, 7 ottobre 1924," in ibid., 3.333–334; "Salvare le ali d'Italia," *Il Popolo d'Italia*, September 26, 1924; "La mistica dell'aviazione," *Critica Fascista*, October 15, 1932, 385–387.

51. "Civiltà nuova" and "L'alto elogio del Duce," *Corriere della Sera*, August 15, 1933. See also Balbo, *La centuria alata*, 9.

52. "Le ali forti e audaci dell'Italia di Mussolini trionfano per la seconda volta dell'Altlantico," *Corriere della Sera*, July 23, 1933.

53. Frontini, *Volare!* 19–20.

54. For the fascist understanding of Balbo's role in fascism, see "Italo Balbo," *Il Giornale d'Italia*, September 13, 1929. For historiographical works on Balbo, see Rochat, *Italo Balbo*; Corner, *Fascism in Ferrara*.

55. Five articles appeared in *Il Giornale d'Italia*: "Crociera aerea italiana in Oriente," June 5, 1929; "Ali tricolori nei cieli d'oriente," June 6, 1929; "Balbo passa in rivista le truppe sovietiche," June 11, 1929; "Con lo stormo di Balbo nei cieli d'oriente," June 12, 1929; "Un volo senza scalo Roma–New York," January 8, 1929. In addition, see "La nuova vittoria dell'ala italiana," *Corriere della Sera*, July 13, 1933. See also Balbo's own account of his European flights: Balbo, *Da Roma a Odessa sui cieli dell'Egeo e del mar Nero* and *Passeggiate aeree sul Mediterraneo*. For his North Atlantic flight, see "Considerazioni di Balbo sulla crociera," *Corriere della Sera*, September 2, 1933, and Balbo, *My Air Armada*.

56. See United States National Archives, Personal papers of Benito Mussolini, T586, no. 1021, reel 111, job 221, De Pinedo. For the Italian scholar Claudio Asciuti, Balbo was critical of the individual flights of De Pinedo and favored the flights of squads because the former were prone to "divismo" and the

latter related to a collective enterprise. See Asciuti, *Il corsaro e il trasvolatore*, 71, 84. See also Argenta, *Ardite imprese*, 119–120. Mussolini, for political reasons, sided with Balbo and gave him full control of the Ministry of Air in 1929. Although the Duce admired De Pinedo, the aviator was sent to Argentina in 1929 as an army attaché and later dismissed from duty in 1932. See "Fue pasado a reserva el Gral. Pinedo," *La Razón*, September 24, 1932. As a private citizen De Pinedo organized a spectacular flight from New York to Baghdad in 1933, but died when his plane crashed in Long Island at the beginning of this flight. See "La tragica fine di De Pinedo a Nuova York," *Corriere della Sera*, September 3, 1933.

57. See Guerri, *Italo Balbo*, 220.

58. See articles in *Il Giornale d'Italia*: "D'Annunzio prepara un volo tra l'Italia e l'America Latina," May 1, 1925; "Casagrande verso l'America," November 6, 1925.

59. See articles in *Il Giornale d'Italia*: "De Pinedo sosta a Rangoon," May 19, 1925; "De Pinedo è giunto a Tokio," September 27, 1925; "Il miracolo dell'ala italiana è compiuto," November 6, 1925; and "I voli transoceanici," *Corriere della Sera*, September 23, 1927.

60. See Eksteins, *Rites of Spring*, 247–252. See also Fritzsche, *A Nation of Fliers*; and Wohl, *The Spectacle of Flight*.

61. "L'incubo di Benedetto Croce," *Il Giornale d'Italia*, September 27, 1925.

62. Mussolini, "Pel Comandante De Pinedo," in Mussolini, *Discorsi del 1925*, 223–224. See also Mussolini's letter to De Pinedo in De Pinedo, *Un volo di 55.000 chilometri*, 9–11.

63. See Cappelli Bajocco, *De Pinedo Aquila d'Italia*, 124–130. For some general examples of fascism's use of Columbus as icon of "Italianness," see "Colombo," *Italia Fascista*, July–August 1939, 8; "Il rimorso di Cristoforo Colombo," *Italia Fascista*, November–December 1942, 2. See also Mussolini, "Discorso di Genova," in *Opera omnia*, 22.138.

64. *Il Popolo d'Italia* published six articles on these events: "De Pinedo trasvolerà oggi l'Atlantico," February 16, 1927; "Il 'Santa Maria' riprenderà subito il suo magnifico volo," February 21, 1927; "L'alto valore morale e politico dell'impresa transoceanica," February 27, 1927; "Il programma dei festeggiamenti nella capitale Argentina," March 2, 1927; "Il commandante De Pinedo accolto trionfalmente al suo arrivo a Buenos Aires," March 3, 1927; "De Pinedo a Mar del Plata," March 6, 1927; a front-page article on March 15, 1927, 1; and "De Pinedo sarà oggi a Terranova," May 20, 1927.

65. Cappelli Bajocco, *De Pinedo Aquila d'Italia*, 155–156.

66. Ibid.,159.

67. "Il discorso dell'on. Mussolini," *Il Messaggero*, October 7, 1927. See also "Italia e Argentina," *Il Popolo d'Italia*, March 3, 1927; "Le leggendarie vicende della crociera aerea: nostra intervista con De Pinedo," *Il Popolo d'Italia*, June 18, 1927; "Il volo sull'Atlantico del sud nella suggestiva narrazione del gen. De Pinedo," *Il Popolo d'Italia*, December 22, 1927.

68. See Archivo del Ministerio de Relaciones Exteriores y Culto, Argentina, División Política, caja 2717, Italia, Embajada Argentina en Italia, expediente 36, año 1928, folio 1.

69. "Desde Cerdeña iniciariase hoy un vuelo a Bs. Aires," *La Prensa*, November 20, 1937; "El próximo vuelo de Mario Stoppani a Buenos Aires," *La Nación*, December 4, 1937; "Vuelo del piloto Mario Stoppani," *La Prensa*, December 18, 1937; "Desde Cádiz llegó ayer a la ciudad de Caravellas, Brasil, el aviador italiano Mario Stoppani," *La Prensa*, December 30, 1937; "La prensa italiana exalta y detalla la proeza de Stoppani," *La Nación*, January 1, 1938. See also Archivo del Ministerio de Relaciones Exteriores y Culto, Argentina, División Política, caja 3838, Italia, Embajada Argentina en Italia, expediente 22, año 1937.

70. See three articles in *Il Giornale d'Italia*: "Il nuovo volo intercontinentale dell'ala fascista," January 26, 1938; January 27, 1938, 1; "L'aviazione fascista dominatrice dello spazio," January 29, 1938. Mussolini's son planned to continue on to Buenos Aires, but I could not confirm in the documentation that he actually made the trip.

71. Italy, Ministero degli Affari Esteri, *I documenti diplomatici italiani*, vol. 14, doc. 572, appunto 1934, 651.

72. On this topic see the comprehensive study by Canistraro, *La fabbrica del consenso*.

73. Virginio Gayda, "Panorama di azione," *Il Giornale d'Italia*, May 23, 1936.

74. "Gli scopi della propaganda," *Il Giornale d'Italia*, May 23, 1936.

75. In his letter to his friend "Rosita," María Rosa Oliver, Ciano boasted about the affinity "of our Latin Spirit." See Archivio Centrale dello Stato, Italia, Archivio Renzo De Felice, B16, F90. The letters are from 1928 and 1929. See also Archivo del Ministerio de Relaciones Exteriores y Culto, Argentina, División Política, caja 3838, Italia, Asuntos varios, expediente 5, año 1937, telegrama cifrado 819.

76. See Archivio Centrale dello Stato, Italia, Ministero della Cultura Popolare, D.G. Serv., Propaganda, B12, Argentina, Varie 5, V8, 900292 / 30, 835407 / 2311.

77. Ibid., B8, Argentina, 1938, I / 4 / 2. As Guariglia put it to Ciano, Argentina

because of these democratic practices was remarkably slow in "the evolution" toward a political "reaction."

78. Guariglia, *Ricordi*, 333.

79. Archivio Centrale dello Stato, Italia, Ministero della Cultura Popolare, D.G. Serv., Propaganda, B9, Argentina, 5 / 1 / 10, T2719 / 1277; ibid., Argentina, 5 / 1 / 7.

80. Ibid., B12, Argentina, Varie 5, V8, 901518, Italiani nell'america del Sud. See also Guariglia, *Ricordi*, 331–333. For Ambassador Guariglia no country was as fast and effective as Argentina with respect to the assimilation of Italians.

81. Archivio Centrale dello Stato, Italia, Ministero della Cultura Popolare, D.G. Serv., Propaganda, B8, Argentina, 1938, I / 4 / 1, pos. 1–23–1, T1589. See also Ettore De Zuani, "L'Argentina e gli inglesi," *Critica Fascista*, October 15, 1940, 405–406.

82. See United States National Archives, Personal papers of Benito Mussolini, T586, job 321, Ministero degli Affari Esteri, cuaderno no. 5 segreto, Argentina, 106975, 106976, 106994, 106995; Guariglia, *Ricordi*, 336.

83. Archivio Centrale dello Stato, Italia, Ministero della Cultura Popolare., D.G. Serv., Propaganda, B8, Argentina, 1938, I / 4 / 2, 307 / 131.

84. See United States National Archives, Personal papers of Benito Mussolini, T586, job 321, Ministero degli Affari Esteri, cuaderno no. 5 segreto, Argentina, 106975, 106976, 106994, 106995. See also Archivio Centrale dello Stato, Italia, Ministero della Cultura Popolare, D.G. Serv., Propaganda, B11, Argentina, 5 / 5; ibid., B7, Argentina, 1937, I / 4 / 35.

85. Archivio Centrale dello Stato, Italia, Ministero della Cultura Popolare, D.G. Serv., Propaganda, B7, Argentina, 1937, I / 4 / 52, T3782 / 1363.

86. For the historiographical discussion on the origins of Peronism, which, of course, included other factors, see Halperín Donghi, *Argentina en el callejón* and *La larga agonía de la Argentina peronista*; Germani, *Política y sociedad en una época de transición*; Murmis and Portantiero, *Estudios sobre los orígenes del peronismo*; Adelman, "Reflections on Argentine Labour and the Rise of Peron"; Torre, *La vieja guardia sindical y Perón: sobre los orígenes del peronismo* and *Los años peronistas*; Rein, *Peronismo, populismo y política*. See also the epilogue of this book and Finchelstein, *La Argentina fascista*, chap. 4.

87. On Italian antifascism in Argentina, see Fanesi, "El antifascismo italiano en Argentina (1922–1945)."

88. See Archivio Centrale dello Stato, Italia, Ministero della Cultura Popolare, D.G. Serv., Propaganda, 16B 4, Argentina, 1930–1933, I / 4; ibid., 16 B4, Argentina, 1934, I / 4 / 6; ibid., B5, Argentina I / 4 / 4; ibid., B10, Argentina, 5 / 1 / 46, pos. 2–2-2; ibid., B8, Argentina, 1938, I / 4 / 2, 307 / 131; ibid., B12, Argentina,

Varie 5, V8.A; ibid., gabinetto B83 570, 2, Gran Consiglio del fascismo, G.I.4.6, mod. 267. In 1937, for example Mussolini's speeches were broadcast in Germany, Austria, Yugoslavia, Hungary, Argentina, Uruguay, Portugal, United States, Brazil, and Switzerland. The speeches were also translated into French, Japanese, Turkish, Chinese, Hindi, Romanian, Greek, and Arabic.

89. Archivio Centrale dello Stato, Italia, Ministero della Cultura Popolare, D.G. Serv., Propaganda, B4, Argentina, 1930–1933, I / 4; ibid., 16 B4, Argentina, 1934, I / 4 / 6.

90. Ibid. See also ibid., B8, Argentina, 1938, I / 4 / 2, 307 / 131.

91. Ibid., 16 B4, Argentina, 1934, I / 4 / 6.

92. See ibid., PB4, Argentina, 1934, I / 4 / 6.

93. See "Le dichiarazioni del Ministro Ciano al Senato," Il Giornale d'Italia, May 23, 1936.

94. See Archivio Centrale dello Stato, Italia, Ministero della Cultura Popolare, D.G. Serv., Propaganda, B5, Argentina, I / 4 / 24, 967161 / 71; ibid., B6, Argentina, I / 4 / 4. See also Archivio, Ministero degli Affari Esteri, Rome, Italy, telespresso 1036 / 1077, July 20, 1937. For Gayda's book see Archivio Centrale dello Stato, Italia, Ministero della Cultura Popolare, D.G. Serv., Propaganda, N.U.P. I.E. B26 F27 147, pos. 1.747, 900237 / 23, pos. 1–2-1; ibid., B8, Argentina, 1938, I / 4 / 3, T1061, pos. 2–1-4; ibid., B12, Argentina, Varie 5, V8.A. See also "Che cosa vuole l'Italia in edizione argentina," Il Giornale d'Italia, January 15, 1941; and Gayda, Que quiere Italia?

95. On this aspect of Italian propaganda, see Archivo del Ministerio de Relaciones Exteriores y Culto, Argentina, División Política, caja 4336, Italia, expediente 17, año 1940; ibid., caja 3981, Guerra Europea, Sugestión chilena sobre actividades fascistas, expediente 201, año 1940, reservado; ibid., caja 4336, Italia, expediente 9, año 1940.

96. See Archivio Centrale dello Stato, Italia, Ministero della Cultura Popolare, D.G. Serv., Propaganda, B4, Argentina, 1934, I / 4 / 4; ibid., B5, Argentina, I / 4 / 4; ibid., B6, Argentina, I / 4 / 4; Archivio, Ministero degli Affari Esteri, Rome, Italy, telespresso 2955, April 19, 1935; ibid., telespresso 1287 / 459, April 18, 1937. The list of papers that published fascist propaganda distributed as news wires by Roma Press included among others the Catholic papers El Pueblo and Los Principios (Córdoba); the conservative La Razón; the provincial mainstream papers La Voz del Interior (Córdoba), El Litoral (Santa Fe), La Tarde, El Norte Argentino, La Gaceta (Tucumán), La Crónica (Jujuy), and El Liberal (Santiago del Estero); the nacionalista papers La Fronda, El Momento Argentino, Crisol, and Bandera Argentina; and the Italian paper in Argentina

Il Mattino d' Italia. In addition, Roma Press gave free news on Argentine fascist developments to Italian fascist publications. *Bibliografia Fascista*, June 1935, 554.

97. Archivio Centrale dello Stato, Italia, Ministero della Cultura Popolare, D.G. Serv., Propaganda, B6, Argentina, I / 4 / 4, T.E. 2331 / 260. See also Archivio, Ministero degli Affari Esteri, Rome, Italy, telespresso 2331 / 260, May 1935.

98. Archivio Centrale dello Stato, Italia, Ministero della Cultura Popolare, D.G. Serv., Propaganda, B9, Argentina, 5 / 1 / 1, pos. 5–1-1–6; 1–19–77; ibid., Propaganda N.U.P.I.E. B16 5.2 Cordoba, pos. A53; ibid., Propaganda, B10, Argentina, 5 / 1 / 46, pos. 2–2-2; ibid., Propaganda, B7, Argentina, 1937, I / 4 / 1, pos. 1, 1658; Archivio, Ministero degli Affari Esteri, Rome, Italy, telespresso 2118, May 19, 1939. *Los Principios* published a regular page entitled "The Page of Italy," which was decorated with the fascist lictor. *El Pueblo*, with a circulation of 50,000 copies often asked for free fascist propaganda related to the Catholic support for fascism in Italy. Like the nacionalista press, *El Pueblo* received not only free news wires but also cash.

99. Archivio Centrale dello Stato, Italia, Ministero della Cultura Popolare, D.G. Serv., Propaganda, B4, Argentina. 1934, I / 4 / 51; ibid., B5, Argentina, I / 4 / 2; ibid., B9, Argentina, 5 / 1 / 1; ibid., B9, Argentina, 5 / 1 / 1; ibid., B10, Argentina, 5 / 1 / 46, pos. 2–2-2; Archivio, Ministero degli Affari Esteri, Rome, Italy, telespresso 4109 / 453, August 20, 1935; ibid., telespresso 3179 / 1142, July 22, 1937; ibid., telespresso 1809, February, 25, 1939. Other nacionalista papers like *El Momento Argentino* received free wires and fascist gifts but, as far as I can tell, no traceable amount of cash.

100. Archivio Centrale dello Stato, Italia, Ministero della Cultura Popolare, D.G. Serv., Propaganda, B8, Argentina, 1938, I / 4 / 83, T.N. 1476; ibid., B9, Argentina, 5 / 1 / 1; ibid., B8, Argentina, 1938, I / 4 / 1, T1589.

101. Ibid., B4, Argentina, 1934, I / 4 / 52; ibid., B4, Argentina, B6, Argentina, I / 4 / 1; ibid., reports B29 71, T8136, T3513, T3144, T2879, T3941; ibid., B11, Argentina, 5 / 5 / 1. The list of provincial papers also included *Córdoba*, *El Orden* (Tucumán), *La Capital* (Rosario), *El Litoral* (Santa Fe), *La Acción* (Rosario), *La Gaceta* (Tucumán), *La Voz de Entre Rios*, and some union journals like *La Tierra* (Federación Agraria) and *Riel*.

102. Archivio Centrale dello Stato, Italia, Ministero della Cultura Popolare, D.G. Serv., Propaganda, B9, Argentina, 5 / 1 / 1.

103. Mussolini, "Al direttore de 'La Razón,'" in *Opera omnia*, 22.446. For some examples of these links, see also Benito Mussolini, "Un artículo de Benito Mussolini: por qué he cambiado de ministros o el relevo de la guardia," *La*

Razón, September 11, 1932; "Mussolini ¿Conquistara el mundo?" *La Razón*, November 18, 1935; "El soldado italiano tiene una sola inspiración: la patria y el Duce," *La Razón*, September 13, 1936; "La ocupación de Abisinia cerraría un ciclo histórico: señalaría el fin de la etapa colonizadora que pudo presagiarse en las hazañas de los primeros navegantes," *La Razón*, September 28, 1936; Giuseppe Bottai, "El amor a Roma," *La Razón*, October 28, 1936.

104. Guariglia, *Ricordi*, 22.

105. Archivio Centrale dello Stato, Italia, Ministero della Cultura Popolare, D.G. Serv., Propaganda, B9, Argentina, 5 / 1 / 7, 1274 / pos. 1-15-26.

106. See *La Razón*, May 8, 1937 (suplemento alemán), 1–31.

107. Archivio Centrale dello Stato, Italia, Ministero della Cultura Popolare, D.G. Serv., Propaganda, B9, Argentina, 5 / 1 / 7.

108. *La Razón*, May 24, 1937 (sección 2), 1–12.

109. Archivio Centrale dello Stato, Italia, Ministero della Cultura Popolare, D.G. Serv., Propaganda, B9, Argentina, 5 / 1 / 7, 1274 / pos. 1-15-26.

110. Ibid., T725, 904273 / 389, 904271 / 377, 904272 / 378, 904274 / 880, 904268 / 374, 904261 / 367, 904264 / 370, 904265 / 371, 904257 / 224, 904258 / 23, 2426, 1441, 904959, 904950 / 454. For the issue of 1936 see also doc. 5188 / 1698. See also Archivio, Ministero degli Affari Esteri, Rome, Italy, telespresso 1957 / 701, May 28, 1937.

111. *La Razón*, May 24, 1937 (sección 2), 1–12.

112. "Las repúblicas Latinas de América son la expresión viviente de Romanidad en el nuevo continente. La estirpe no solo no muere, sino que no cambia con las transmigraciones. Los pioneros antes de pensar en recoger los frutos de las nuevas tierras donde ponen el pie, cuidan instintivamente de establecer las bases de la raza. Es el hombre latino, la sociedad latina, que ha dado la fisonomía y ha hecho arraigar la civilidad en una gran parte del Nuevo Continente. Si un ciudadano romano de los tiempos de Augusto renaciera en el Uruguay, en el Paraguay, en la Argentina, en el Brasil, en uno cualquiera de los Estados de la América Latina, sentiría el mismo latido de corazones, la misma genialidad de las mentes, el florecimiento de inteligencias como en las tierras del imperio. . . . En el curso de los siglos, Italia estuvo siempre presente en toda la tierra latina de América. . . . La Italia fascista, elevada al rango de Italia imperial, envía hoy a las hermanas de América, y esencialmente a la República Argentina—que por su desarrollo cultural las sintetiza—su saludos afectuoso y augural, en la seguridad de que en el nuevo imperio ellas sabrán ver el imperio de Roma, hoy todavía garantía de civilización, de gloria, de justicia y de progreso en el mundo." See *La Razón*, May 24, 1937, 10. See also

Archivio Centrale dello Stato, Italia, Ministero della Cultura Popolare, D.G. Serv., Propaganda, B 9, Argentina, 5/1/7, 904950/454. For the issue of 1936, see also doc. 5188/1698.

113. See De Felice, *Mussolini il duce*. For a discussion of this topic, see Corner, "Italian Fascism." See also Finchelstein, "The Fascist Canon."

114. On both sides of the Atlantic, fascism did not only cater to intellectuals. For a criticism of the view that nacionalismo was restricted to writers and theorists, see Finchelstein, *Fascismo, liturgia e imaginario*, 10–27.

115. Archivio Centrale dello Stato, Italia, Ministero della Cultura Popolare, D.G. Serv., Propaganda, B 4, Argentina, 1934, I/4/4; ibid., B9, Argentina, 5/1/1; ibid., B5, Argentina, I/4/26; United States National Archives, Personal papers of Benito Mussolini, T586, job 321, Ministero degli Affari Esteri, quaderno no. 5 segreto, Argentina, 106992.

116. Archivio Centrale dello Stato, Italia, Ministero della Cultura Popolare, D.G. Serv., Propaganda, B10, Argentina, 5/1/46, pos. 2-2-2.

117. For some examples, see "Un partito fascista è sorto anche in Argentina," *Universalità Fascista*, July–August 1932, 375; "La rifrazione del fascismo nell'America Latina," *Gerarchia*, October 1932, 848–853; "Gli sviluppi del fascismo Argentino," *Universalità Fascista*, February 1934, 253; Sandro Volta, "Decadenza democratica, fascismo e pseudofascismo nell'America del Sud," *Civiltà Fascista*, April 1934, 310–317; "Argentina," *Bibliografia Fascista*, January 1935, 90; "Mosca si attende dal processo uno stato di tensione europea," *Corriere Padano*, January 30, 1937; "Un altro processo attende quello di Mosca," *La Vedetta d'Italia* (Fiume), January 30, 1937; Carlo Foa, "Nazionalismi sudamericani," *Gerarchia*, July 1937, 480; Mario Da Silva, " 'Fascismi' latino-americani," *Critica Fascista*, December 15, 1937, 44–47.

118. Archivio Centrale dello Stato, Italia, Ministero della Cultura Popolare, D.G. Serv., Propaganda, B5, Argentina, I/4/12.

119. J.L., "El fascismo y los obreros," *La Nueva República*, May 5, 1928; "Vida Intelectual," *Criterio*, October 30, 1930, 575.

120. See, for example, United States National Archives, Personal papers of Benito Mussolini, T586, job 321, Ministero degli Affari Esteri, quaderno no. 5 segreto, Argentina, 106992; Archivio Centrale dello Stato, Italia, Ministero della Cultura Popolare, D.G. Serv., Propaganda, B4, Argentina, 1934, I/4/4; ibid., B9, Argentina, 5/1/1; ibid., B5, Argentina, I/4/26. See also Zanatta, *Del estado liberal a la nación católica*, 52.

121. Archivio Centrale dello Stato, Italia, Ministero della Cultura Popolare, D.G. Serv., Propaganda, B10, Argentina, 5/1/10, T.N. 3930, pos. 2-3-8, 1941.

122. See ibid., B9, Argentina, 5/1/5, pos. 1-2b-3, prot. no. 20084, 3636. See also Archivo del Ministerio de Relaciones Exteriores y Culto, Argentina, División Política, caja 2717, Italia, Embajada Argentina en Roma, expediente II, año 1928.

123. Archivo General de la Nación, Argentina, Archivo Agustín P. Justo, caja 36, doc. 101. See also *Nueva Política* 1 (June 1940): 28; Bruno Jacovella, "Los Italianos en la Argentina," *Nuevo Orden*, June 4, 1941, 7; H. Sáenz y Quesada, "¿Qué sería una política imperial argentina?" *Nueva Política* 9 (February 1940): 19; Ignacio Anzoátegui, "El almirante," *Sol y Luna* 5 (1940); "Cristóbal Colón," *Nueva Política* 17 (November 1941): 28.

124. See "Del Momento," *El Momento Argentino*, March 16, 1936. See also "La bandera tricolor siempre triunfante" and "Europa: he ahí a tu Italia!" *El Momento Argentino*, March 16, 1936; "La victoria romana," *Aduna*, May 15, 1936; "Las colectividades extranjeras," *Liberación*, September 9, 1941; Casajs, *Guerra al eje*, 125.

125. As Borges once argued, it was Nazism and not fascism that created a myth about technological warfare. However, as Borges recognized, Italian air power played no small role in the conquest. Borges wrote: "En 1936, casi toda la fuerza de los tiranos deriva de su posesión de la técnica. Wells venera los chauffeurs y los aviadores; la ocupación tiránica de Abisinia fue obra de los aviadores y de los chauffeurs—y del temor, tal vez un poco mitológico, de los perversos laboratorios de Hitler." See Jorge Luis Borges, "Wells previsor," *Sur* 6.26 (November 1936): 126. On Borges and fascism, see chap. 4 of Finchelstein, *El canon del Holocausto*.

126. "Hace un año se inició la conquista de Abisinia, que hoy ya no existe, pese a la confabulación mundial antifascista," *Crisol*, October 4, 1936. On the notion of vital space in fascist Europe, see Rodogno, *Fascism's European Empire*.

127. "[Italia] logra la civilización de un pueblo bárbaro con la expansión forzosa de sus connacionales, demasiados estrechos en la vieja Italia" ("Del Momento," *El Momento Argentino*, March 16, 1936). See also "Habrá un mitin de homenaje a Italia," *Bandera Argentina*, December 30, 1936; *Crisol*, October 4, 1936; "La victoria romana," *Aduna*, May 15, 1936.

128. Archivio Centrale dello Stato, Italia, Ministero della Cultura Popolare, D.G. Serv., Propaganda, B4, Argentina, 1934, I/4/6; and ibid., B5, Argentina, I/4/3. See also Sergio Villamil, "Un hombre y un pueblo," *Crisol*, December 17, 1933; and "Fiasco," *El Tábano* (Tucumán), May 9, 1935.

129. Finchelstein, *Fascismo, liturgia e imaginario*, 113–130.

130. For a typical example, see "El Mussolini Argentino: General Fasola Castaño,"

El Momento Argentino, March 16, 1936, 1. See also "Hace falta un Mussolini," *Bandera Argentina*, October 25, 1932, 1; "El fascismo en marcha," *Bandera Argentina*, October 29, 1932, 1; "Precio de sangre," *Bandera Argentina*, January 3, 1933; "Dictaduras efímeras y dictaduras permanentes," *Bandera Argentina*, April 5, 1933, 1; " Queremos un Uriburu," *Bandera Argentina*, May 3, 1933, 1; "Libertad," *Aduna*, October 15, 1933; "Una antología mussoliniana," *Crisol*, October 15, 1936; "A catorce años de Fascismo," *Crisol*, October 28, 1936; Juan Manuel, "Así canta Repetto," *La Fronda*, January 23, 1937; "Como terminar con el comunismo," *Clarinada* 6.77 (September 1943): 2–3; Sánchez Sorondo, *Memoria*, 35; Ibarguren, *Orígenes del nacionalismo argentino*, 135, 237.

131. Archivio Centrale dello Stato, Italia, Ministero della Cultura Popolare, D.G. Serv., Propaganda, B4, Argentina, 1934, I / 4 / 52; and ibid., B4, Argentina, 1934, I / 4 / 51; ibid., B9, Argentina, 5 / 1 / 1, T1874, pos. 1-16-39. See also more generally, Archivio Fundación IWO, Argentina, caja Organización Popular contra el Antisemitismo, Correspondencia panfletos, publicaciones C1936–1937, C1939.

132. Archivio Centrale dello Stato, Italia, Ministero della Cultura Popolare, D.G. Serv., Propaganda, B5, Argentina, I / 4 / 12, T2623, pos. I / 4 / 12.

133. Ibid., B4, Argentina, 1934, Movimento fascista in Argentina, I / 4 / 8, T906144, T4347 / 673. The fascist ambassador, Arlotta, told his Italian superiors that he had a "total favorable opinion" of Villegas Oromí. On the Legión de Mayo, see also Archivo General de la Nación Argentina, Archivo Uriburu, legajo 12, sala 7 2588, docs. 286–287; ibid., legajo 20, sala 7 2596, doc. 10; Archivo General de la Nación Argentina, Archivo Agustín P. Justo, caja 49, doc. 233; ibid., caja 45, doc. 67.

134. On clericofascists in Italy, see Pollard, "Conservative Catholics and Italian Fascism."

135. Archivio Centrale dello Stato, Italia, Ministero della Cultura Popolare, D.G. Serv., Propaganda, B4, Argentina, 1934, I / 4 / 6. See also Alberto El Argentino, "Frente nacionalista: Dios y el destino de una patria," *Bandera Argentina*, December 16, 1933.

136. See Alfredo Tarruella, "Benito Mussolini y las juventudes nacionalistas," *Bandera Argentina*, September 6, 1935, 2.

137. The possibility of signing a trade agreement between Italy and Argentina was a major concern of the Argentine government. Argentina had always had a trade deficit with Italy, and Ezequiel Ramos Mexía, a nacionalista fascist sympathizer was sent to Italy in 1933 to meet with Mussolini in order to promote the Italian importation of Argentine goods. Some Argentine nacionalistas correctly believed that the administration was doing them and the

nacionalista officers in the army a favor by sending a nacionalista emissary to meet with Mussolini, but Saavedra Lamas, the Argentine foreign minister, was seriously displeased about the venture. Saavedra Lamas knew that Ramos Mexía had a direct relation with President Justo (in fact, Ramos Mexía reported directly to the president) and he may have known about Justo's dealings with nacionalismo. Nonetheless Saavedra Lamas decided to make public the diplomatic exchanges regarding the special envoy's political opinions on fascism. In these exchanges, he bluntly told Ramos Mexía to keep quiet. Ramos Mexía responded that he did not abide by the "old-fashioned molds" of behavior that Mussolini himself had "shattered in pieces." As a "nacionalista" he claimed, he could not stop manifesting his "defense of nacionalismo," which he equated with a defense of fascism. This episode shows the limits of President Justo's instrumental use of nacionalismo and Italian fascism. The Argentine administration was unhappy with the result of Ramos Mexía's mission not only for his "nacionalista" declaration for fascism but also because he was considered to have conceded too much to Mussolini. There may, however, have been some connection between Argentina's concessions and Mussolini's agreement to sign the Latin American antiwar pact put forward by Saavedra Lamas in 1933–1934. In urging Italy to sign the pact Saavedra Lamas argued that Italy should play a role "morally representing Latin America in Europe." This was music to Mussolini's ears, and Italy signed the pact. But Saavedra Lamas later invited Poland to sign the pact as well, and he thus in practice undercut the "Latin" argument about Italy and Europe. On Ramos Mexía, see Archivo del Ministerio de Relaciones Exteriores y Culto, Argentina, División Política, caja 3298, Italia, expediente 5, año 1933, telegramas cifrados, N318, 321, 532, 539, 333, 570, 655, N20 RE M. See Italy, Ministero degli Affari Esteri, *I documenti diplomatici italiani*, vol. 5, doc. 426, Promemoria, 1933, p. 464; ibid., vol. 14, doc. 440, T2109 / 199 r, 1933, p. 482; ibid., vol. 14, doc. 495, appunto 1933, p. 554; ibid., vol. 14, doc. 604, T336 / 24 r, 1934, p. 691; ibid., vol. 14, doc. 616, T137 / 19 r, 1934, p. 702; ibid., vol. 14, doc. 789, T370 / 69 r, 1934, p. 877; ibid., vol. 14, doc. 796, T1027 / 34 r, 1934, p. 883. See also "Puntualizose el alcance de los juicios del Sr. Ramos Mexía," *La Nación*, April 14, 1933; "Ramos Mexía se declaró partidario de la inflación," *La Nación*, May 3, 1933; "Las actitudes del jefe de la misión italiana," *La Prensa*, May 5, 1933; "Han producido desagrado al gobierno las declaraciones del embajador Ramos Mexía," *La Prensa*, May 6, 1933; Carlo Dall'Ongaro, "Intervista col Presidente della Repubblica Argentina," *Il Giornale d'Italia*, December 11, 1932; Archivo del Ministerio de Relaciones Exteriores y Culto, Argentina, División Política, caja 3538, Italia,

Política interna, expediente 15, año 1935; Archivo General de la Nación Argentina, Archivo Agustín P. Justo, caja 70, docs. 59, 60, 77, 86, 88.

138. On Goyeneche, see Archivio Centrale dello Stato, Italia, Ministero della Cultura Popolare, D.G. Serv., Propaganda, B9, Argentina, 5/1/8; Archivo del Ministerio de Relaciones Exteriores y Culto, Argentina, División Política, caja 22, Italia, telegrama cifrado, N511, N34, Estrictamente reservado y muy confidencial, folio 1, June 4, 1943. On Ramos Mexía, see ibid., caja 3298, Italia, expediente 5, año 1933, telegramas cifrados, N318, 321, 532, 539, 333, 570, 655, N20 RE M; Archivo General de la Nación Argentina, Archivo Agustín P. Justo, caja 70, docs. 59, 60, 77, 86, 88. On Lavalle, see *Bandera Argentina*, March 23, 1933, 1.

139. Fresco had been an earlier admirer of Uriburu. As the Speaker of the House in the Argentine Congress he had visited Italy and met with Mussolini in Rome. He described in great detail to the Argentine press how he was able to personally "study Mussolini," namely, how he could engage in eye contact with the Duce and how he "had the feeling of having found a friend." For the Italian fascist press and for many of its readers, Fresco was an "eminent political man [*eminente uomo politico*]" who had surrendered to "the potent fascination of the Duce's persona." Interviewed by *Il Messagero* and asked about his impression of fascist Italy, Fresco argued: "I cannot have a better opinion about it." Fresco was particularly interested in corporativism and highlighted the "great effort of rebirth that the fascist regime and its great leader have given to Italy." Mussolini valued power above all and saw in Fresco a politician with a future. When Fresco became the governor of Buenos Aires, the largest Argentine province, an institutional executive position second in importance to the presidency, Mussolini would tell Argentine visitors, "I always remember him with sympathy." However the Duce's "sympathy" was not sufficient for Fresco to be what the Italians wanted from him, namely, an imitator of fascism, and in 1938 in his report to Ciano, Ambassador Guariglia secretly complained that Fresco wanted to "find 'original Argentine solutions' to Argentine problems." As a governor, Fresco established mandatory Catholic education in state schools and social measures inspired in social Catholicism that Perón himself would later acknowledge as being a precedent for Peronism. Fresco defined his social politics as both nacionalista and Catholic, and he opposed communism and universal suffrage in his writings. See Archivio Centrale dello Stato, Italia, Ministero della Cultura Popolare, D.G. Serv., Propaganda, B5, Argentina, 1/4/3; Archivio, Ministero degli Affari Esteri, Rome, Italy, telespresso 6659/957, November 27, 1934; ibid., telespresso 1676/610, April, 18, 1937. See also "Política: una entrevista con el Doctor

Fresco," *Córdoba*, May 13, 1935. See Archivo del Ministerio de Relaciones Exteriores y Culto, Argentina, División Política, caja 3538, Italia, expediente 5, año 1935. See "Il presidente della Camera Argentina ammirato delle realizzazioni fasciste," *Il Messaggero*, February 4, 1935. On the fascist appreciation of Fresco, see Luigi Federzoni, *Parole fasciste al Sud-America*, 22. See also Archivio Centrale dello Stato, Italia, Ministero della Cultura Popolare, D.G. Serv., Propaganda, B7, Argentina, 1937, I / 4 / 21; ibid., B10, Argentina, 5 / 1 / 46; ibid., B8, Argentina, 1938, I / 4 / 1. Mussolini once said that Federzoni told him about the significance of Fresco's tenure in the province of Buenos Aires.

140. As the Italian fascists recognized, both in secret reports and more openly in an article published in Mussolini's newspaper, Sánchez Sorondo was an early advocate of fascism, "not our only friend on the River Plate but . . . the most convinced [*il più convinto*]." The most important fascist paper praised Sánchez Sorondo for his anticommunist credentials and defined him as "a great politician and also a great humanist" who "knows everything about us, about our revolution." To be sure, Sánchez Sorondo was not alone in having "a deep admiration" a "love" for Mussolini. But the fascist paper drew its readers' attention to the specificity of Sánchez Sorondo's brand of fascism and the "grandiosity and the difficulty of his efforts" in the context of a country that remained too fixated on liberalism: "The battle that he initiated in order to create in Argentina a party that could resemble fascism . . . has not been improvised. Argentina has a political and a moral climate that is different to ours. Naturally Sánchez Sorondo is not copying, but if the appearance [*timbro*] is not identical, the spirit is." Sánchez Sorondo's admiration for fascism led to a two-month visit to fascist Italy, where he had been invited by the fascist regime to "study the works of fascism." Invited by the Turin section of the Partido Fascista Argentino, Sánchez gave a speech in that city. Later he went to Rome, where he gave a lecture titled "Italy in Argentina," which was attended by many fascist dignitaries, including Count Ciano. Sánchez Sorondo met many times with Ciano in order to talk about fascism and was surprised to learn about Ciano's deep knowledge on Argentine developments. In typical nacionalista fashion, Sánchez had private meetings with the Duce and the pope. The meeting with the pope provided Sánchez Sorondo with the opportunity to give the Holy Father a collection of his own anticommunist speeches, which Sánchez identified with the pope's own battle against communism. Much more interesting was the meeting of the Argentine senator with the Duce. As Sánchez Sorondo later told the United Press, he conversed with Mussolini—surely one of the best primary sources on the subject—

"about [his] current studies on fascism," taking the opportunity to sell himself to the fascist leader. He found the Duce "charming" and was impressed by his "simplicity [*sencillez*] and human qualities." It is highly doubtful that Mussolini would have really enjoyed the meeting with Sánchez Sorondo, given his well-documented impatience with listening to explanations. It is likely that Mussolini talked more than Sánchez. In his own recollection of the meeting, Sánchez Sorondo emphasized his own political role and the importance of the Argentine anticommunist battle. He seemed to be more interested in talking about himself and the transnational importance of his own fight against the common enemy than in listening to anything the Duce had to say: "Mr. Mussolini wanted to know my opinion on a variety of Argentine social problems and among other things, I told him: the only Argentine political question that may possibly be a concern for the whole world and to Christian civilization as well is the fight against communism." Sánchez Sorondo's trip to fascist Italy and his later visit to Nazi Germany and to the Spanish fascist front in the Civil War enhanced his status within nacionalismo. But the boost was not permanent. After his ultimately unsuccessful anticommunist project and the failure of the Ethiopian campaign, Sánchez Sorondo lost momentum and could not rise above his reputation as nothing more than a fascist fellow traveler. See "Un argentino in Italia: Sanchez Sorondo," *Il Popolo d'Italia*, May 7, 1937. See also "Viajeros sudamericanos han llegado a Genova," *La Nación*, April 9, 1937. See also United States National Archives, Personal papers of Benito Mussolini, T586, job 321, Ministero degli Affari Esteri, cuaderno no. 5, segreto, Argentina, 106995; and Archivio Centrale dello Stato, Italia, Ministero della Cultura Popolare, D.G. Serv., Propaganda, B7, Argentina, 1937, I / 4 / 52, 5. See Archivo del Ministerio de Relaciones Exteriores y Culto, Argentina, División Política, caja 3838, Italia, expediente 11, año 1937. See also "El Conde Ciano recibió al Dr. Sánchez Sorondo," *La Nación*, April 14, 1937; "Dará una conferencia en Roma el senador Sánchez Sorondo," *La Prensa*, May 8, 1937; "Conferencia del doctor Sánchez Sorondo," *La Prensa*, May 9, 1937; "Recorrerá Italia el Dr. Sánchez Sorondo," *La Prensa*, May 11, 1937; "Declaraciones del Senador doctor M. Sánchez Sorondo," *La Prensa*, August 8, 1937; Archivo del Ministerio de Relaciones Exteriores y Culto, Argentina, División Política, caja 3838, Italia, expediente 11, año 1937. See also "Fue recibido por Mussolini el doctor Sánchez Sorondo," *La Prensa*, April 15, 1937.

141.   See *Bandera Argentina*, March 23, 1933, 1. A similar survey was conducted by the Italian fascist press in Argentina; see Scarzanella, *Fascisti in Sud America*.

142.   Rodolfo Irazusta, "Entre gallos y medianoche," *La Voz del Plata* 1.1 (1942): 1.

143. Ernesto Palacio, "Reflexiones sobre la unidad," *Nuevo Orden* 1.16 (October 30, 1940). See also "El fascismo en marcha," *Bandera Argentina*, October 29, 1932, 1.

144. See José María Rosa, "Rectificación," *Bandera Argentina*, April 13, 1933, 1. For the criticism on Rosa, see *Bandera Argentina*, April 5, 1933, 1; and "La propaganda de la A.N.A., vista desde Rosario," *Bandera Argentina*, August 14, 1932.

145. Archivio Centrale dello Stato, Italia, Archivio Asvero Gravelli, B4 F4, 1.

146. Ibid., Ministero della Cultura Popolare, D.G. Serv., Propaganda, B5, Argentina, I / 4 / 26; ibid., B4, Argentina, 1934, I / 4 / 4, 902625 / 1012, 1–5; Archivio, Ministero degli Affari Esteri, Rome, Italy, telespresso 1690 / 199, March 16, 1934.

147. Archivio Centrale dello Stato, Italia, Ministero della Cultura Popolare, D.G. Serv., Propaganda, B4, Argentina, 1934, I / 4 / 63, B7-1011, prot. 44230512, 442 / 1506, B7-1011 3478.

148. Ibid., B5, Argentina, I / 4 / 26, prot. 038-7779.

149. Ibid., B5, Argentina, I / 4 / 26, 905456.

150. Archivo General de la Nación Argentina, Archivo Agustin P. Justo, caja 49, doc. 29.

151. See Finchelstein, *Fascismo, liturgia e imaginario*, 134.

152. "[We are] inspired in the purest fascist nacionalismo based in the sacred trilogy of God, patria, and home." Archivo General de la Nación Argentina, Archivo Agustín P. Justo, caja 49, doc. 29. See also Finchelstein, *Fascismo, liturgia e imaginario*, 133–134.

153. Archivo General de la Nación Argentina, Archivo Agustín P. Justo, caja 36, doc. 271.

154. See Archivo General de la Nación Argentina, Ministerio del Interior, año 1935, L37, no. 30029.

155. Bertoni, *Patriotas, cosmopolitas y nacionalistas*, 1–12, 166–211. See also Barbero and Devoto, *Los nacionalistas*, 15–24; Solberg, *Immigration and Nationalism*.

156. Juan de los Palotes, "Septembrismo o fascismo," *Bandera Argentina*, January 18, 1933, 3. See also "Definiciones," *El Fortin*, January 1, 1941 (2 quincena); Hector Bernardo, "El sombrío panorama de la política argentina," *El Rioplatense*, November 14, 1942, 1–2; Archivo General de la Nación Argentina, Archivo Agustín P. Justo, caja 36, doc. 277, Reaccion, 1 quincena, June 1935, no. 1.

157. Archivo General de la Nación Argentina, Archivo Agustín P. Justo, caja 46, doc. 120. See also, for Lugones Sr., "Guardia Argentina: propósitos." I want to thank Miss Carmen Lugones for giving me Lugones's personal copy of this text.

158. The Radical Party distributed pamphlets with this argument. Some are in the Argentine national archive: Archivo General de la Nación Argentina, Archivo Agustín P. Justo, caja 49, docs. 162–165.

159. "El nacionalismo tiene un programa máximo que consiste fundamentalmente en reunir en un solo haz (fascismo) las fuerzas políticas, espirituales, morales y económicas, bajo el signo de lo nacional para asegurar los objetivos básicos de la vida de una nación: el bien común o sea la felicidad de todos y la potencia del Estado." See Juan Carulla, "Carta a un nacionalista de San Martín," *Bandera Argentina*, December 27, 1936.

160. Federico Ibarguren, *La aristocracia y la cultura*, 6. For Federico Ibarguren, the leaders of nacionalismo should be not only the leaders of the nation but an "aristocracy" "born from the war." Ibarguren wanted to create the leadership of the future. For him, the latter constituted a new form of aristocracy, not the "prostituted" aristocratic class of the past but one that conveys at the same time "differentiation, power, unicity. These are its three indivisible coordinates. In other words, the permanent acknowledgment of hierarchies, justice imposed upon self-sacrifice, and the transcendent communion of man with the divinity and with the world in which he lives."

161. Archivio Centrale dello Stato, Italia, Ministero della Cultura Popolare, D.G. Serv., Propaganda, B5, Argentina, I / 4 / 4. See also Enrique P. Osés, "Los triunfos del socialismo," *El Momento Argentino*, April 28, 1934. See also Osés, *Medios y fines del nacionalismo*, 25–26, 66–67, 72–73.

162. See Julio Irazusta, "El problema del régimen," *Nuevo Orden* 1.5 (August 15, 1940); Ernesto Palacio, "Los equívocos del nacionalismo," *Nuevo Orden* 2.52 (July 9, 1941).

163. On clericofascist anti-Semitism, see Finchelstein, "Sexo, raça e nacionalismo."

164. Leopoldo Lugones, "La moral sin dogmas," *La Nación*, May 17, 1936.

165. Leopoldo Lugones, "Vida y materia," *La Nación*, July 12, 1936.

166. Leopoldo Lugones, "El escritor ante la libertad," *La Nación*, May 16, 1937.

167. "Así se da el caso de que los procesos de reacción americana siguen un camino inverso a los europeos. Aquí es la conciencia nacionalista e imperialista la que los inicia, y luego buscan un acomodo con los principios católicos y con la Iglesia. Allí son los grupos católicos que los inician, buscando luego la colaboración de los instrumentos y estilos fascistas. Aquí es la fuerza y la violencia la que llama luego, para decorarse, a los principios. Allí son los principios los que llaman, para defenderse a la fuerza." See José María Pemán, "Pasemos a la escucha," *Sol y Luna* 4 (1940): 91.

4. A "Christianized Fascism"

1. Pico, *Carta a Jacques Maritain*, 13–14, 7–8, 20, 21, 36, 40–41, 43. Pico's book had been submitted to Catholic censorship and thereby had the imprimatur of Bishop Antonio Rocca.

2. See my criticism of this historiography in the introduction to my book *Fascismo, liturgia e imaginario*, 10–27.

3. Italian fascist propagandists in particular made efforts to reach out to a group of influential mainstream Catholic priests who were prominent among the Argentine clericofascists. Archivio Centrale dello Stato, Italia, Ministero della Cultura Popolare, D.G. Serv., B11, Argentina, 5 / 5 / 1; ibid., B7, Argentina, 1937, I / 4 / 18; United States National Archives, Personal papers of Benito Mussolini, no. 430, reel 33, job 32, 015390, 106992. See also *Critica Fascista*, May 15, 1924, 470–471; "La formazione del clero argentino," *Il Giornale d'Italia*, January 4, 1929. For a Nazi appreciation of the role of the church in Argentina, see "Die Judenfrage in Argentinien," Politisches Archiv des Auswärtigen Amtes (Germany), *AA / PA*, Inland II A / B, Akten betr. Judenfrage in Argentinien. I want to thank Haim Avni for sharing this Nazi document with me. See also Finchelstein and Speyer, "El hilo pardo."

4. The notable exception was, of course, the early fascist Leopoldo Lugones Sr., who nonetheless "returned" to Catholicism in the mid-1930s. See Deutsch, *Las Derechas*, 196; and Devoto, *Nacionalismo, fascismo y tradicionalismo en la Argentina moderna*, 77–105, 144–149.

5. Archivo General de la Nación Argentina, Archivo Agustín P. Justo, caja 45, doc. 97.

6. "El clero argentino está muy lejos aún de sentir la influencia de los acontecimientos y las enseñanzas de la persecución anticatólica de Alemania y defienden a Hitler y Mussolini a capa y espada, siendo ardientes sostenedores en general de los regímenes totalitarios y de los gobiernos de fuerza." See *El congreso de la solidaridad de los pueblos*, 35–36. See also Amadeo, *El falso dilema*, 85–86. For a similar argument with respect to the Vatican, see Edmundo Guibourg, "Los caminos que llevan a Roma," *Crítica*, March 17, 1940. For an influential text in this context, see the Spanish translation of a book by the Brazilian intellectual María Lacerda de Maura, *Clericalismo y fascismo*.

7. Archivo Fundación IWO, Argentina, caja Organización Popular contra el Antisemitismo, Correspondencia panfletos, publicaciones C1936–1937, C1939, doc. 1029 / 12. "Los fanatismos caen fatalmente en contradicción," *Vida Nuestra*, September 27, 1934.

8. Raúl González Tuñón saw a clear alliance, an "acción conjunta," of priests and nacionalistas to propagate "clerical fascism" through "Catholic papers" such as *El Pueblo* and *Crisol*. González Tuñón, *8 Documentos de hoy*, 16, 31, 44. For a similar view, see Troise, *Significado de la reacción espiritualista y católica de la pos-guerra*. See also Archivo General de la Nación Argentina, Archivo Agustín P. Justo, caja 46, doc. 136; Archivo Fundación iwo, Correspondencia panfletos, publicaciones C1936–1937, C1939, doc. 1029 / 12. *Crisol* was founded by Father Molas Terán and later directed by Enrique Osés. For early Catholic praise of *Crisol*, see "Crisol," *Criterio*, February 4, 1932, 135. See also *Criterio*, May 26, 1932, 199; *Criterio*, June 9, 1932, 245.

9. For the former fascist writer Eugenia Silveyra de Oyuela, the very extension of Argentine fascism was related to its identification with Catholicism. See Eugenia Silveyra de Oyuela, "Del buen uso del nombre 'católico,'" *Orden Cristiano* 3.61 (March 15, 1944): 239–240. Father Carlos Cuchetti, a member of the same liberal Catholic group that Silveyra de Oyuela belonged to, argued during a show on Radio Mitre that "true nacionalismo, as a Christian movement, does not hate or denigrate the foreigner. True nacionalismo does not feel more patriotic when bravely shouting, 'Death to the Jews.'" See Carlos Cuchetti, "El falso nacionalismo," *Orden Cristiano* 1.2 (October 5, 1941): 8. The liberal Catholics writing in *Orden Cristiano* were particularly critical of the conflation of Catholicism with fascism and Nazism, with the anti-Semitism of those movements, and their approval of the measures and programs that constituted the Holocaust. They also criticized the Slovakian president, Father Tisso, for equating Catholicism and fascism. See the following articles in *Orden Cristiano*: "Nuestra posición," 1.1 (September 15, 1941): 5–6; Agustín Luchia Puig, "La buena tolerancia," 1.1 (September 15, 1941): 7; "Sobre confusionismo . . . ," 3.54 (December 1, 1943): 113; Emilio Miras, "¿Quienes son los peores enemigos de la Iglesia?" 3.55 (December 15, 1943): 128; "Tribuna," 3.55 (December 15, 1943): 134; Eugenia Silveyra de Oyuela, "Rosas y los católicos," 3.57 (January 15, 1944): 161–162, and 3.58 (February 15, 1944): 195; Emilio Miras, "Catolicismo sin catolicidad," 3.57 (February 15, 1944): 206; Adriana Cross, "Motivos de confusión," 3.66 (June 1, 1944): 351. For more on this topic, see Zanatta, *Del estado liberal a la nación católica*; Lvovich and Finchelstein, "L'Holocauste et l'Eglise argentine." On the Argentine Catholic Church, see also Caimari, *Perón y la Iglesia Católica*; and Luis Alberto Romero, "Una nación católica: 1880–1946," in Altamirano, *La Argentina en el siglo XX*.

10. See Zanatta, *Del estado liberal a la nación católica*, 114–122, 185–197.

11. See ibid., 287; and Collotti, *Fascismo, fascismi*, 33. See also Deutsch, *Las Derechas*, 240–244.

12. See my criticism in *Fascismo, liturgia e imaginario*, 10–27.

13. As Loris Zanatta has observed, the links between nationalism and Catholicism were almost structural. A case in point is the creation by the institutional church of a "Christian order" of nacionalistas that provided paramilitary security during the International Eucharistic Congress of 1934. Zanatta, *Del estado liberal a la nación católica*; and Ibarguren, *Orígenes del nacionalismo argentino*, 248. I find Zanatta's work illuminating; recently I have argued that it opens new historical pathways for Argentine historiography. See my *Fascismo, liturgia e imaginario*, 25–27. Although I agree with Zanatta's understanding of the relationship between Catholicism and nacionalismo as symbiotic, in this chapter I want to present this symbiosis as part of nacionalista self-understanding. In other words, nacionalista and clericonacionalista priests claimed they were indissolubly linked, but this discourse hid many contradictions and avoided real dialogue on the question. In this sense, while the institutional church criticized "exaggerated nacionalismo," nacionalistas never saw themselves as exaggerating anything. I see this chapter as complementing Zanatta's more institutionally oriented approach.

14. Enrique Osés, "Contra una mentalidad," *Crisol*, September 27, 1932, 1.

15. The nacionalista third way that Osés presented differs from the revolutionary dimensions of generic fascism, tracing back to ideas of Georges Sorel, which are emphasized by historians such as Zeev Sternhell or Alberto Spektorowski. On the centrality of these authors see my *Fascismo, liturgia e imaginario*, 23–24; and my review of Alberto Spektorowski, "The Origins of Argentina's Revolution of the Right," *The Americas* 60.4 (2004): 672–673.

16. Archivio Centrale dello Stato, Italia, Ministero della Cultura Popolare, D.G. Serv., Propaganda, B5, Argentina, I / 4 / 12. See also Archivo General de la Nación Argentina, Archivo Agustín P. Justo, caja 36, doc. 277, reaccion 1 quincena June 1935, no. 1; ibid., doc. 271; *Nueva Idea* 1.1 (January 19, 1935).

17. The Argentine members of fascism, in the view of *Mundo Israelita*, were Catholic priests, military in active duty, and nacionalistas who conflated Catholicism and patriotism with anti-Semitism and other practices of victimization. For this newspaper, nacionalismo was composed of "an imported reactionary group" that wanted to defend "capitalist privilege." But its presentation of the nacionalistas as importing their ideology from Europe contradicted the newspaper's description of European fascisms as anti-Christian. See its articles "La internacional negra," November 28, 1931, 1; "La Legión

Cívica y los judíos," March 5, 1932, 1; June 11, 1932, 1; October 4, 1930, 1. See also Archivo General de la Nación Argentina, Archivo Agustín P. Justo, caja 45, doc. 97.

18. Enrique Osés, "Ni derecha ni izquierda son el nacionalismo," *Crisol*, October 6, 1936.

19. "La espada cristiana," *Crisol*, October 8, 1936. See also Carlos M. Silveyra, "Unidad nacionalista," *Clarinada* 44 (December 31, 1940): 2; Raúl Guillermo Carrizo, "El ideal democrático y el Nuevo Orden," *Nuevo Orden*, August 22, 1940; Jerónimo del Rey (Leonardo Castellani), "Glosa," *Nuevo Orden*, March 19, 1941; Bruno Jacovella, "La insuficiencia vital del nacionalismo," *Nuevo Orden*, March 26, 1941; *Nuevo Orden*, May 21, 1941; *Nueva Política* 5 (October 1940): 4; Nimio de Anquín, "Liberalismo subrepticio y libertad cristiana," *Nueva Política* 12 (June 1941): 6–11; *Nueva Política* 13 (July 1941): 3–4; Alberto Ezcurra Medrano, "Libertad y totalitarismo," *Nueva Política* 15 (August 1941): 16–18; César Pico, "La Prudencia Católica frente al conflicto ruso-alemán," *Nueva Política* 15 (September 1941): 19–23; "Doce de octubre," *Nueva Política* 16 (October 1941): 3; Alberto Ezcurra Medrano, "Libertad y totalitarismo," *Nueva Política* 28 (May 1943): 10–13. See also Archivo General de la Nación Argentina, Archivo Agustín P. Justo, caja 49, doc. 232; ibid., caja 36, doc. 277, reacción 1 quincena June 1935, no. 1.

20. All through his tenure in *Crisol*, and later as director of *La Maroma*, *El Pampero*, and *El Federal*, Osés argued for a link between Catholicism and nacionalismo. This was not a difficult task for Osés, who tended to see theoretical nuances and the acknowledgment of tensions or contradictions as liabilities for the expansion of nacionalismo. Bringing clericofascist theory to the nacionalista masses was one of Osés's most successful achievements. In *El Pampero*, for example, some slogans were frequently repeated. The paper presented nacionalismo and Catholicism as an undivided ideological unity embodied in the Argentine male. One slogan said, for example: "I am Argentine: the Southern Cross talks to me about [our] superior destiny." Another one stated: "I am Argentine: inside me lives the America that prays to Christ and speaks Spanish." Argentina as a Catholic entity that finally in 1943 followed nacionalista politics was "a favorite daughter of providence," and the alliance between nacionalista politics and the church could confirm the "superior destiny" of the nacionalista nation. See *El Pampero*, July 9, 1943. For other examples, see "Lo que queremos y lo que no queremos," *Crisol*, October 18, 1936; "¿Por qué Buenos Aires, llamase Buenos Aires?" *Crisol*, October 13, 1936. See also *Crisol*, March 30, 1940; *El Pampero*, July 7, 1943; *El Pampero*, July 10, 1943;

El Pampero, November 4, 1943; *El Federal*, September 4, 1944; *El Federal*, February 13, 1945. On Osés, see also Archivo General de la Nación Argentina, Archivo Agustín P. Justo, caja 104, docs. 17, 51, 149, doc. sin numero, foliado no. 1235; ibid., caja 104 bis, docs. 271, 407.

21.   "Brevísimo relato del origen y fundación de las Diócesis argentinas," *El Pueblo*, November 22, 1942, 356–357. See "La enseñanza católica en las escuelas," *Crisol*, October 10, 1936, 1; "La campaña socialista contra la enseñanza religiosa," *Bandera Argentina*, September 23, 1939. See also Archivio, Ministero degli Affari Esteri, Rome, Italy, telespresso 4057 / 2918, June 28, 1938.

22.   "El Dr. Nimio de Anquín pide sea reconsiderada su exoneración," *Crisol*, September 9, 1939. See also "Sólo el nacionalismo puede crear en las masas una conciencia política," *Bandera Argentina*, April 23, 1935, 1; *Nueva Política* 22 (June 1942). For the nacionalista Miguel Piccone, "the universal fight against the city of Christ" that "the Judeo-Marxists" proposed was going to be defeated by the "Argentine people, for whom Catholicism and patriotism are the same name for the same unshakeable reality." Miguel Piccone, "El plan de dominación mundial y el frente político religioso," *El Federal*, March 27, 1944.

23.   Catholicism for *Clarinada* meant nacionalismo, insofar as nationalism and Catholicism could not "live without each other." See "Alter ego contesta a 'porteño nacionalista,'" *Clarinada* 2.16 (August 1938). *Clarinada* itself was viewed by many priests and bishops as defending a nacionalista and Catholic common ground. Thus the Catholic newspaper *El Pueblo* advertised in *Clarinada*; the bishop of Santiago del Estero, Monsignor Rodriguez Olmos, "blessed" the journal's "Catholic readers"; and Father Meinvielle praised it for being a "vigoroso luchador contra el monstruo comunista." "Dos saludos que nos honran," *Clarinada* 2.23 (March 31, 1939). See also Virgilio Filippo, *El monstruo comunista*, 426–427.

24.   *Clarinada* 1.8 (December 1937).

25.   *Clarinada* 2.23 (March 31, 1939).

26.   Ibid.

27.   *Clarinada* 1.8 (December 1937). See also Delfina Bunge de Gálvez, "La fascinación soviética," *Criterio*, July 30, 1931, 142.

28.   See for example *Clarinada* 6.73 (February, 1943): 34. See also *Criterio*, April 8, 1937, 327–332, and April 15, 1937, 350–356. See also Archivo del Ministerio de Relaciones Exteriores y Culto, Argentina División Política, Santa Sede, caja 3987, expediente 2, año 1938, N24 / RE.

29.   *Clarinada* 1.8 (December 1937). See also Silveyra, *El comunismo en la Argentina*,

1st ed., 536; 2nd ed., 541. For the liberal criticism of this idea, see de Alvear, *Democracia*, 211–213; and Amadeo, *El falso dilema*, 9, 72.

30. "La Iglesia y la lucha anticomunista," *La Razón*, March 19, 1937. For the center Right, and not only for the nacionalistas, the timing of the encyclical coincided with a discussion in the Argentine Senate about the banning of communist activities in the country. This project united the church, the conservatives, and the nacionalistas. For them, banning communism was a direct outcome of the pope's dictum. This line of thought was expressed, for example, in the editorials of the center Right newspaper *La Razón*, which had longstanding anticommunist and profascist leanings, as we saw in the previous chapter.

31. Gómez Forgues, *Comunismo y religión*, 8.

32. Archivo General de la Nación Argentina, Archivo Agustín P. Justo, caja 54, doc. 12. For European rightist observers, however, the expansion of communism was not so apparent. See, for example, Emmanuel Bertrand, *Frontières: Revue de politique étrangère*, April 10, 1936, 202–206.

33. See Varela, *Las hordas comunistas*. *Criterio* considered Varela's book to be one of the best on the question. See *Criterio*, May 24, 1934, 75–76. See Gustavo Franceschi's positive review of Napal's book in *Criterio*, July 21, 1932, 70.

34. "Nacionalismo y catolicismo," *Clarinada* 1.8 (December 1937). Like most nacionalista media, *Clarinada* saw in the Italian fascists an instrument of God. Mussolini himself was, in their view, a willing follower of Vatican policies. In short, Italian fascism was for these nacionalistas a form of nationalism. See also "Defensa de la moral pública," *Crisol*, March 28, 1940; "La hora que viene," *Aduna*, November 20, 1933. In addition to the continuous publishing of the papal encyclicals, *Clarinada*'s director, Carlos Silveyra, proposed the paper's slogan as the best rhymed expression of the imperatives of nacionalismo: "A Dios rogando y con el mazo dando" ("As Argentines and Catholics: praying to God while punishing with the club"). See Carlos M. Silveyra, "Dos años de vida," *Clarinada* 2.23 (March 31, 1939). For an ironic, antifascist denunciation of *Clarinada* as a "theoretical" publication, see Archivo Fundación iwo, Argentina, caja Organización Popular contra el Antisemitismo, Correspondencia panfletos, publicaciones C1936–1937, C1939, docs. 23, 139-13.

35. Silveyra had been an early and fanatic admirer of Uriburu. He wrote to Uriburu in order to share with the general a clericofascist *uriburista* poem that Silveyra's blind mother (Eugenia Encina) had written. The poem was entitled "¡Gracias Señor!" and included these lines: "Gracias te doy señor, porque a mi Patria / En la hora de oprobio y de vergüenza / Le diste un hijo esclarecido y

fuerte / Grande entre grandes! / Es el valiente que su vida arriesga / Para sacar del cieno a la Argentina / Y la cubre de gloria inmarcesible / Con noble esfuerzo / Es Uriburu que en Setiembre surge / Con sus virtudes de varon insigne, / Más alto que las cumbre de los Andes! / Es nuestro heroe!" See Archivo General de la Nación Argentina, Archivo Uriburu, legajo 20, sala 7 2596, doc. 47, carta dated February 21, 1932.

36. See, for example, Nimio de Anquín, "La clase media y la virtud de prudencia en Aristóteles," *Sol y Luna* 4 (1940).

37. In other words, Ezcurra considered nacionalista thought and practice as the political incarnation of the dictum of the Catholic Church. Nacionalismo represented politics in the same way that the Argentine Catholic Church represented more celestial aspects of the sacred truth that nacionalismo embraced. Ezcurra equated nacionalista "Catholic" politics with corporatism, anti-individualism, and anti-Marxism. Ezcurra Medrano, *Catolicismo y nacionalismo*, 22–23. Ezcurra Medrano was a contributor to Osés's newspaper, *Crisol*, and a member by marriage of the Uriburu family. See "Hoy contrae enlace Alberto Ezcurra Medrano," *Crisol*, October 9, 1936.

38. *Criterio* and the *Cursos de Cultura Católica* were both founded in 1922 by Atilio Dell'Oro Maini, César Pico, and Tomás D. Casares and both were Catholic forums of *"seglares."* They had official recognition from the church, and a representative of the Buenos Aires archbishop belonged to *Criterio*'s editorial board. See Ernesto Palacio, "Crítica literaria," *Criterio*, October 18, 1928, 86. Loris Zanatta states that *Criterio* in its first two years had a symbiotic relationship with the nacionalista group of *La Nueva Republica*. See Zanatta, *Del estado liberal a la nación católica*, 47; *Criterio*, January 16, 1930, 70. The archbishop of Buenos Aires thought that Dell'Oro Maini, Pico, and Casares had too much autonomy and no right to represent the Catholic Church. Thus, both *Cursos* and *Criterio* were increasingly appropriated by the clergy between 1929 and 1932. By the early 1930s, *Criterio* already called itself "the doctrinal journal of Catholicism" (*Criterio*, January 30, 1930, 134).

39. See Zanatta, *Del estado liberal a la nación católica*, 45, 114–115, 195; Casares, *Los Cursos de Cultura Católica*, 14. See also Barbero y Devoto, *Los nacionalistas*, 88.

40. Casares, *El orden civil*, 30. Like Casares, Federico Ibarguren, a young nacionalista of the nacionalista group Liga Republicana, presented an apocalyptic notion of the place of the sacred in politics as a divine response to "modern man" and his seemingly atavistic traits (his "carnivalistic postures" and "Dionysian" tendencies), as embodied in liberal mass politics. For Ibarguren, "nothing of what is immutable stands still." The young Ibarguren believed

that an imminent "collective expiation" would "open the eyes" of those who would "see through the shadows of darkness." Ibarguren included the Argentine nacionalistas and Mussolini among those who represented "the voice of the strong," who would make the right choice between "Catholicism" and "anarchy." See the following by Ibarguren: *La aristocracia y la cultura*, 42; *Orígenes del nacionalismo argentino*, 173–174, 238, 244, 253; and "León Bloy: 'Peregrino de lo absoluto,'" *La Nación*, August 2, 1936.

41.   See Ezcurra Medrano, *Catolicismo y nacionalismo*, 30.

42.   Casares, *Catolicismo y acción política*, 10. See also Casares, *Los Cursos de Cultura Católica*, 15. The coming of the Spanish Civil War, soon followed by the Second World War, only strengthened these shared feelings about apocalyptic threats and clericofascist solutions. Many nacionalistas and clericofascists saw these two wars as the inevitable product of liberalism, sensualism, Protestantism, Masonry, communism, and Judaism. For most of them, an Argentine civil war was imminent, and a Catholic solution seemed to be at hand in order to avoid the conversion of "Christian women into prostitutes" and the mass killings by "Jews" of Argentine men and the enslavement of the survivors. See "Izquierda unidas, derechas discutiendo . . . ," *El Pueblo*, February 26, 1937; Archivo General de la Nación Argentina, Archivo Agustín P. Justo, caja 54, doc. 73; Franceschi, *Visión espiritual de la guerra*; and, by an unnamed author, *El judío sin careta*, back cover. See also Alberto Molas Terán, "Del laicismo al soviet judío," *Criterio*, November 26, 1931, 270–271; and Alberto Molas Terán "¿Por qué niegan a Dios los judíos del soviet?" *Criterio*, December 3, 1931, 301–302.

43.   The canon also included Mussolini and the nacionalistas Felipe Yofre and Carlos Silveyra, the leader of the nacionalista group Patria and the publisher of *Clarinada* 2.19 (November 1938). See also "Incomprensión," *Clarinada* 1.8 (December 1937).

44.   See Zanatta, *Del estado liberal a la nación católica*, 51. See also *Criterio*, September 11, 1930, 344; *Criterio*, October 9, 1930, 461–462; "El camino a seguir," *Criterio*, December 18, 1930, 781.

45.   See Archivo General de la Nación Argentina, Archivo Uriburu, legajo 2, sala 7 2578, doc. 230; ibid., sala 7 2599, doc. 251.

46.   See "Una entrevista con el General Uriburu," *Criterio*, October 16, 1930, 500. See also "El general José F. Uriburu," *Criterio*, May 5, 1932, 133.

47.   Gustavo J. Franceschi, "El despertar nacionalista," *Criterio*, October 20, 1932, 55.

48.   This "invention" of a Catholic tradition had many venues of diffusion, including the journal *Archivum*, which was entirely dedicated to Catholic nation

building from a disciplinary "historical" perspective; many bishops and "secular" nacionalistas contributed to it. The publication represented a formal endeavor of self-glorification that complemented *Criterio*. Once again Father Franceschi came to represent this political project. Father Francisco Avella Cháffer, a Catholic priest and historian who was a prolific contributor to *Archivum*, remembers that Franceschi was always seen as a master to be emulated. Many nacionalistas shared Father Avella's admiration and considered Franceschi a "Christian warrior," the embodiment of the "sword" and the "cross." This opinion was not restricted to the Right or the clergy alone, as the editors of the mainstream literary journal *Síntesis*, for example, considered that Franceschi's opinion expressed the "official" opinion of the Catholic Church. See *El Pueblo*, "Archivum," June 13, 1943, 9. See also *Archivum* 2.1 and 2.2 (1944) (interview with Father Avella Cháffer, Buenos Aires, June 1998). Ignoring the fact that I am an Argentine Jew, Father Avella confided to me his high regard for the "French" Father Franceschi as well as his intimate feeling "that Jews are everywhere and dominate the press." See also Lizardo Zia, "Semblanzas: Monseñor Franceschi," *Criterio*, June 8, 1933, 231. The editors of *Síntesis* included Martin S. Noel, Emilio Ravignani, Guillermo de Torre, Arturo Capdevila, and Jorge Luis Borges, among others. See *Síntesis* 3.34 (March 1930): 5.

49.　Franceschi was a central figure in Argentine cultural life and even took part in an advertisement for Yacimientos Petrolíferos Fiscales (Y.P.F.), the nationalized oil consortium. His face appeared in half-page ads in newspapers arguing that the consortium affirmed Argentine nationalism by providing economic independence to the country. See *La Razón*, August, 7, 1936; and *La Fronda*, January 26, 1937. Yacimientos Petrolíferos Fiscales was headed by Ricardo Silveyra, the brother of Carlos Silveyra, director of *Clarinada*. See Joseph, *Argentine Diary*, xxxvi; José E. Assaf, "Una generación rebelde," *Criterio*, August 30, 1934, 438–439.

50.　See three articles by Gustavo J. Franceschi in *Criterio*: "El despertar nacionalista," October 20th, 1932, 55; "El negocio de la guerra," April 13, 1933, 31–33; "Equívocos," May 31, 1934, 102. Some years later the Argentine Conference of Bishops would use Franceschi's words. See *Revista Eclesiástica del Arzobispado de Buenos Aires*, July 1936, 438.

51.　Gustavo J. Franceschi, "Anticomunismo," *Criterio*, August 16, 1934, 376. See also "La Acción Católica y el gobierno italiano," *Criterio*, June 11, 1931, 355–356; "Catolicismo y fascismo," *Criterio*, July 16, 1931, 73–74; "Cursos de Cultura Católica: conferencia del R., Julio Meinvielle," *Criterio*, October 1, 1931, 7. See also Gustavo J. Franceschi, "Problemas de doctrina," *Criterio*, January 16, 1936, 57, and his "Severidad, violencia," *Criterio*, February 20, 1936, 173–176. As we will see below, Franceschi was not the only nacionalista member of the clergy who warned that nacionalismo might deploy an instrumental view of Catholicism, a view that he and others identified with the French right-wing ideology of Charles Maurras and the Action Française. Franceschi's concern was an expression of worry rather an assessment of nacionalista ideology at large. It would be misleading to ignore the importance of the model of Action Française—which, for example, the brothers Julio and Rodolfo Irazusta were often so enthusiastic about. But it would be equally wrong to project their "Maurrasianism" onto the entire movement and assume that there was a unique Catholic identity. See Julio Irazusta, "Maurras," in his *Actores y espectadores*, 142–144; Julio Irazusta, *Memorias*; Rodolfo Irazusta, *Escritos políticos completos*, 1.44. Some historians share this instrumental vision with their limited Maurrasian sources, namely, the Irazusta brothers, and put forward a functionalist view that downplays the importance of religious beliefs and fascist ideology within nacionalismo. See Zuleta Álvarez, *El nacionalismo argentino*; and Devoto, *Nacionalismo, fascismo y tradicionalismo*, 195–205. In my own approach I emphasize nacionalista agency and stress the need to incorporate nacionalista self-understanding into the picture. Most nacionalistas, including some members of the founding publication *La Nueva República*, did not see a contradiction between their political practices and their religious beliefs, and after Maurras's excommunication by the pope, they were not willing to fully identify with his position. Even the Maurrasian Rodolfo Irazusta asserted in 1928 that Argentina was inherently, and not functionally, a "Catholic state." His brother Julio noted some years later "the weakness of the Maurrasian argumentation when confronted with the realities of Argentine politics." Maurrasianism was often an ingredient of the ideological cocktail of some nacionalistas, but it never achieved the importance of a doctrinal element, and some nacionalistas even presented it as "profoundly" anti-Christian and atheistic. In short, most nacionalistas believed that the church should use them, as it was supposedly "using Mussolini." See de Laferrere, *Literatura y política*, 121. See also "Nuestro Programa," *La Nueva República*, December 1, 1927; Luis Enrique, "Marginando," *Criterio*, February 6, 1930, 172; Luis Enrique, "Marginando," *Criterio*, March 20, 1930, 371; Julio Meinvielle, "El estado gendarme," *Criterio*, January 1, 1931, 13; Rodolfo Irazusta, "La política," *La Nueva República*, May 5, 1928, 1; and Julio Irazusta, "Nuevas glosas a la manifestación de los Cuatro Cancilleres," *La Voz del Plata*,

September 30, 1942. For other criticism of Maurras, see "Política nacional," *Nueva Política* 28 (May 1943): 5; "Maurras," *La Fronda*, January 13, 1937.

52. Later in 1937, he defined Nazism as the "lesser evil" when compared with communism. Franceschi often presented Nazism as a form of totalitarianism. See Gustavo J. Franceschi, "Hitler," *Criterio*, May 18, 1933, 152. For an earlier Catholic criticism of the leader of the "Germanic fascist movement," see "Una figura del año: Hitler," *Criterio*, December 24, 1931, 396. See also Julio Finguerit, "Ingredientes del hitlerismo," *Criterio*, August 4, 1932, 70. The type of racism and anti-Catholicism that the Nazis proposed was not acceptable for Franceschi as he saw it in Munich in 1933. See also Gustavo J. Franceschi, "La voz de una Iglesia," *Criterio*, August 30, 1934, 429; and Gustavo J. Franceschi, "Nacionalsocialismo y dignidad humana," *Criterio*, October 7, 1937, 125–127.

53. Archivio Centrale dello Stato, Italia. Ministero della Cultura Popolare, D.G. Serv., B7, Argentina, 1937, I / 4 / 18, T105.

54. Franceschi, *Discursos*, 252–266. Franceschi gave speeches in central venues such as the the Teatro Colón. At the funeral of the archbishop of Buenos Aires he gave a speech at the cathedral, and he would give speeches in honor of the different papal nuncios.

55. Archivio Centrale dello Stato, Italia. Ministero della Cultura Popolare, D.G. Serv., B7, Argentina, 1937, I / 4 / 18, gabinetto 90433 / 747. See also Archivio, Ministero degli Affari Esteri, Rome, Italy, telespresso 212638, April 1937. Franceschi had his first impression of fascism in Italy during a visit in 1922. The Italian people, he argued, were determined to eliminate democracy and "communist agitation." For Franceschi, fascism was in "profound consonance" with the "mentality, the aspirations, the historical legacy, the needs, the total idiosyncrasy of the Italian people." Writing from Rome in 1933 Franceschi gave a more critical assessment of Italian "nacionalismo" (i.e., fascism): "It has spread in the sons of Italy a huge pride about their nationality and a prodigious zeal. I know about its past and present excesses. . . . But I would prefer a thousand times all its undeniable excesses, to the indifferences or the weaknesses in character of many of our own citizens." In 1937, Franceschi once again reminded his readers that fascism was widely accepted because it had "reestablished discipline, life, and the traditions of the fatherland." See Franceschi, *La angustia contemporánea*, 166–168; and three articles by Franceschi in *Criterio*: "Por la dignidad nacional," May 4, 1933, 104; "¿Vamos hacia la paz?" May 11, 1933, 128; "Haga patria," November 25, 1937, 294.

56. Franceschi, *La angustia contemporánea*, 252–266.

57. See Franceschi, *Keyserling*, 158. See also "Convergencias y divergencias," *Criterio*, July 13, 1933, 351.

58. Thus, Franceschi saw himself many times "at the antipodes of Mussolini," particularly when dealing with the secularist tendencies of fascism. Whereas in 1933 he saw the Duce "as the first politician of Europe and the world in the current time" but also as a "remarkable orientator" and in 1936 as a "political remedy," in 1939 he had already come to the conclusion than fascism was following Nazi patterns and therefore was at odds with the Catholic Church. However, in 1940, after the rapid victories of the Axis he declared the definitive death of liberalism as a regime. He continued to regard totalitarianism as being at odds with Christianity but now advocated its usefulness. A "Christian regime of collective life" would be achieved, at least in Europe, he said, after a "totalitarian phase." Gustavo J. Franceschi, "Orientación social de las dictaduras," *Criterio*, June 15, 1933, 249. See also by Franceschi in *Criterio*: "Estado totalitario, estado cristiano," June 29, 1933, 296–299; "El caso Lindbergh," January 2, 1936, 8; and "La Cruz en el mundo contemporáneo," April 6, 1939, 320–321; see also Franceschi, *Visión espiritual de la guerra*, 94–95, 133, and especially 103.

59. Gálvez saw generic fascism as "bringing the church to its right place." Manuel Gálvez, "Interpretación de las dictaduras," *Criterio*, October 11, 1928, 43–44. See also Gálvez, *Este pueblo necesita*; Archivo General de la Nación Argentina, Archivo Agustín P. Justo, caja 45, doc. 146.

60. Gustavo J. Franceschi, "La lección del Brasil," *Criterio*, March 19, 1936, 272. See also "Ante la patria," *Criterio*, May 25, 1933, 173; and Leonardo Castellani, "Postales," *Criterio*, August 3, 1933, 420–421.

61. Franceschi saw totalitarianism as a European pattern deriving from the Renaissance, liberalism, and secularization: (all by Franceschi, in *Criterio*) "La absurda guerra," April 13, 1939, 342; "Pueblos pacíficos, estadistas guerreros," April 20, 1939, 368; "¿Totalitarismo o liberalismo?" April 27, 1939, 390. Although Franceschi often presented totalitarianism as a term that encompassed Stalinism and fascism, and even wrote a book on totalitarianism, he did not equate the "extremism" of the Left with that of the Right. In his view, whereas the former "nullifies the sense of nationality," the latter "intensifies it" ("Arbitrariedad y vida," April 28, 1938, 465).

62. Franceschi, "Argentina," January 27, 1938, 79. See also Franceschi, "Catolicismo rioplatense," *Criterio*, January 5, 1939, 5–9.

63. By Franceschi, writing in *Criterio*: "Equívocos," May 31, 1934, 102; "Laicismo,"

June 21, 1934, 173–176; "Patria y tradición," June 28, 1934, 197–199; "Balance de un cincuentenario," July 26, 1934, 293–296; "La inquietud de esta hora," August 2, 1934, 318; "Religión y moral," November 29, 1934, 369–370; "Una dictadura inaceptable" and "Comentarios," September 30, 1937, 101–103; "Un gesto inoportuno," December 2, 1937, 317–321. See also Justo Franco, "El peligro de la escuela laica," *Criterio*, December 10, 1931, 337.

64. Franceschi, *Criterio*, September 21, 1933, 56.

65. Franceschi saw Brazil as developing a healthy response to the widespread communist threat in that country, whereas Mexico was "a substantially and openly antireligious tyranny." Franceschi, "La lección del Brasil," *Criterio*, March 19, 1936, 272; Franceschi, "Dos medidas," *Criterio*, March 26, 1936, 294. See also, for a converging argument, Luis Barrantes Molina, "El enemigo oculto," *El Pueblo*, December 25, 1942, 9.

66. "We had two obligations [with respect to nationalism]: first to make it stronger and second to avoid its losing popularity due to party politicking, conflict over flags [*banderías*], or by way of its impregnation with erroneous doctrines." Franceschi, "Argentina," *Criterio*, January 27, 1938, 78.

67. José E. Assaf, "Hacia la nueva democracia," *Criterio*, June 1, 1933, 202–203; and T.P. y T., "Adunismo," *Criterio*, June 1, 1933, 204. See also Hildebrando (pseud. of A. H. Varela), "La marcha sobre Buenos Aires," *Bandera Argentina*, September 6, 1933, 2.

68. Franceschi, "La inquietud de esta hora," *Criterio*, August 2, 1934, 319–320.

69. See Archivo General de la Nación Argentina, Archivo Agustín P. Justo, caja 36, doc. 277, reacción 1 quincena June 1935, no. 1, "440. aniversario de la encíclica 'Rerum Novarum'"; J.L., "El fascismo y los obreros," *La Nueva República*, May 5, 1928; "León XIII, Encicl. Rerum Novarum," *La Nueva República*, June 2, 1928, 1; Enrique Osés, "De Rerum Novarum," *Criterio*, May 14, 1931, 227–228; Enrique Osés, "Nuestra doctrina social," *Criterio*, May 5, 1932, 127; "Bases económicas de la acción nacionalista argentina," *Bandera Argentina*, January 3, 1933; "Nacionalismo económico," *Bandera Argentina*, January 3, 1933; "Federación de Círculos Católicos de Obreros" *Crisol*, October 4, 1936; "El problema de la tierra debe ser base de la acción nacionalista," *Bandera Argentina*, December 15, 1936; "Debe ser función del nacionalismo elevar el 'standard' de vida argentino," *Bandera Argentina*, December 16, 1936; "Es un acontecimiento trascendental para el país la compra del FC Central Córdoba," *Bandera Argentina*, December 29, 1936; Julio Meinvielle, "Pastor Angelicus," *Sol y Luna* 2 (1939); "Dolor argentino," *Crisol*, March 27, 1940; *Crisol*, March 29, 1940; Juan Carlos Moreno, "La 'Rerum Novarum' frente al problema obrero,'" *El Res-*

taurador, June 12, 1941, 4; Fresco, *Habla el gobernador de Buenos Aires*, 21. See also also Archivio Centrale dello Stato, Italia, Ministero della Cultura Popolare, D.G. Serv., B4, Argentina, 1934, Movimento fascista in Argentina, I / 4 / 8; Archivo General de la Nación Argentina, Archivo Agustín P. Justo, caja 49, doc. 170, and ibid., caja 54, doc. 12.

70. Franceschi, agreeing with many nacionalistas, such as Osés, argued that the conservative Right favored the wrong kind of dictatorship and had a "liberal mentality wrapped in Catholic sentimentality." See articles by Franceschi in *Criterio*: "Burguesismo y comunismo," November 1, 1934, 265–268; "Páginas de doctrina," February 13, 1936, 154; "La lección del Brasil," April 16, 1936, 366; "¿Comunista o católico?" April 30, 1936, 414; "El recurso revolucionario," November 24, 1932, 177; and more generally "Las revoluciones políticas," December 29, 1932, 295–297.

71. Franceschi, "El recurso revolucionario," *Criterio*, November 24, 1932, 177; and more generally Franceschi, "Las revoluciones políticas," *Criterio*, December 29, 1932, 295–297.

72. Franceschi, "Iglesia y política," *Criterio*, May 10, 1934, 29–32; Franceschi, "Lo concreto," *Criterio*, April 2, 1936, 318; Franceschi, "La eterna acusación," *Criterio*, December 16, 1937, 365–368. See also Luis Barrantes Molina, "Cambios de táctica liberal," *El Pueblo*, June 2, 1943, 9.

73. *El Pueblo*, December 1941, 1.

74. See "Gracias colegas," *Bandera Argentina*, October 30, 1932, 2. See also Archivo General de la Nación Argentina, Archivo Agustín P. Justo, caja 49, doc. 247.

75. Franceschi even visited Israel in 1952. See Allan Metz, "Gustavo Juan Franceschi and the Jews: The Overcoming of Prejudice by an Argentine Prelate."

76. See the following by Luis Barrantes Molina, writing in *El Pueblo*: "La democracia, el comunismo y la Iglesia," February 5, 1937, 13; "Democracia no es, obligatoriamente, liberalismo," September 24, 1942, 9; "Nuestro gobernante y los deseos del Papa," October 1, 1942, 9; "Para establecer el nuevo orden," November 23 and 24, 1942, 9; "Los dictadores de hoy," January 3, 1943, 9; "Democracia no es liberalismo," May 19, 1943, 9. For Franceschi, the cases of Portuguese fascism and the French Vichy regime represented examples of "functional" and corporative democracy. See Franceschi, *Visión espiritual de la guerra*, 86, and also 107, 119.

77. "Una lección de democracia nueva ha dictado al mundo Benito Mussolini," *Bandera Argentina*, August 11, 1932, 1; and Franceschi, "Democracia," *Criterio*, December 1, 1932, 199. On Mussolini, fascism, and democracy, see chapter 1.

78. Luis Barrantes Molina, "El 1 de mayo y el cristianismo," *El Pueblo*, April 29, 1943, 8; Barrantes Molina, "La democracia que nos falta y que debemos construir," *El Pueblo*, November 1, 1942, 8.

79. For Sturzo's position, see Luigi Sturzo, "Lo que queda de las monarquías europeas," *Criterio*, November 6, 1930, 595–596; and Sturzo, "A propósito del corporativismo," *Criterio*, November 11, 1937, 254–255. The fact that Sturzo published some antifascist articles in *Criterio* counters to some degree my argument about the fascist leanings of the journal. However, *Criterio* never embraced fascism as fully as it embraced nacionalismo; in publishing Sturzo, it declared a continuing ambivalence with regard to fascism. Typically, Argentine fascists never complained about Sturzo's presence in the pages of *Criterio*, while the Italian fascist paper in Argentina certainly did complain. See *Criterio*, December 16, 1937, 370–371. See also *Criterio*, January 7, 1937, 28.

80. See Luis Barrantes Molina, "Fascismo y totalitarismo," *El Pueblo*, February 22 and 23, 1937, 4.

81. Ibid.

82. Luis Barrantes Molina, "Diversas formas del ateismo," *El Pueblo*, February 12, 1943, 8. See also Barrantes Molina, "El mal no está en la democracia," *El Pueblo*, September 17, 1942, 9; Barrantes Molina, "La única salvación de la humanidad," *El Pueblo*, October 16, 1942, 9. See also "La crueldad de la guerra," *La Voz del Plata*, June 30, 1943, 5; Barrantes Molina, "Judaismo y comunismo," *El Pueblo*, September 12, 1936; Archivo Fundación iwo, Buenos Aires, Argentina, caja Organización Popular contra el Antisemitismo.

83. In this and other matters, Franceschi and Barrantes expressed the view of the hierarchy. Having been personally blessed by the pope with a prestigious title, Prelado Doméstico de Su Santidad, in one of his visits to Rome, Franceschi always stood with Rome as the Argentine church itself did. In short, if historians want to know what the Argentine Catholic hierarchy was thinking, they must pay attention to what Franceschi said. However, though he had gone along with a variety of changing stances in the institution of the church, Franceschi was not a mere reproducer of institutional ideology but a central figure in the reformulation and constant refashioning of these positions. His intellectual autonomy was restricted, but he pushed it to the limits without crossing the line as many other clericofascists would do. His long journey from illiberal and nacionalista sympathizer to his abrupt embrace of democracy in 1944–1945 and his anti-Peronism of 1955 followed the changing policies of the Vatican and the Argentine hierarchy during this period. See Franceschi,

La democracia cristiana; Pbro. J. B. Lectora, "El Padre Santo y los totalitarismos," *El Pueblo*, January 10, 1943, 9.

84. Franceschi, "Frente al comunismo," *Criterio*, October 25, 1934, 243.

85. Franceschi, *Criterio*, September 21, 1933, 56.

86. Eugenia Silveyra de Oyuela, "El gobierno totalitario no está contra el dogma católico," *Clarinada* 5.54–55 (October–November 1941): 2–4. This article was first published in 1937, when she belonged to the nacionalista movement. See also Silveyra de Oyuela, "Confusionismo intelectual," *El Pueblo*, February 11, 1937.

87. Eugenia Silveyra was a rabid clericofascist who, during the war, had an astonishing rebirth as a leading intellectual in the sparsely populated group of Catholic Christian democrats who favored the Allies. In 1956, without acknowledging her own recent past, she presented nacionalismo as being part, with the majority of Argentine Catholics, of a united front of military, priests, and "laicos" that she ironically called "nazionalistas" (note the z of Nazi) or "católicos nacionalistas." She presented this front as being confused about the teaching of the church, to the extent that in the 1930s "in order to be a 'good Argentine Catholic' one had to be a complete nacionalista, who desired the victory of the Axis, venerated Franco, and hated the Jews" ("la confusión llegó a tal extremo que, para ser 'buen católico argentino' era menester ser un completo nacionalista: anhelar el triunfo del Eje, venerar a Franco y odiar a los judíos"). See Silveyra de Oyuela, "Del buen uso del nombre 'catolico,'" *Orden Cristiano* 3.61 (March 15, 1944): 239–240. See also Silveyra de Oyuela, *Nacionalismo y neo-peronismo*, 12–13, 21–23. For a rabid nacionalista criticism of Eugenia Silveyra's turn to the center Left, see *Nueva Política* 18 (December 1941): 27; and Miguel Piccone, "El plan de dominación mundial y el frente político religioso," *El Federal*, March 27, 1944.

88. "Monseñor Franceschi y el fascismo," *Bandera Argentina*, September 16, 1933, 2.

89. See Franceschi, "Contestando a un ataque," *Criterio*, September 14, 1933, 32; César Pico, "Democracia y catolicismo," *La Fronda*, September 11, 1933. See also "El clero, la 'política' y 'La Vanguardia,'" *Crisol*, October 15, 1936; *Nueva Política* 20 (March 1942): 30.

90. Franceschi, "Nacionalismo," *Criterio*, September 21, 1933.

91. For Ezcurra, the link between nacionalismo and the church was unbreakable. However, this did not mean that the church was nacionalista per se. Ezcurra argued that the church should not be implicated in nacionalista political practice. See Ezcurra Medrano, *Catolicismo y nacionalismo*, 6. In this sense,

Ezcurra made explicit an implicit warning expressed in the collective pastoral letter of the Argentine episcopate that warned against the danger of "exaggerated nacionalismo." There were many ways to read the pastoral letter. Enrique Osés, for example, argued that it could never refer to nacionalismo because its only "exaggerated" tendencies were "in accordance" with the teachings of the church. Osés concluded, "God above all for the salvation of our souls and the patria above all for the salvation of our patria." Enrique Osés, "Nuestras almas y nuestra patria," *El Federal*, February 7, 1944. In daily political practice, the separation advocated by Ezcurra (and the higher echelons of the church in Buenos Aires that were at ease with the conservative rule of President Justo), was not so easy to enforce for those nacionalistas, militants, and priests that took part in practices related to the myth of Uriburu in plazas, churches, and newsrooms, or incorporated the Catholic religion in their daily ideology and practices. Thus, nacionalista leaders sent religious salutations for Easter, nacionalista intellectuals wrote poems to the cardinal of Buenos Aires, and varied groups of priests regularly wrote about religion and politics in nacionalista and fascist journals that continuously reproduced papal encyclicals, nacionalista religious poems, and even liturgical texts. See "Los partidos políticos y el comunismo," *El Pueblo*, February 26, 1937; *El Pueblo*, October 8, 1942, 9. See *Revista Eclesiástica del Arzobispado de Buenos Aires*, July 1936; "El mensaje del vicario de Cristo y la Argentinísima verdad del nacionalismo," *El Federal*, September 4, 1944. See also Zanatta, *Del estado liberal a la nación católica*, 192–193. For the appreciation of the Justo administration by the higher echelons of the institutional church, see Archivo General de la Nación Argentina, Archivo Agustín P. Justo, caja 46. See also "La oración del presidente," *Criterio*, October 25, 1934, 245. For the myth of Uriburu and Catholicism, see chapter 2, and Finchelstein, *Fascismo, liturgia e imaginario*, chap. 1. For colorful examples of the conflation between religion and politics in nacionalismo, see also "Movimiento nacionalista," *Crisol*, March 20, 1940, 1; Guillermo Carabajal, "Salve Cardenal Copello," *El Momento Argentino*, March 16, 1936; Ernesto Vallazza, "Navidad," *Bandera Argentina*, December 25, 1936; *Crisol*, September 1939. See also Archivo General de la Nación Argentina, Archivo Agustín P. Justo, caja 36, doc. 277.

92.   For Meinvielle, as well as for Franceschi, who regularly praised Meinvielle's approach to the question, nacionalismo had to be careful not to fall into the errors of the Maurrasian Right, or those of a sector of Italian fascism or "Hitlerian paganism." Meinvielle's longstanding role as theoretical advisor and even founder of nacionalista publications goes from the early 1920s to the

time of his violent death in an apparent car crash 1973. Meinvielle was the intellectual behind, for example, the neofascist Tacuara group during the 1960s. Meinvielle directed nacionalista publications such as *Nuestro tiempo* and *Balcón* and regularly contributed articles to *Crisol, El Pueblo, Criterio, Sol y Luna*, and many other nacionalista and Catholic publications. Sánchez Sorondo, *Memorias*, 64.

93. Meinvielle, a rabid anti-Semite, believed that the ultimate battle would be between the Christian and the Antichrist as represented by the Jews, and found himself in the position of trying to explain how it was the Nazis (the present-day pagans) who would have to fight that fight. He argued that the Nazis, although reluctant to join the Christians, were unconsciously working as an "instrument of the church" and that they were going to end up destroyed in their apocalyptic battle against communism. Each would destroy the other, and the "Christian new order" would reign in the world. After this event unfolded, Meinvielle claimed, Catholicism would return to Mexico, a new Christian prince probably of French, Italian, or Spanish origin would fight the resurgence of "Jewish communism," while Muslims would start converting to Christianity in mass numbers. From then on, the real apocalyptical era would begin. See Meinvielle, *Los tres pueblos bíblicos en su lucha por la dominación del mundo*, 27, 55, 74, 84, 86–87, 97, 99; Meinvielle, *Entre la Iglesia y el Reich*, 67; Meinvielle, *El judío*, 114, 131. In its favorable review of *Entre la Iglesia y el Reich*, *Criterio* particularly praised this point; see *Criterio*, November 11, 1937, 243–244.

94. Meinvielle, *Los tres pueblos bíblicos en su lucha por la dominación del mundo*, 57, 62.

95. Meinvielle, *Concepción católica de la política*, 27.

96. Arias made a visit to Argentina in 1933 and later, with the blessing of the pope, returned as an exile after the imposition of the Italian racial laws of 1938. Arias was a Jewish convert to Catholicism. During his exile, he was clearly opposed by the more radical Argentine anti-Semites. But an important group of nacionalistas and priests including Franceschi, Meinvielle, and César Pico were among his greatest admirers. Moreover, Arias wrote for Catholic and nacionalista publications such as *Criterio* and *Sol y Luna*. Arias's influence should not be framed under a mimetic or derivative model of fascism insofar as he was perhaps the only Italian fascist to tell nacionalistas what they wanted to hear. He was able to engage in a dialogue with nacionalistas like Meinvielle because he presented a model of Catholic-oriented fascism that never existed in the Italian peninsula, other than among a small group of intellectuals. See Pico, *Carta a Jacques Maritain*, 13. See also Franceschi, "Sociedad civil y cato-

licismo," *Criterio*, September 7, 1933, 5. When Arias died in 1942, *Sol y Luna* identified his thought with that of Argentine nacionalismo. *Sol y Luna* 2 (1939): 10, 27; and Gino Arias, *Manuel de Economía Política*. For a nacionalista criticism of Arias, see, for example, Raúl Larra, "El escritor argentino y la conciencia nacional," *Reconquista*, December 17, 1939. On Arias and his visit to Argentina in 1933, see Archivio, Ministero degli Affari Esteri, Rome, Italy, telespresso 5226/586, August 8, 1933. Other Italian fascists might have been aware of Arias's success in Argentina. Tellingly, during his visit to Argentina, Luigi Federzoni copied Arias in presenting fascism as partly driven by Catholicism and anticommunism. He stressed the (debatable) notion that fascism was all about the values of "religion, family, nationalism, justice, and labor." If the Argentines needed to see fascism as connected to the church, Federzoni told them, "Fascism is the militant and intrepid defender of the Latin and Christian West," and presented Mussolini, as Pope Pius XI had done, as the "man of providence." Luigi Federzoni, *Parole fasciste al Sud-America*, 11–13.

97. Meinvielle, *Un juicio católico sobre los problemas nuevos de la política*, 44.

98. Meinvielle, "Catolicismo y nacionalismo," *El Pueblo*, October 18, 1936, 3. See also "Contra bandera roja, 'Bandera Argentina,'" *Bandera Argentina*, August 1, 1932, 2.

99. Meinvielle, *Concepción católica de la economía*, 70–71, 252–255; and Meinvielle, *Los tres pueblos bíblicos en su lucha por la dominación del mundo*, 83. The church had to keep fascist "dynamism" in check: "Fascism cannot be judged a static phenomenon. It is a movement moved by a powerful dynamism aiming for a reintegration into order that even unwillingly takes fascism into Christian politics." Within the context of the politics of the sacred, Meinvielle argued, the importance of fascism was necessarily a "secondary one." And its character was "provisory." Meinvielle understood politics as "the prudence of governing the multitude in order to guarantee its temporal good." See Meinvielle, *Un juicio católico sobre los problemas nuevos de la política*, 9, 38. See also F. Castellano Torres, "La crisis del idealismo," *Criterio*, May 17, 1934, 60–61.

100. See Meinvielle, *Un juicio católico sobre los problemas nuevos de la política*, 9.

101. Ibid., 52–53.

102. Meinvielle, *Concepción católica de la política*, 2nd ed., 187.

103. Ibid. See also Meinvielle, *Entre la Iglesia y el Reich*; and Franceschi, "Nacionalsocialismo y dignidad humana," *Criterio*, October 7, 1937, 127.

104. Meinvielle, *Concepción católica de la economía*, 255–256. For those Catholic nacionalistas who presented nacionalismo as rooted in Catholicism and who also denied the pagan or non-Catholic tendencies of Hitler and Mussolini, see,

for example, Pedro Clamori, "La apostasía de las masas," *Nuevo Orden* 45 (May 21, 1941): 7; "Cultura contra barbarie," *El Pampero*, June 22, 1943, 3.

105. Meinvielle, "Catolicismo y nacionalismo," *El Pueblo*, October 18, 1936, 3; Meinvielle, *Concepción católica de la economía*, 255–256; Meinvielle, *Un juicio católico sobre los problemas nuevos de la política*, 55–56.

106. Meinvielle, *Un juicio católico sobre los problemas nuevos de la política*, 53–54.

107. Filippo, *Musica de Ideas*, 183–184.

108. For Filippo there was a straight continuum between colonial Argentina and independent Argentina in this respect. For example, he notes that Viceroy Liniers's "memorable reconquista . . . despertó este suelo sin independizarse de su Dios" (memorable reconquista [from the British invaders of the River Plate] awoke this [Argentine] soil without severing its ties to its God). Filippo, *Conferencias radiotelefónicas*, 407–408; Filippo, *El Reinado de Satanás*, 2.291–302; Filippo, *Sistemas genialmente antisociales*, 3.269.

109. Filippo, *Confabulación contra la Argentina*, 1, 64; and Filippo, *Hablan los jefes del comunismo*, 5.

110. For Filippo the "nefarious infiltration of Jews" and their plans for communism represented this very possibility. Filippo, "Martillo de los herejes," *El Pueblo*, June 13, 1943, 9.

111. However, Filippo agreed with Franceschi in seeing communism as "the most complete totalitarianism." He also agreed with Meinvielle in differentiating his own anti-Semitism from Nazi "racial imperialism." Filippo was somewhat ambivalent about the Nazi persecution of Jews, which he believed to be legitimate, while also criticizing its potential anti-Christian repercussions. Filippo, *Confabulación contra la Argentina*, 212. See also the following, all by Filippo: *El monstruo comunista*, 10, 408, 411, 423; *¡Defiéndete!* 52–53, 58–59, 63, 66; *Quienes tienen las manos limpias?* 56, 120–122; *Drama de barbarie y comedia de civilización*, 308–309; *El Reinado de Satanás*, 2.15; *Habla el Padre Filippo*, 67; *Hablan los jefes del comunismo*, 52.

112. The need to distance himself from the Nazis was not only ecclesiastical but personal. Because of his links with the more pro-Nazi forces within nacionalismo, particularly the group associated with *Clarinada* and its relentless anti-Semitism, Filippo was constantly accused of a being a Nazi himself. He was presented as a Nazi in antifascist cartoons and people often asked him if he was a Nazi. He explicitly denied this charge many times, even claiming that he was not a member of any political party or that he did not speak for the Argentine church but for himself. Of course, these statements did not imply that he was not a nacionalista, because he saw nacionalismo not as a political

party but as a dynamic movement working for the church. See Archivo Centro de Documentación e Investigación de la Cultura de Izquierdas en Argentina, Carpeta panfletos antifascistas; and the following, all by Filippo: *Confabulación contra la Argentina*, 41, 110; *Hablan los jefes del comunismo*, 123–124; *Confabulación contra la Argentina*, 100; *Drama de barbarie y comedia de civilización*, 251. See also, all by Filippo, *Quienes tienen las manos limpias?* 29, 56; *El Reinado de Satanás*, 15; *Democracia sana y democracia falaz*, 88; *Sistemas genialmente antisociales*, 15; *Hablan los jefes del comunismo*, 182.

113.   In the pages of *Clarinada*, Filippo denied that he was a Nazi and claimed: "Hay que hacer obra de argentinos genuinamente nacionalista" (Genuinely nacionalista Argentine works need to be done); "Más datos sobre la democracia inglesa," *Clarinada* 5.53 (June 30, 1941).

114.   "Nacionalismo sano, sí; nacionalismo enfermizo, exagerado, egoísta, despectivo y agresivo, no." Filippo, *Confabulación contra la Argentina*, 214. Having being accused by the liberal Catholic *Orden Cristiano* of being a "nacionalista," Filippo denied that he was a "jingoistic" nacionalista, arguing that he was a "sane" one: Filippo, *Hablan los jefes del comunismo*, 205; and *Quienes tienen las manos limpias?* 27–28. See also Guillermina Oliveira de Ramos, "Una incomprensible actitud," *Orden Cristiano* 1.1 (September 15, 1941): 13–14. For an earlier use of the term "nacionalismo sano" to describe Argentine nacionalismo, see Rodolfo Irazusta, "La política: nacionalismo imperial," *La Nueva República*, May 5, 1928.

115.   Like many other nacionalistas, Filippo really liked Mussolini—particularly due to the Duce's "patriotism," "mysticism," "love for the workers," and "military genius"—and even recommended that his readers and the listeners of his radio show read Mussolini's works. However, Filippo often downplayed human agency when thinking about politics and argued "that everything moves because of religion." Filippo, *Habla el Padre Filippo*, 49–50. See also Filippo, *Drama de barbarie y comedia de civilización*, 133–139; and *Quienes tienen las manos limpias?* 91–94.

116.   He did not care much for the "audacious" attitudes of Mussolini, though he regarded fascism "as a form of dictatorship not condemned by the Holy See." Filippo, *Confabulación contra la Argentina*, 27, 179; and *Drama de barbarie y comedia de civilización*, 210.

117.   Filippo, *El monstruo comunista*, 414–415.

118.   Filippo, *Tratado de amistad y negocio de amor*, 115–116; Filippo, *Conferencias radiotelefónicas*, 418; Filippo, *Confabulación contra la Argentina*, 85.

119.   Filippo, *Confabulación contra la Argentina*, 298, 345.

120. See Gabriel Riesco, *Liberalismo y catolicismo*, 9, 21. See also Riesco, *El problema de la guerra actua*, 22, 37, 43–44, 55; Riesco, "Estatismo moderno," *El Pueblo*, November 22, 1942, 9; Riesco, "Disolución espiritual," *El Pueblo*, November 1, 1942, 9.

121. Riesco, *El destino de la Argentina*, 34.

122. Ibid., 49, 263–264. Nazism was in direct opposition to the church. Riesco argued that "liberal Catholicism" or "Nazi Catholicism" were contradictions in terms. Like Barrantes, Franceschi, Filippo, and Meinvielle, Riesco embraced the "providential" regime of Franco in Spain and made explicit his repudiation of both liberalism and totalitarianism. Riesco's conception of democracy was related to his criticism of a liberal Argentina that for a "hundred years" had lived in a state of decay and "outside its historical reality." He presented Argentina's organization and cosmopolitan structure as being directed by liberalism, Masonry, and Judaism and thereby as a polity that was foreign to the very "essence" of Argentina. For Riesco, the essence of Argentina was Catholicism, and the need to give the church its place in Argentine society and culture oriented his own political choice, which he defined as "neither liberal nor totalitarian."

5. Debating Global Totalitarianism

1. Jacques Maritain, a French-born intellectual, was perhaps the most influential and important Catholic philosopher of the twentieth century.

2. See Zanatta, *Del estado liberal a la nación católica*, 198–205; and Deutsch, *Las Derechas*, 243. See also Sánchez Sorondo, *Memorias*, 34; Compagnon, *Jacques Maritain et l'Amérique du Sud*, 109–135.

3. Jacques Maritain, "Le sens de la condamnation," in Doncoeur, *Pourquoi Rome a parlé*, 379. See also Maritain, *Antimoderne*, 15.

4. Before his antifascist turn, Maritain also denounced exclusivist Eurocentrism, colonization, and the victimization of the natives of the Americas and racism in general. But this was not part of the Argentine canonical reading of Maritain, either in the nacionalista sources of the past or among their historians in the present. All Maritain's rather subversive statements on these topics represented countercanonical instances of his earlier texts and were definitely at odds with the core of Argentine Catholicism and nacionalismo. Most Argentine nacionalistas simply denied them and agreed with what they considered to be more important in Maritain. Namely, they were attracted to his neo-Thomist idea that temporal power was highly dependent upon the spiritual

power of the church. See Maritain, *The Things That Are Not Ceasar's*, 64–66, 81–85, 95, 96, 101–106. The French original edition of this book was published in 1927 as *Primauté du spirituel*. For an analysis of the problems in reading canons, see LaCapra, *Representing the Holocaust*, 19–41.

5. See Maritain, *The Things That Are Not Ceasar's*, 127–131, 153–155.

6. See also "Una visita a Maritain," *Criterio*, October 1, 1931, 243. Criterio received special collaborations that Maritain would send from France. For an early example, see Maritain, "Santo Tomás y la unidad de la cultura cristiana," *Criterio*, November 29, 1928, 299–300. Before Maritain's visit, Criterio published a laudatory poem by the Nicaraguan Hispanist Pedro Cuadra. See *Criterio*, April 2, 1936, 328.

7. In addition, *Criterio* published an anti-Semitic piece by Maritain, in which he claimed that the "Jewish spirit" was behind "all modern revolutions." See Maritain, "Nota sobre la cuestión judía," *Criterio*, August 9, 1934, 356–357. See also Leonardo Castellani, "Los domingos de Meudon," *La Nación*, August 16, 1936; Leonardo Castellani, "Jacques Maritain," *Sur* 6.23 (August 1936): 62–67; *Criterio*, August 16, 1934, 375, 392. Federico Ibarguren, "Una visión católica del momento actual," *La Nación*, March 16, 1936; Llambias, Berraz, and Amadeo, *Jacques Maritain ante el problema estético y social*. Castellani recommended that readers "read the last works of Maritain"; he observed that he had minor "objections" to some "details" of Maritain's most recent works but that nonetheless, he felt they were valuable: "Una cosa sé: que [su] vision del mundo actual . . . me parece profunda, fundada, justa; y notoriamente oportuna en la Argentina" (Castellani, "Jacques Maritain," 66).

8. Halperín Donghi, *Argentina y la tormenta del mundo*, 104.

9. See Ziprian de Lagraña, "Sobre Maritain, el comunismo y los judíos," *Crisol*, October 14, 1936.

10. Maritain, *Humanisme intégral*, 294–304; Maritain, *Problemas espirituales y temporales de una nueva cristiandad*, 206–220.

11. Maritain, *The Things That Are Not Ceasar's*, 64–66, 81–85, 95, 96, 101–106.

12. Maritain, "Carta sobre la independencia," *Sur* 6.22 (July 1936): 66–67, 70, 73, 76, 78, 85.

13. "Maritain hablará sobre León Bloy," *Crisol*, October 1, 1936. See also *Criterio*, June 3, 1937, 99–100. See also "Diez cosas," *Crisol*, October 4, 1936.

14. See Archivo Fundación IWO, Argentina, caja Organización Popular contra el Antisemitismo, Correspondencia panfletos, publicaciones C1936–1937, C1939, doc. 139-5. See also "Maritain, el pasquín y la asociación hebraica," *Crisol*, October 7, 1936; Enrique Osés, "Cuando el filósofo baja de su tejado," *Crisol*,

October 11, 1936: Bruno Jacovella, "El judío es el enemigo del pueblo cristiano," *Crisol*, October 13, 1936. See also "Condenó el antisemitismo, en una conferencia sobre León Bloy, el filósofo J. Maritain," *Noticias Gráficas*, October 10, 1936. For a similar argument that stresses that Maritain did not represent the "authority" of the church, see "Audacias hebreas," *Criterio*, May 27, 1937, 80–81.

15. Franceschi debated with *Sur*, accusing the publication of advocating an "irreligious state." *Sur*, in turn, asked for a "better clergy more interested in the eternal question rather than in the transitory deals of politics." The journal asked Franceschi and the church to return to the Argentine liberal tradition based in the complete separation of church and state. Franceschi argued that even though he and the church were apolitical, "the church cannot be silent or disengaged from politics" if "Christian principles are threatened." See Franceschi, " 'Sur' y Criterio," *Criterio*, September 23, 1937, 77–79, and "Posición de Sur," *Sur* 7.35 (August 1937): 8. For a nacionalista view of *Sur* that was similar to that of Franceschi, see *Crisol*, September 12, 1939. The Italian fascist propaganda informers also regarded *Sur* as "filocomunista." See Archivio Centrale dello Stato, Italia, Ministero della Cultura Popolare, D.G. Serv., Propaganda, B9, Argentina, 5 / 1 / 8.

16. Maritain, "Conferencia de Jacques Maritain a propósito de la 'Carta sobre la independencia,' " and "Debate," *Sur* 6.27 (December 1936): 9, 11, 25–28. María Rosa Oliver, the "red friend" of the fascist Count Ciano, was present at the debate and asked him about leftist tendencies in "evangelical principles." Maritain used the question as a way of putting forward progressive principles. In answer to other questions posed by a member of the audience, Maritain justified the use of violent means such as coups d'état to suppress fascist "aggressions," and he criticized the doctrine of "preemptive war" in a possible implicit reference to Mussolini's invasion of Ethiopia. He did not want to talk explicitly about the situation in Spain, however. See 41–42, 47, 49–50. On Ciano and Oliver, see chapter 3, note 75.

17. See Archivo Fundación IWO, Argentina, caja Organización Popular contra el Antisemitismo, Correspondencia panfletos, publicaciones C1936–1937, C1939, doc. 139-5. "Un filósofo al servicio de la confusión social," *Crisol*, October 8, 1936.

18. The Italian fascist writer Ungaretti was also present in the debate. Maritain made reference to his presence but the Italian, unlike Castellani, remained silent during the entire debate. "Debate," *Sur* 6.27 (December 1936): 58–60.

19. Ibid.

20. The international meeting gathered more than eighty international writers, including such bestselling authors as Stefan Zweig and Emil Ludwig; fascists and nacionalistas, including Filippo Tommaso Marinetti, Giuseppe Ungaretti, and Mario Puccini (all from Italy); and other writers, such as Victoria Ocampo and Eduardo Mallea (Argentina), Alcides Arguedas (Bolivia), Sanín Cano (Colombia); Jules Romains, Benjamin Crémieux, and Jean Giraudoux (all from France); Sophia Wadia (India), Majid Khadduri (Iraq),Toson Shimazaki (Japan), and Alfonso Reyes (Mexico). See PEN Club, *XIV Congreso Internacional de los P.E.N. Clubs.* See also United States National Archives, Personal papers of Benito Mussolini, T586, 430, reel 33, job 32, 015390, 106995.

21. Archivo Fundación IWO, Argentina, caja Organización Popular contra el Antisemitismo, Correspondencia panfletos, publicaciones C1936–1937, C1939, doc. 139-5; "Marginando Sucesos," *Crisol,* October 1, 1936. For an earlier anti-Semitic criticism of Ludwig, see Juan Sepich, "Las falsificaciones de Emil Ludwig," *Criterio,* August 7, 1930, 175–176. See also *Criterio,* November 15, 1928, 205–206.

22. Father Filippo, who had been an enthusiastic reader of Maritain, obsessively annotated his personal copies of Maritain's book and expressed particular interest in the anticommunist venues where Maritain published. In his annotations to *Cristianismo y democracia,* a later antifascist book by Maritain, Filippo wrote in the margins that the French philosopher enacted a "wrongly applied Catholic idealism" and also that Maritain thought with a "Jewish logic" and "does not understand well what communism is." See the Cornell University Library's copy of Maritain's *Cristianismo y democracia* (1944), annotated by Filippo; see 30, 124. See also *Nueva Política* 2 (July 1940): 28–29. The "new Christianity" that Maritain associated with a more or less pluralistic "temporal regime" was readily taken as a symbol by Argentine antifascism, including the Catholic liberals who contributed to the journal *Orden Cristiano* and their most outspoken representative, the former fascist Eugenia Silveyra de Oyuela. The idea of using the new Maritain for antifascist political purposes was widely criticized. Ironically, the nacionalista intellectual Delfina Bunge de Gálvez accused *Orden Cristiano* of using the church for political purposes. Without noticing the extent of the nacionalista use of the papal encyclicals, she criticized liberal Catholics for their instrumental reading of them. Bunge's complaint against Catholic antifascism was clearly heard by the institutional church: Cardinal Copello promptly forbade Catholics to read *Orden Cristiano,* and other bishops did the same. See Zanatta, *Del estado liberal a la nación católica,* 282. See Eugenia Silveyra de Oyuela, "Jacques Maritain.

¿Por qué no somos racistas?" *Orden Cristiano* 3.52 (November 1, 1943): 74. See also "Nacionalismo y aislacionismo," *Orden Cristiano* 3.53 (November 15, 1943): 94; *Orden Cristiano* 3.54 (December 1, 1943): 104; José Andino, "Maritain y la democracia," *Orden Cristiano* 3.71 (August 15, 1944): 439. See also Delfina Bunge de Gálvez, "Catolicismo de guerra," *El Pueblo*, November 1, 1942 (suplemento cátedra), and Delfina Bunge de Gálvez, "Catolicismo de guerra," *Criterio*, October 22, 1942, 185–188. Bunge alluded to their readings of the encyclical "Non abbiamo bisogno" (1931), in which Pope Pius XI criticized the frictions between fascism and the Catholic action. For a reading of this encyclical that does not condemn fascism as a whole, see *Criterio*, July 7, 1932, 15. In 1938, *Sur* published Maritain's book on anti-Semitism. See Maritain, *Los judíos entre las naciones*.

23. Gustavo J. Franceschi, "Ante un palacio," *Criterio*, July 1, 1937, 198. For the exchange between Franceschi and Maritain on this question, see Jacques Maritain and Gustavo J. Franceschi, "Puntualizaciones," *Criterio*, September 16, 1937, 53–57. Another nacionalista priest who kept his admiration for Maritain was Juan Sepich. See *Sol y Luna* 1 (1938): 183.

24. Cardinal Santiago Copello of Argentina sent Franceschi to Spain to represent Argentine Catholicism. See *Criterio*, May 13, 1937, 33; Gustavo J. Franceschi, "Crueldad," *Criterio*, May 20, 1937, 53. See also *Revista Eclesiástica del Arzobispado de Buenos Aires*, November 1936, 753; Sánchez Sorondo, *Memorias*, 37.

25. Gregorio Maldonado, "La nueva cristiandad de Maritain a la luz de los nuevos documentos pontificios," *Criterio*, June 10, 1937, 131–134. For a critique of this critique, see Manuel V. Ordoñez, "Sobre la nueva cristiandad de Maritain," *Criterio*, June 17, 1937, 158. See also Gregorio Maldonado, "Respuesta a Manuel V. Ordoñez," *Criterio*, June 24, 1937, 175; Rafael Pividal, "Defensa de Maritain," *Criterio*, June 24, 1937, 178–180; Gregorio Maldonado, "Respuesta a D. Rafael Pividal"; and the response by a group of Uruguayan Catholics, "Sobre la nueva cristiandad de Maritain," *Criterio*, July 1, 1937, 206.

26. Julio Meinvielle, "Los desvaríos de Maritain," *Criterio*, July 8, 1937, 227. See also Meinvielle, *Qué saldrá de la España que sangra*.

27. Many women partook of the nacionalista movement. The Legión Cívica Argentina, for example, had a "rama femenina," whereas other nacionalista organizations were explicitly based on gender differences such as the Asociación Damas Patria y Hogar. Traditional gender distinctions were particularly emphasized by nacionalista men in their writings. See, for example, Juan E. Carulla, "El voto femenino," *La Nueva República*, April 28, 1928, 1; Juan Bautista Teran, *El divorcio, conferencia*, 40; "Legión Cívica Argentina," *Crisol*, Octo-

ber 4, 1936; Villafañe, *Chusmocracia*, 29. On this topic, see also the path-breaking contributions of Sandra McGee Deutsch, "The Visible and Invisible Liga Patriótica Argentina"; Deutsch, *Counter Revolution in Argentina*; Deutsch, *Las Derechas*, 234–238; Deutsch, "What Difference Does Gender Make?" For an analysis of nacionalista notions of masculinity, see Finchelstein, *Fascismo, liturgia e imaginario*, 113–130.

28. Julio Meinvielle, "Los desvaríos de Maritain," *Criterio*, July 8, 1937, 227–228; Meinvielle, "Carta a Jacques Maritain de César Pico," *Criterio*, August 5, 1937, 330–331; Meinvielle, "Contestación a Jacques Maritain," *Criterio*, August 5, 1937, 356–360; Meinvielle, "De la guerra santa," *Criterio*, August 19, 1937, 378–383.

29. Jacques Maritain, "Posiciones," *Criterio*, August 12, 1937, 349.

30. Maritain, *Los rebeldes españoles no hacen una "guerra santa"* and *Sobre la guerra santa*, 62.

31. In his native France, many Catholics shared Maritain's choice for Christian democracy. The Catholic writer François Mauriac criticized the "conflation of fascism and Christianity" that was happening in Spain. The Argentine nacionalistas saw this conflation in positive terms. See "Mauriac fija la actitud de los católicos frente a la guerra de España," *La Razón*, July 1, 1938, 3.

32. Meinvielle, *Un juicio católico sobre los problemas nuevos de la política*, 41–42, 51; Pico, *Carta a Jacques Maritain sobre la colaboración*, 56.

33. Pico, *Carta a Jacques Maritain sobre la colaboración*, 56; César Pico, "Totalitarismo," *Sol y Luna* 3 (1939).

34. Leonardo Castellani, "Teoría y práctica," *Cabildo*, May 28, 1944. Also in Castellani, *Las canciones de Militis*.

35. "Carta del Emperador Carlos V a Benito Mussolini," in Castellani, *Las canciones de Militis*, 227–228.

36. Castellani appreciated the deep Christian tenets of "Catholic nacionalismo" in its "efforts to think Christian [*pensar en cristiano*] and for not breaking, in the midst of the inevitable violence of political battles, the modules of the evangelic ideal. They are nervous in this battle, disturbed very much by their weapons, often they kneel as much as they can, although they are even able to bitch during an 'Our Father.'" Jerónimo del Rey (Leonardo Castellani), "Política y Teología," *Nuevo Orden*, January 29, 1941, 8.

37. Leonardo Castellani, "Teoría y práctica," *Cabildo*, May 28, 1944; and Castellani, "Como salir," *Cabildo*, April 23, 1944. See also Castellani, *Las canciones de Militis*, 134.

38. Riesco asserted that "la argentinidad es la concreción de la hispanidad en

nuestra realidad nacional." See Gabriel Riesco, *El destino de la Argentina*, 249. See my criticism of this historiography: Finchelstein, *Fascismo, liturgia e imaginario*, 10–14.

39. Riesco, *El destino de la Argentina*, 145, 171–176, 181, 199, 210–211, 262–263. See also Riesco, *Nuestra misión histórica*, 9, 12–13, 113, 119, 121–123, 143, 151, 163.

40. For Franceschi, Guernica had been "intentionally" attacked by the "reds." Gustavo J. Franceschi, "El eclipse de la moral," *Criterio*, May 27, 1937, 77; Franceschi, *En el humo del incendio*. See also A. H. Varela, "Dios en España," *Criterio*, September 9, 1937, 41; Julio Meinvielle, "Pastor Angelicus," *Sol y Luna* 2 (1939): 114. See also Archivio Centrale dello Stato, Italia, Ministero della Cultura Popolare, D.G. Serv., B7, Argentina, 1937, I / 4 / 18, T105.

41. For the liberal birth of Argentina, see Halperin Donghi, "Argentina: Liberalism in a Country Born Liberal," in Love and Jacobsen, *Guiding the Invisible Hand*.

42. Rodó especially made reference to Argentina at the end of his influential work *Ariel*, when he argued that Buenos Aires (like Latin America at large) was at the risk of becoming a victim of U.S.-inspired cosmopolitanism. "Already there exist, in our Latin America, cities whose material grandeur and apparent civilization place them in the first rank; but one may fear lest a touch of thought upon their exterior, so sumptuous, may make the shining vessel ring hollow within; lest our cities too—though they had their Moreno, their Rivadavia, their Sarmiento, cities which gave initiative to an immortal revolution that, like a stone cast on water, spread the glory of their heroes and the words of their tribunes in ever-widening circles over a vast continent—may end like Tyre or Sidon, or as Carthage ended." See Rodó, *Ariel*, 134.

43. For an analysis of Hispanism before nacionalismo, see Moya, *Cousins and Strangers*, 340–384. Moya argues: "Mid-nineteenth century liberals had dreamed about capitalist modernization. Now that it had come—not as a pure ideal but as a complex and messy reality—nationalists dreamed about an idealized precapitalist and premodern past; about a pastoral, patrician, and patriarchal Argentina where gauchos were loyal and servants knew their place, free of Russian anarchists, French pimps, and Neapolitan thieves. In this atmosphere, the Spanishness that earlier liberals had wanted to eradicate as an impediment to progress became a nostalgic emblem of the idealized past" (364). For other important comparative analyses of hispanidad and nacionalismo, see Zuleta Álvarez, *España en América*; González Calleja, "El hispanismo autoritario español y el movimiento nacionalista argentino," 599–642.

44. The term "hispanidad" had been defined earlier in the *Diccionario de la Real*

Academia Española as a synonym for "a peculiar way of speaking Spanish outside of Castellan rules." Miguel Unamuno had also used the term to refer to a liberal cultural project that was shared by speakers of the Spanish language. But it was Vizcarra who extended the use of the term beyond linguistics and in geographical and "Catholic" terms. See González Calleja, "El hispanismo autoritario español y el movimiento nacionalista argentino," 613.

45. De Maeztu, *Defensa de la hispanidad*, 8, 16, 19–21, 36, 39, 73, 105–106, 109, 132–135, 168–169, 184, 216–217, 288–289. Interestingly, Maeztu located the genealogy of the vocational concept of hispanidad in the writings of Father Vizcarra, whom he identified as a Spanish priest. On Vizcarra, see Zanatta, *Del estado liberal a la nación católica*, 45, 162, 295.

46. See *Criterio*, February 16, 1930, 198; "El momento español," *Criterio*, December 18, 1930, 782.

47. Ramiro de Maeztu, "Las aguas de Rousseau," *Criterio*, December 4, 1930, 723–724. See also González Calleja, "El hispanismo autoritario español y el movimiento nacionalista argentino," 609.

48. *Criterio*, July 12, 1934, 243.

49. "¿Qué hace América ante la tragedia de España?" *Crisol*, October 13, 1936; "La causa de los nacionalistas españoles es una causa de cultura universal," *La Fronda*, January 21, 1937; Luis Barrantes Molina, "El movimiento militar de Franco no es sedición," *El Pueblo*, February 18, 1937, 4.

50. García Morente, *Idea de la hispanidad*, 12–17, 22, 25, 55, 129; *Sol y Luna* 2 (1939): 174; Pemán, *Seis conferencias pronunciadas en Hispano América*, 9–11, 28, 37, 43, 87, 95, 99; Pemán, *El paraíso y la serpiente*, 7–15, 20–21. See also Pemán, *Cartas a un escéptico en materias de formas de gobierno*, 86, 153. See also Tovar, *El imperio de España*, 9–16; de Ascanio, *España imperio*, 3, 11, 14, 18, 27–32, 43, 115–122, 127, 168–171; Cereceda, *Historia del imperio español y de la hispanidad*, 8–9, 265–275; Díaz de Robles, *El ideal hispánico a través de la historia*, 19, 54, 60, 65–66, 109–112, 126–127; José Millán Astray, "Emoción de la hispanidad," in Asociación Cultural Hispano-Americana, *Voces de Hispanidad* (Madrid, 1940), 45–52. Tellingly, *hispanistas* like de Maeztu or Díaz de Robles criticized the Argentine author Domingo Sarmiento as the icon of the anti-Hispanic intellectual.

51. Archivo del Ministerio de Relaciones Exteriores y Culto, Argentina División Política, mueble 7, casilla 22, Guerra Europea, expediente 258, año 1940. See ibid., folio 3.

52. Ibid., expediente 20, año 1940. See also the reports in the Spanish press: "Las cosas claras," *Informaciones* (Madrid), November 26, 1941; "Discurso de Serrano Suñer en nombre de España," *Informaciones* (Madrid), November 26,

1941; "El ministro español de Asuntos Exteriores, recibido por el Fiuhrer-canciller," *Arriba*, November 28, 1941.

53. Villafañe, *Chusmocracia*, 43.

54. For some examples, see Marcelo Sánchez Sorondo, "Dialéctica del imperio," *Sol y Luna* 1 (1938): 107, 109–110; Armando Cascella, "Hay que retomar la ruta del virreynato," *Nuevo Orden*, August 8, 1940; Héctor Saenz Quesada, "¿Qué sería una Política imperial argentina?" *Nueva Política* 9 (February 1941): 16–19; *Nueva Política* 10 (March 1941): 4–5; Héctor Sáenz y Quesada, "¿Un continente con contenido?" *El Restaurador*, June 12, 1941, 4; Font Ezcurra, *La unidad nacional*, ix; "Buenos Aires cabeza del sexto continente," *Nueva Política* 19 (February 1942): 3; Marcelo Sánchez Sorondo, "Hispano América o South America," *Nueva Política* 19 (February 1942): 11–13; Federico Ibarguren, "Democracia, socialismo, nacionalismo," *Nueva Política* 24 (August 1942): 17; *Nueva Política* 25 (October 1942): 3.

55. Pemán, who "fell in love" with the "real" Argentina, "the land of *asado* and *dulce de leche*, of verses of Lugones and *coplas* of gauchos," presented an orientalizing idea of this country as the reservoir of the true classic Spain. Pemán, *El paraíso y la serpiente*, 6.

56. "¡Cuánto más limpia y altamente se hace un poco de fascismo cuando no hay una Etiopía que conquistar, ni un Túnez que recordar, ni una Austria que sorber!" José María Pemán, "Pasemos a la escucha," *Sol y Luna* 4 (1940): 91.

57. See ibid., 90, 92.

58. An exception to this trend was the case of Rómulo Carbia, the Argentine nacionalista and anti-Semitic historian, who, in his major book, published in fascist Spain by the Council of Hispanidad, claimed that Spain as a concept "transcends the limits of political geography" insofar as it represented "the Christian-Catholic way of life." Carbia, *Historia de la leyenda negra hispanoamericana*, and "La Iglesia en la 'Leyenda Negra' hispanoamericana," *Sol y Luna* 2 (1939).

59. Leopoldo Lugones, "España y nosotros," in de Madariaga, *Diez Maestros*, 119–120, 122, 126, 128. See also Lugones, *Poemas solariegos*, 6; Rodolfo Irazusta, "La política: nacionalismo imperial," *La Nueva República*, May 5, 1928, 1; Pedro García, "Horacio Quiroga político," *La Nueva República*, May 5, 1928, 2; Irazusta and Irazusta, *La Argentina y el imperialismo británico*, 62–63, 158, 184, 192–193, 199; Fresco, *Habla el gobernador de Buenos Aire*, 41–42; "El mundo hispanoparlante," *Bandera Argentina*, September 23, 1939; Rodolfo Irazusta, "Estamos como en 1890," *Reconquista*, November 15, 1939; *Nueva Política* 10 (March 1941): 3; Enrique Harriague Coronado, "Sigue el reajuste del estatuto colonial," *La*

Voz del Plata, September 30, 1942, 4; Ibarguren, *Rosas y la tradición hispano-americana*, 5; *Combate* 1.2 (June–July 1943); Lastra, *Bajo el signo nacionalista*, 20, 23, 58, 66; Guardia Argentina, Propósitos.

60. For a prenacionalista example, see Ingenieros, *La evolución sociológica argentina*, 17, 46, 86, 90, 93–100, 105, 187.

61. For a theoretical approach to this issues, see Stoler, "Intimidations of Empire. Predicaments of the Tactile and the Unseen," 1–22.

62. *Criterio*, February 13, 1931, 157; Irazusta and Irazusta, *La Argentina y el imperialismo britanico*; Doll, *Acerca de una política nacional*, 153; Enrique Osés, "Como se hacen campañas britanicas desde un diario que no es argentino," *Crisol*, September 9, 1939; Rodolfo Irazusta, "El peligro alemán," *Reconquista*, November 26, 1939; Héctor Sáenz y Quesada, "¿Un continente con contenido?" *El Restaurador*, June 12, 1941, 4; Archivo General de la Nación Argentina, Archivo Agustín P. Justo, caja 104, doc. 112.

63. On this topic, see chapter 1. See also Rodolfo Irazusta, "Los ingleses y el progreso argentino," *Reconquista*, November 30, 1939; Archivo General de la Nación Argentina, Archivo Agustín P. Justo, caja 104, doc. 111.

64. See Carulla, *Problemas de cultura*, 16–21. See also César Pico, "Cultura greco-latina," *Criterio*, March 15, 1928, 47; and Pico, "El valor esencial de la cultura europea," *Criterio*, April 19, 1928, 199–200.

65. Pico, *Doctrina y finalidades del comunismo*, 5, 12–13.

66. Gustavo J. Franceschi, "Panamericanismo," *Criterio*, September 2, 1937, 6.

67. See Carulla, *Problemas de cultura*, 44. See also "La capa dorada del presidente Calles," *Criterio*, March 8, 1928, 17; César Pico, "Hacia la hispanidad," *Sol y Luna* 9 (1942): 136.

68. See Halperín Donghi, *El revisionismo histórico argentino*, and "El revisionismo histórico argentino como visión decadentista de la historia nacional," in his *Ensayos de historiografía*; Cattaruzza, "Algunas reflexiones sobre el revisionismo histórico"; Quattrocchi-Woisson, *Los males de la memoria*; Deutsch, *Las Derechas*, 223–224.

69. Borges, *Obras completas en colaboración*, 74, 80–81.

70. "El nacionalismo de nuestros nacionalistas," *Sur* 7.37 (October 1937): 105.

71. For the Italian fascist criticism of the reception of Spanish fascism in Argentina, see Archivio Centrale dello Stato, Italia. Ministero della Cultura Popolare, D.G. Serv., B10, Argentina, 5 / 1 / 10.

72. See, for example, "Hombres e ideas José María Pemán," *El Restaurador*, June 12, 1941.

73. On this topic, see Newton, *The "Nazi Menace" in Argentina*. See also Newton,

"The 'Nazi Menace' in Argentina Revisited"; Buchrucker, "Latin America in the Time of the Nazis"; Klich, "Los Nazis en la Argentina"; Finchelstein and Speyer, "El hilo pardo."

74. Archivo del Ministerio de Relaciones Exteriores y Culto, Argentina, División Política, mueble 7, casilla 21, Guerra Europea, expediente 210, año 1940; ibid., casilla 21, Guerra Europea, expediente 197, año 1940; ibid., casilla 17, Guerra Europea, expediente 172, año 1940; ibid., casilla 17, Guerra Europea, expediente 168, año 1940. The more successful joint engagement between allied propaganda and Argentine antifascism, though, was the creation in the Argentine Congress of the commission to inquire into "anti-Argentine" activities by Nazi spies. See also ibid., casilla 35, Guerra Europea, expediente 210, año 1940. Roosevelt's speech was expectedly criticized by the German press and the German ambassador in Buenos Aires. See also ibid., casilla 41, Guerra Europea, expediente 486, año 1942; "Una nota del gobierno alemán relativa a manifestaciones del presidente Roosevelt," *La Nación*, November 4, 1941.

75. See Valle, *El decreto del poder ejecutivo sobre asociaciones extranjeras*, 8–9, 10, 30–31.

76. Silveyra, *La cuestión nazi en la Argentina*, 20–21; Carlos M. Silveyra, *Norteamérica se cava su fosa*; Biblioteca Nacional Argentina, folleto 274464.

77. See the copy of Carlos M. Silveyra, *El comunismo en la Argentina*, in the Hitler collection of the Library of Congress, Washington, D.C., Library of Congress call number Rare Books HX5, S55 1936, Third Reich Collection.

78. Borges, of course, was agnostic, and he used Nazi anti-Catholicism as a powerful tool against the deeply Catholic nacionalistas. Borges hyperbolized the artificiality of nacionalismo, even ironically arguing (with dubious logic) that Hitler may have been justified in his actions though the "germanófilos" were surely not. Borges, "Definición del germanófilo," *El Hogar*, December 13, 1940. Also in Borges, *Obras completas*, 4.441.

79. "Somos Germanófilos," *Clarinada* 5.50 (June 30, 1941).

80. For antifascist views on this question, see the extensive archival materials at the Jewish cultural institute in Buenos Aires, particularly: Archivo Fundación iwo, Argentina, caja Organización Popular contra el Antisemitismo, Correspondencia panfletos, publicaciones C1936–1937, C1939, docs. 13, 22 / 16, 61, 139, 139-13, 139-14, 139-19, 139-21. See also "La acción hitlerista en la Argentina," *Mundo Israelita*, July 22, 1933, 1; Ernesto Giudici, "Por el pacto fascista entregan Latinoamérica a Hitler," November 15, 1937; *El Corresponsal Argentino: servicio de información del Comité contra el racismo y el antisemitismo de la Argentina*, May 5, 1939, 1; "Los métodos alemanes en el antisemismo argentino," *Mundo*

Israelita, March 27, 1937, 1; Boletín de la Organización Popular contra el antisemitismo, N13, 1942.

81. See "El lirismo ingenuo del 'nazismo,'" *El Pueblo*, February 14, 1937, 8. For a lay nacionalista example of the explicit presentation of Nazism as "racismo exagerado," see Un Católico, "Los dos conceptos: la verdad católica sobre la unidad de la especie humana y las falsas construcciones del racismo," *Bandera Argentina*, March 28, 1940. Even before the Nazi takeover, *Bandera Argentina* informed its readers about the structural aspects of Nazism and its internal party regulations and handbooks. In 1932, an envoy from the Nazis arrived in Buenos Aires in order to organize the Nazi party section in Argentina. See "Se encuentra en ésta el delegado del partido nacional socialista," *Bandera Argentina*, November 22, 1932, 3. During the years of Nazi rule many nacionalistas praised Nazism for its economic and military successes and highlighted its anticapitalist tendencies, its supposed working-class nature, and radical social tendencies. The journal *Aduna*, for example, presented the Nazis as the "defender of Christian civilization" against communism and Judaism: "Ejemplos para la Nueva Argentina," *Aduna*, March 31, 1935. See also "El pueblo contra la libertad," *Aduna*, January 31, 1935, and "La lucha contra el comunismo," *Aduna*, May 15, 1936. See also Archivo Fundación iwo, caja Organización Popular contra el Antisemitismo, Correspondencia, C1933, C1935, doc. 13. For some examples see *Crisol*, October 1, 1936. See also Carlos M. Silveyra, *La cuestión nazi en la Argentina*, 18–19, 21. The nacionalistas never talked about Nazism's anti-Catholic trends. Moreover, even the Nazis in Argentina, that is to say, the Nazi members of the German community, when dealing with Argentine nacionalistas presented Germans as a "Christian people" and did not engage in any pagan arguments whatsoever. For some examples, see "Contra la dignidad y la masculinidad," *Bandera Argentina*, March 29, 1933, 1; "La obra de Hitler," *Bandera Argentina*, April 5, 1933, 3; "Los nazis se tienen fe," *Crisol*, October 1, 1936; "El tercer Reich en su vi aniversario," *Bandera Argentina*, March 29, 1939, 1. Up to the end of the Nazi regime the nacionalista press supported Hitler and his military and genocidal campaigns. See Lvovich and Finchelstein, "L'Holocauste et l'Eglise argentine."

82. See "Son unánimes las simpatías de fascistas y nazistas por los nacionalistas españoles," *Crisol*, October 1, 1936; Santiago de Estrada, "Sobre historia," *Sol y Luna* 1 (1938): 130.

83. Archivo General de la Nación Argentina, Ministerio del Interior, año 1932, L13, n. 18990R. The Argentine canonical edition of the writings of Oliveira Salazar

represented an important effort to widely diffuse Portuguese fascism in Argentina. See Salazar, *El pensamiento de la revolución nacional*. Catering to the Argentines, the Portuguese fascists explicitly stated that nacionalismo represented the essence of the thought and practice of the Portuguese dictator. For the reception, see for example: "Oliveira Salazar: dueño del momento en Portugal," *Aduna*, September 30, 1935; "La carrera y el carácter de Oliveira Salazar," *Aduna*, October 15, 1935; "Oliveira Salazar," *Aduna*, October 31, 1935; "Decálogo del Nuevo Estado Portugués," *Aduna*, September 6, 1936; "Los principios y la acción," *Sol y Luna* 7 (1942): 168, 171; Filippo, *Confabulación contra la Argentina*, 199; Luis Barrantes Molina, "Fascismo y totalitarismo," *El Pueblo*, February 22 and 23, 1937, 4; Meinvielle, *Los tres pueblos bíblicos en su lucha por la dominación del mundo*, 69; Meinvielle, *Un juicio católico sobre los problemas nuevos de la política*, 57; Meinvielle, *Entre la Iglesia y el Reich*, 71.

84. Villafañe, *La miseria de un país rico*, 23, 37, 114, 182, 184, 229; Federico Ibarguren, "La tradición hispanoamericana en nuestra emancipación política," *Sol y Luna* 3 (1939): 12; *Nueva Política* 10 (March 1941): 3.

85. For an Italian fascist critical assessment of Spanish fascist propaganda in Argentina, see Archivio Centrale dello Stato, Italia. Ministero della Cultura Popolare, D.G. Serv., B10, Argentina, 5 / 1 / 10. For the Spanish fascist perspective on Latin American propaganda, see Payne, *Fascism in Spain*, 344. See also Rein, *The Franco-Perón Alliance*.

86. See Finchelstein, *La Argentina fascista*, chaps. 4 and 5. See also Spektorowski, *Argentina's Revolution of the Right*, 173–200; and Buchrucker, *Nacionalismo y peronismo.*.

87. Leopoldo Lugones, "La copa de Jade," *La Nación*, January 28, 1937; Lugones, "La Campana," *La Nación*, October 17, 1937.

88. Lugones, *Política revolucionaria*, 55. See also the following, all by Lugones, "España y nosotros," in de Madariaga, *Diez Maestros*, 126; "El escritor ante su obra," *La Nación*, March 28, 1937; "Vida y materia," *La Nación*, July 12, 1936; "El escritor ante la libertad," *La Nación*, May 16 and June 13, 1937; "La guerra de los ideólogos," *La Nación*, October 31, 1937; "Los dos balances," *La Nación*, December 26, 1937; "Conciencia de escritor," *La Nación*, January 16, 1938. See also Castellani, *Sentir la Argentina*, 5, 16.

89. For Lugones, beauty was "the manifestation of the divinity in the harmony of the creation" ("la manifestación de la divinidad en la armonía de lo creado"). See Lugones, "El decoro estético," *La Nación* January 26, 1936. On this topic, Lugones went back to his early claim that the Latin people was aes-

thetic in nature, while Nordic peoples and the Jews had an essentially ethical nature.

90. Ibid. See also the following, all by Lugones, *La organización de la paz*, 9 and 66; "Ante una nueva perspectiva del gobierno del mundo," *La Fronda*, January 16, 1933, 7; "Vida y materia," *La Nación*, July 12, 1936; and *Estudios helénicos*, 19–21.

91. Lugones, *Política revolucionaria*, 89.

92. Ibid., 55.

93. Lugones, "La libertad del arte," *La Nación*, February 16, 1936; and Lugones, "El decoro estético," *La Nación*, January 26, 1936.

94. Lugones, *Prometeo*, 5; Spektorowski, "The Making of an Argentine Fascist."

95. Lugones, "El decoro estético"; Lugones, "La moral sin dogmas," *La Nación*, May 17, 1936.

96. "La materialización del arte progresaba hacia el mismo fin, que ahora tocamos en el mamarracho sistemático—vale decir fealdad impúdica—la jazz de los negros, la infame lubricidad del tango y del fox, el nudismo precursor del amor libre: todas cosas de mono, según bien se echa de ver" (Lugones, "El decoro estético").

97. "Eso, por último, Freud, para quien toda la vida humana se desarrolla como sujeto y como objeto morales, entre dos determinantes: el amor físico, por supuesto, apetito carnal, y el odio; o sea el imperio del instinto, motor principal de la inteligencia, bajo las sendas expresiones significativas de Eros y Ananké o fatalidad (*Malestar en la Civilización*)." See Lugones, "La formación del ciudadano," *La Nación*, February 13, 1938.

98. "Mientras que Dios no es otra cosa que la idealización asimismo bi-polarizada, del Totem o bestia-mascota que poseen algunas tribus salvajes." Lugones, "La formación del ciudadano." On Lugones and his notion of Argentines as a European, "white," and "beautiful" race, see Lugones, *Estudios helénicos*, 19–21; Lugones, "Castellano de América," *La Nación*, July 26, 1936.

99. See Lugones, "La formación del ciudadano." Only at the end of his life was Lugones engaged in an anti-Semitism that was clericofascist, but it was never as extreme as that of most nacionalistas.

100. For an analysis of this topic, see Finchelstein "The Anti-Freudian Politics of Argentine Fascism."

101. See Emilio De Martino, "Il compiacimento del Duce," *Corriere della Sera*, June 12, 1934, 4; *La Prensa*, June 11, 1934; Carli, "Olimpionica"; and Martin, *Football and Fascism*. See also Eduardo Galeano, "La guerra o la fiesta," *Brecha* (Montevideo), June 1, 2002; and his *El fútbol a sol y sombra y otros escritos*.

102. Canadian historian Ronald Newton, in his remarkable study of Nazi activities in Argentina, observed the extensive links between the German ministry of propaganda and the Argentine nacionalistas. Newton presents a reality, the German purchase of space in Argentine nacionalista newspapers, as evidence of the exclusive Nazi character of the "natives," or what he calls "Creole fascism." See Newton, *The "Nazi Menace" in Argentina*. In their institutional history of Argentine foreign relations, the historian Carlos Escudé and his collaborators claim that while the Germans conducted a propaganda campaign, there was no similar endeavor by the Italian fascist regime and its institutions in Argentina. Escudé, *Historia general de las relaciones exteriores de la república argentina*, vol. 9.

103. See Archivo del Ministerio de Relaciones Exteriores y Culto, Argentina, División Política, caja 22, Italia, telegrama cifrado, N511, N34, Estrictamente reservado y muy confidencial, folio 1, June 4, 1943.

104. Gramsci, *Socialismo e fascismo*, 101.

105. Archivo General de la Nación Argentina, Archivo Agustín P. Justo, caja 36, doc. 271; *Nueva Idea* 1.1 (January 19, 1935).

106. The Argentine tradition of relative secularity within a more "religious" Latin American context brings this clerical turn into more dramatic relief. Liberal Argentina for example, had broken diplomatic relations with the Vatican between 1885 and 1899. Between 1922 and 1953 there were open conflicts between the Argentine state and the Vatican. See Zanatta and Di Stefano, *Historia de la Iglesia argentina*.

107. Point 25 reads: "Nuestro Movimiento incorpora el sentido católico—de gloriosa tradición y predominante en España a la reconstrucción nacional. / La Iglesia y el Estado concordarán sus facultades respectivas, sin que se admita intromisión o actividad alguna que menoscabe la dignidad del Estado o la integridad nacional." Primo de Rivera, *Doctrina de F.E. de las J.O.N.S* and *Papeles póstumos de José Antonio*, 169.

108. Codreanu argued in his "manual" that the movement was like a "temple" and that its members should pray to God for the triumph of the movement. But the leader had an almost equal standing with the sacred and did not seem to ask instructions from above. God had called for the existence of Romanian fascism and its actions were accomplished "in the name of God," but there was no predestination. See points 7, 10, 12, 22, 37, 42, 47, 54, 64, 80–83, 89, 93, and see especially point 9 of the "ten commandments" in Codreanu, *Manual del jefe*.

109. See for example, "La espada cristiana," *Crisol*, October 8, 1936.

110. See Zanatta, *Del estado liberal a la nación católica*.

111. Alberto Franco, "Teología y política: breve disertación sobre la violencia," *Crisol*, October 20, 1936.

112. See Archivo General de la Nación Argentina, Archivo Agustín P. Justo, caja 49, docs. 162–165, 174, 180. See also Enrique Osés, "El Frente Nacional que no encaja en el alma nacional," *Crisol*, October 13, 1936; Osés, "Al cruce de unos argumentos deleznables e inconsistentes," *Crisol*, October 22, 1936; "Llamamiento al deber de los católicos," *Bandera Argentina*, March 28, 1940. See also the transcript of an intercepted telephone conversation between Osés and an anonymous nacionalista, Archivo General de la Nación Argentina, Archivo Agustín P. Justo, caja 104, doc. 51.

113. Pierre Drieu la Rochelle, "Estado de las ideologías europeas," *La Nación*, May 31, 1936; Drieu la Rochelle, "Dos civilizaciones en Europa," *La Nación*, November 14, 1937. It is interesting to note that on the same page, the paper published an article on Freud by Stefan Zweig. See also Drieu la Rochelle, "Sobre la palabra democracia," *La Nación*, August 30, 1936. For a criticism of the French fascist with regard to his lack of knowledge of Catholicism, see Gustavo J. Franceschi, "Monsieur Drieu La Rochelle y el tomismo," *Criterio*, July 14, 1932.

114. See *Combate* 1.2 (June–July 1943); Ernesto Palacio, "La situación del país y la situación de los escritores," *Reconquista*, December 10, 1939.

115. See "La perdida perla Austral," *Choque*, January 3, 1941, 5. See also *Criterio*, February 13, 1931, 157; *Reconquista*, November 20, 1939; Irazusta and Irazusta, *La Argentina y el imperialismo británico*, 29, 32, 62–63; *Liberación: órgano oficial de la Alianza de la Juventud Nacionalista*, September 9, 1941, 11; and the pamphlet *Finis Inglaterra* (Buenos Aires: El Momento Argentino, 1941), in Archivo Cedinci. For the history of Argentine education and nationalism, see Luis Alberto Romero, *La Argentina en la escuela*. For a provoking analysis of the issue of Malvinas in Argentina, see Palermo, *Sal en las heridas*.

116. See Bibliothèque de documentation internationale contemporaine, Nanterre, France, Fonds Argentine, F7380, Recueil Guerre de Malouines, Documents 312, doc. 68456, Ángel B. Armelin, Homilía, May 5, 1982, Universidad de Buenos Aires. See also Finchelstein, *La Argentina fascista*.

117. For a dissection of revisionist and neorevisionist trends, see Tulio Halperín Donghi in an interview by Mariana Canavese and Ivana Costa, "Entrevista: Tulio Halperín Donghi: la serena lucidez que devuelve la distancia," *Clarín, Ñ*, May 5, 2005. See also Alejandro Cattaruzza, "Algunas reflexiones sobre el

revisionismo histórico," and "Descifrando pasados"; Catturazza and Eujanian, *Políticas de la historia*. See also Cattaruzza, *Los usos del pasado*.

118. Archivo General de la Nación Argentina, Archivo Agustín P. Justo, caja 49,
docs. 166, 168, 169, 170, 173; ibid., caja 36, doc. 277; *Crisol*, March 20, 1940, 1.

119. On these two issues Argentina is not different from other countries in the western hemisphere such as the United States, Paraguay, Bolivia, and Canada.

120. See Irazusta and Irazusta, *La Argentina y el imperialismo británico*, 198–199;
"Carta de Juan Carlos Moreno," *Reconquista*, November 30, 1939; Doll, *Acerca
de una Política nacional*, 153; Enrique Osés, "Como se hacen campañas bri-
tánicas desde un diario que no es argentino," *Crisol*, September 9, 1939.

121. Domingo F. Sarmiento famously stated: "¿Lograremos exterminar a los indios? Por los salvajes de América siento una invencible repugnancia sin po-
derlo remediar. Esa canalla no son más que unos indios asquerosos a quienes
mandaría colgar ahora si reapareciesen. Lautaro y Caupolicán son unos indios
piojosos, porque así son todos. Incapaces de progreso, su exterminio es pro-
videncial y útil, sublime y grande. Se los debe exterminar sin ni siquiera
perdonar al pequeño, que tiene ya el odio instintivo al hombre civilizado"
(Sarmiento, *El Nacional*, November 25, 1876). For Ernesto Palacio the idea that
natives contributed to the formation of Argentine nationality was an "invention": "Esta invención polémica, repito, no fue nunca sentida verdaderamente
por el pueblo de nuestra campaña, que conoció al indio antes de que fuese
exterminado" (Palacio, *La historia falsificada*, 63). Palacio argued that Argentine gauchos were not "mestizos" but "white" people "happy" about the
extermination of the Indians (64). See also "La crisis intelectual," *Bandera
Argentina*, July 6, 1939; Archivo General de la Nación Argentina, Archivo
Roca Hijo, legajo 6, sala 7 3107, doc. 97. For the victim's perspective, see
Curruhuinca-Roux, *Las matanzas del Neuquén*. For an overview see Seoane,
Argentina, 19.

122. Torres, *Algunas maneras de vender la patria*, 7. See also Archivo General de la
Nación Argentina, Archivo Agustín P. Justo, caja 49, docs. 174–175, 233, 236;
ibid., caja 36, doc. 277; ibid., caja 46, doc. 120; Rodolfo Irazusta, "Las falsas
adaptaciones," *Criterio*, October 5, 1933, 104–105; Rodolfo Irazusta, "Aclaración
sobre la democracia," *Criterio*, September 21, 1933, 59; "Dictaduras efímeras y
dictaduras permanentes," *Bandera Argentina*, April 5, 1933, 1; *Bandera Argentina*,
December 24, 1936; Carlos Ibarguren Jr., "Nacionalistica," *Nueva Política* 7
(December 1940): 16; "Duelo criollo," *La Fronda*, August 20, 1942; Lastra, *Bajo
el signo nacionalista*, 49.

123. Archivo General de la Nación Argentina, Archivo Agustín P. Justo, caja 45, doc. 67.

Epilogue

1. Mussolini received Goyeneche against the advice of some fascist officials and gave him a private audience. The Duce clearly saw that Goyeneche was an officious secret representative of the Argentine conservative president Castillo. At this time Castillo himself was turning to the nacionalistas for their political support and regularly courted nacionalista leaders like Manuel Fresco or Enrique Osés. See Archivio Centrale dello Stato, Italia, Ministero della Cultura Popolare, D.G. Serv., Propaganda, Bio, Argentina, 5/1/6, fon. 1361, T8477, pos. 5.1.6.7, T33348, T27770, T1238. See also Archivo del Ministerio de Relaciones Exteriores y Culto, Argentina, División Política, caja 22, Italia, telegrama cifrado, N511, N34, Estrictamente reservado y muy confidencial, folio 1, June 4, 1943. For Castillo's policies toward the nacionalistas see Archivo General de la Nación Argentina, Archivo Agustín P. Justo, caja 104, docs. 149, 109; ibid., caja 49, doc. 274. After the meeting, Goyeneche wrote to Mussolini and asked him to write to President Castillo, since "one timely suggestion from you could change the path of our [Argentine] domestic policy." Goyeneche was bluntly asking Mussolini to meddle in Argentine politics. See Archivio, Ministero degli Affari Esteri, Rome, Italy, appunto April 13, 1943, and carta April 6, 1943.

2. See Archivo del Ministerio de Relaciones Exteriores y Culto, Argentina, División Política, caja 22, Italia, "Entrevista concedida por el señor Mussolini al señor Juan Carlos Goyeneche," expediente 7, año 1943, folios 1–4. See also Archivio, Ministero degli Affari Esteri, Rome, Italy, appunto March 13, April 13, 1943.

3. See Halperín Donghi, "Del fascismo al peronismo," in his *Argentina en el callejón,* 29–55. See also Germani *Authoritarianism, Fascism, and National Populism*; Finchelstein, "Fascismo y peronismo."

4. See "La missione militare argentina esalta l'organizzazione delle Forze Armate Italiana," *Il Giornale d'Italia,* September 12, 1940. See also Archivo del Ministerio de Relaciones Exteriores y Culto, Argentina, División Política, mueble 7, casilla 1, Guerra Europea, expediente 14, año 1939, telegrama, Rome, July 4, 1940.

5. Hannah Arendt, "The Seeds of a Fascist International," 149.

6. See *L'Antidiario,* July 9–16, 1950, and July 16–23, 1950, 342–343.

7. For an influential study of the role of *letrados* in Argentine history, see Halperín Donghi, *Una nación para el desierto argentino*.

8. Archivo General de la Nación Argentina, Archivo Agustín P. Justo, caja 49, doc. 274, and ibid., caja 104, docs. 83, 26. An intelligence report from 1942 argued that nacionalistas had not been dangerous before Fresco's leadership and also argued nacionalista allies of Fresco including General Molina were using the secret service to spread nacionalista propaganda among the military. Other reports argued that Fresco had a totalitarian expansionist policy toward Bolivia. See also Archivo Fundación IWO, Argentina, caja Organización Popular contra el Antisemitismo, Correspondencia, C1936, 1942, 1943. On Fresco's tenure as covernor of Buenos Aires, see Halperín Donghi, "El populismo de Manuel Fresco a la luz de su impacto electoral"; Béjar, *El régimen fraudulento*, 139–166.

9. Archivo General de la Nación Argentina, Archivo Agustín P. Justo, caja 104, doc. 112.

10. The new archival evidence that I have gathered shows that my point about Osés's early support for the military option was not an all-or-nothing choice, as I suggested in my book *Fascismo, liturgia e imaginario* (see 143). See Archivo General de la Nación Argentina, Archivo Agustín P. Justo, caja 104, doc. 149 and doc. sin numero, foliado no. 1235; ibid., caja 104 bis, docs. 318, 407.

11. Finchelstein, *Fascismo, liturgia e imaginario*, 131–144. See also Archivo General de la Nación Argentina, Archivo Agustín P. Justo, caja 49, docs. 203, 232; ibid., caja 104 bis, doc. 271.

12. See Archivo Cedinci, Documentos del GOU (Group of United Officers). On Perón and GOU, see Potash, *El ejército y la política en la Argentina*, 1.263–340; Halperín Donghi, *La república imposible*, 300–315; Spektorowski, *Argentina's Revolution of the Right*, 176–200.

13. I would like to thank one of the two anonymous readers for suggesting this point.

14. See Finchelstein, *La Argentina fascista*, chap. 4; Halperín Donghi, *Argentina en el callejón*, 135–175. On Peronism, fascism, and nacionalismo, see also Spektorowski, *Argentina's Revolution of the Right*, 173–200; and Buchrucker, *Nacionalismo y peronismo*.

15. For an intelligent assessment of Peronism, see Plotkin, "Perón y el peronismo." See also Torre, "Interpretando (una vez más) los orígenes del peronismo"; Adelman, "Reflections on Argentine Labour and the Rise of Perón"; Zanatta, *Il peronismo*. For the structural approaches, see Germani, *Política y sociedad en una época de transición*; Murmis and Portantiero, *Estudios sobre los*

orígenes del peronismo. On Peronism and populism, see Laclau, *Politics and Ideology in Marxist Theory.* For the mythical dimensions of Peronism, see Plotkin, *Mañana es San Perón* and *El día que se inventó el peronismo.*

16. See Romero, *Las ideas políticas en la Argentina,* 244–245. See also Halperín Donghi, *La Argentina y la tormenta del mundo,* 240–241; Spektorowski, *Argentina's Revolution of the Right.*

17. Borges had personal reasons to be against Peronism as well. During the years of his regime, Perón had fired Borges from his position at a municipal library and designated him municipal inspector for chickens.

18. Archivio Centrale dello Stato, Italia, Ministero della Cultura Popolare, D.G. Serv., Propaganda, gabinetto B43 263 5, Autografi del Duce, anno 13, no. 27.3, N5.

19. See Finchelstein, "Fascism Becomes Desire."

20. LaCapra, *Representing the Holocaust.*

21. On Himmler, see LaCapra, *Writing History, Writing Trauma,* 136–140. See Evola, *Imperialismo pagano* and "Legionarismo ascetico: colloquio col capo della Guardia di Ferro," *Il Regime Fascista,* March 22, 1938 (reprinted in Evola, *La tragedia della Gueradia di ferro*). For an analysis of the Romanian case, see Ioanid, *The Sword of the Archangel.* For an analysis of Spanish fascism, see Saz, *Fascismo y franquismo.*

22. Mussolini, "Nel quinto anniversario della fondazione dei fasci: Roma, 24 marzo 1924," in *La nuova politica dell'Italia,* 3.32; Archivo del Ministerio de Relaciones Exteriores y Culto, Argentina, División Política, caja 2293, Italia, expediente 1, año 1924. See Schmitt, *The Concept of the Political,* 19–79. As Jorge Dotti has demonstrated in his work on the Argentine reception of Schmitt, many nacionalistas regarded this Nazi thinker highly, and after 1945 he was offered a teaching position in Buenos Aires (Dotti, *Carl Schmitt en Argentina,* 121–122).

23. Gentile, *Le religioni della politica,* 206.

24. In September 20, 2001, President George W. Bush said of Osama Bin Laden and his supporters: "By sacrificing human life to serve their radical visions— by abandoning every value except the will to power—they follow in the path of fascism, and Nazism, and totalitarianism." See http://www.whitehouse .gov/news/releases/2001/09/20010920_8.html. For an analysis of the transnational ideological dimensions of Islamic extremism, I refer to two books by my colleague Faisal Devji: *Landscapes of the Jihad* and *The Terrorist in Search of Humanity.*

25. On the notion of negative sublime, see LaCapra, *History and Memory after Auschwitz*, 27–30; *Representing the Holocaust*, 100–110; and *Writing History, Writing Trauma*, 94.

26. See Archivio Centrale dello Stato, Italia, Mostra della rivoluzione fascista, B91, F154, sala Dotrinna SF 2, "tabelloni murali," Dottrina; and Mussolini, *Fascism*, 25. In the Italian version, referring to the period prior to 1789, Mussolini had stated, "Non si torna indietro" (Mussolini, *Opera omnia*, 34.128).

27. Arendt, "Ideology and Terror," 310–314. See also her *The Origins of Totalitarianism*, 389–392.

28. Traverso, *The Origins of Nazi Violence*. On the anti-Enlightenment, see Sternhell, *Les anti-Lumières*.

29. Franceschi, *La angustia contemporánea*.

30. See Ibarguren, *La inquietud de esta hora*.

31. Gustavo J. Franceschi, "Frente al comunismo," *Criterio*, October 25, 1934, 243.

32. "Yendo hasta la raíz del mal, se ha podido ver que ni el parlamentarismo ni el liberalismo general de nuestras instituciones permitirían una defensa eficaz contra el comunismo, el espíritu judaico, la desorganización marxista y la ruina general de la economía." Gustavo J. Franceschi, *Criterio*, September 21, 1933, 56. *Criterio* was the only Catholic journal in Argentina that had the official approval of the institutional church. See "Tribuna," *Orden Cristiano* 3.70 (August 1, 1944): 434.

33. Finchelstein, "Sexo, raça e nacionalismo."

34. Arendt, *The Origins of Totalitarianism*, 7–8.

35. See Blumenberg *The Legitimacy of the Modern Age*; LaCapra, *Representing the Holocaust*, 169–203. For an analysis of Blumenberg, see Palti, "In Memoriam," 503–524. See also Casanova, *Public Religions in the Modern World*.

36. Finchelstein, "The Anti-Freudian Politics of Argentine Fascism."

37. Meneses, *Cartas de juventud de J. L. Borges*, 15.

38. "Es una guerra santa la que ha de librar en bien del país": Juan Carulla, "Carta a un nacionalista de San Martín," *Bandera Argentina*, December 27, 1936.

39. Ernesto Palacio, "El único remedio para la enfermedad que nos aqueja," *Reconquista*, November 22, 1939.

40. See Castellano, *El psicoanálisis de Freud*; Genta, *Curso de psicología*.

41. Scalabrini Ortiz, *El hombre que está solo y espera*, 67.

42. Bunge de Gálvez, "Sueños con los muertos," *La Nación*, March 6, 1938. See also Bunge de Gálvez, "Un punto de vista católico: en torno a algunas teorías de Freud," *La Nación*, June 7, 1936.

43. Ramón Doll, "El sueño de la patria," *Liberación: órgano oficial de la Alianza de la Juventud Nacionalista*, September 9, 1941, 2.

44. Vezzetti, *Aventuras de Freud en el país de los argentinos*; Plotkin, *Freud in the Pampas*. See also the illuminating collection edited by Mariano Plotkin, *Argentina on the Couch*.

45. Enrique Osés, "Una fuerza nueva y distinta entre todas," *Crisol*, October 16, 1936. See also "Nacionalismo argentino al pueblo de la Nación," *La Nación*, June 1, 1936; "Hay que dar al alma nacional un sentido heroico de la vida," *Bandera Argentina*, December 24, 1936; "Hoy los bárbaros no asedian a Roma," *Bandera Argentina*, December 30, 1936; "Nuestros propósitos," *Clarinada* 2.23 (March 31, 1939); *Sol y Luna* 5 (1940); Villafañe, *La tragedia argentina, de la acción parlamentaria*, 44; Ibarguren, *Orígenes del nacionalismo argentino*, 304.

46. Eugenia Silveyra de Oyuela, "El gobierno totalitario no está contra el dogma católico," *Clarinada* 5.54–55 (October–November 1941): 2–4.

47. See Finchelstein, *Fascismo, liturgia e imaginario*, 144.

Bibliography

Archival Sources

ARCHIVIO CENTRALE DELLO STATO, ITALIA (ROME, ITALY)
Series: Archivi Fascisti. Segreteria Particolare del Duce.
  Carteggio ordinario.
Series: Archivi Fascisti. Segreteria Particolare del Duce.
  Carteggio riservato.
Series: Archivio Asvero Gravelli
Series: Archivio Renzo De Felice
Series: Ministero della Cultura Popolare. D.G. Serv. Propaganda.
Series: Ministero della Cultura Popolare. D.G. Serv. Propaganda. N.U.P.I.E.
Series: Ministero della Cultura Popolare. D.G. Serv. Propaganda. Reports.
Series: Mostra della Rivoluzione Fascista
Series: PNF Senatori e Consiglieri Nazionali
Series: SPD CR RSI
Series: Collez. Muss. (B. Mussolini Personal Library Collection)

ARCHIVIO, MINISTERO DEGLI AFFARI ESTERI (ROME, ITALY)

ARCHIVO CEDINCI (CENTRO DE DOCUMENTACIÓN E INVESTIGACIÓN DE LA
CULTURA DE IZQUIERDAS EN ARGENTINA), BUENOS AIRES, ARGENTINA
Series: Fondo Solari
Series: Fondo Repetto
Series: Documentos del Gou
Series: Volantes C-A1
Carpeta panfletos antifascistas

Bibliography

ARCHIVO DE RAÚL SCALABRINI ORTIZ
Papeles Reconquista
Recortes

ARCHIVO DEL MINISTERIO DE RELACIONES EXTERIORES Y CULTO,
BUENOS AIRES, ARGENTINA
Series: División Política
Series: Guerra Europea

ARCHIVO GENERAL DE LA NACIÓN ARGENTINA, BUENOS AIRES, ARGENTINA
Series: Archivo Roca Hijo
Series: Archivo Agustín P. Justo
Series: Archivo José F. Uriburu
Series: Archivo Manuel Gálvez
Series: Ministerio del Interior

ARCHIVO FUNDACIÓN IWO (INSTITUTO JUDÍO DE INVESTIGACIONES),
BUENOS AIRES, ARGENTINA
Series: Organización Popular contra el Antisemitismo: Correspondencia; Recortes
Series: Boletines DAIA 1935–1976

BIBLIOTECA NACIONAL ARGENTINA, BUENOS AIRES, ARGENTINA

BIBLIOTHÈQUE DE DOCUMENTATION INTERNATIONALE CONTEMPORAINE,
NANTERRE, FRANCE
Dossier France. GF Delta 143. B.P. 14.6.21.n 162.
Dossier France. Daniel Guerin. F Delta 721. 51/1.
Fonds Argentine. F.P. 7380. Recueil. Guerre de Malouines. Documents. 312. Doc.
68456.

UNITED STATES NATIONAL ARCHIVES
Personal papers of Benito Mussolini, together with some official records of the Italian Foreign Office and the Ministry of Culture, 1922–1944, received from the Archivio Ministero degli Affari Esteri, Rome, Italy, by the Department of State, Washington, D.C. National Archives T586.
Papers of Count Ciano (Lisbon Papers) received from the Archivio Ministero degli Affari Esteri, Rome, Italy, by the Department of State, Washington, D.C. National Archives T. 816, no. 430.

Journals and Newspapers

ARGENTINA

Acción Antijudía Argentina

Aduna

Agrupación Argentina Amigos de Italia

Ahora

Antología

Archivum

Argentina Libre

Bandera Argentina

Cabildo

Choque

Clarinada

Combate

Córdoba

Crisol

Criterio

Crítica

Crónica (Rosario)

Deutsche La Plata Zeitung

El Buho

El Corresponsal Argentino

El Diario de Buenos Aires

El Federal

El Fortín

El Litoral (Santa Fe)

El Momento Argentino

El Pampero

El Pueblo

El Restaurador

El Rioplatense

El Tábano (Tucumán)

Fastras

Il Mattino d'Italia

Jornada

La Acción (Rosario)

La Fronda

Bibliography

La Gaceta (Tucumán)

La Maroma

La Nación

La Nueva República

La Picana

La Prensa

La Razón

La República

La Vanguardia

La Voz del Interior

La Voz del Plata

Liberación: Órgano Oficial de la Alianza de la Juventud Nacionalista

Los Principios

Mundo Israelita

Noticias Gráficas

Nueva Idea

Nuevo Orden

Nueva Palabra

Nueva Política

Orden Cristiano

Proa

Reacción

Reconquista

Revista Eclesiástica del Arzobispado de Buenos Aires

Síntesis

Sol y Luna

Sur

Tribuna (Rosario)

Última Edición

Vida Nuestra

ITALY

Bibliografia Fascista

Civiltà Fascista

Corriere della Sera

Corriere Padano

Critica Fascista

Gazzetta del Popolo

Gazzetta di Venezia

Gerarchia

Giornale d'Italia

Il Lavoro

Il Mattino (Naples)

Il Messaggero

Il Piccolo

Il Popolo d'Italia

Il Regime Fascista

Il Secolo xix

Italia Fascista

La Difesa della Razza

La Riviera: Settimanale della Liguria di Ponente

La Sera

La Tribuna

La Ultime Notizia (Trieste)

La Vedetta d'Italia (Fiume)

L'Idea Nazionale

L'Impero

Universalità Fascista

COLOMBIA

El Espectador

El Siglo

El Tiempo

MEXICO

El Nacional

SPAIN

Arriba

Informaciones

Other Sources

Adamson, Walter L. *Avant-Garde Florence: From Modernism to Fascism*. Cambridge, Mass.: Harvard University Press, 1993.

——. "Avant-garde Modernism and Italian Fascisim: Cultural Politics in the Era of Mussolini." *Journal of Modern Italian Studies* 6.2 (2001).

Bibliography

Adelman, Jeremy. "Reflections on Argentine Labour and the Rise of Perón." *Bulletin of Latin American Research* 11.3 (1992).

——. *Republic of Capital: Buenos Aires and the Legal Transformation of the Atlantic World*. Stanford: Stanford University Press, 1999.

Agamben, Giorgio. *Remnants of Auschwitz: The Witness and the Archive*. New York: Zone Books, 1999.

Albónico, Aldo. *L'America latina e l'Italia*. Rome: Bulzoni, 1984.

Allardyce, Gilbert. "What Fascism Is Not: Thoughts on the Deflation of a Concept." *American Historical Review* 84.2 (1979).

Alonso, Paula. *Between Revolutions and the Ballot Box: The Origins of the Argentine Radical Party*. Cambridge: Cambridge University Press, 2000.

Altamirano, Carlos, ed. *La Argentina en el siglo xx*. Buenos Aires: Ariel, 1999.

——. "De la historia política a la historia intelectual: reactivaciones y renovaciones." *Prismas: Revista de Historia Intelectual* 9 (2005).

——. *Para un programa intelectual y otros ensayos*. Buenos Aires: Siglo Veintiuno Editores, 2005.

——. *Peronismo y cultura de izquierda*. Buenos Aires: Temas, 2001.

Alzogaray, Julio L. *Trilogía de la trata de blancas: rufianes-policía-municipalidad*. Buenos Aires: n.p., 1933.

Amadeo, Tomás. *El falso dilema: fascismo o bolcheviquismo*. Buenos Aires: Librería del Colegio, 1939.

——. *El fascismo y su jefe*. Buenos Aires: n.p., 1926.

Anderson, Benedict. *Imagined Communities: Reflections on the Origin and Spread of Nationalism*. London: Verso, 1983.

Andreoli, Anna Maria, Giovanni Caprara, and Elena Fontanella, eds. *Volare! Futurismo, aviomania, tecnica e cultura italiana del volo, 1903–1940*. Rome: De Luca, 2003.

Arad, Yitzhak, Israel Gutman, and Abraham Margaliot, eds. *Documents on the Holocaust*. Lincoln: University of Nebraska Press, 1999.

Ardemagni, Mirko. *Viaggio alla Terra del Fuoco e in Patagonia*. Milan: Giacomo Agnelli, 1929.

Arendt, Hannah. "Ideology and Terror: A Novel Form of Government." *Review of Politics* 15.3 (1953).

——. *The Origins of Totalitarianism*. New York: Meridian, 1959.

——. "The Seeds of a Fascist International." In *Essays in Understanding, 1930–1954*, ed. Jerome Kohn. New York: Harcourt Brace, 1994.

Argenta, Guido. *Ardite imprese*. Turin: Gribaudo Editore, 1995.

Arias, Gino. *Manual de economía política*. Buenos Aires: Lajouane, 1942.

Bibliography

Asciuti, Claudio. *Il corsaro e il trasvolatore: le crociere celesti di D'Annunzio e Balbo.* Genova: Bozzi Editore, 1990.

Baily, Samuel L. *Immigrants in the Lands of Promise: Italians in Buenos Aires and New York City, 1870–1914.* Ithaca: Cornell University Press, 2004.

Bajtin, Mijail. *La cultura popular en la Edad Media y en el Renacimiento.* Buenos Aires: Alianza, 1994.

Balbo, Italo. *La centuria alata.* Milan: Mondadori, 1934.

——. *Da Roma a Odessa sui cieli dell'Egeo e del mar Nero.* Milan: Fratelli Treves, 1929.

——. *My Air Armada.* London: Hurst and Blackett, 1934.

——. *Passeggiate aeree sul Mediterreneo.* Milan: Fratelli Treves, 1929.

Baldoli, Claudia. *Exporting Fascism: Italian Fascists and Britain's Italians in the 1930s.* Oxford: Berg, 2003.

Barbero, María Inés, and Fernando Devoto. *Los nacionalistas, 1910–1932.* Buenos Aires: Ceal, 1983.

Bataille, Georges. *Visions of Excess: Selected Writings, 1927–1939.* Minneapolis: University of Minnesota Press, 1985.

Béjar, María Dolores. *El régimen fraudulento: la política en la provincia de Buenos Aires, 1930–1943.* Buenos Aires: Siglo Veintiuno Editores, 2005.

Belardelli, Giovanni. "L'antisemitismo nell'ideologia fascista." *Ricerche di Storia Politica* 10.3 (2007).

Beltrametti, Giulia. "L'autorappresentazione totalitaria del fascismo italiano: storia di un'invenzione politica." *Storia e Memoria* 2 (2005).

Ben Dror, Graciela. *Católicos, nazis y judíos: la Iglesia argentina en los tiempos del Tercer Reich.* Buenos Aires: Lumiere, 2003.

Ben-Ghiat, Ruth. *Fascist Modernities: Italy, 1922–1945.* Berkeley: University of California Press, 2001.

——. "Italian Fascists and National Socialists: The Dynamics of a Difficult Relationship." In *Art, Culture and the Media under the Nazis,* ed. Richard Etlin. Chicago: University of Chicago Press, 2002.

——. "A Lesser Evil? Italian Fascism in/and the Totalitarian Equation." In *The Lesser Evil: Moral Approaches to Genocide Practices in a Comparative Perspective,* ed. Helmut Dubiel and Gabriel Motzkin. New York: Routledge, 2004.

Benjamin, Walter. *Illuminations.* New York: Schocken, 1969.

——. "Theories of German Fascism." *New German Critique* 17 (1979).

Berezin, Mabel. *Making the Fascist Self: The Political Culture of Interwar Italy.* Ithaca: Cornell University Press, 1997.

Bertagna, Federica. *La inmigracion fascista en la Argentina.* Buenos Aires: Siglo Veintiuno Editores, 2007.

Bibliography

Bertonha, João Fábio. *O fascismo e os imigrantes italianos no Brasil.* Porto Alegre: Edipucrs, 2001.

———. *Fascismo, nazismo, integralismo.* São Paulo: Ática, 2000.

Bertoni, Lilia Ana. *Patriotas, cosmopolitas y nacionalistas: la construcción de la nacionalidad argentina fines del siglo XIX.* Buenos Aires: Fondo de Cultura Económica, 2001.

Bessel, Richard, ed. *Fascist Italy and Nazi Germany: Comparisons and Contrasts.* Cambridge: Cambridge University Press, 1996.

Bioy Casares, Adolfo. *Descanso de caminantes.* Buenos Aires: Sudamericana, 2001.

Bisso, Andrés. *Acción Argentina: un antifascismo nacional en tiempos de guerra mundial.* Buenos Aires: Prometeo, 2005.

———. *El antifascismo argentino.* Buenos Aires: Cedinci Editores, 2007.

Blanco, Alejandro. *Razón y modernidad: Gino Germani y la sociología en la Argentina.* Buenos Aires: Siglo Veintiuno Editores, 2006.

Blumenberg, Hans. *The Legitimacy of the Modern Age.* Cambridge, Mass.: MIT Press, 1983.

Borges, Jorge Luis. *El Aleph.* Buenos Aires: Emecé, 1965.

———. *Obras completas.* Buenos Aires: Emecé, 1996.

———. *Obras completas en colaboración.* Buenos Aires: Emecé, 1997.

Bosworth, R. J. B. *The Italian Dictatorship: Problems and Perspectives in the Interpretation of Mussolini and Fascism.* London: Arnold, 1998.

———. "Mito e linguaggio nella politica estera italiana." In *La politica estera italiana, 1860–1985,* ed. R. J. B. Bosworth and Sergio Romano. Bologna: Il Mulino, 1991.

———. *Mussolini's Italy: Life under the Fascist Dictatorship, 1915–1945.* New York: Penguin, 2006.

Bracher, Karl Dietrich. *The German Dictatorship: The Origins, Structure, and Effects of National Socialism.* New York: Holt, Rinehart and Winston, 1970.

———. "The Role of Hitler: Perspectives of Interpretation." In *Fascism: A Reader's Guide: Analyses, Interpretations, Bibliography,* ed. Walter Laqueur. Berkeley: University of California Press, 1976.

Bracher, Karl Dietrich, and Leo Valiani. *Fascismo e nazionalsocialismo.* Bologna: Il Mulino, 1986.

Braun, Emily. *Mario Sironi and Italian Modernism: Art and Politics under Fascism.* Cambridge: Cambridge University Press, 2000.

Brennan, James, ed. *Peronism and Argentina.* Wilmington, Del.: SR Books, 1998.

Brower, Benjamin Claude. *A Desert Named Peace: The Violence of France's Empire in the Algerian Sahara, 1844–1902.* New York: Columbia University Press, 2009.

Buchrucker, Cristián. "Latin America in the Time of the Nazis." *Patterns of Prejudice* 31.3 (1997).

——. *Nacionalismo y peronismo: la Argentina en la crisis ideológica mundial, 1927–1955.* Buenos Aires: Sudamericana, 1987.

Budde, Gunilla, Sebastian Conrad, and Oliver Janz, eds. *Transnationale Geschichte: Themen, Tendenzen und Theorien.* Göttingen: Vandenhoeck and Ruprecht, 2006.

Burrin, Philippe. *Fascisme, nazisme, autoritarisme.* Paris: Seuil, 2000.

Caimari, Lila. *Perón y la Iglesia Católica: religión, estado y sociedad en la Argentina, 1943–1955.* Buenos Aires: Ariel, 1995.

Calvino, Italo. "Il Duce's Portraits." *New Yorker,* January 6, 2003.

Campi, Alessandro. *Che cos'è il fascismo? Interpretazioni e prospettive di ricerche.* Rome: Ideazione Editrice, 2003.

Canavese, Mariana, and Ivana Costa. "Entrevista: Tulio Halperín Donghi, la serena lucidez que devuelve la distancia." *Clarín, Ñ,* May 5, 2005.

Canistraro, Philip, *La fabbrica del consenso: fascismo e mass media.* Rome: Laterza, 1975.

Cappelli Bajocco, Marcellina. *De Pinedo Aquila d'Italia.* Rome: Librería del Littorio, n.d.

Carbia, Rómulo D. *Historia de la leyenda negra hispanoamericana.* Madrid: Publicaciones del Consejo de la Hispanidad, 1944.

Carli, Maddalena. *Nazione e rivoluzione: il "socialismo nazionale" in Italia, mitologia di un discorso rivoluzionario.* Milan: Edizioni Unicopli, 2001.

——. "'Olimpionica': tra fascistizzazione e italianizzazione dello sport nella propaganda fascista dei tardi anni Venti." *Memoria e Ricerca* 27 (2008).

——. "Par la volonté du Chef et par l'oeuvre du Parti: le mythe du chef dans la Guide Historique de l'Exposition de la Révolution Fasciste." *Cahiers du Centre de Rechereches Historiques* 31 (2003).

Carmagnani, Marcello. *El otro Occidente: América Latina desde la invasión europea hasta la globalización.* Mexico City: Fondo de Cultura Económica, 2004.

Carulla, Juan E. *Al filo del Medio Siglo.* Buenos Aires: Huemul, 1964.

——. *Problemas de cultura: "Defensa de Occidente" y otros temas.* Buenos Aires: El Ateneo, 1927.

Casajs, Victoriano. *Guerra al eje.* Buenos Aires: Editorial La Mazorca, 1943.

Casanova, José. *Public Religions in the Modern World.* Chicago: University of Chicago Press, 1994.

Casanova, Julián. "Civil Wars, Revolutions and Counterrevolutions in Finland, Spain, and Greece (1918–1949): A Comparative Analysis." *International Journal of Politics, Culture, and Society* 13.3 (2000).

Casanova, Julián, with Francisco Espinosa, Conxita Mir, and Francisco Moreno Gómez. *Morir, matar, sobrevivir: la violencia en la dictadura de Franco*, Barcelona: Crítica, 2002.

Casares, Tomás D. *Catolicismo y acción política*. Buenos Aires: La Junta Parroquial del Santísimo Redentor–A.C.A, 1932.

———. *Los Cursos de Cultura Católica: discurso pronunciado en el acto inaugural de las clases el día 10 de mayo de 1933*. Buenos Aires: n.p., 1933.

———. *El orden civil*. Buenos Aires: n.p., 1932.

Cassels, Alan. *Mussolini's Early Diplomacy*. Princeton: Princeton University Press, 1970.

Castellani, Leonardo. *Las canciones de Militis: seis ensayos y tres cartas*. Buenos Aires: Ediciones Dictio, 1973.

———. *Conversación y crítica filosófica*. Buenos Aires: Espasa-Calpe, 1941.

———. *Freud en cifras*. Buenos Aires: Cruz y Fierro, 1966.

———. *Sentir la Argentina: Leopoldo Lugones*. Buenos Aires: Adsum, 1938.

Castellano, Filemón. *El psicoanálisis de Freud*. Buenos Aires: Difusión, 1941.

Cattaruzza, Alejandro. "Algunas reflexiones sobre el revisionismo histórico." In *La historiografía argentina en el siglo xx*, ed. Fernando Devoto. Buenos Aires: Ceal, 1993.

———. "Descifrando pasados: debates y representaciones de la historia nacional." In *Crisis económica, avance del estado e incertidumbre política, 1930–1943*, ed. Alejandro Cattaruzza. Buenos Aires: Sudamericana, 2001.

———. "La historia política en el fin de siglo: ¿retorno o transformación?" In *Historia a debate*, ed. Carlos Barros and Carlos Aguirre Rojas. Santiago de Compostela: HAD, 1996.

———. *Historia y política en los años 30: comentarios en torno al caso radical*. Buenos Aires: Biblos, 1991.

———. *Marcelo T. de Alvear: el compromiso y la distancia*. Buenos Aires: Fondo de Cultura Económica, 1997.

———. *Los usos del pasado*. Buenos Aires: Sudamericana, 2007.

Cattaruzza, Alejandro, and Alejandro Eujanian. *Políticas de la historia, Argentina, 1860–1960*. Buenos Aires: Alianza, 2003.

Cereceda, Feliciano. *Historia del imperio español y de la hispanidad*. Madrid: Razón y Fe, 1940.

Chakrabarty, Dipesh. *Provincializing Europe: Postcolonial Thought and Historical Difference*. Princeton: Princeton University Press, 2000.

Chalmers, D., M. do Carmo Campello, and A. Boron, eds. *The Right and Democracy in Latin America*. New York: Praeger, 1992.

Chartier, Roger. "Elias, proceso de la civilización y barbarie." In *El Holocausto, los alemanes y la culpa colectiva: el debate Goldhagen*, ed. Federico Finchelstein. Buenos Aires: Eudeba, 1999.

Chase, Allan. *Falange: The Axis Secret Army in the Americas.* New York: G. P. Putnam's Sons, 1943.

Chiaramonte, José Carlos. *Nación y estado en Iberoamérica: el lenguaje político en tiempos de la independencia.* Buenos Aires: Sudamericana, 2004.

Ciarlantini, Franco. *Viaggio in Argentina.* Milan: Alpes, 1928.

Ciccarelli, Orazio. "Fascism and Politics in Peru during the Benavides Regime, 1933–39: The Italian Perspective." *Hispanic American Historical Review* 70.3 (1990).

Cisneros, Andrés, and Carlos Escudé. *Historia general de las relaciones exteriores de la República Argentina.* Buenos Aires: Grupo Editor Latinoamericano, 1999.

Codreanu, Corneliu Zelea. *Manual del jefe: hacia una aristocracia de la virtud.* Barcelona: Editorial Ojeda, 2004.

Cohen, Deborah, and Maura O'Connor, eds. *Comparison and History: Europe in Cross-National Perspective.* New York: Routledge, 2004.

Cohen, Jean L., and Andrew Arato. *Civil Society and Political Theory.* Cambridge, Mass.: MIT Press, 1992.

Colarizi, Simona. *L'opinione degli Italiani sotto il regime.* Bari: Laterza, 1991.

Collotti, Enzo, ed. *Fascismo e antifascismo: rimozioni, revisioni, negazioni.* Rome: Laterza, 2000.

——. *Il fascismo e gli ebrei: le leggi razziali in Italia.* Rome: Laterza, 2003.

——. *Fascismo e politica di potenza: politica estera, 1922–1939.* Milan: La Nuova Italia, 2000.

——. *Fascismo, fascismi.* Milan: Sansoni Editore, 1994.

Comisión Nacional sobre la Desaparación de Personas (Conadep). *Nunca Más.* Buenos Aires: Eudeba, 1984.

Compagnon, Olivier. *Jacques Maritain et l'Amérique du Sud: le modèle malgré lui.* Paris: Presses Universitaires du Septentrion, 2003.

Conferencia Interamericana. *Diario de la Conferencia Interamericana de Consolidación de la Paz*, nos. 1–23. Buenos Aires: 1936.

El congreso de la solidaridad de los pueblos (realizado en Paris—setiembre de 1937). Buenos Aires: Alerta, 1937.

Corner, Paul, *Fascism in Ferrara, 1915–1925.* Oxford: Oxford University Press, 1975.

——. "Italian Fascism: Whatever Happened to Dictatorship?" *Journal of Modern History* 74.2 (2002).

——. *Riformismo e fascismo: l'Italia fra il 1900 e il 1940.* Rome: Bulzoni, 2002.

Croce, Benedetto. *Scritti e discorsi politici, 1943–1947.* Bari: Laterza, 1963.

Cuneo, Niccolo. *Storia dell'emigrazione italiana in Argentina, 1810–1870.* Milan: Garzanti, 1940.

Curcio, Carlo. *La politica demografica del fascismo.* Milan: Mondadori, 1938.

Curruhuinca, Roux. *Las matanzas del Neuquén: crónicas mapuches.* Buenos Aires: Plus Ultra, 1985.

Cuzzi, Marco. *L'internazionale delle camicie nere: i CAUR, Comitati d'azione per l'universalita' di Roma, 1933–1939.* Milan: Mursia, 2005.

Daechsel, Markus. "Scientism and Its Discontents: The Indo-Muslim 'Fascism' of Inayatullah Khan al-mashriqi." *Modern Intellectual History* 3.3 (2006).

Danner, Mark. "Abu Ghraib: The Hidden Story." *New York Review of Books,* October 7, 2004.

De Alvear, Marcelo T. *Democracia.* Buenos Aires: Manuel Gleizer, 1936.

De Ascanio, Alfonso. *España imperio: el nuevo humanismo y la humanidad.* Ávila: Librería religiosa Sigirano Díaz, 1939.

De Caprariis, Luca. " 'Fascism for Export'? The Rise and Eclipse of the Fasci Italiani all'Estero." *Journal of Contemporary History* 35.2 (2000).

De Felice, Renzo. "Il fenomeno fascista." *Storia Contemporanea,* no. 10 (1979).

——. *Interpretations of Fascism.* Cambridge, Mass.: Harvard University Press, 1977.

——. *Mussolini il duce: gli anni del consenso, 1929–1936.* Turin: Einaudi, 1974.

——. *Storia degli ebrei italiani sotto il fascismo.* Turin: Einaudi, 1993.

De Grand, Alexander, *Fascist Italy and Nazi Germany.* New York: Routledge, 1995.

——. *Italian Fascism: Its Origins and Development.* Lincoln: University of Nebraska Press, 2000.

De Grazia, Victoria. *How Fascism Ruled Women: Italy, 1922–1945.* Berkeley: University of California Press, 1992.

De la Guardia, Carmen, and Juan Pan-Montojo. "Reflexiones sobre una historia transnacional." *Studia histórica (Historia contemporánea)* 16 (1998).

De Laferrere, Alfonso. *Literatura y política.* Buenos Aires: Manuel Gleizer, 1928.

De Madariaga, Salvador, ed. *Diez maestros.* Buenos Aires: Talleres Gráficos Argentinos L. J. Rosso, 1935.

De Maeztu, Ramiro. *Defensa de la hispanidad.* 2nd, enl. ed. Madrid: Gráfica Universal, 1935.

De Pinedo, Francesco. *Un volo di 55.000 chilometri.* Milan: A. Mondadori, 1927.

De Privitellio, Luciano. *Agustín P. Justo: las armas en la política.* Buenos Aires: Fondo de Cultura Económica, 1997.

De Sagastizábal, Leandro. *La edición de libros en la Argentina.* Buenos Aires: Eudeba, 1995.

De Vecchi, Antonio E. *La prensa argentina y el momento actual de Italia.* La Plata: Olivieri, 1941.

Degreff, Walter. *260 manifiestos judíos auténticos: modernos y antiguos, recogidos traducidos y comentados por el autor de 'judiadas.' "* Buenos Aires: F. A. Colombo, 1937.

———. *Esperanza de Israel.* Buenos Aires: F. A. Colombo, 1938.

———. *Sión el último imperialismo.* Buenos Aires: n.p., 1937.

Del Boca, Angelo. *I gas di Mussolini: il fascismo e la guerra d'Etiopia.* Rome: Editori Riuniti, 1996.

Dennis, David B. *Beethoven in German Politics, 1870–1989.* New Haven: Yale University Press, 1996.

Deutsch, Sandra McGee. *Counter Revolution in Argentina, 1900–1932: The Argentine Patriotic League.* Lincoln: University of Nebraska Press, 1986.

———. *Las Derechas: The Extreme Right in Argentina, Brazil, and Chile, 1890–1939.* Stanford: Stanford University Press, 1999.

———. "Los nacionalistas argentinos y la sexualidad, 1919–1940." *Reflejos: Revista del Departamento de Estudios Españoles y Latinoamericanos, Hebrew University of Jerusalem* 10 (2001–2002).

———. "Verso un'internazionale nazionalista: le relazioni internazionali della 'Liga Patriótica Argentina,' 1919–22." *Ricerche di Storia Politica* 2 (2002).

———. "The Visible and Invisible Liga Patriótica Argentina, Gender Roles and the Right Wing." *Hispanic American Historical Review* 64.2 (1984).

———. "What Difference Does Gender Make? The Extreme Right in the ABC Countries in the Era of Fascism." *Estudios Interdisciplinarios de América Latina y el Caribe* 8.2 (1997).

Devji, Faisal. *Landscapes of the Jihad: Militancy Morality Modernity.* Ithaca: Cornell University Press, 2005.

———. *The Terrorist in Search of Humanity: Militant Islam and Global Politics.* New York: Columbia University Press, 2008.

Devoto, Fernando. *Historia de la inmigración argentina.* Buenos Aires: Sudamericana, 2003.

———. *Historia de los italianos en la Argentina.* Buenos Aires: Editorial Biblos, 2006.

———. *Nacionalismo, fascismo y tradicionalismo en la Argentina moderna: una historia.* Buenos Aires: Siglo Veintiuno Editores, 2002.

Di Meglio, Gabriel. *¡Mueran los salvajes unitarios! La Mazorca y la política en tiempos de Rosas.* Buenos Aires: Sudamericana, 2007.

Díaz de Robles, Enrique. *El ideal hispánico a través de la historia.* La Coruña: El ideal gallego, 1937.

Bibliography

Doll, Ramón. *Acerca de una política nacional*. Buenos Aires: Difusión, 1939.

Doncoeur, Paul. *Pourquoi Rome a parlé*. Paris: Spes: 1927.

Dore, Grazia. *La democrazia italiana e l'emigrazione italiana in Argentina*. Brescia: Morcelliana, 1964.

Dos Santos, Viviane Teresinha, and Maria Luiza Tucci Carneiro. *Os seguidores do Duce: os italianos fascistas no Estado de São Paulo*. São Paulo: Arquivo do Estado: Imprensa Oficial, 2001.

Dotti, Jorge Eugenio. *Carl Schmitt en Argentina*. Rosario: Ediciones Homo Sapiens, 2000.

Eatwell, Roger. *Fascism: A History*. London: Chatto and Windus, 1995.

——. "On Defining the 'Fascist Minimum': The Centrality of Ideology." *Journal of Political Ideologies* 1.3 (1996).

——. "Reflections on Fascism and Religion." *Totalitarian Movements and Political Religions* 4.3 (2003).

——. "Towards a New Model of Generic Fascism." *Journal of Theoretical Politics* 4.2 (1992).

Eksteins, Modris. *Rites of Spring*. Boston: Mariner Books, 2000.

Espigares Moreno, J. M. *Lo que me dijo el Gral: Uriburu*. Buenos Aires: Talleres Gráficos Durruty y Kaplan, 1933.

Evola, Julius. *Imperialismo pagano: il facismo dinanzi al pericolo euro-cristiano*. Rome: Casa Editrice "Atanor," 1928.

——. *La tragedia della Guardia di ferro*. Rome: Fondazione Julius Evola, 1996.

Ezcurra Medrano, Alberto. *Catolicismo y nacionalismo*. Buenos Aires: Adsum, 1939.

Falasca-Zamponi, Simonetta. "Fascism and Aesthetics." *Constellations* 15.3 (2008).

——. *Fascist Spectacle: The Aesthetics of Power in Mussolini's Italy*. Berkeley: University of California Press, 1997.

Fanesi, Rinaldo. "El antifascismo italiano en Argentina, 1922–1945." *Estudios migratorios latinoamericanos* 4.12 (1989).

Federzoni, Luigi. *Parole fasciste al Sud-America*. Bologna: Zanichelli, 1938.

Filippo, Virgilio. *Confabulación contra la Argentina*. Buenos Aires: Lista Blanca, 1944.

——. *Conferencias radiotelefónicas*. Buenos Aires: Tor, 1936.

——. *¡Defiéndete!* Buenos Aires: Escuelas Gráficas del Colegio Pío IX, 1941.

——. *Democracia sana y democracia falaz*. Buenos Aires: Lista Blanca, 1945.

——. *Drama de barbarie y comedia de civilización*. Buenos Aires: Lista Blanca, 1944.

——. *Habla el Padre Filippo: conferencias radiotelefónicas trasmitidas desde L.R.8, Radio Sarmiento de BS. As*. Buenos Aires: Tor, 1941.

——. *Hablan los jefes del comunismo*. Buenos Aires: Lista Blanca, 1945.

——. *Los judíos: juicio histórico científico que el autor no pudo transmitir por L.R.S Radio París*. Buenos Aires: Tor, 1939.

——. *El monstruo comunista: conferencias radiotelefónicas irradiadas el año 1938, los domingos a las 13 desde L.R. 8 Radio París de Bs. Aires*. Buenos Aires: Tor, 1939.

——. *Música de ideas*. Buenos Aires: Tor, 1936.

——. *Páginas místicas*. Buenos Aires: n.p., 1946.

——. *El Plan Quiquenal de Perón*. Buenos Aires: Lista Blanca, 1948.

——. *Quienes tienen las manos limpias? Estudios sociológicos*. Buenos Aires: Tor, 1939.

——. *El reinado de Satanás: conferencias irradiadas dominicalmente a las 13 horas desde L.R.8, Radio Paris de BS. As*. Vol. 2. Buenos Aires: Tor, 1937.

——. *Sistemas genialmente antisociales: conferencias irradiadas dominicalmente a las 13 horas desde L.R.8, Radio Paris de BS. As*. Vol. 3. Buenos Aires: Tor, 1938.

——. *Tratado de amistad y negocio de amor*. Buenos Aires: Librería Editorial Santa Catalina, 1944.

Finchelstein, Federico. "The Anti-Freudian Politics of Argentine Fascism: Antisemitism, Catholicism and the Internal Enemy, 1932–1945." *Hispanic American Historical Review* 87.1 (2007).

——. *La Argentina fascista: los orígenes ideológicos de la dictadura*. Buenos Aires: Sudamericana, 2008.

——. *El canon del Holocausto*. Buenos Aires: Prométeo, 2009.

——. "Fascism Becomes Desire: On Freud, Mussolini and Transnational Politics." In *The Transnational Unconscious*, ed. Mariano Plotkin and Joy Damousi. London: Palgrave: 2009.

——. *Fascismo, liturgia e imaginario: el mito del general Uriburu y la Argentina nacionalista*. Buenos Aires: Fondo de Cultura Económica, 2002.

——. "Fascismo y peronismo." *Clarín, Ñ*, December 13, 2003.

——. "The Fascist Canon: Renzo De Felice and the Writing of History." *Forum Italicum* 40.1 (2006).

——. "The Holocaust Canon: Rereading Raul Hilberg." *New German Critique* 96 (2005).

——, ed. *El Holocausto, los alemanes y la culpa colectiva: el debate Goldhagen*. Buenos Aires: Eudeba; Buenos Aires University Press, 1999.

——. "Irving, el negador de la historia." *Clarín, Ñ*, February 25, 2006.

——. "Sexo, raça e nacionalismo: a construção católica do del estereótipo corporal judaico na Argentina." In *O anti-semitismo nas Americas: memória e história*, ed. Maria Luiza Tucci Carneiro. São Paulo: Editora da Universidade de São Paulo–Fapesp, 2007.

Finchelstein, Federico, and Esteban Speyer. "El hilo pardo: una mirada nazi sobre Argentina." *Espacios de Crítica y Producción: Publicación de la Facultad de Filosofía y Letras–Universidad de Buenos Aires*, no. 26 (2000).

Finis Inglaterra. Buenos Aires: El Momento Argentino, 1941.

Flores, Marcello, ed. *Nazismo, fascismo, communismo*. Milan: Mondadori, 1998.

Focardi, Filippo. *La guerra della memoria: la Resistenza nel dibattito politico italiano dal 1945 a oggi*. Rome: Laterza, 2005.

Fogu, Claudio. "Fascism and Philosophy: The Case of Actualism." *South Central Review* 23.1 (2006).

——. *The Historic Imaginary: Politics of History in Fascist Italy*. Toronto: University of Toronto Press, 2003.

Font Ezcurra, Ricardo. *La unidad nacional*. Buenos Aires: Editorial La Mazorca, 1941.

Forment, Carlos. *Democracy in Latin America, 1760–1900*. Chicago: University of Chicago Press, 2003.

Franceschi, Gustavo J. *La angustia contemporánea*. Buenos Aires: Coni, 1928.

——. *La democracia cristiana*. Buenos Aires: Ediciones Criterio, 1956.

——. *Discursos*. Buenos Aires: Tálleres Gráficos M. Reynes, 1930.

——. *En el humo del incendio*. Buenos Aires: Difusión, 1938.

——. *Keyserling*. Buenos Aires: Atenas, 1929.

——. *Visión espiritual de la guerra*. Buenos Aires: Difusión, 1940.

Fresco, Manuel. *Habla el gobernador de Buenos Aires . . . Capital y trabajo. Caridad cristiana. El Sarmiento auténtico. Ley de estabilidad y escalafón del magisterio*. La Plata: n.p., 1938.

Freud, Sigmund. *Moses and Monotheism*. New York: Vintage: 1967.

——. *The Standard Edition of the Complete Psychological Works of Sigmund Freud*. Edited by James Strachey, in collaboration with Anna Freud. London: Hogarth Press, 1961.

Friedlander, Saul. *Memory, History, and the Extermination of the Jews of Europe*. Bloomington: Indiana University Press, 1993.

——. "Nazism: Fascism or Totalitarianism." In *The Rise of the Nazi Regime: Historical Reassessments*, ed. Charles S. Maier, Stanley Hoffmann, and Andrew Gould. Boulder: Westview Press, 1986.

Fritzsche, Peter. *A Nation of Fliers: German Aviation and the Popular Imagination*. Cambridge, Mass.: Harvard University Press, 1992.

Frontini, Gesualdo Manzella. *Volare!* Quaderni Fascisti 15. Florence: Bemporad, 1927.

Furet, François, and Ernst Nolte. *Fascism and Communism*. Lincoln: University of Nebraska Press, 2001.

Galeano, Eduardo. *El fútbol a sol y sombra y otros escritos*. Buenos Aires: Editorial Catálogos, 1995.

———. "La guerra o la fiesta." *Brecha* (Montevideo), June 1, 2002.

Gallardo, Ángel. *Memorias para mis hijos y nietos*. Buenos Aires: Academia Nacional de la Historia, 1982.

Gallardo, Luis F. *La mística del adunismo*. Buenos Aires: n.p., 1933.

Gálvez, Manuel. *Este pueblo necesita*. Buenos Aires: A. García Santos, 1934.

García Morente, Manuel. *Idea de la hispanidad*. Buenos Aires: Espasa-Calpe, 1939.

Gayda, Virginio. *Que quiere Italia?* Buenos Aires: Ediciones Modernas Luz, 1941.

Gelman, Jorge. *Rosas, estanciero*. Buenos Aires: Capital Intelectual, 2005.

Genta, Jordan B. *Curso de psicología*. Buenos Aires: Kapelusz, ca. 1939.

Gentile, Emilio. *Il culto del littorio: la sacralizzazione della politica nell'Italia fascista*. Rome: Laterza, 1993.

———. "L'emigrazione italiana in Argentina nella politica di espansione del nazionalismo e del fascismo." *Storia Contemporanea* 17.3 (1986).

———. "Fascism and the Italian Road to Totalitarianism." *Constellations* 15.3 (2008).

———. "Fascism, Totalitarianism and Political Religion: Definitions and Critical Reflections on Criticism of an Interpretation." *Totalitarian Movements and Political Religions* 5.3 (2004).

———. *Fascismo: storia e interpretazione*. Rome: Laterza, 2002.

———. *Le origini dell'ideologia fascista*. Bari: Laterza, 1975; 2nd ed. Bologna: Il Mulino, 1996.

———. "La politica estera del Partito fascista: ideologia e organizzazione dei fasci italiani all'estero, 1920–1930." *Storia Contemporanea* 26.6 (1995).

———. *Le religioni della politica: fra democrazie e totalitarismi*. Rome: Laterza, 2001.

Germani, Gino. *Autoritarismo, fascismo y populismo nacional*. Buenos Aires: Temas, 2003. English version, *Authoritarianism, Fascism, and National Populism* (New Brunswick, N.J.: Transaction Books, 1978).

———. *Política y sociedad en una época de transición: de la sociedad tradicional a la sociedad de masas*. Buenos Aires: Paidós, 1962.

Ghosh, Amitav, and Dipesh Chakrabarty. "Reflections. A Correspondence on Provincializing Europe." *Radical History Review* 83 (2002).

Gillette, Aaron. *Racial Theories in Fascist Italy*. London: Routledge, 2002.

Gilman, Sander. *The Jew's Body*. New York: Routledge, 1991.

Ginzburg, Carlo. *Wooden Eyes: Nine Reflections on Distance*. New York: Columbia University Press, 2001.

Glave, Guido. *Economía dirigida de la democracia corporativa argentina*. Buenos Aires: Imprenta L. L. Gotelli, 1936.

Gobetti, Piero. *On Liberal Revolution.* New Haven: Yale University Press, 2000.

Gómez Forgues, Máximo. *Comunismo y religión.* Buenos Aires: Editorial La Mazorca, 1943.

González Calleja, Eduardo. "El hispanismo autoritario español y el movimiento nacionalista argentino: balance de medio siglo de relaciones políticas e intelectuales, 1898–1946." *Hispania* 67.226 (2007).

González Tuñón, Raúl. *8 Documentos de hoy.* Buenos Aires: n.p., 1936.

Gorelik, Adrián. "Buenos Aires y el país: figuraciones y una fractura." In *La Argentina en el siglo xx,* ed. Carlos Altamirano. Buenos Aires: Ariel, 1999.

———. *Miradas sobre Buenos Aires: historia cultural y crítica urbana.* Buenos Aires: Siglo Veintiuno Editores, 2004.

Gramsci, Antonio. *Socialismo e fascismo: l'Ordine Nuovo, 1921–1922.* Turin: Einaudi, 1978.

Grandi, Dino. *Le origini e la missione del fascismo.* Bologna: Capelli, 1922.

Gregor, A. J. "Fascism, Marxism and Some Considerations Concerning Classification." *Totalitarian Movements and Political Religions* 3.2 (2002).

Griffin, Roger, ed. *International Fascism: Theories, Causes and the New Consensus.* London: Arnold Publishers, 1998.

———. *Modernism and Fascism: The Sense of a Beginning under Mussolini and Hitler.* London: Palgrave, 2007.

———. *The Nature of Fascism.* New York: St. Martin's Press, 1991.

———. "'The Primacy of Culture: The Current Growth (or Manufacture) of Consensus within Fascist Studies." *Journal of Contemporary History* 37.1 (2002).

Grillo, María Victoria. "El antifascismo italiano en Francia y Argentina: reorganización política y prensa,1922–1930." In *Fascismo y antifascismo en Europa y Argentina-Siglo xx,* ed. Judith Casali de Babot and María Victoria Grillo. Tucumán: Universidad Nacional de Tucumán, 2002.

Groppo, Bruno, and Patricia Flier, eds. *La imposibilidad del olvido: recorridos de la memoria en Argentina, Chile y Uruguay.* La Plata: Ediciones Al Margen, 2001.

Guariglia, Raffaele. *Ricordi, 1922–1946.* Naples: Edizioni Scientifiche Italiane, 1950.

Guerin, Daniel. *Fascisme et grand capital.* Paris: Gallimard, 1936.

Guerra, Francois-Xavier. *Modernidades e independencias: ensayos sobre las revoluciones hispánicas.* Madrid: Mapfre, 1992.

Guerri, Giordano Bruno. *Italo Balbo.* Milan: Garzanti, 1984.

Gunther, John. *Inside Latin America.* New York: Harper and Brothers, 1941.

Gurian, Waldemar. "'Totalitarianism as Political Religion." In *Totalitarianism,* ed. Carl J. Friedrich. New York: Grosset and Dunlap, 1964.

Gutiérrez, Leandro H., and Luis Alberto Romero. *Sectores populares, cultura y política: Buenos Aires en la entreguerra.* Buenos Aires: Sudamericana, 1995.

Guy, Donna J. *Sex and Danger in Buenos Aires: Prostitution, Family, and Nation in Argentina.* Lincoln: University of Nebraska Press, 1991.

Halperín Donghi, Tulio. "Argentina: Liberalism in a Country Born Liberal." In *Guiding the Invisible Hand: Economic Liberalism and the State in Latin American History,* ed. Joseph Love and Nils Jacobsen. New York: Praeger, 1988.

——. *Argentina en el callejón.* Buenos Aires: Ariel, 1995.

——. *La Argentina y la tormenta del mundo: ideas e ideologías entre 1930 y 1945.* Buenos Aires: Siglo Veintiuno Editores, 2003.

——. *La democracia de masas.* Buenos Aires: Paidós, 1983.

——. *Ensayos de historiografía.* Buenos Aires: Ediciones el Cielo por Asalto, 1996.

——. *El espejo de la historia: problemas argentinos y perspectivas latinoamericanas.* Buenos Aires: Sudamericana, 1987.

——. *La larga agonía de la Argentina peronista.* Buenos Aires: Ariel, 1994.

——. "Mitre y la formulación de una historia nacional para la Argentina." *Anuario del IEHS* 11 (1996).

——. *Una nación para el desierto argentino.* Buenos Aires: Prometeo, 2005.

——. "El populismo de Manuel Fresco a la luz de su impacto electoral." In *La investigación social hoy,* ed. Darío Cantón and Raúl Jorrat. Buenos Aires: Instituto Gino Germani, 1997.

——. *La república imposible, 1930–1945.* Buenos Aires: Ariel, 2004.

Harootunian, Harry. "The Future of Fascism." *Radical Philosophy* 136 (2006).

Hennessy, Alistair. "Fascism and Populism in Latin America." In *Fascism: A Reader's Guide: Analyses, Interpretations, Bibliography,* ed. Walter Laqueur. Berkeley: University of California Press, 1976.

Herf, Jeffrey. *The Jewish Enemy: Nazi Propaganda During World War II and the Holocaust.* Cambridge, Mass.: Harvard University Press, 2006.

Herrero, Alejandro, and Fabián Herrero, eds. *Las ideas y sus historiadores: un fragmento del campo intelectual en los años noventa.* Santa Fe: Universidad Nacional del Litoral, 1996.

Hilberg, Raul. *The Destruction of the European Jews.* New York: Holmes and Meier, 1985.

Horkheimer, Max, and Theodor W. Adorno. *Dialectic of Enlightenment.* Stanford: Stanford University Press, 2002.

Ibarguren, Carlos. *La inquietud de esta hora: liberalismo, corporativismo, nacionalismo.* Buenos Aires: Librería y Editorial La Facultad, 1934.

Bibliography

Ibarguren, Carlos Jr. [hijo]. *Roberto de Laferrère (periodismo-política-historia)*. Buenos Aires: Eudeba, 1970.

Ibarguren, Federico. *La aristocracia y la cultura*. Buenos Aires: Ediciones de la Liga Republicana, n.d.

———. *Orígenes del nacionalismo argentino, 1927–1937*. Buenos Aires: Celcius, 1969.

———. *Rosas y la tradición hispanoamericana*. Buenos Aires: Ediciones de la Liga Republicana, 1942.

Ingenieros, José. *La evolución sociológica argentina: de la barbarie al imperialismo*. Buenos Aires: Librería J. Menendez, 1910.

Ioanid, Radu. "'The Sacralised Politics of the Romanian Iron Guard." *Totalitarian Movements and Political Religions* 5.3 (2004).

———. *The Sword of the Archangel: Fascist Ideology in Romania*. Boulder: East European Monographs, 1990.

Ipsen, Carl. *Dictating Demography: The Problem of Population in Fascist Italy*. Cambridge: Cambridge University Press, 1996.

Irazusta, Julio. *Actores y espectadores*. Buenos Aires: Sur, 1937.

———. *Genio y figura de Leopoldo Lugones*. Buenos Aires: Eudeba, 1969.

———. *Memorias: historia de un de historiador a la fuerza*. Buenos Aires: Ediciones Culturales Argentinas, 1975.

Irazusta, Rodolfo. *Escritos políticos completos*. Buenos Aires: Editorial Independencia, 1993.

Irazusta, Rodolfo, and Julio Irazusta. *La Argentina y el imperialismo británico*. Buenos Aires: Condor/Tor, 1934.

Isnenghi, Mario. *Intellettuali militanti e intellettuali funzionari: appunti sulla cultura fascista*. Turin: Einaudi, 1979.

Italy, Ministero degli Affari Esteri. *I documenti diplomatici italiani, 1922–1935*. Rome: Librería dello Stato, 1953.

Italy, Senato del Regno. *Discorso del capo del governo ministro degli affari esteri*. Rome: Senato del Regno, 1928.

Joseph, Gilbert M., ed. *Reclaiming the Political in Latin American History: Essays from the North*. Durham: Duke University Press, 2001.

Joseph, Gilbert M., and Daniel Nugent, eds. *Everyday Forms of State Formation: Revolution and the Negotiation of Rule in Modern Mexico*. Durham: Duke University Press, 1994.

Josephs, Ray. *Argentine Diary: The Inside Story of the Coming of Fascism*. New York: Random, House, 1944.

———. *Latin America. Continent in Crisis*. New York: Random House, 1948.

El judío sin careta: los protocolos de los sabios de Sión, el libro más importante de la historia. Buenos Aires: n.p., 1936.

Justo, Luis. "Argentina: Torture, Silence, and Medical Teaching." *British Medical Journal* 326.7403(June 21, 2003).

Kahan, Emmanuel. "El nacionalismo autoritario argentino: discursos, enemigos y liturgia, estudios actuales en el campo historiográfico argentino." *Sociohistórica* 13–14 (2003–2004).

Kallis, Aristotle. *Fascist Ideology: Territory and Expansionism in Italy and Germany, 1922–1945*. London: Routledge, 2000.

Kershaw, Ian. *The Nazi Dictatorship: Problems and Perspectives of Interpretation*. London: Arnold, 2000.

Kershaw, Ian, and Moshe Lewin, eds. *Stalinism and Nazism: Dictatorships in Comparison*. Cambridge: Cambridge University Press, 1997.

Klein, Marcus. "The Legión Cívica Argentina and the Radicalisation of Argentine Nacionalismo during the *Década Infame*." *Estudios Interdisciplinarios de América Latina y el Caribe* 13.2 (2002).

Klich, Ignacio. "Los Nazis en la Argentina: revisando algunos mitos." *Ciclos* 5.9 (1995).

———. "Perón, Braden y el antisemitismo: opinión pública e imagen internacional." *Ciclos* 2.2 (1992).

Knowlton, James, and Truett Cates. *Forever in the Shadow of Hitler? Original Documents of the Historikerstreit, the Controversy Concerning the Singularity of the Holocaust*. Atlantic Highlands: Humanities Press, 1993.

Knox, MacGregor. *Common Destiny: Dictatorship, Foreign Policy, and War in Fascist Italy and Nazi Germany*. Cambridge: Cambridge University Press, 2000.

———. *To the Threshold of Power, 1922–33: Origins and Dynamics of the Fascist and National Socialist Dictatorships*. Cambridge: Cambridge University Press, 2007.

Koonz, Claudia. *The Nazi Conscience*.Cambridge, Mass.: Harvard University Press, 2003.

Kristeva, Julia. *Powers of Horror: An Essay on Abjection*. New York: Columbia University Press, 1982.

LaCapra, Dominick. *History and Memory after Auschwitz*. Ithaca: Cornell University Press, 1998.

———. *History in Transit: Experience, Identity, Critical Theory*. Ithaca: Cornell University Press, 2004.

———. *Representing the Holocaust: History, Theory, Trauma*. Ithaca: Cornell University Press, 1994.

———. *Rethinking Intellectual History: Texts, Contexts, Language*. Ithaca: Cornell University Press, 1983.

———. "Tropisms of Intellectual History." *Rethinking History* 8.4 (December 2004).

———. *Writing History, Writing Trauma*. Baltimore: Johns Hopkins University Press, 2001.

Lacerda de Maura, María. *Clericalismo y fascismo*. Rosario: Argos, 1936.

Laclau, Ernesto. *Politics and Ideology in Marxist Theory: Capitalism—Fascism—Populism*. London: New Left Books, 1977.

Lagomarsino, Albérico S. *La cuestión judía: su estudio analítico y crítico*. Buenos Aires: n.p., 1936.

Larsen, Stein Ugelvik. *Fascism outside Europe*. New York: Columbia University Press, 2001.

Lastra, Bonifacio. *Bajo el signo nacionalista: escritos y discursos*. Buenos Aires: Editorial Alianza, 1944.

Ledeen, Michael. *Universal Fascism: The Theory and Practice of the Fascist International, 1928–1936*. New York: H. Fertig, 1972.

Levi, Primo. *Conversazioni e interviste, 1964–1987*. Turin: Einaudi, 1997.

———. *The Drowned and the Saved*. New York: Vintage, 1989.

Llambias, Héctor, Manuel A. Berraz, and Mario Amadeo. *Jacques Maritain ante el problema estético y social*. Buenos Aires: Voluntad, 1936.

Lomnitz, Claudio. *Deep Mexico Silent Mexico: An Anthropology of Nationalism*. Minneapolis: University of Minnesota Press, 2001.

———. *Modernidad indiana: nueve ensayos sobre nación y mediación en México*. Mexico City: Planeta, 1999.

Love, Joseph, and Nils Jacobsen, eds. *Guiding the Invisible Hand: Economic Liberalism and the State in Latin American History*. New York: Praeger, 1988.

Luconi, Stefano. *La "diplomazia paralela": il regime fascista e la mobilitazione politica degli italo-americani*. Milan: Franco Angeli, 2000.

Lugones, Leopoldo. *Estudios helénicos*. Buenos Aires: Biblioteca Argentina de Buenas Ediciones Literarias, 1923.

———. *La patria fuerte*. Buenos Aires: Circulo Militar-Biblioteca del oficial, 1930.

———. *Poemas solariegos*. Buenos Aires: Babel, 1928.

———. *Política revolucionaria*. Buenos Aires: Anaconda, 1931.

———. *Prometeo: un proscripto del sol*. Buenos Aires: Talleres de Otero, 1910.

Lugones, Leopoldo Jr. *Mi padre: biografía de Leopoldo Lugones*. Buenos Aires: Centurión, 1949.

Lvovich, Daniel. *El nacionalismo de derecha: desde sus orígenes a Tacuara*. Buenos Aires: Capital Intelectual, 2006.

———. *Nacionalismo y antisemitismo en la Argentina.* Buenos Aires: Vergara, 2003.

———. "Peronismo y antisemitismo: historia, memorias, mitos." In *La memoria de las cenizas: historia, trauma, representación,* ed. Pablo Dreizik. Buenos Aires: Presidencia de la Nación Argentina, Secretaría de Cultura, 2001.

Lvovich, Daniel, and Finchelstein, Federico. "L'Holocauste et l'Église argentine: perceptions et réactions, 1933–1945." *Bulletin trimestriel de la Fondation Auschwitz/ Driemaandelijks tijdschrift van de Auschwitz Stichting* 76–77 (2002).

Lynch, John. *The Spanish American Revolutions, 1808–1826: Old and New World Origins.* Norman: University of Oklahoma Press, 1994.

Mack Smith, Denis. *Mussolini.* New York: Knopf, 1982.

———. *Mussolini's Roman Empire.* New York: Penguin, 1977.

Maier, Charles S. *Among Empires: American Ascendancy and Its Predecessors.* Cambridge, Mass.: Harvard University Press, 2006.

———. *In Search of Stability: Explorations in Historical and Political Economy.* Cambridge: Cambridge University Press, 1987.

———. *Recasting Bourgeois Europe.* Princeton: Princeton University Press, 1988.

Malanni, Esteban J. *Comunismo y judaísmo.* Buenos Aires: Editorial La Mazorca, 1944.

Manzella Frontini, Gesualdo. *Volare!* Quaderni Fascisti 15. Florence: Bemporad, 1927.

Maresca, Silvio, and Norberto Galasso. "Debate: peronismo no es fascismo. El filósofo Silvio Maresca y el historiador Norberto Galasso refutan enérgicamente la nota publicada por el historiador Federico Finchelstein." *Clarín, Ñ,* December 20, 2003.

Mariátegui, José Carlos. *La escena contemporánea.* Lima: Editorial Minerva, 1922.

———. *Fascismo sudamericano, los intelectuales, la revolución y otros artículos inéditos, 1923–1924.* Lima: Centro de Trabajo Intelectual Mariátegui, 1975.

Maritain, Jacques. *Antimoderne.* Paris: Éditions de la Revue des Jeunes, 1922.

———. *Cristianismo y democracia.* Buenos Aires: Biblioteca Nueva, 1944.

———. *Freudismo y psicoanálisis: conferencias pronunciadas en la Facultad de Filosofía y Letras de Buenos Aires.* Buenos Aires: Instituto de Filosofía, Universidad de Buenos Aires, 1938.

———. *Humanisme intégral.* Paris: Aubier, 1936.

———. *Los judíos entre las naciones.* Buenos Aires: Sur, 1938.

———. *Primauté du spirituel.* Paris: Plon, 1927.

———. *Problemas espirituales y temporales de una nueva cristiandad.* Madrid: Signo, 1935.

———. *Los rebeldes españoles no hacen una "guerra santa."* Madrid: Ediciones Españolas, 1937.

——. *Sobre la guerra santa*. Buenos Aires: Sur, 1937.

——. *The Things That Are Not Ceasar's*. London: Sheed and Ward, 1930.

Martin, Simon. *Football and Fascism: The National Game under Mussolini*. Oxford: Berg, 2005.

Mason, Tim. "Moderno, modernità, modernizzazione: un montaggio." *Movimento Operaio e Socialista* 1–2 (1987).

Megaro, Gaudenz. *Mussolini in the Making*. New York: Houghton Mifflin, 1938.

Mehlman, Jeffrey. *Legacies of Anti-Semitism in France*. Minneapolis: University of Minessota Press, 1983.

Meinvielle, Julio. *Concepción católica de la economía*. Buenos Aires: Cursos de Cultura Católica, 1936.

——. *Concepción católica de la política*. 1st ed. 1932. 2nd ed., Buenos Aires: Cursos de Cultura Católica, 1941.

——. *Entre la Iglesia y el Reich*. Buenos Aires: Adsum, 1937.

——. *Un juicio católico sobre los problemas nuevos de la política*. Buenos Aires: Gladium, 1937.

——. *El judío*. Buenos Aires: Antídoto, 1936.

——. *Qué saldrá de la España que sangra*. Buenos Aires: Edición del Secretariado de Publicaciones de la Asociación de los Jóvenes de la Acción Católica, 1937.

——. *Los tres pueblos bíblicos en su lucha por la dominación del mundo*. Buenos Aires: Adsum, 1937.

Meldini, P. *Mussolini contro Freud: la psicoanalisi nella pubblicistica fascista*. Florence: Guaraldi, 1976.

Meneses, Carlos. *Cartas de juventud de J. L. Borges, 1921–1922*. Madrid: Editorial Orígenes, 1987.

Metz, Allan. "Gustavo Juan Franceschi and the Jews: The Overcoming of Prejudice by an Argentine Prelate." *Church History* 62.2 (1993).

Michaelis, Meir. *Mussolini and the Jews: German-Italian Relations and the Jewish Question in Italy, 1922–45*. Oxford: Clarendon Press, 1978.

Middlebrook, Kevin J., ed. *Conservative Parties, the Right, and Democracy in Latin America*. Baltimore: Johns Hopkins University Press, 2000.

Millán Astray, José. "Emoción de la hispanidad." In *Asociación Cultural Hispano-Americana: Voces de Hispanidad*. Madrid: Gráficas Afrodisio Aguado, 1940.

Molinari Morales, Tirso. *El fascismo en el Perú: la Unión Revolucionaria, 1931–1936*. Lima: Universidad Nacional Mayor de San Marcos, Fondo Editorial de la Facultad de Ciencias Sociales, 2006.

Mondolfo, Rodolfo. *Per la comprensione storica del fascismo*. Bologna: Capelli, 1922.

Bibliography

Mosse, George L. *The Crisis of German Ideology: Intellectual Origins of the Third Reich.* New York: Howard Fertig, 1998.

——. *The Fascist Revolution: Toward a General Theory of Fascism.* New York: Howard Fertig, 1998.

——. *The Image of Man: The Creation of Modern Masculinity.* New York: Oxford University Press, 1996.

——. *Masses and Man: Nationalist and Fascist Perceptions of Reality.* New York: Howard Fertig, 1980.

——. *Nationalism and Sexuality: Respectability and Abnormal Sexuality in Modern Europe.* New York: Howard Fertig, 1985.

——. *The Nationalization of the Masses: Political Symbolism and Mass Movements in Germany from the Napoleonic Wars through the Third Reich.* Ithaca: Cornell University Press, 1991.

——. *Nazism: A Historical and Comparative Analysis of National Socialism.* New Brunswick: Rutgers University Press, 1978.

Moya, José C. *Cousins and Strangers: Spanish Immigrants in Buenos Aires, 1850–1930.* Berkeley: University of California Press, 1998.

——. "The Positive Side of Stereotypes: Jewish Anarchists in Early Twentieth-Century Buenos Aires." *Jewish History* 18.1 (2004).

Mugnaini, Marco. "L'Italia e l'America Latina,1930–1936: alcuni aspetti della politica estera fascista." *Storia delle Relazioni Internazionali* 2.2 (1986).

Murmis, Miguel, and Juan Carlos Portantiero. *Estudios sobre los orígenes del peronismo.* Buenos Aires: Siglo Veintiuno Editores, 1971.

Musiedlak, Didier. "Religion and Political Culture in the Thought of Mussolini" *Totalitarian Movements and Political Religions* 6.3 (2005).

Mussolini, Benito. *Discorsi del 1925.* Milan: Alpes, 1926.

——. *Discorsi del 1925–1930.* 6 vols. Milan: Alpes, 1926–1930.

——. *Discorsi del 1927.* Milan: Alpes, 1928.

——. *Fascism: Doctrine and Institutions.* Rome: Ardita, 1935.

——. *La nuova politica dell'Italia: discorsi e dichiarazioni.* Milan: Alpes, 1925.

——. *Opera omnia.* 36 vols. Florence: La Fenice, 1951–63.

Mutsuki, Noriko. *Julio Irazusta: treinta años de nacionalismo argentino.* Buenos Aires: Editorial Biblos, 2004.

Myers, Jorge. *Orden y virtud: el discurso republicano en el régimen rosista.* Bernal: Universidad Nacional de Quilmes, 1995.

Nállim, Jorge. "Del antifascismo al antiperonismo: Argentina libre, . . . Antinazi y el surgimiento del antiperonismo político e intelectual." In *Fascismo/antifascismo, peronismo/antiperonismo: conflictos políticos e ideológicos en Argentina, 1930–1955*, ed. Marcela García. Madrid: Editorial Iberoamericana, 2006.

Navarro Gerassi, Marysa. *Los nacionalistas*. Buenos Aires: Jorge Álvarez, 1968.

Neiburg, Federico. *Los intelectuales y la invención del peronismo: estudios de antropología social y cultural*. Buenos Aires: Alianza, 1998.

Neocleous, Mark. *Fascism*. Minneapolis: University of Minnesota Press, 1997.

Neumann, Franz. *The Democratic and the Authoritarian State: Essays in Political and Legal Theory*. New York: Free Press, 1957.

Newton, Ronald. "Ducini, prominenti, antifascisti: Italian Fascism and the Italo-Argentine Collectivity, 1922–1945." *The Americas* 17.3 (1986).

——. " 'The Nazi Menace' in Argentina Revisited." *Patterns of Prejudice* 31.3 (1997).

——. *The "Nazi Menace" in Argentina, 1931–1947*. Stanford: Stanford University Press, 1992.

——. "¿Patria? ¿Cuál patria? Italo-argentinos y Germano-argentinos en la era de la renovación nacional fascista, 1922–1945." *Estudios Migratorios Latinoamericanos* 7.22 (1992).

Nolte, Ernst. *La guerra civil europea, 1917–1945*. In *Nacionalsocialismo y bolchevismo*. Mexico City: Fondo de Cultura Económica, 1994.

——. *Three Faces of Fascism: Action Française, Italian Fascism, National Socialism*. New York: Mentor, 1969.

Novaro, Marcos, and Vicente Palermo. *La dictadura militar, 1976–1983*. Buenos Aires: Paidós, 2003.

Orsina, Giovanni, ed. *Fare storia politica: il problema dello spazio pubblico nell'eta' contemporanea*. Soveria Mannelli, Catanzaro: Rubbettino, 2000.

Osés, Enrique P. *Medios y fines del nacionalismo*. Buenos Aires: Editorial La Mazorca, 1941.

——. *Sarmiento el indeseable*. Buenos Aires: Ediciones de "Asociación Amigos de Crisol," ca. 1939.

Paggi, Leonardo. "Antifascism and the Reshaping of the Democratic Consensus in Post-1945 Italy." *New German Critique* 67 (1996).

Palacio, Ernesto. *La historia falsificada*. Buenos Aires: Difusión, 1939.

Palermo, Vicente. *Sal en las heridas*. Buenos Aires: Sudamericana, 2007.

Palti, Elias. "In Memoriam: Hans Blumenberg (1920–1996), an Unended Quest." *Journal of the History of Ideas* 58.3 (1997).

——. "Temporalidad y refutabilidad de los conceptos políticos." *Prismas: Revista de Historia Intelectual* 9 (2005).

Panunzio, Sergio. *Diritto, forza e violenza: lineamenti di una teoria della violenza*. Bologna: Capelli, 1921.

Passerini, Luisa. "Memories of Resistance, Resistances of Memory." In *European Memories of the Second World War*, ed. Helmut Peitsch. New York: Berghahn, 1999.

Pavone, Claudio. *Alle origini della Repubblica: scritti su fascismo, antifascismo, e la continuità dello stato*. Turin: Bollati Boringhieri, 1995.

———. "La Resistenza in Italia: alcuni nodi interpretativi." *Ricerche di Storia Politica* 5.1 (2002).

Paxton, Robert. *The Anatomy of Fascism*. New York: Knopf, 2004.

Payne, Stanley G. *Fascism: Comparison and Definition*. Madison: University of Wisconsin Press, 1980.

———. *Fascism in Spain, 1923–1977*. Madison: University of Wisconsin Press, 1999.

———. "Historical Fascism and the Radical Right." *Journal of Contemporary History* 35.1 (2000).

———. *A History of Fascism, 1914–1945*. Madison: University of Wisconsin Press, 1995.

Payne, Stanley G., David J. Sorkin, John S. Tortorice, eds. *What History Tells: George L. Mosse and the Culture of Modern Europe*. Madison: University of Wisconsin Press, 2004.

Pemán, José María. *Cartas a un escéptico en materias de formas de gobierno*. Burgos: Cultura Española, 1937.

———. *El paraíso y la serpiente: notas de un viaje por tierras de la hispanidad*. Madrid: Escelicer, 1942.

———. *Seis conferencias pronunciadas en Hispano América*. Madrid: Sucesores de Rivadeneyra, 1941.

PEN Club. *LXIV Congreso Internacional de los P.E.N. Clubs*. Buenos Aires: La Bonaerense, 1937.

Pergher, Roberta. "Impero immaginario, impero vissuto: recenti sviluppi nella storiografia del colonialismo italiano." *Ricerche di Storia Politica* 10.1 (2007).

Persello, Ana Virginia. *El partido radical: gobierno y oposición, 1916–1943*. Buenos Aires: Siglo Veintiuno Editores, 2004.

———. *El radicalismo en crisis, 1930—1943*. Rosario: Fundación Ross, 1996.

Piccato, Pablo. "¿Modelo para armar? Hacia un acercamiento crítico a la teoría de la esfera pública." In *Actores, espacios y debates en la historia de la esfera pública en la ciudad de México*, ed. Cristina Sacristán and Pablo Piccato. Mexico City: Instituto Mora, 2005.

———. "Public Sphere in Latin America: A Map of the Historiography." *Social History* (forthcoming).

Picciotto Fargion, Liliana. *Il libro della memoria: gli Ebrei deportati dall'Italia, 1943–1945*. Milan: Mursia, 1991.

Bibliography

Pico, César. *Carta a Jacques Maritain sobre la colaboración de los católicos con los movimientos de tipo fascista*. Buenos Aires: Francisco A. Colombo, 1937.

——. *Doctrina y finalidades del comunismo*. Santiago: Editorial Difusión Chilena, 1942.

Plotkin, Mariano, ed. *Argentina on the Couch: Psychiatry, State, and Society, 1880 to the Present*. Albuquerque: University of New Mexico Press, 2003.

——. *El día que se inventó el peronismo*. Buenos Aires: Editorial Sudamericana, 2007.

——. *Freud in the Pampas: The Emergence and Development of a Psychoanalytic Culture in Argentina*. Stanford: Stanford University Press, 2001.

——. "Freud, Politics, and the Porteños: The Reception of Psychoanalysis in Buenos Aires, 1910–1943." *Hispanic American Historical Review* 77.1 (1997).

——. *Mañana es San Perón—Propaganda, rituales políticos y educación en el régimen peronista, 1946–1955*. Buenos Aires: Eduntref, 2007.

——. "Perón y el peronismo: un ensayo bibliográfico." *Estudios Interdisciplinarios de América Latina y el Caribe* 2.1 (1991).

Pollard, John. "Conservative Catholics and Italian Fascism: The Clerico-Fascists." In *Fascists and Conservatives: The Radical Right and the Establishment in Twentieth Century Europe*, ed. Martin Blinkhorn. London: Allen and Unwin, 1991.

Pombeni, Paolo. "Fascismo e nazismo nella storia politica nazionale: una svolta storiografica?" *Contemporanea* 3 (2004).

Potash, Robert. *El ejército y la política en la Argentina*, vol. 1, 1928–1945. Buenos Aires: Hyspamerica, 1985.

Poulantzas, Nicos. *Fascism and Dictatorship: The Third International and the Problem of Fascism*. London: New Left Books, 1974.

Pratt, Mary Louise. *Imperial Eyes: Travel Writing and Transculturation*. New York: Routledge, 1992.

Primo de Rivera, José Antonio. *Doctrina de F.E. de las J.O.N.S.* Valladolid: Ediciones Libertad, 1936.

Primo de Rivera y Urquijo, Miguel, ed. *Papeles póstumos de José Antonio*. Barcelona: Plaza y Janés, 1996.

Prislei, Leticia. *Los orígenes el fascismo argentino*. Buenos Aires: Edhasa, 2008.

Puccini, Mario. *L'Argentina e gli Argentini*. Milan: Garzanti, 1939.

Puget, Janine, and Rene Kaës. *Violencia de estado y psicoanálisis*. Buenos Aires: Centro Editor de America Latina, 1991.

Quartara, Giorgio. *Un viaggio nel Sud-America*. Milan: Fratelli Bocca, 1939.

Quattrocchi-Woisson, Diana. *Los males de la memoria: historia y política en la Argentina*. Buenos Aires: Emecé, 1998.

Rabinbach, Anson. "Legacies of Antifascism." *New German Critique* 67 (1996).

——. "Moments of Totalitarianism." *History and Theory* 45 (2006).

Rein, Raanan. *Argentina, Israel, and the Jews: Perón, the Eichmann Capture and After.* Bethesda: University Press of Maryland, 2003.

——. *The Franco-Perón Alliance: Relations between Spain and Argentina, 1946–1955.* Pittsburgh: University of Pittsburgh Press.

——. *Peronismo, populismo y política: Argentina, 1943–1955.* Buenos Aires: Editorial de Belgrano, 1998.

Riesco, Gabriel. *El destino de la Argentina.* Buenos Aires: Grupo de Editoriales Católicas, 1944.

——. *Liberalismo y catolicismo.* Buenos Aires: Imprenta Guadalupe, 1938.

——. *Nuestra misión histórica.* Buenos Aires: Imprenta Guadalupe, 1941.

——. *El problema de la guerra actual.* Buenos Aires: Difusión, 1940.

Rivarola, Rodolfo. *La constitución Argentina contra las sanciones de Ginebra.* Buenos Aires: Imprenta A. Guido Buffarini, 1935.

Roberts, David. "Myth Style and Substance in the Totalitarian Dynamic in Fascist Italy." *Contemporary European History* 16.1 (2007).

Rochat, Giorgio. *Italo Balbo: aviatore e ministro dell'aeronautica, 1926–1933.* Ferrara: Italo Bovolenta Editore, 1979.

Rock, David. *Authoritarian Argentina: The Nationalist Movement, Its History and Its Impact.* Berkeley: University of California Press, 1993.

——. *El radicalismo argentino, 1890–1930.* Buenos Aires: Amorrortu, 1977.

Rodgers, Daniel, Frederick Cooper, Pierre-Yves Saunier, Michael Werner, and Bénédicte Zimmerman. "Penser l'histoire croisée: entre empirie et réflexivité." *Annales: Histoire, Sciences Sociales* 58 (2003).

Rodó, José Enrique, *Ariel.* Boston: Houghton Mifflin, 1922.

Rodogno, Davide. *Fascism's European Empire: Italian Occupation During the Second World War.* Cambridge: Cambridge University Press, 2006.

Rodríguez Molas, Ricardo. *Historia de la tortura y el orden represivo en la Argentina.* Buenos Aires: Eudeba, 1984.

Roldán, Mary. "The Local Limitations to a National Political Movement: Gaitan and Gaitanismo in Antioquia." In *Political Cultures in the Andes, 1750–1950,* ed. Nils Jacobsen and Cristóbal Aljovín de Losada. Durham: Duke University Press, 2005.

Romero, José Luis. *El ciclo de la revolución contemporánea.* Buenos Aires: Huemul, 1980.

——. *La experiencia Argentina.* Buenos Aires: Fondo de Cultura Económica, 1989.

——. *Las ideas políticas en la Argentina.* Buenos Aires: Fondo de Cultura Económica, 1996.

Bibliography

——. *El pensamiento político de la derecha latinoamericana*. Buenos Aires: Paidós, 1970.

——. *Situaciones e ideología en Latinoamérica*. Buenos Aires: Sudamericana, 1986.

——. *La vida histórica*. Buenos Aires: Sudamericana, 1988.

Romero, Luis Alberto, ed. *La Argentina en la escuela: la idea de nación en los textos escolares*. Buenos Aires: Siglo Veintiuno Editores, 2003.

——. *Breve historia contemporánea de la Argentina*. Buenos Aires: Fondo de Cultura Económica, 2001.

——. "Católicos en movimiento: activismo político en una parroquia de Buenos Aires, 1935–1946." *Estudios Sociales* 8.14 (1998).

——. *La crisis argentina*. Buenos Aires: Siglo Veintiuno Editores, 2003.

——. "La democracia y la sombra del proceso." In *Argentina, 1976–2006: entre la sombra de la dictadura y el futuro de la democracia*, ed. Hugo Quiroga and César Tcach. Rosario: Homo Sapiens, 2006.

——. *Libros baratos y cultura de los sectores populares: Buenos Aires en la entreguerra*. Buenos Aires: Centro de Investigaciones Sociales sobre el Estado y la Administración, 1986.

Rossanvallon, Pierre. "Para una historia conceptual de lo político (nota de trabajo)." *Prismas: Revista de Historia Intelectual* 6 (2002).

Rousso, Henry, ed. *Stalinisme et nazisme: histoire e mémoire comparées*. Brussels: Complexe, 1999.

Ruiz Guiñazú, Alejandro. *La Argentina ante sí misma: reflexiones sobre una revolución necesaria*. Buenos Aires: Guillermo Kraft, 1942.

Ruiz Moreno, Isidoro. *Historia de las relaciones exteriores argentinas, 1810–1955*. Buenos Aires: Editorial Perrot, 1961.

Sabatini, Davide. *L'internazionale di Mussolini: la diffusione del fascismo in Europa nel progetto politico di Asvero Gravelli*. Rome: Edizioni Tusculum, 1997.

Sabato, Hilda. *The Many and the Few: Political Participation in Republican Buenos Aires*. Stanford: Stanford University Press, 2001.

——. "La reacción de América: la construcción de las repúblicas en el siglo xix." In *Europa, América y el mundo: tiempos históricos*, ed. Roger Chartier and Antonio Feros. Madrid: Marcial Pons, 2006.

Said, Edward W. *Orientalism*. New York: Vintage Books, 1979.

Saitta, Sylvia. *Regueros de tinta: el diario Crítica en la década de 1920*. Buenos Aires: Sudamericana, 1998.

Salazar, Oliveira. *El pensamiento de la revolución nacional*. Buenos Aires: Poblet, 1938.

Salgó, Eszter. "Recenti studi sul fascismo." *Bolletino di Storiografia* 6 (2003).

Salvaneschi, Nino. *Lavoratori nostri d'oltralpe*. Quaderni fascisti 13. Florence: Bemporad, 1928.

Sánchez Sorondo, Marcelo. *Memorias: conversaciones con Carlos Payá*. Buenos Aires: Sudamericana, 2001.

Santinon, Renzo. *I fasci italiani all'estero*. Rome: Settimo Sigillo, 1991.

Sarfatti, Michele. *Gli ebrei nell'Italia fascista: vicende, identita', persecuzione*. Turin: Einaudi, 2000.

Sarlo, Beatriz. *Tiempo pasado: cultura de la memoria y giro subjetivo, una discusión*. Buenos Aires: Siglo Veintiuno Editores, 2005.

Savarino, Franco. "Juego de ilusiones: Brasil, México y los 'fascismos' latino-americanos frente al fascismo italiano." *Historia Crítica* 37 (2009).

Saz, Ismael. *Fascismo y franquismo*. Valencia: Universitat de València, 2004.

Sazbón, José. "Conciencia histórica y memoria electiva." *Prismas: Revista de Historia Intelectual* 6 (2002).

———. "El sujeto en las ciencias humanas." *Estudios: Filosofía Práctica e Historia de las Ideas* 1.1 (2000).

Scalabrini Ortiz, Raúl. *El hombre que está solo y espera*. Buenos Aires: Gleizer, 1931.

Scarzanella, Eugenia, ed. *Fascisti in Sud America*. Florence: Le Lettere, 2005.

Schieder, Wolfgang. "Fatal Attraction: The German Right and Italian Fascism." In *The Third Reich between Vision and Reality: New Perspectives on German History, 1918–1945*, ed. Hans Mommsen. Oxford: Berg, 2001.

Schmitt, Carl. *The Concept of the Political*. New Brunswick: Rutgers University Press, 1976.

Schnapp, Jeffrey. *Anno X—La Mostra delle Rivoluzione Fascista del 1932: genesi, sviluppo, contesto culturale-storico, ricezione*. Rome: Istituti Editoriali e Poligrafici Internazionali, 2003.

———. *Staging Fascism: 18 BL and the Theatre of Masses for the Masses*. Stanford: Stanford University Press, 1996.

Senkman, Leonardo, ed. *El antisemitismo en la Argentina*. Buenos Aires: Ceal, 1989.

———. *Argentina, la segunda guerra mundial y los refugiados indeseables, 1933–1945*. Buenos Aires: Grupo Editor Latinoamericano, 1991.

Seoane, María. *Argentina: el siglo del progreso y la oscuridad*. Buenos Aires: Crítica, 2004.

Sergi, Jorge. *Historia de los italianos en la Argentina*. Buenos Aires: Editora Italo Argentina, 1940.

Sharp, Rolland Hall. *South America Uncensored*. New York: Green, 1945.

Silveyra, Carlos M. *El comunismo en la Argentina: origen–desarrollo–organización actual*. 1st ed. 1936. 2nd ed., Buenos Aires: Editorial Patria, 1937.

———. *La cuestión nazi en la Argentina*. Buenos Aires: Editorial Patria, 1939.

———. *Norteamérica se cava su fosa: por haber bombardeado al centro católico del mundo*

Bibliography

Roma el Vaticano y sus iglesias obligando al Santo Padre a orar entre sus ruinas.
Buenos Aires: Editorial Patria, ca. 1940.

Silveyra de Oyuela, Eugenia. *Nacionalismo y neo-peronismo: réplica a Mario Amadeo.*
Buenos Aires: Cuadernos Republicanos, 1956.

Simonini, Augusto. *Il linguaggio di Mussolini.* Milan: Bompiani, 2004.

Solberg, Carl. *Immigration and Nationalism: Argentina and Chile, 1890–1914.* Austin:
University of Texas Press, 1970.

Sorba, Carlotta, et al. "Sguardi transnazionali." *Contemporanea* 1 (2004).

Sørensen, Gert, and Robert Mallett, eds. *International Fascism, 1919–45.* London:
Frank Cass, 2002.

Spackman, Barbara. *Fascist Virilities: Rhetoric, Ideology, and Social Fantasy.* Minneapolis: University of Minnesota Press, 1996.

Spektorowski, Alberto. *Argentina's Revolution of the Right.* Notre Dame: University
of Notre Dame Press, 2003.

——. "The Making of an Argentine Fascist: Leopoldo Lugones—From Revolutionary Left to Radical Nationalism." *History of Polical Thought* 17.1 (1996).

Steigmann-Gall, Richard. "Nazism and the Revival of Political Religion Theory."
Totalitarian Movements and Political Religions 5.3 (2004).

Steinberg, Michael P. *Austria as Theater and Ideology: The Meaning of the Salzburg Fes-
tival.* Ithaca: Cornell University Press, 2000.

——. *Listening to Reason: Culture, Subjectivity, and Nineteenth-Century Music.* Princeton: Princeton University Press, 2004.

——, ed. *Walter Benjamin and the Demands of History.* Ithaca: Cornell University
Press, 1996.

Sternhell, Zeev. *Les anti-Lumières du xviiie siècle à la guerre froide.* Paris: Fayard, 2006.

——. *La droite révolutionnaire, 1885–1914: les origines françaises du fascisme.* Paris: Gallimard, 1997.

——. "Fascism: Reflections on the Fate of Ideas in Twentieth-Century History."
Journal of Political Ideologies 5.2 (2000).

——. "Fascist Ideology.'" In *Fascism: A Reader's Guide, Analyses, Interpretations,
Bibliography,* ed. Walter Laqueur. Berkeley: University of California Press, 1976.

——. "How to Think about Fascism and Its Ideology." *Constellations* 15.3 (2008).

——. *Neither Right nor Left: Fascist Ideology in France.* Berkeley: University of California Press, 1986.

Sternhell, Zeev, with Mario Sznajder and Maia Asheri. *The Birth of Fascist Ideology:
From Cultural Rebellion to Political Revolution.* Princeton: Princeton University
Press, 1994.

Stoler, Ann Laura. "Intimidations of Empire: Predicaments of the Tactile and the

Unseen." In *Haunted by Empire. Geographies of Intimacy in North American History*, ed. Ann Laura Stoler. Durham: Duke University Press, 2006.

——. "On Degrees of Imperial Sovereignty." *Public Culture* 18.1 (2006).

Stoler, Ann Laura, and Frederick Cooper. "Between Metropole and Colony: Rethinking a Research Agenda." In *Tensions of Empire: Colonial Cultures in a Bourgeois World*, ed. Ann Laura Stoler and Frederick Cooper. Berkeley: University of California Press, 1997.

Stone, Marla. "The Changing Face of the Enemy in Fascist Italy." *Constellations* 15.3 (2008).

——. *The Patron State*. Princeton: Princeton University Press, 1998.

Suckert, Curzio (Malaparte). *Italia barbara*. Turin: Gobetti, 1925.

——. *L'Europa vivente: teoria storica del sindicalismo nazionale*. Florence: La Voce, 1923.

Tacchi, Francesca, Adrian Lyttelton, and Anna Rossi-Doria. "Discussioni: l'abbiccì del fascismo." *Passato e Presente* 61 (2004).

Talmon, Jacob L. *The Origins of Totalitarian Democracy*. New York: Norton, 1970.

Terán, Juan Bautista. *El divorcio, conferencia*. Buenos Aires: Librería del Colegio, 1932.

Terán, Oscar. *Positivismo y nación en la Argentina*. Buenos Aires: Puntosur, 1987.

——. *Vida intelectual en el Buenos Aires fin-de-siglo*. Buenos Aires: Fondo de Cultura Económica, 1997.

Todorov, Tzvetan. *Face à l'extrême*. Paris: Seuil, 1991.

Torre, Juan Carlos, ed. *Los años peronistas, 1943–1955*. Buenos Aires: Sudamericana, 2002.

——. "Interpretando (una vez más) los orígenes del peronismo." *Desarrollo Económico* 28.112 (1989).

——. *La vieja guardia sindical y Perón: sobre los orígenes del peronismo*. Buenos Aires: Editorial Sudamericana–Instituto Torcuato Di Tella, 1990.

Torres, José Luis. *Algunas maneras de vender la patria*. Buenos Aires: Editorial Yunque, 1940.

Los torturados: la obra criminal de Leopoldo Lugones (hijo), relato de las víctimas. Buenos Aires: Estampa, 1932.

Tovar, Antonio. *El imperio de España*. Madrid: Ediciones Afrodisio Aguado, 1941.

Traverso, Enzo. *À feu et à sang: de la guerre civile européenne, 1914–1945*. Paris: Stock, 2007.

——. "De l'anticommunisme: l'histoire du xxe siècle relue par Nolte, Furet et Courtois." *L'Homme et la Société* (2001).

——. *The Origins of Nazi Violence*. New York: New Press, 2003.

——. *Le passé, mode d'emploi—histoire, mémoire, politique*. Paris: La Fabrique, 2005.

——. *La pensée dispersée*. Paris: Lignes, 2004.

——. *Il totalitarismo: storia di un dibattito*. Milan: Mondadori, 2002.

Trindade, Heélgio. "La cuestión del fascismo en América Latina." *Desarrollo Económico* 23.91 (1983).

——. *O nazi-fascismo na América Latina: mito e realidade*. Porto Alegre: Universidad Federal do Rio Grande do Sul Editora, 2004.

Troise, Emilio. *Significado de la reacción espiritualista y católica de la pos-guerra: ¿Qué es el fascismo?* Buenos Aires: Socorro Rojo Internacional, ca. 1930.

Truett, Samuel, and Elliott Young. "Making Transnational History: Nations, Regions, and Borderlands." In *Continental Crossroads: Remapping U.S.-Mexico Borderlands History*, ed. Samuel Truett and Elliott Young. Durham: Duke University Press, 2004.

Turi, Gabriele. *Il fascismo e il consenso degli intellettuali*. Bologna: Il Mulino, 1980.

——. *Giovanni Gentile: una biografia*. Florence: Giunti, 1995.

United Kingdom. *Documents on German Foreign Policy*. Series D (1937–1945). Vol. 6. London: Her Majesty's Stationery Office, 1956.

United States, Department of State. *Consultation among the American Republics with Respect to the Argentine Situation*. Washington, D.C.: U.S. GPO, 1946.

Valle, R. E. *El decreto del poder ejecutivo sobre asociaciones extranjeras*. Buenos Aires: Argumentos, 1939.

Vander, Fabio. "Estetica e fascismo." *Bolletino di Storiografia* 6 (2001–2002).

Varela, Antonio Hilario. *Las hordas comunistas*. Buenos Aires: n.p., 1932.

Ventrone, Angelo. *La seduzione totalitaria: guerra, modernità, violenza politica, 1914–1918*. Rome: Donzelli, 2003.

Vezzetti, Hugo. *Aventuras de Freud en el país de los argentinos: de José Ingenieros a Enrique Pichon-Rivière*. Buenos Aires: Paidós, 1996.

——. *Freud en Buenos Aires, 1910–1939*. Buenos Aires: Puntosur, 1989.

——. *Pasado y presente: guerra, dictadura y sociedad en la Argentina*. Buenos Aires: Siglo Veintiuno Editores, 2002.

——. "Las promesas del psicoanálisis en la cultura de masas." In *Historia de la vida privada en la Argentina*, ed. Fernando Devoto and Marta Madero. Vol. 3. Buenos Aires: Taurus, 1999.

Villafañe, Benjamín. *Chusmocracia: continuación de hora obscura y la ley suicida*. Buenos Aires: Imprenta Mercatali, 1937.

——. *La miseria de un país rico*. Buenos Aires: El Ateneo, 1927.

——. *La tragedia argentina, de la acción parlamentaria*. Buenos Aires: n.p., 1943.

Volt (Vincenzo Fani). *Programma della destra fascista*. Florence: La Voce, 1924.

Welles, Summer. *The Time for Decision*. New York: Harper and Brothers, 1944.

Wohl, Robert. *The Spectacle of Flight: Aviation and the Western Imagination, 1920–1950*. New Haven, Conn.: Yale University Press, 2005.

Wood, Ellen Meiksins. *Empire of Capital*. London: Verso, 2005.

Zagarrio, Vito. "Fascismo e intellettuali." *Studi Storici* 22.2 (1981).

Zanatta, Loris. *Del estado liberal a la nación católica: Iglesia y Ejército en los orígenes del peronismo*. Bernal: Universidad Nacional de Quilmes, 1996.

———. "I fasci in Argentina negli anni Trenta." In *Il fascismo e gli emigrati*, ed. E. Franzina and M. Sanfilippo. Rome: Laterza, 2003.

———. *Perón y el mito de la nación católica: Iglesia y Ejército en los orígenes del peronismo, 1943–1946*. Buenos Aires: Sudamericana, 1999.

———. *Il peronismo*. Rome: Carocci, 2008.

Zaretsky, Eli. *Secrets of the Soul: A Social and Cultural History of Psychoanalysis*. New York: Knopf, 2004.

Žižek, Slavoj. *Did Somebody Say Totalitarianism? Five Interventions in the (Mis)use of a Notion*. New York:Verso, 2002

———. "Learning to Love Leni Riefenstahl." *In These Times*, September 10, 2003.

———. *The Sublime Object of Ideology*. New York: Verso, 1989.

———. "The Two Totalitarianisms." *London Review of Books*, March 17, 2005.

Zuccotti, Susan. *The Italians and the Holocaust: Persecution, Rescue, and Survival*. New York: Basic Books, 1987.

Zuleta Álvarez, Enrique. *España en América: estudios sobre la historia de las ideas en Hispanoamérica*. Buenos Aires: Editorial Confluencia, 2000.

———. "Historia de una revista nacionalista Nueva Política (1940–1943)." In *Cuando opinar es actuar: revistas argentinas del siglo xx*, ed. Noemi Girbal-Blacha and Diana Quattrocchi-Woisson. Buenos Aires: Academia Nacional de la Historia, 1999.

———. *El nacionalismo argentino*. Buenos Aires: La Bastilla, 1975.

———. "El nacionalismo argentino y la historiografía contemporánea." In *Noveno Congreso Nacional y Regional de Historia Argentina, Rosario, 26–28 de septiembre de 1996*. Buenos Aires: 1996.

———. "Presencia de Irazusta en la Argentina contemporánea." In *Homenaje a Julio Irazusta*, ed. Enrique Zuleta Álvarez, Mario Guillermo Saravi, and Enrique Díaz Araujo. Mendoza: Editorial "Diario la Tarde," 1984.

Zunino, Pier Giorgio. *L'ideologia fascista*. Bologna: Il Mulino, 1985.

———. *Interpretazione e memoria del fascismo: gli anni del regime*. Rome: Laterza, 1991.

———. *La Repubblica e il suo passato: il fascismo dopo il fascismo, il comunismo, la democrazia: le origini dell'Italia contemporanea*. Bologna: Il Mulino, 2003.

Index

FEDERICO FINCHELSTEIN is assistant professor of history at The New School for Social Research and Eugene Lang College of The New School in New York City. He is the author of El Canon del Holocausto (2009), La Argentina fascista: los orígenes ideológicos de la dictadura (2008), and Fascismo, liturgia e imaginario: el mito del general Uriburu y la Argentina nacionalista (2002).

Made in the USA
San Bernardino, CA
15 March 2018